M000217109

DAILY
DEVOTIONS
FOR MEN

MORNING & EVENING EDITION

365 DAYS OF
BIBLE WISDOM

DAILY
DEVOTIONS
FOR MEN

365 DAYS OF
BIBLE WISDOM

BARBOUR BOOKS
An Imprint of Barbour Publishing, Inc.

MORNING AND EVENING. . .RECEIVE CHALLENGE AND ENCOURAGEMENT FROM GOD'S WORD

It is good to proclaim your unfailing love in the morning,
your faithfulness in the evening.

PSALM 92:2 NLT

Morning and evening. Day and night. Sunrise and sunset.

This daily rhythm reverberates throughout the first chapter of Genesis and echoes hundreds of times throughout the Bible until the closing pages of Revelation.

This relentless daily rhythm speaks of Creation and Fall, and of judgment and promise and provision. It describes the Plagues on Egypt, the giving of the Ten Commandments on Mount Sinai, the Cloud by day and Fire by night, and Joshua's meditations on the five books of Moses.

What's more, this daily rhythm reminds us of prayers and sacrifices, of Goliath's taunts against Israel's army, of Gideon's tests of God's will, of the meals brought to Elijah by ravens, of repeated wilderness fasts forty times over, and of three times over inside the deep.

Yes, the unstoppable daily rhythm of sunrise and sunset will continue at the Lord's command until the New Heavens and New Earth. Until then, we're wise to ponder the truths of God's Word both day and night. As we do, God's rich promises give us renewed hope, courage, and strength to persevere.

Each morning and evening, may this particular 365-day devotional collection speak regularly to *your* heart and life.

GOD IS THERE FOR YOU

The righteous cry out, and the LORD hears them;
he delivers them from all their troubles.

PSALM 34:17 NIV

Those who have lived the Christian life for any length of time have likely had a good chance to learn an important lesson about a life of faith. The lesson: God never promised that it would be easy or that there wouldn't be times of difficulty.

Indeed, any effort to find a scriptural promise telling us that the Christian life is a trouble-free life would end in frustration and failure. In fact, Jesus promised quite the opposite when He said, "In this world you will have trouble. But take heart! I have overcome the world" (John 16:33).

Yes, in this world, we're going to face times of trouble. But there is one promise God has made repeatedly in His written Word for believers facing times of difficulty. Time and time again, He tells us, "I'll be there for you."

God is our loving heavenly Father, and He's also a devoted Friend who is there for us in our times of greatest trouble. And not only that, He provides us all we need to emerge from the difficult times as overcomers.

With a Friend like Him, who needs. . .*anything else*?

GOD-HONORING HUMILITY

Humble yourselves, therefore, under God's mighty hand,
that he may lift you up in due time.

1 PETER 5:6 NIV

It's probably fair to say that pride is at the heart of nearly every sin we can commit against God and against others. Pride causes people to boast about themselves and to tear others down. Pride causes people to believe they can do for themselves what God has promised to do for them, and that leads to a lack of prayer. Pride causes conflicts between people, and it keeps us from confessing our sins to one another and to God so that we can be reconciled.

This list of the terrible results of human pride could go on and on, but when you read it, it is no small wonder that God has said, "I hate pride" (Proverbs 8:13).

God hates human pride, but He loves humility, which can be defined as the acknowledgment that apart from Him, we are nothing and can do nothing of value. When we are humble, in effect we are confessing that we have nothing to offer God apart from what He has already done.

So build your life on the words of the apostle Peter. Humble yourself before God. Don't seek to be exalted on your own, but wait patiently for God to give you what you are due.

READ YOUR BIBLE!

Your word is a lamp for my feet, a light on my path.
PSALM 119:105 NIV

Life is busy, isn't it? We spend eight-plus hours a day, five-plus days a week working, and then we have to make time for family, for friends, and for church and church-related activities. Sometimes we're squeezed for time, and one of the first casualties is time alone with God in prayer and Bible reading.

The psalmist who wrote today's scripture verse understood that the Word of God gives believers direction and lights the way as we follow its leading. But the apostle Paul had much more to say about what the Bible does for us: "All Scripture is God-breathed and is useful for teaching, rebuking, correcting and training in righteousness, so that the servant of God may be thoroughly equipped for every good work" (2 Timothy 3:16–17).

So the words recorded in scripture lead and guide us, rebuke and correct us, and teach us what it means to be righteous. Can there be any question as to how important it is that we spend time reading God's Word?

Reading books and other materials about the Bible are good, and attending group Bible studies probably are even better. But nothing should ever take the place of spending time alone with God, reading and meditating on His written Word.

YOUR CONSCIENCE CAN BE YOUR GUIDE

*Holding on to faith and a good conscience, which some have
rejected and so have suffered shipwreck with regard to the faith.*

1 TIMOTHY 1:19 NIV

God has given human beings the wonderful gift of a conscience—a
sense of right and wrong. But the human conscience was exposed
to damage when sin entered into the human experience, when
Adam and Eve chose to disobey the one commandment God had
given them (see Genesis 3). Since that moment, sin has damaged
the conscience of every human being.

When you first received the free gift of salvation through Jesus
Christ, God placed His Holy Spirit within you. Part of the Holy
Spirit's role in your Christian life is to alert you when you're about
to make a choice that doesn't please God. That is partly what Jesus
meant when He told His followers that the Spirit would "guide you
into all the truth" (John 16:13).

When God's Holy Spirit is inside you, He allows you to better
understand the truths of scripture, which are the basis for every
decision we make. And when we have the Spirit playing that role
in our lives, we can safely allow our conscience to be our guide.

LEARNING CONTENTMENT

I know what it is to be in need, and I know what it
is to have plenty. I have learned the secret of being
content in any and every situation, whether well fed
or hungry, whether living in plenty or in want.

<small>PHILIPPIANS 4:12 NIV</small>

Modern advertisers and marketers have tapped into something about our fallen human nature that makes too many of us easy marks as customers who buy what we don't need and oftentimes can't afford.

The world around us does all it can to make us believe that we don't have everything we need, and if we're not careful, we can find ourselves falling into attitudes of discontent because we don't have the newest and best things.

The apostle Paul had learned that contentment has less to do with his setting in life (he was in a Roman prison when he wrote to the Philippian church), with his possessions (he had few), or with physical provision (he had apparently experienced real hunger) and everything to do with the fact that he was doing what God had called him to do.

Paul is an amazing example of what true contentment looks like. While we too often feel the pangs of discontent because we don't have the latest and best (fill in the blank), Paul knew how to feel content when he didn't even have a place to stay, enough to eat, or safe travels.

THE IMPORTANCE OF PLANNING

The plans of the diligent lead to profit
as surely as haste leads to poverty.

PROVERBS 21:5 NIV

The word *planning* sometimes gets a bad rap among certain segments of the Christian world. Some of us don't think it's important to make a plan; instead, they would rather keep their options open and let the Holy Spirit guide their every step on the fly.

Other believers, when God gives them a vision for something, want to plan everything out to the smallest detail so that they don't head out in the wrong direction.

Is either approach necessarily wrong? Like many things in the Word of God, there is usually a point of balance between moving out when God calls you to move and making sure you have a plan of action.

There may be times when God directs you to move out immediately (see Abram in Genesis 12:1–4), but in most instances, when He gives you a vision for something He wants to accomplish through you, it's wise to avoid rushing into it before you carefully plan and weigh your options.

So by all means, have a plan. But just make sure that you prayerfully and humbly submit your planning process to God so that He can guide you in every step you take.

GOD HONORS HARD WORK

*A sluggard's appetite is never filled, but the
desires of the diligent are fully satisfied.*

PROVERBS 13:4 NIV

It might be hard at times to believe it (especially when it's time
to get up each Monday morning), but from the very beginning,
God intended for man to work. His first assignment for Adam was
to live in the Garden of Eden and "to work it and take care of it"
(Genesis 2:15). Sadly, when Adam and Eve sinned, work turned into
toil—and it has been that way ever since (see Genesis 3).

But the fact still remains that it is God's will that each man work
and produce. Not only that, He warns against laziness in today's
scripture and encourages us to work hard and with diligence.
He tells us that laziness leads to poverty and that those who
demonstrate diligence in their work will find that their needs are
met.

So work hard. Approach what you do for a living with
commitment and passion. And as you work so you can provide
well for yourself and your family, don't forget Paul's words: "So
whether you eat or drink or whatever you do, do it all for the glory
of God" (1 Corinthians 10:31).

BEING "REAL" WITH GOD

Immediately the boy's father exclaimed, "I do believe; help me overcome my unbelief!"

MARK 9:24 NIV

It's amazing how desperation can often bring out the best in people. When the chips are down and when our backs are against the wall (pick your own cliché here), we're often forced to get real with one another. . .and with God.

The man who spoke the words in today's scripture verse was at a point where he had no choice but to turn to Jesus for help. He apparently knew enough about Jesus to know that He had miraculously healed many people. But it is equally apparent that he had his doubts as to whether Jesus could help *him*.

Jesus responded to this man's kernel of faith. . .and to his honesty. He healed the man's son and then used the incident to teach His followers some things about real, mountain-moving, demon-repelling faith.

Jesus repeatedly and consistently taught His followers that they could do anything if they had faith. Those same promises hold true for us today. But in those times when we wonder if we have "enough" faith, when we wonder if God can reach down and make a difference in our lives, our best first step might be to confess honestly, "I do believe, Lord. Help me overcome my unbelief."

FORGIVE YOURSELF!

*Therefore, there is now no condemnation
for those who are in Christ Jesus.*

ROMANS 8:1 NIV

Some Christian men haven't quite mastered what it takes to let go of the past. They walk around filled with regret and guilt, believing deep down that even though they've given themselves over to Jesus Christ, God still intends to lower the boom on them for the terrible things they've done.

The Bible calls our spiritual enemy, Satan, the "accuser of our brothers and sisters" (Revelation 12:10) and a "liar" (John 8:44), and he loves few things more than tormenting believers with reminders of their sinful pasts. But the Bible also tells us that there is no condemnation for those of us who belong to Jesus and that our sins are forgiven and buried in a sea of divine forgetfulness (see Micah 7:19).

So no matter what you've done in your past, no matter how awful a sinner you believe you were before Jesus found you, forgave you, and cleansed you, forgive yourself. Let go of your sinful past (God already has) and move on into the wonderful, full life God has given you through the sacrifice of His Son.

BEING PATIENT WITH GOD

Wait for the Lord; be strong
and take heart and wait for the Lord.

PSALM 27:14 NIV

It's so commonly spoken that it's become something of a Christian cliché, but in light of today's scripture verse, it bears repeating here: "God answers prayers in one of three ways—yes, no, and not yet."

Of course we're happy to receive that "Yes" from God, and sometimes we can understand why He says "No." But that "Not yet"—that one can really mess with us. When we pray for something we know is God's will (say, the salvation of a loved one or personal spiritual revival), we're often flummoxed when it doesn't happen right away. So we keep praying—sometimes over a period of years—and waiting.

The scriptural truth of the matter is that God often makes His people wait before He answers their requests. We may not understand why we have to wait, so we must cling to the truth that God's ways and thoughts are different from ours (see Isaiah 55:8).

So be patient and keep seeking God. He has made literally hundreds of promises in scripture, and His track record of keeping them still stands at one hundred percent.

Our part of this grand bargain is to wait patiently, knowing that God's very nature keeps Him from letting us down.

GOSSIP—STOP IT!

*A gossip betrays a confidence,
but a trustworthy person keeps a secret.*

PROVERBS 11:13 NIV

Gossip is one of those all-too-common sins that we might think of as a "little" one. . .certainly not on par with the "biggies" like adultery, murder, or theft.

But when you look at what the Bible has to say about gossip, you'll find that God takes it very, very seriously.

In the first chapter of Paul's letter to the Romans, he writes about God's punishment on sinful humans for their lawlessness. He goes on to provide a list of sinful individuals whose behavior makes them deserving of God's judgment. Right there in verse 29 is the word *gossips.*

Let's get real with ourselves here. God hates gossip, and He hates it because it destroys what He has created and has worked so hard to restore and protect—the name of another person. So let's be very careful not just what we say *to* another person, but also what we say *about* him or her. Let's think before we speak about another. Let's ask ourselves first if what we are about to say is true. Then let's ask ourselves if our words are loving and helpful. . . or if they just damage another's reputation.

And if the words we are about to speak don't pass muster, let's keep them to ourselves.

SEEING GOD IN CREATION

"But ask the animals, and they will teach you, or the birds in the sky, and they will tell you; or speak to the earth, and it will teach you, or let the fish in the sea inform you. Which of all these does not know that the hand of the LORD has done this?"

JOB 12:7–9 NIV

There are all kinds of settings in which you can spend time with God and enjoy His presence. Today's verse teaches us that we can see the greatness of God and experience His presence in a setting too few of us get to enjoy these days: in nature.

Ask believers who enjoy spending time outdoors (hiking, camping, fishing, hunting, and other activities), and they'll likely tell you that natural settings are places where they see God's greatness and creativity, where they communicate with Him. . . and where He communicates with them.

Job certainly understood this truth. He had apparently pondered the greatness of God in the natural world around him.

Your time with God in a natural setting should never take the place of time spent in fellowship with other believers, and it should never crowd out "quiet time" spent reading God's Word and praying. But, as Job points out, you can find great blessing in seeing God's handiwork and experience His presence when you spend time enjoying creation and everything in it.

KINGDOM WORK—JUST KEEP AT IT!

*Let us not become weary in doing good, for at the proper time we
will reap a harvest if we do not give up.*

GALATIANS 6:9 NIV

Think of some of the great preachers in Christian history. From the
apostles Peter and Paul all the way through the centuries to men
like Billy Graham, certain preachers are exceptional in our eyes
because the results of their work are both obvious and tremendous.

But it's not like that for every kingdom laborer. Far from it!

God never promised us that working for Him would be easy—or
that we'd see a huge harvest of souls or large numbers of lives
changed through that work. We don't always see the results of
our hard work for the kingdom of God in the short run; in fact,
we may not see them at all this side of heaven. But Galatians 6:9
promises us that if we persevere in our good work for the Lord,
we *will* share with Him in the joy of seeing the furthering of His
eternal kingdom.

So when you begin to wonder whether you're making a
difference in the world around you, don't give up. Just keep
doing what God has laid on your heart to do, and He'll take care
of the rest.

THE FATHER'S DELIGHT

"The LORD your God is with you, the Mighty Warrior who saves. He will take great delight in you; in his love he will no longer rebuke you, but will rejoice over you with singing."

ZEPHANIAH 3:17 NIV

The Old Testament prophet Zephaniah wrote his prophecy during a very difficult time for the nation of Israel. His message is one of coming judgments on God's chosen people. But the book ends with wonderful promises of restoration—restoration of the loving, close relationship between God and His people.

The third chapter of Zephaniah is a series of promises and encouragements, all of which God directs at His people today. It tells us that God isn't just a God who loves His people but also a God who takes delight in us—such delight that His heart breaks out in song.

The promises in today's scripture verse point to a time when God " 'will wipe every tear from their eyes. There will be no more death' or mourning or crying or pain, for the old order of things has passed away" (Revelation 21:4).

This is the beginning of eternal life in the paradise that is heaven, the beginning of an eternity in the presence of the One who will no longer correct or rebuke us—and who will celebrate our presence as much as we do His.

A MOST IMPORTANT COMMAND

*...ver claims to love God yet hates a brother or sister is a liar.
For whoever does not love their brother and sister, whom they
have seen, cannot love God, whom they have not seen.
And he has given us this command: Anyone who loves
God must also love their brother and sister.*

1 JOHN 4:20-21 NIV

Let's face it: some people are very difficult to love. They're too
loud, too opinionated, too overbearing, too unlearned, too. . .you
get the point. But the apostle John has some very strong words
as to how we as followers of Christ are to relate to even the most
unlovable among us.

If you can't love someone who's right in front of you, John taught,
then how can you say you love a God you can't even see? That's
putting John's message rhetorically, for of course the answer is
that saying we love God but not the people He's placed in our
lives makes us. . .well, liars.

Ouch!

So when you encounter one of the "unlovable"—and there
are plenty of them out there!—love them the way Jesus loved,
unconditionally and sacrificially. And when your words and acts
of love don't change them in the least, love them all the more. It's
God's job to change people. It's your job to love them the same
way He loves you.

DIVINE FORGETFULNESS

"I, even I, am he who blots out your transgressions, for my own sake, and remembers your sins no more."

ISAIAH 43:25 NIV

If you think about it, part of the message behind today's verse might seem to contradict the very nature of God. Sure, we can grasp—and celebrate in—the fact that God forgives our sins and cleanses us from all unrighteousness. But how can a God who knows everything that has happened or will happen in eternity past and in eternity future forget something?

Let's put this in human perspective for just a moment. Suppose your spouse—or someone else close to you—does or says something to cause you pain or loss. It may be a matter of simple carelessness, or it could have been something done intentionally. Either way, you've decided that it is far better to forgive that person and restore the relationship than it is to cling to wrongs done and let it die. You can't literally forget the offense committed, but you can forget any thought of punishing that person for what he or she has done to you.

God's "forgetfulness" is a lot like that. He remembers sins we've committed against Him, but when we come to Him in humble repentance, He forgives us and casts away any thought of vengeance against us.

CHOOSING FRIENDS WISELY

Do not make friends with a hot-tempered person,
do not associate with one easily angered, or you may
learn their ways and get yourself ensnared.

PROVERBS 22:24–25 NIV

People with bad tempers can be very unpleasant to be around. Sure, they can be good company—as long as other people and life itself are treating them the way they deserve to be treated. But when some offense comes, the ill-tempered can react with unkind words and unkind (or even violent or dangerous) actions.

The Bible includes some simple but very sound wisdom when it comes to dealing with hot-tempered people: stay clear! Sure, we're going to encounter people with bad tempers (and other sinful attitudes and behaviors), but today's passage advises us to avoid socializing too much with these kinds of people.

Our God is all-knowing and all-wise, and He understands far better than we do that we tend to adopt the behaviors of those closest to us. He also knows that a person with a bad temper is headed for disaster, and He will do everything He can to make sure His people don't end up in the same place.

That includes giving us this simple bit of wisdom: don't spend your time with a hothead!

ONE-ON-ONE INTERVENTIONS

Better is open rebuke than hidden love. Wounds from a friend can be trusted, but an enemy multiplies kisses.

Proverbs 27:5-6 niv

Confrontation is uncomfortable for most people. We don't like being told that we're harboring sinful or unhealthy attitudes or taking part in actions that displease God or cause others pain. And it can be even harder to be "that guy"—the one who must somehow summon the courage it takes to confront a friend who so desperately needs it.

But the Bible tells us that a true friend is one who is willing to risk the friendship and say what needs to be said to a brother or sister in the Lord who is either living with obvious sin or has some kind of "blind spot" that keeps him or her from living or thinking in a way that pleases God.

It's easy to decide to just mind your own business when your friend strays from God's standards of living and thinking. But today's verse teaches us that part of being a real friend is being willing, no matter how uncomfortable it may be, to speak difficult truth to those you love—and to do it gently and firmly.

Do you have that kind of friend? And can you *be* that kind of friend?

"I'LL PRAY FOR YOU"

DAY 10 – MORNING

*"My intercessor is my friend as my eyes pour out
tears to God; on behalf of a man he pleads
with God as one pleads for a friend."*

Job 16:20–21 NIV

The Bible has a lot to teach us about how to pray, when to pray, and what to pray for. One type of prayer the Word tells us to engage in regularly is called "intercession," which is a type of prayer in which we "stand in the gap" before God on behalf of another person.

But just how important is it to God that His people intercede in prayer for others? So important that Jesus, His very own Son, spends His time in heaven interceding for us this very moment (see Hebrews 7:23–28).

When a friend, a family member, or a brother or sister in Christ is hurting and in need of a touch from the hand of God, it's always good to offer comfort by promising to pray for that person. But as you spend time with the Lord, please be sure to make good on that promise. God loves to answer His people's prayers, and He is absolutely delighted to answer prayers of loving concern when we offer them up to Him.

So don't forget to make intercession for others a regular part of your prayer life. Someone may very well be counting on you.

FRIENDS WITH GOD

"I no longer call you servants, because a servant does not know his master's business. Instead, I have called you friends, for everything that I learned from my Father I have made known to you."

JOHN 15:15 NIV

When we approach the work we do for a living in the right way, we can take great joy in that work. But there is something extra special about the work we do in helping our friends. There's something about getting our hands dirty in simple tasks like helping him move or spending a Saturday helping him paint his home, or in more "emotional" ways like offering a listening ear during times of trouble that bring you closer to your friend.

The same is true of the greatest Friend you'll ever know—Jesus, who demonstrated His love for His friends by laying down His own life for us (see John 15:13). When we walk closely with Him, listen to Him, and follow His leading, He calls us His own friends (John 15:14).

Jesus is such a loving Friend that He walked the earth for more than thirty years for us, taught us, died for us, was raised from the grave for us, and now resides in heaven, where He constantly pleads our case before His heavenly Father (see Hebrews 7:25).

As the old hymn says, "What a Friend we have in Jesus!"

THIS IS LIFE

"Now this is eternal life: that they know you, the only true God, and Jesus Christ, whom you have sent."

JOHN 17:3 NIV

We've all seen those T-shirts bearing the none-too-profound message that "Football Is Life," "Baseball Is Life," or "Basketball Is Life."

There are a lot of easily observable things about American culture, and one of them is that we are absolutely obsessed with sports—youth and high school sports (especially for those of us who have children competing), college sports, and professional sports alike.

There's nothing wrong with enjoying spectator sports—as long as you put them in their proper place in your life. These things are not life, just an enjoyable part of it. When they become an obsession, when they dominate your thinking and the way you live, then they become idols—and we know how God feels about idols!

For the believer, life isn't the work we do, in the recreation we enjoy on the weekends, or in the sports teams we follow. Real life—abundant life and everlasting life—is found in knowing God through Jesus Christ, the One He sent so that we could live eternally.

So feel free to root for your team and to enjoy watching a game. But never forget that these things don't define or make your life.

YOUR PLACE IN THE BIG PICTURE

What, after all, is Apollos? And what is Paul? Only servants,
through whom you came to believe—as the Lord has assigned to
each his task. I planted the seed, Apollos watered it, but God has
been making it grow.

1 CORINTHIANS 3:5–6 NIV

Read most every list of the most important/influential people in the history of Western civilization, and you're likely to find the name of the apostle Paul mentioned prominently. Of course, Paul was largely responsible for spreading Christianity throughout the known world, and we can't forget that he wrote most of the New Testament.

But you only need to read today's scripture passage to know that Paul's response to being held in such high esteem in such a list would be along the lines of "I'm nobody!" Paul understood that God had given him a big assignment, but he also understood that it was God, not him, who was worthy of the glory for the results.

God has given us, His servants, responsibilities that are but small parts in the bigger plan of salvation for others. Our job is to sow the seeds by telling others the truth about salvation through Jesus Christ and to water those seeds through prayer. God's part is to illuminate the message we present (to make the seed grow) and bring people to Him through the work of His Holy Spirit.

BE CAREFUL WHAT YOU LOOK AT

"I made a covenant with my eyes not to look lustfully at a young woman."

JOB 31:1 NIV

You probably know this already, but if you were to poll those at your weekly men's Bible study about their top struggle in the Christian walk, it would probably have something to do with sexual lust. They'd likely tell you that their eyes go where they shouldn't, and then it's only a matter of moments before the mind follows.

It probably wouldn't come as news to you if someone were to tell you that it's not easy to avoid seeing lust-inducing images in today's world. We live in an R-rated world, and even movies and television shows containing a PG rating often, if not usually, include scenes that can cause the mind to wander to places God doesn't want it to go.

So how do we win this seemingly overwhelming battle? It's a matter of commitment—or, as Job put it, making a covenant with your eyes not to look at images that cause you to stumble into lustful thinking.

So far as it depends on your personal choices, make a covenant with your eyes not to intentionally view lust-inducing images. And when you make a commitment to focus on the right things—namely your love for your family and your God—you will find yourself winning the battle for your mind.

STOP YOUR GRIPING!

*Do everything without grumbling or arguing, so that
you may become blameless and pure, "children of God
without fault in a warped and crooked generation."*

PHILIPPIANS 2:14–15 NIV

Let's face it—life can sometimes feel like one frustrating situation
after another. Who among us, when circumstances put the squeeze
on us, hasn't felt like just griping and complaining to anyone who
will listen?

While the Bible contains some examples of godly men who
complained to God (David and Job, for example), it also warns
us against grumbling and complaining, and also shows us that
having a complaining attitude and mouth can have very negative
consequences (see Numbers 14).

When we complain, we separate ourselves from God and His
peace, and we also ruin our testimony for Christ to a lost and hurting
world. After all, who wants to listen to someone offering answers
when that person constantly gripes about his own life?

So in those times when you don't think life is being fair to you,
remember to do as the apostle Paul instructed and "give thanks
in all circumstances; for this is God's will for you in Christ Jesus"
(1 Thessalonians 5:18). Also remember God's promise that "in all
things God works for the good of those who love him, who have
been called according to his purpose" (Romans 8:28).

GIVING WITH THE RIGHT MOTIVES

*"So when you give to the needy, do not announce it with trumpets,
as the hypocrites do in the synagogues and on
the streets, to be honored by others. Truly I tell you,
they have received their reward in full."*

MATTHEW 6:2 NIV

We may not want to admit it, but it can be easy to wonder *What's in it for me?* when we think of giving to others. Jesus understood this part of fallen human nature, and that's why He told His followers not to seek human recognition when we give.

When we think of the word *giving*, our minds usually go to the financial. But God also calls us to give of our time, of our efforts, of any other of the gifts He's given us. But no matter what we find ourselves in a position to give, the principle stands the same. When we give, we're to do it in a way so that only God—and sometimes the recipient—knows about it.

So give—give generously. But when you give, make sure your heart and mind are free of any desire for human recognition or any other earthly reward. When you give with a pure heart that is motivated by the desire to glorify God and bless others, God will honor your giving and bless you in return.

PUT YOUR TRUST IN GOD

Trust in the Lᴏʀᴅ with all your heart and lean not on your own
understanding; in all your ways submit to him,
and he will make your paths straight.

Pʀᴏᴠᴇʀʙs 3:5–6 ɴɪᴠ

No matter your level of education, you don't have all the answers to whatever life throws at you. Whether it's a difficult predicament, unexpected turn of events or a tragic loss, you may find yourself struggling to solve a problem and unable to explain why something negative has happened.

Friend, God has all the answers. You don't need to look any further or seek comfort from anyone else. He has your best interest at heart. He knows what you need. All you have to do is submit to Him, praise Him for the successes in your life, and turn to Him at times of hardship. The Lord will guide you through every situation no matter the circumstances. But, you must ask Him to direct you and you must seek God's will in everything you do.

Turn every area of your life over to God. There's no halfway with Him. You can't choose to follow the Lord some of the time and ignore Him other times. If you make Him a vital part of everything you do, He will lead you because you will be working to accomplish His will. God knows what is best for you. He is a better judge of what you need than you are, so you must trust Him completely in every choice you make.

IT'S ALL GOOD

*And we know that in all things God works for
the good of those who love him, who have
been called according to his purpose.*

ROMANS 8:28 NIV

God works in everything for your good. He doesn't pick and choose situations. He doesn't care about you only on certain days. He loves you every second of every minute of every hour of every day. You may face hardships. You may have people speaking ill about you. You may endure unbearable physical or emotional suffering. But even when something bad happens to you, God can turn any circumstance around for your long-term betterment.

Remember, God is always working for your benefit and He is always trying to accomplish His will through you. It's not your will, however. It's His will for you that He wants to help you fulfill. God makes this promise not to everyone, but to those who are filled by the Holy Spirit, those who love Him, those who put Him first in their life, those who don't care about worldly treasures, and those who determine heaven is their first priority.

If you love God with all your heart, soul, and mind and live your daily life acting out this unconditional love through your interactions with others, He will take care of the rest for you. All you have to do is believe in Him, exercise your faith, and work toward building His kingdom.

TO GOD BE THE GLORY

Humble yourselves, therefore, under God's mighty hand, that he may lift you up in due time.

1 Peter 5:6 NIV

It's easy to take credit for your success and accomplishments when you did all the hard work. You put in long hours studying when you were in school and made many sacrifices along the way to earn that diploma. You worked tirelessly at your job and spent countless nights working overtime shifts to prove yourself worthy of that promotion. So it's no wonder you soak in all the praise when everything pays off.

But what about God? Remember Him? He created you. He blessed you with the gifts you needed to get excellent grades, to work diligently, and to achieve great things. He put you in position to be right where you are at this moment. Have you thanked Him today? Have you given Him the credit? Humble yourself, exalt Him, and tell others about the wonders He has done in your life.

Stop worrying about your social standing, your position on the corporate ladder, and your status. God doesn't care about such trivial things. His recognition is more important than what anyone else thinks of you. He will bless you far greater than you can imagine. He will give you an abundance of blessings. Now, humbly obey Him, and He will honor you either in this lifetime or in the next or both.

HELP ONE ANOTHER

*"The King will reply, 'Truly I tell you, whatever you
did for one of the least of these brothers and
sisters of mine, you did for me.'"*

MATTHEW 25:40 NIV

How often do you pass the homeless person on the street corner
and look away, avoiding eye contact and continuing on your way
instead of offering help—food, drink, clothing, shelter, or money?
Would you ignore that person if it were Jesus Himself standing right
before you? Certainly, you wouldn't. So, look for opportunities to
extend a hand to someone in need.

Jesus specifically says that whatever you do for someone else,
you do for Him. Whether you give a drink to someone thirsty, food
to someone hungry, clothes to someone who needs it, or whether
you visit someone in prison or in a shelter, or look after someone
who is sick, you are giving to the Lord. He's watching you.

Friend, be thankful for all your blessings and be mindful that
others may not be so fortunate. Don't take what you have for
granted. Share what God has given you with someone who has less
than you. Perhaps you don't have much to give in the way of food
or money or clothing. But it doesn't cost anything to go see an
elderly person and lend a listening ear. It's free to visit someone in
prison and offer a word of encouragement. Please consider doing
something selfless today.

CAREFUL WHAT YOU SAY

"But I say, if you are even angry with someone, you are subject to judgment! If you call someone an idiot, you are in danger of being brought before the court. And if you curse someone, you are in danger of the fires of hell."

MATTHEW 5:22 NLT

You know that you should not commit murder. It's against the law and breaks the fifth commandment. But anger is a great sin too. It's a dangerous emotion that can lead to violence and even murder. Even to a lesser degree, anger is an awful sin because it causes bitterness, emotional pain, mental anguish, and spiritual damage. Simply being angry with someone goes against God's law to love one another. It prevents you from developing a closer relationship with God.

When you express anger, you aren't acting in Christlike manner. Instead, you are moving away from the example He set for you in the way He lived His life. Jesus didn't fight back when the soldiers crucified Him. He didn't curse at them or raise His voice in anger.

When someone makes you mad, rather than retaliating with hurtful words or physical violence, remember how Jesus responded to His critics and the men who put Him on the cross. Exercise self-control and try to respond in a manner that would please God. He will hold you accountable for your attitude, so train yourself to control your thoughts and that will make it easier for you to show restraint and avoid anger.

WALK YOUR TALK

"Prove by the way you live that you have repented of your sins and turned to God."

MATTHEW 3:8 NLT

Some Jewish leaders followed the Old Testament laws and oral traditions passed down for generations. John the Baptist criticized these leaders, calling them hypocrites for being too legalistic, and he accused them of using religion to advance their political power. John the Baptist challenged them to change their behavior and prove through their actions and by the way they lived their lives—not through words or rituals—that they had turned to God.

Friend, you've heard these sayings: "Practice what you preach" and "actions speak louder than words." You may say that you're a Christian. You read the Bible. You go to church. You offer tithes. You follow the rigid rules in your particular denomination. But do you truly practice what you preach? Do you walk your Christian talk? Do others see Christ in you in your daily life and activities?

Only you and God know the answer to that important question. God knows your true heart. He knows your intentions. He looks beyond your words and your religious practices and ultimately will judge you based on your behavior. Your actions speak louder than your words. Today, make sure that you put your Christian faith into practice.

GIVE ME STRENGTH

*I can do all things through
Christ who strengthens me.*

PHILIPPIANS 4:13 NKJV

The apostle Paul turned to Christianity after condemning and even murdering Christians. He eventually dedicated his life to serving Christ, and his journey led him to abundant wealth, extreme poverty, and everything in between. He was imprisoned for several years, but still wrote this joyful letter from prison.

When Paul says he "can do all things through Christ," he's not talking about superhuman ability to accomplish goals that satisfy his selfish purpose. Paul learned to get by with whatever he had whether it was little or nothing. He focused on what he should do—serve the Lord—instead of what he should have. Paul set his priorities in order and was grateful for all that God gave him. Paul faced many trials and tribulations, but he found joy in spreading God's Word and was not deterred by any trouble he encountered along the way.

You also "can do all things through Christ." You can accomplish any task, overcome any adversity, and survive any trouble if you come to the Lord and ask Him to strengthen you. He will not grant you the power to accomplish anything that does not serve His interests, but He will help you every step of the way as you build your faith and develop a relationship with Him.

FORGIVE ME, FATHER

*Restore to me the joy of your salvation,
and make me willing to obey you. Then I will teach
your ways to rebels, and they will return to you.*

PSALM 51:12–13 NLT

Have you ever felt disconnected from God because of your sin? Perhaps you are so embarrassed by your actions that you feel unworthy of being in the Lord's presence at church. David felt this way when he sinned with Bathsheba. In this prayer, he cries out to God: "Restore to me the joy of your salvation." David truly repented of his sin and asked for forgiveness.

God wants you to be close to Him, but sin drives a wedge between you and Him. Unconfessed sin pushes you further away from God, and it can separate you entirely from Him if you don't confront it, beg Him for forgiveness, and learn to obey Him. You may end up suffering earthly consequences for your sin. For example, adultery may lead to divorce. Fraud may lead to imprisonment. But God's forgiveness gives you the joy of a relationship with Him.

Once you experience that joy, like David, you will want to share it with others. David wanted to teach "rebels" and help them "return" to the Lord. You can help your friends and relatives by telling them about the joy of God's forgiveness and your fellowship with Him.

A SHINING LIGHT

Jesus replied, "My light will shine for you just a little longer. Walk in the light while you can, so the darkness will not overtake you. Those who walk in the darkness cannot see where they are going. Put your trust in the light while there is still time; then you will become children of the light." After saying these things, Jesus went away and was hidden from them.

JOHN 12:35–36 NLT

Jesus was speaking to a crowd of people in Jerusalem when they asked Him how the Son of God could possibly die. He explained to them He would only be with them in person for a short time and urged them to take advantage of His presence on earth. He was the light of the world, trying to show them how to walk out of darkness. If they followed Him, they would enjoy eternal salvation with His Father in heaven.

As a Christian, God wants you to bear Christ's light to the world. He wants you to let your light shine for others to see. Can those around you see Christ in you? Is your light shining brightly? Or has it dimmed?

Tomorrow, get up and go out there and spread the Word of the Lord. Be a shining light for someone else to see. Be a blessing to someone. Inspire someone to come to the Lord by illuminating your light to the world around you.

CRITICAL SELF-ANALYSIS

*I realize how kind God has been to me, and so I tell each
of you not to think you are better than you really are.
Use good sense and measure yourself by the
amount of faith that God has given you.*

ROMANS 12:3 CEV

It's important to have self-esteem and healthy confidence in the talents, skills, and abilities God has given you. However, you should not overestimate your worth by basing your evaluation of yourself on worldly standards. The true measure of your worth to the Lord isn't found in your bank statements, your job title, the size of your house, or cost of your luxury vehicle.

You must be honest and accurate in your self-evaluation, ignoring the world's standards of success and achievement. Your true value to God is demonstrated in the amount of faith that you have, not the total sum of your material possessions. All that you have is a gift from God. Recognizing, acknowledging, and being grateful for God's blessings will keep you from becoming too prideful, arrogant, or conceited. It will lead you to true humility because whatever you are, God made you so. He wants you to use the gifts He's given you rather than waste them, but He wants you to understand and appreciate why you have those skills.

DEFEATING TEMPTATION

Don't blame God when you are tempted! God cannot be tempted
by evil, and he doesn't use evil to tempt others.
We are tempted by our own desires that drag us off
and trap us. Our desires make us sin, and when
sin is finished with us, it leaves us dead.

JAMES 1:13–15 CEV

Often, you hear people say: "God is tempting me." Nothing could be further from the truth. It is not God who is tempting you. It's Satan who is tempting you.

Temptation comes from the evil desires within you. It begins with a simple thought and can escalate into a wrong action if you allow it. God tests you, but He does not tempt you. He allows you to be tempted because He wants you to strengthen your faith and rely on Christ for help. You can resist temptation by praying for God's guidance and direction in those situations and obeying His Word.

People often blame others for their sins. You hear sayings like: "The devil made me do it." No, you made yourself do it. You allowed yourself to succumb to the evil one's temptation. Don't make excuses and shift the blame to someone else. A Christian will accept responsibility for their sins, confess them to God, and ask for forgiveness. You can defeat temptation by stopping it in its evil tracks before it becomes too strong and you lose self-control.

CHOOSE WORDS CAREFULLY

"No weapon formed against you shall prosper, and every tongue
which rises against you in judgment You shall condemn.
This is the heritage of the servants of the LORD,
and their righteousness is from Me," says the LORD.

ISAIAH 54:17 NKJV

You may face a situation when someone is talking bad about you, perhaps even slandering your name. Your first inclination is to defend yourself and retaliate against that person. But Isaiah tells you that no one can injure you with words and accusations. You must be firm in your beliefs and stand up for righteousness.

Words can be weapons. They can hurt you deeply. But God will protect you. There is nothing that anyone can say about you that will damage your relationship with the Lord. He has a special place prepared for His Christian servants, and no person and no weapon can destroy it. People have mocked, ridiculed, and harassed Christians for thousands of years, and they will continue to do so. Have no fear, however. God will punish the wicked according to His will. You don't have to take matters into your own hands and seek vengeance. Simply pray that the attacks, lies, and harassment stop and God renounces the evildoers.

ROOTED IN CHRIST

And now, just as you accepted Christ Jesus as your Lord, you must
continue to follow him. Let your roots grow down into him,
and let your lives be built on him. Then your faith
will grow strong in the truth you were taught,
and you will overflow with thankfulness.

COLOSSIANS 2:6–7 NLT

Once you receive Jesus Christ as your Lord and Savior, it's the beginning of your new life with Him. But you can't stop there. Rather, you must build your relationship with Jesus by following His leadership, studying His Word, learning from His example, and obeying His teachings. Christ wants to help you and guide you through problems that arise in your daily life, and He asks that you commit to Him and submit yourself to His will. Be rooted in Him by drawing on His Word and putting the lessons you've learned into action. You will be protected from those who try to take you away from your Christian faith and tempt you with false answers if you call on Christ for strength.

You need constant nourishment to build your faith. You can feed your soul by reading daily scripture and studying and meditating on the Word. Let Christ be your strength and be free from human regulations.

SPREAD THE WORD

For I am not ashamed of the gospel, because it is the power of God that brings salvation to everyone who believes: first to the Jew, then to the Gentile.

ROMANS 1:16 NIV

If you have a favorite pizza place, you tell your friends. You don't hesitate to tell someone about a great experience you had at a restaurant, a hotel, a vacation resort, and so much more. So why do many Christians keep quiet about Christ? You know the Savior of the universe. You know the greatest man who ever lived. Don't be shy about sharing the Good News. Don't feel embarrassed to embrace your Christian faith and share it with others.

Paul was not ashamed to preach the Gospel. He withstood strong opposition and even went to prison for his beliefs, but he boldly and consistently found ways to preach the Word of the Lord.

If the people closest to you don't know you are a Christian, you aren't doing your job. You have the best news anyone should ever want to hear. Jesus changes lives and saves souls. Tell them. Give them an opportunity to hear how the Lord has worked wonders in your life. They may be ready to hear it and accept Him if only you would speak up.

TROUBLED WATERS

"When you pass through the waters, I will be with you;
and when you pass through the rivers, they will not sweep
over you. When you walk through the fire, you will not
be burned; the flames will not set you ablaze."

Isaiah 43:2 niv

Life is full of good moments. . .and unpleasant ones. There are days that feel like a breath of fresh air and life is great, and there are days that feel as if the seconds and minutes take forever. It could be that you received bad news about someone dear to you or news about something you expected to happen that did not go the way you had hoped.

Many people go through life thinking days are endless and bad moments will carry on for a while, but you need to remember that God is in control and that He is always right by your side. The Lord is not just someone who can be counted on when things go wrong, but also when things go right. He longs for a relationship with His children. He wants a relationship with you just like a relationship you have with a best friend. He wants His children to run to Him first with good news and first with bad news.

When you have a bad moment, count on Him to comfort you, solve the problem, and be the first one there for you. Likewise, when you have a good moment, run to Him and thank Him for it. Friend, through deep waters, hills, and floods, He will carry you. Just rely on Him with all your understanding and He will see you through.

A LOVING HEART

We love each other because he loved us first.

1 JOHN 4:19 NLT

One of the most difficult things human beings face is to love the way God loves His children. Many people go through life with so much anger, hurt, resentment, and hate in their hearts. It's easy to hate, but so much harder to love.

Take time today to reflect on how God loves His children, how He has blessed everyone with many gifts, talents, and abilities to suit their own need, how He protects you and keeps you safe from harm. God's love is pure. It is the source for all human love. It has no boundaries and needs no explanation, and it can spread like a wildfire.

Friend, have you ever thought about why God loves you the way He does? Have you ever tried to be as loving as He is? It is truly wonderful to be able to love the way God loves. There's something uniquely special about a loving heart that cures sadness, melts any hurt, and mends broken hearts. Next time someone treats you as less than you would like, remember that God loves you and cares about you. So, try to live like Christ in love.

OPEN DOORS

*"I know all the things you do, and I have opened a door
for you that no one can close. You have little strength,
yet you obeyed my word and did not deny me."*

REVELATION 3:8 NLT

Many Christians in the world today seek many opportunities, whether it's for a career change or marriage or something new and different. Doors open and close all the time. But how do you know which door to choose? How do you know which one God intended for you to walk into?

Many Christians forget the simplest rules of following Christ because they are so intent on getting ahead. They lie and even deny God to advance in their careers or lives in general. Not every open door in front of you is from God. You must remember that if you open a door that takes you away from Him, then it isn't from Him. If it made you disobey Him or break any of His laws, you must close that door immediately.

You may wonder, "What can I do? Why didn't that door come my way?" The devil is deceiving. He comes to you when you're at your worst, at your lowest point, and presents a key to your solution. Friend, be aware of his conniving presence when you're going through difficult times.

Pray to the Lord to direct you and ask the Holy Spirit to guide you to the door that God has for you. He will always provide for you, and He will never leave you or forsake you. He has a door for you that will come open just at the right time, a door that no man can ever close. All you have to do is believe that simple truth and walk through it.

PRAY FOR EVERYTHING

*"Ask and it will be given to you; seek and you will find;
knock and the door will be opened to you."*

MATTHEW 7:7 NIV

Many believers pray every day for different things. Some pray for more money, a new job, a new place to live. Some pray for health, happiness, and success. Some pray for it all. There's no limit on what you can pray about or ask the Lord to provide.

Often, people misinterpret this verse and focus their prayers on material things because God says He will give you whatever you ask. But Jesus is telling you to shift your attention from your daily wants and desires. Instead, ask God to show you more about Him, ask Him for wisdom, and ask for His patience and His understanding.

The Lord wants His children to have a relationship with Him just like a father has with his son or daughter. As a father tries to give his children whatever they ask for, our Father in heaven wants to give us more. Our Father is more generous and more gracious than any father on earth; He gives us much more than what we can ask for or imagine.

Jesus tells you to be persistent in your prayer and your pursuit of a relationship with God. Don't give up if He doesn't answer your prayer requests immediately. God knows what you need most, and He will provide when the time is right.

CHOOSE FRIENDS WISELY

Do not be misled: "Bad company
corrupts good character."

1 CORINTHIANS 15:33 NIV

When you were a child, your parents probably told you to stay away from the troublemakers at school because they didn't want you to go down the wrong path with them. As an adult, you are careful to avoid people who don't do the right things. Even your girlfriend or wife may not want you to hang out with certain friends, especially single guys who enjoy partying a little too much and are often preoccupied with chasing women.

As a Christian, you certainly should be mindful of the people you surround yourself with on a daily basis. Be careful not to associate too closely with unbelievers, for those who deny the resurrection of Christ can take you away from Him and cause your faith to waver.

Also, be wary of friends who don't know the Lord and speak out against Him. Their influence can be greater than you may think. They could you fill your mind with doubt and force you to question what you stand for in Christianity. Unbelievers live for today, for the moment, for instant gratification and satisfaction. They don't believe they will one day answer to God, so they do whatever pleases them on any given day. Avoid this type of person. Don't sacrifice eternal rewards for happiness today.

SEEING ISN'T BELIEVING

For we live by faith, not by sight.

2 CORINTHIANS 5:7 NIV

Sight is a beautiful thing. Many of God's wonderful creations are admired visually. Everything from the sun to the moon to the mountains to the oceans was created by God. Many people rely on what they see to make decisions, to take the next step in life, so they know exactly where they are headed.

Although the ability to see everything around you is one of God's amazing gifts to His children, He asks you to rely more on faith. Friend, faith is knowing that God is your eyes. He sees what you don't see and He knows what you don't know. Your future is His past. He has a plan for your life and He knows which way is better for you. Trust in Him to guide you, to hold your hand and take you to places you never considered going or imagined you could go.

Faith is a powerful thing. It is hope and light in the midst of darkness. Facing the unknown can cause fear and anxiety because you don't know what will happen. Fear of death is natural, for you don't want to leave loved ones behind. But if you believe in Jesus Christ and eternal life with Him, you will have hope and confidence in the most important thing you cannot see.

DON'T WORRY, BE HAPPY

Don't worry about anything; instead, pray about everything.
Tell God what you need, and thank him for all he has done.

PHILIPPIANS 4:6 NLT

Worry can sometimes consume your mind to the point of frustration. Perhaps you are worried about tomorrow, worried about your children, worried about paying your bills or rent, worried about your health, worried about a loved one, worried about a relationship, worried about what to do when faced with a difficult decision. Your brain plays tricks on you, makes your thoughts race round and round to help you find an answer, and you become obsessed with the problem instead of the solution.

Next time you worry, stop thinking. Hit the pause button in your mind. God asks His children to come to Him for counsel. He asks that you run to Him first before you even consult your best friend. Worrying does nothing to make tomorrow better. It is wasted energy. It's wasted time. Worrying doesn't allow you to appreciate what God does for you. He takes care of your tomorrow.

Come to God with all your burdens; open your heart and mind and believe that He will resolve all your problems and will provide for your tomorrow. He will take your worries away and give you peace and happiness for today and every day. So worry less, pray more.

HE WILL FIND YOU

*"For the Son of Man has come to seek
and to save that which was lost."*

Luke 19:10 NKJV

Many believers go through life with no known destination, no direction, and no purpose. You may be questioning what you are intended to do with your life. You may feel that you have no clue where you are and where you are going. Perhaps you have been searching for years and can't seem to find any answers.

Friend, have you tried to search for God in your life? Has He taken precedence in your life? Is He involved in every decision you make and every step you take? God searches for you. No matter how far you go and how badly you mess up, He longs for you. He searches for His lost sheep until He finds them, but He wants the ones looking for a relationship with Him. Seek Him today and He will answer all the questions you were searching to find answers for.

Simply sit down and talk to God about your life and He will direct you. He will tell you what your purpose is. Life has a greater meaning when you and God meet at the perfect place and the perfect time. That time is when you are ready to find Him. Don't waste any more days wandering aimlessly. Make that time now.

HARD WORK PAYS OFF

Do your work willingly, as though you were serving the
Lord himself, and not just your earthly master.

COLOSSIANS 3:23 CEV

You work hard day and night to provide for your family. You try your best and put in long hours at your job to impress your bosses. Some days you feel valuable. . .and some days you wonder why you work so hard. Your job doesn't pay that well, or your boss doesn't appreciate you. You sometimes feel as if you are invisible. No one notices what you do or the long hours you put in. The one who does notice is your Father in heaven. He watches over you, He sees your dedication, your hard work, and your loyalty. Sometimes your work doesn't pay off, but God sees how much effort you are putting in so you can get that promotion or that new job, so you can fulfill your duties as a husband and a father. Remember, you are called to be the priest, protector, and provider of your household.

Friend, always remember that the Lord will reward all your hard work. He will promote you in the midst of a market crash. He will take you higher and open doors for you even if you are underqualified. Trust Him and always be faithful. He sees your work and He'll give you what you deserve at the right time.

LEAD BY EXAMPLE

*Direct your children onto the right path,
and when they are older, they will not leave it.*

PROVERBS 22:6 NLT

Children are a precious gift from God, a blessing greater than any other. It's your responsibility as a parent to raise your children to know God, to love Him and to fear Him. Teach them to glorify His name in their words, in their thoughts, and in their actions. But you must do it yourself. You can't be a hypocrite. Show them by your example, and they will learn to follow your path.

Parents often want to make important decisions for their children, but that won't help them in the future. They need to stand on their own, recognize right from wrong, and make smart decisions for themselves. By raising them in the Church, teaching them the ways of the Lord, and impressing upon them the importance of a relationship with Christ, you will allow your children to grow up knowing this is the best path to take, and they will not take a detour away from it, away from God.

Don't worry about the distractions in the world or the negative influences that impact others. If your children are grounded in faith, they won't go wrong.

TRAIN YOUR SOUL

Have nothing to do with godless myths and old wives' tales; rather, train yourself to be godly. For physical training is of some value, but godliness has value for all things, holding promise for both the present life and the life to come.

1 Timothy 4:7–8 NIV

You spend a lot of time working on your outward appearance, eating healthy food, exercising, and doing whatever you can to ensure you look your best. There's so much emphasis placed on outer beauty, and you have to work hard to keep up.

But are you in shape spiritually as well as physically? Your spiritual health is more important. Your physical health can fail you whether it's sickness, disease, and ultimately, death. But your spiritual health will sustain you. It will carry you through the difficult times. It will help you endure tragedy and anything that goes wrong.

You have to focus more on your spiritual well-being because it will benefit you the most in the long run. It will always be with you, guiding you along. So, before you go to the gym, make sure to train your spiritual muscles today. Use the abilities God has given you to help others around you and be a serviceable member of the Church.

NEVER TOO LATE

Then he said, "Jesus, remember me when you come into your Kingdom." And Jesus replied, "I assure you, today you will be with me in paradise."

LUKE 23:42–43 NLT

When Jesus was hanging on the cross, two criminals were crucified along with him. One of them mocked Jesus, telling Him if He is the Messiah, He should save Himself and them. But the other criminal defended Jesus, admitted his own sin, and asked for mercy. This man showed unwavering faith, so Jesus assured him he would join Him in the kingdom of heaven.

Friend, it's never too late to turn to the Lord. Even on your dying day, God is ready to welcome you home. If you accept His son, Jesus Christ, as your Lord and Savior, your place in heaven is assured, just like how Jesus assured this criminal that he was accepted. But how much more fulfilling would your life be if you made the decision right now rather than waiting until you were on your deathbed. God doesn't care what you have done in the past.

You are already forgiven. Turn to Him, accept Him, and reap the rewards of His blessings. You don't know when you will take your last breath. Be prepared. Eternal salvation can be yours this moment if you're ready.

BE STRONG IN SUFFERING

That is why we never give up. Though our bodies are dying, our spirits are being renewed every day. For our present troubles are small and won't last very long. Yet they produce for us a glory that vastly outweighs them and will last forever!

2 CORINTHIANS 4:16–17 NLT

Whenever you face problems at work, at home, or in your relationships, it's easy to want to quit. Paul faced daily struggles and persecution that wore him down. But even when he was sent to prison, Paul never gave up on his goal to spread the Good News.

No matter the hardships you face, the pain or anger, the fatigue or criticism, focus on your inner strength from the Holy Spirit and continue to push forward. You have an eternal reward waiting for you, so don't give it up because you are feeling too much pressure today. Commit yourself to serving the Lord and He will empower you, turning your weakness into strength. Don't allow your troubles to diminish your faith. There is purpose in your suffering, even though you may never understand it. God can show His power through you. Your problems are opportunities for Him to work through you and for you to witness for Him.

LEAVING A LASTING LEGACY

A good man leaves an inheritance to his children's children,
and the wealth of the sinner is stored up for the righteous.

PROVERBS 13:22 NASB

Most people think of their legacy as the money, property, or possessions they pass on after death. That's the clear context of Proverbs 13:22. Of course we want to leave that kind of legacy and care for our wives, children, and grandchildren. It's one way we show our love for them and keep our promises—something every godly man should do.

Our legacy is much more than the material things we leave. Our legacy is spiritual, moral, and relational. It's the influence of our lives on those we love, those we know, our communities, and our world. Our true legacy is our impact in the world. Everyone leaves that kind of legacy—the good and godly person and the sinner alike. They just leave very different types of legacies.

So, what should we do? We should live with our legacy in mind and ask—at every decision point, at every moment of temptation, and at every opportunity to serve God and His kingdom—what we want to leave behind. Which choice will make us, our wives, children, grandchildren, and most importantly, God, proud of us? We should do that!

In coming days we'll look at factors that can add up to a legacy to be proud of in terms of our personal core, our character, our commitments, and our conduct.

AT THE CORE: IDENTITY

*Therefore, if anyone is in Christ, the new creation
has come: The old has gone, the new is here!*

2 CORINTHIANS 5:17 NIV

Who are you?

Men answer that question in many ways. We can answer it in terms of our relationships as sons, husbands, and fathers or in terms of our work or the sports we love and play. We can answer it in terms of our nationality, ethnicity, personal history, family, or generation. In fact, we are all of these and much, much more. Who we are is not one thing but the combination of many things that make each of us unique individuals.

But at the core of every man is one thing that defines how he sees himself. This fundamental identity shapes the person we become, defines all our relationships, and guides all of our decisions. That core identity can come to us by virtue of our birth. Sometimes it's forced on us by society because of the color of our skin, our last name, or the circumstances we grew up in.

But the true core of our lives, the single most important thing about us is always chosen. As Christians, we chose Christ. That fact should be the most important thing anyone knows about us. It's the choice out of which all other choices flow, that impacts everything else in life. It affects how we see ourselves, those around us, our purpose in the world, and our sense of right and wrong.

So, who are you? Is your identity in Christ the most important truth about your life?

AT THE CORE: VALUES

What is more, I consider everything a loss because of
the surpassing worth of knowing Christ Jesus my Lord,
for whose sake I have lost all things. I consider
them garbage, that I may gain Christ.

PHILIPPIANS 3:8 NIV

A man's values are those things most important to him.

Every day we are confronted with choices that rest on and often reveal what we truly value. Often the greatest challenge is sorting out competing values and choosing between good things. Is advancing our career more valuable than time with our children? Is work more important than worship? Are our hobbies more valuable than our wives' happiness? Do we value that purchase more than staying out of debt and the financial well-being of our family? Do we value momentary pleasure more than our purpose?

In this verse, Paul expresses his greatest value. Nothing, absolutely nothing was more valuable to him than knowing Jesus. He willingly let go of everything else and considered it little more than garbage compared to the insurmountable value of Christ in his life. Paul's core value echoed Christ's statement that loving God is the greatest commandment.

Are we like Paul, ready to value our relationship with God more than our ambition, pride, pleasure, and our desire for success, money, and status? Can we give them up? The answer to that question has a profound impact on each man, his family, and his future.

AT THE CORE: PRIORITY

Therefore, since we have so great a cloud of witnesses surrounding us, let us also lay aside every encumbrance and the sin which so easily entangles us, and let us run with endurance the race that is set before us, fixing our eyes on Jesus, the author and perfecter of faith, who for the joy set before Him endured the cross.

HEBREWS 12:1–2 NASB

Living out our values means establishing priorities.

Some things are important and worthy of our time, investment, and energy. Other things are great if we get to them. But there are things that we shouldn't do, not because they are sinful but because they distract us from what is more important.

These verses give us a way to think about our priorities. First, we should eliminate sin and everything that hinders a godly life. Things that interfere with our life in Christ or distract us from our calling should never end up on our "to do" lists. Second, we should live the life God has called us to with perseverance. Staying spiritually, emotionally, relationally, and physically healthy and happy is a priority. Fulfilling our responsibility as God's ambassadors, sons, husbands, and fathers in ways that honor God and further His kingdom isn't optional. Those responsibilities must be our priority. Finally, we should do all that while staying focused on Jesus and delighting in the joy of a life well lived.

No one disputes the wisdom found in these verses. It's just hard to understand and harder to live by. That should not keep us from trying. Achieving what's most important in life is always challenging and always worth it!

AT THE CORE: PRINCIPLES

*Trust in the LORD with all your heart and lean not on
your own understanding; in all your ways submit
to him, and he will make your paths straight.*

PROVERBS 3:5-6 NIV

Lofty ideals are fine. But a man's life is full of difficult choices, and we are often tempted to compromise our values and priorities. How can we live out our values and priorities in the challenging reality of everyday life?

First, trust God completely! The pressure we feel and the fears we face are very real. Christ's followers can and do experience very painful consequences for their faith. But we can trust God to make all things right and to reward those who serve Him.

Second, don't trust yourself! All of us have spent our lives immersed in cultures and societies that don't honor God. We learned how this world works. God's ways are so counterintuitive that our instinct is to think and act like those around us. Don't do it!

Third, submit every action and decision to God, His will, and His ways. This kind of submission isn't weak—it's incredibly strong. Submitting to God means we don't give in to the world around us or its temptations and pressures. That takes real strength and courage.

Finally, we do it God's way and walk His paths. The temptation is to wrest control over our lives from God and follow a path that makes sense to us. Adam and Eve tried that. It's never a good idea. His ways are always the best ways.

AT THE CORE: WISDOM

Be very careful, then, how you live—not as unwise but as wise, making the most of every opportunity, because the days are evil.

EPHESIANS 5:15–16 NIV

No man wants to live with the consequences of an unwise or foolish decision. But many do. Looking back, we can't believe we were that foolish and shortsighted. In these few verses, Paul outlines guidelines for acting wisely.

First, recognize the reality of our times. Paul encouraged his readers to act wisely "because the days are evil." We too live in evil times when honoring God is disparaged as intolerant and bigoted, while sinful behavior and lifestyles are celebrated. Wisdom sees our world for what it is, dangerous and destructive.

Second, be careful how you live! We can't risk acting recklessly or carelessly. Our marriages, children, the cause of Christ, and our own futures are at stake. It's all too easy to be tempted by the pleasures of a sinful world. We may enjoy it for a time, but in the end that life destroys what we value most.

Finally, we should make the most of every opportunity. Paul's instruction is crystal clear in the context of the rest of the letter. Making the best use of time, making the most of every opportunity rests on understanding and doing the will of God (Ephesians 5:17). The truly wise man seizes every circumstance, every choice, and every challenge as an opportunity to make the most out of doing God's will. It's the surest way to a wise and noble life.

AT THE CORE: LOVE

"A new command I give you: Love one another. As I have loved you,
so you must love one another. By this everyone will know
that you are my disciples, if you love one another."

JOHN 13:34–35 NIV

Love is a word with so many meanings and shades of meaning that it's hard to know what a person means when they use the word. But in these verses what Christ means is clear.

First, love isn't optional. It's a command!

Second, love is mutual. We are to love each other.

Third, the standard of our love for others is Christ's love for us. That's a tall order!

Fourth, Christian love is our surest witness. Our words don't mean much if we don't love each other.

But what does it mean to love like Christ? That isn't an easy question to answer. While there are many definitions, one practical way to think about love is "always acting in the other person's best interest." Isn't that what Christ did for us?

This kind of love isn't selfish. It's focused on the other person. It's not passive; it's active. It's not emotional; it's biblical. It doesn't cower in fear of the consequences; it's courageous.

But what is in the other person's best interest? Here are some litmus tests. When you pray, ask for godly wisdom and the leading of the Holy Spirit. What does the Bible teach? If the Bible isn't clear, ask for wise, mature Christian counsel.

AT THE CORE: SPIRITUAL VITALITY

*He answered, " 'Love the Lord your God with all your heart
and with all your soul and with all your strength and with
all your mind'; and, 'Love your neighbor as yourself.' "*

LUKE 10:27 NIV

Every relationship, no matter how intense or important, can fade and lose its luster.

There is no relationship more important to any man than his relationship with God because every other relationship depends on it. When a man loses his connection to God, his relationship with his wife, his children, his friends, and everyone else in his life suffers.

We are called to love God with all our heart, soul, mind, and strength. The question is how? Maintaining and developing a deeper, more vital relationship with God requires what all successful relationships demand—time, intention, practice, and service.

Great relationships take time. The problem isn't God. He'll give us all the time we want. The problem is we don't take time to pray, worship, study His Word, and listen to His voice.

Great relationships aren't accidental. They are intentional. We have to want spiritual vitality and intentionally do what must be done to experience a greater degree of God's presence.

Great relationships require practice. We have to actively and consistently do what builds our relationship with God.

Finally, great relationships mean we serve. We invest our time, creativity, and energy into those things that benefit the other person. Serving brings us close to the heart of God.

If we stop working at any relationship, it grows cold. We must intentionally and habitually invest time and energy into those practices that bring us close to God.

CHARACTER THAT MATTERS: PASSION

*Whatever you do, work at it with all your heart, as working for
the Lord, not for human masters, since you know that you
will receive an inheritance from the Lord as a reward.
It is the Lord Christ you are serving.*

COLOSSIANS 3:23–24 NIV

We all pursue our passions, and our passions inevitably drive our lives in their direction. That's not the question. The real question is—what are those passions?

Sadly many men settle "for grime when [they] could reach for glory" (Carl F.H. Henry). Their passions burn for power, possessions, pleasures and pride. They settle for paths that give temporary pleasure but are ultimately unfulfilling and destructive.

Paul made it clear that the only passion worth living and dying for is an all-consuming passion for God and His work in the world. Nothing can take its place. Nothing is as satisfying or rewarding. Most Christian men wouldn't disagree. But most of us don't pursue that passion. We are distracted by the shiny baubles of the world, dig for fool's gold, and end up empty and exhausted.

William Borden, heir to the great Borden Dairy fortune, was a student at Yale when he found his passion for Christ. He followed that passion and led the great Christian student movement of the early twentieth century. He turned his back on his family's business and fortune and pursued his call to serve God in China. He died on the way and is buried in Cairo, Egypt.

In his journal Borden wrote, "No reserves. No retreats. No regrets." Passion!

CHARACTER THAT MATTERS: GENEROSITY

Remember this: Whoever sows sparingly will also reap sparingly,
and whoever sows generously will also reap generously.

2 CORINTHIANS 9:6 NIV

Generosity is long remembered. So is stingy selfishness!

Scrooge, the main character in Dickens's *A Christmas Carol*, has become the epitome of stingy selfishness, of a man so concerned with himself he ignored the needs of all those around him, including his family, his employees, and his neighbors. But after his dramatic encounter with the ghosts of Christmas past, present, and future, he becomes so generous that "it was always said of him, that he knew how to keep Christmas well, if any man alive possessed the knowledge."

Like Scrooge, we would do well to consider generosity in light of our past, present, and future. God is generous with His children in giving us far more than we need and treating us far better than we deserve. His generosity is best expressed in His most generous gift, His own Son, Jesus. It's impossible to imagine a more generous gift to any less deserving.

Today's verse reminds us that both stingy selfishness and joyous generosity have consequences in the future. A large measure of our future joy, in this world and the next, depends on generosity today. True generosity isn't about how much; it's possible to give a great deal and not be truly generous. Generosity is a matter of the heart attuned to a generous God. It is the result of gratitude for what He has done and trusting in what He will do.

CHARACTER THAT MATTERS: HONESTY

An honest answer is like a kiss on the lips.

PROVERBS 24:26 NIV

Very few would disagree with the old maxim coined by Benjamin Franklin that "honesty is the best policy." But there are times when honesty seems like the worst possible "policy"!

We aren't always as honest as we could or should be. We shade the truth to avoid embarrassment, save money, or stay out of trouble. Sometimes we exaggerate or downplay the truth so others will think better of us than they would if they knew the whole truth. Some men are pretty clever in the ways they are less than honest. They may not be lying, but they certainly aren't "truthing" either!

The problem with being less than honest is that the truth always and inevitably comes out. Then we are not only guilty for whatever we tried to hide but guilty of not being honest about it. Often the dishonesty ends up hurting us more than whatever we tried to hide.

Honesty can be painful and costly for us and sometimes for others. But in the end, honesty always costs less.

CHARACTER THAT MATTERS: GROWING

For this reason, since the day we heard about you, we have not stopped praying for you. We continually ask God to fill you with the knowledge of his will through all the wisdom and understanding that the Spirit gives, so that you may live a life worthy of the Lord and please him in every way: bearing fruit in every good work, growing in the knowledge of God.

COLOSSIANS 1:9–10 NIV

Great men know there is always more to learn and they are ready to learn it. In fact, all of us want the people we deal with—our physicians, attorneys, financial advisors, and others—to be learners. We want the best they can give us now, not what they learned years ago. We expect them to keep up!

But we all know men who aren't learners. Sometimes it's pride. They don't believe others have anything to teach them. Sometimes it's insecurity. They don't believe they can master new things. But most of the time, it's just neglect and laziness. We're comfortable without the hard work of learning, so why put out the effort?

People can get away with that in some things but never in their spiritual lives. Today's verses make it clear that "a life worthy of the Lord" is a life that is growing in the knowledge of God through the wisdom and understanding of the Spirit. The truth is that no matter how much we know of God and His wisdom, there is always more to know.

Have you learned something new about God this week, this month, or this year?

COMMITMENTS THAT MATTER: GOD

*Now all has been heard; here is the conclusion of the
matter: fear God and keep his commandments,
for this is the duty of all mankind.*

ECCLESIASTES 12:13 NIV

We all make commitments. And, we all know some commitments matter more than others. If we can't keep our commitment to have coffee with a friend, it's not a big deal. If we don't keep our commitments to our wives and children, it's a very big deal!

What we are committed to shapes and makes up much of our lives. There are some things to which we must make unwavering, permanent commitments if we expect to leave a legacy that matters.

The first and most fundamental commitment any Christian man must make is his commitment to God and the Christian life. It has to be a non-negotiable. No matter what comes, no matter what challenges we face, no matter how great our successes or failures, our commitment to God is the anchor that holds in the storm and the compass that guides our days.

There are plenty of examples of men who have given up on their commitment to God and following Him. All of them have some things in common. First, in a moment of trial and temptation, they wavered and broke their commitment. Second, their grip on God gradually loosened. Finally, in the end they and those they loved suffered, and they left a woeful legacy.

How committed to God are you today? Are you wavering? Are you losing your grip?

COMMITMENTS THAT MATTER: FAMILY

But if a widow has children or grandchildren, these should learn first of all to put their religion into practice by caring for their own family and so repaying their parents and grandparents, for this is pleasing to God.

1 TIMOTHY 5:4 NIV

Next to a man's commitment to God, there is no commitment more important than his commitment to be a godly son, brother, husband, and father. Nothing will leave a more lasting impact on the generations to come, and nothing will matter more to him in the end.

Sadly, it seems that many men have abandoned their critical role in the family to pursue their own wants, needs, and desires. They seem to care little for the impact of their choices on their wives, children, and future generations. Being a godly husband and father just doesn't seem important. Nothing could be further from the truth!

We are called to lead our families in faithfully following God, to willingly sacrifice, to love our spouses like Christ loved the church, and to guide our children to a life devoted to God and His service. We are called to be protectors, providers, and examples of godly living.

It's true: There is no such thing as a perfect man, husband, or father. We all make mistakes, have regrets, and wish we had done some things differently. But perfection isn't required. A commitment to live for God and lead and love our family is.

COMMITMENTS THAT MATTER: GOD'S PEOPLE

Do nothing out of selfish ambition or vain conceit.
Rather, in humility value others above yourselves,
not looking to your own interests but each
of you to the interests of the others.

PHILIPPIANS 2:3–4 NIV

"To live above with the saints we love, oh that will be glory! To live below with the saints we know, that's another story!"

To leave a godly legacy, we must be committed not only to God and our family but to the people of God, His church. That's not always easy. All too often pain and conflict erupt in the church. It's easy to be disappointed, discouraged, and disillusioned. But that doesn't mean we should walk away from God's people.

Today's verse challenges us in several ways. First, we are not to act out of selfish ambition or vain conceit. All too often our disappointment comes from bruised egos and taking offense. Our commitment to the church must go beyond our wants and needs and rest on a deep loyalty to the family of God.

Second, we are to value others. Even those who hurt and disappoint us are valuable and worthy of our grace and forgiveness. We too need grace, forgiveness, and loyalty when we fail and disappoint others.

Finally, we should care about and do what is good for others. It's God's church and they are God's people. Perhaps the most powerful question we can ask is "What can I do for you?" We are all guilty of asking "What can the church do for me?"

COMMITMENTS THAT MATTER: GOD'S WORK IN THE WORLD

"Therefore go and make disciples of all nations, baptizing them in the name of the Father and of the Son and of the Holy Spirit, and teaching them to obey everything I have commanded you."

MATTHEW 28:19–20 NIV

God is at work in the world! Many doubt it or ignore it, but it's still true. Also, God will accomplish His plans and purposes. . .with or without us!

The only real issue is whether or not we will be part of what God is doing. In the end, the best life is one fully devoted to the greatest cause. Nothing can match the grandeur, significance, or value of being on a mission with God.

Sadly, there are many myths and misunderstandings. Serving God isn't a profession. It's a lifestyle. Serving God doesn't mean giving up everything we enjoy. God isn't a killjoy! Nor does it mean leaving the life we have and love and going to some faraway place. We can serve God right where we are. We think we're too busy. A man's day is crowded with responsibilities and obligations, and many think they don't have time. But we all know we make time for what is most important to us.

Every man is gifted and called to serve God, and each of us is uniquely equipped and positioned to make a difference in the world right where we are. . .if we'll do it.

That's the real question, isn't it? Will we?

COMMITMENTS THAT MATTER: PRESENCE

"And surely I am with you always, to the very end of the age."
MATTHEW 28:20 NIV

It's one of the most comforting promises in the entire Bible. Jesus is God Emmanuel, God with us who never leaves or forsakes us.

Presence matters. Being with those we love matters to our wives, children, and friends. Sometimes just being there, just being with those we love is the very best thing we can do. Being there for those we love only happens if we make it a priority. But it's not always easy.

There are times when being away from family isn't a man's choice. Work and other obligations can demand long absences or that we miss important moments. That's not the point. Our wives and children understand that.

Here are some suggestions. First, make your presence a priority. Family events go on your calendar first! Build the rest of your life around them. Second, find a way to be with your wife and kids every day. Give them your time no matter how tired or stressed you are. When you are with them, be WITH them. Leave the briefcase, the hassles, and the worries at work and focus on them. When you can't be there, find a way to be there. Skype, telephone, email, write notes and cards, Facebook message or Twitter, send flowers or gifts. Do something that shows your thoughts and your heart are with them. You'll never regret it.

Finally, make sure that when your kids and grandchildren leaf through the family photo albums, they'll find pictures of you!

COMMITMENTS THAT MATTER: FUTURE

*I consider that our present sufferings are not worth
comparing with the glory that will be revealed in us.*

ROMANS 8:18 NIV

Some men live in the past. Others live only in the present. All of us should live with an eye on the future.

The future is life's great, undiscovered territory. We know the past. At least we think we do. We can see the present, at least most of it. But no one accurately and truly knows the future. All we can do is make our best guess. There are too many unknown factors that are completely out of our control for us to predict the future. We just wish we could.

But this is a world of cause and effect, of action and reaction. What we choose today always and inevitably matters in the future. Sometimes what we think is a trivial decision has the greatest impact. And we know that God has revealed great truths and magnificent wisdom. So how do we live with an eye on the future?

First, don't let the past determine the future. Whatever happened in the past need not control our present decisions or future lives. Second, act ethically not expediently. Make wise long-term decisions not easy short-term choices. Third, trust God, His will and His ways, not what you see around you. Remember God, not our present circumstances, controls the future.

Finally ask yourself, "Do I want this choice to be part of the story of my life I tell my children or grandchildren?"

COMMITMENTS THAT MATTER: REPUTATION

Here is a trustworthy saying: Whoever aspires to be an overseer desires a noble task. Now the overseer is to be above reproach.

1 TIMOTHY 3:1–2 NIV

Reputation matters to your legacy.

A man's reputation is what others think of him and what kind of man they think he is. Some men build false reputations. They are good at pretending to be what they are not. They are like Dr. Jekyll who kept his Mr. Hyde carefully hidden. But no man is clever enough or careful enough to keep the truth about himself secret all of his life. And when the truth comes out, his carefully constructed reputation is shattered. Building a good reputation can take a lifetime. Destroying it only takes one act or one failure.

Our family, our friends, the church, and the cause of Christ suffer or benefit from our reputation. Rightly or wrongly, others draw conclusion about them from what they know of us.

The surest and best way to build a reputation is to follow the admonition in this verse, to live "above reproach." First, don't lead a double life. If you have a "Mr. Hyde" lurking somewhere, kill him! Second, pay attention to biblical standards and live well within those margins. Third, ask yourself what others, especially those outside the faith, will think if you act in a certain way. If it dishonors the gospel in their minds, don't do it.

Finally, leave a reputation worth living up to, not one the church or your wife, children, and grandchildren will have to live down.

CONDUCT THAT MATTERS: LISTEN

"Now then, my children, listen to me; blessed are those who keep my ways. Listen to my instruction and be wise; do not disregard it."

PROVERBS 8:32–33 NIV

Listening is always harder than talking. We all want others to know how we feel, to understand why we act and see things as we do. When people don't listen to us, we feel insignificant and disrespected.

It's easy to forget other people need the same thing from us. When we don't listen to our wives, children, friends, and coworkers, they feel ignored, uncared for, and mistreated. But when we listen well, we open the door to greater intimacy and understanding; we build trust and strengthen the bonds of our relationships. That's why listening is so important.

Before anyone else, we need to listen to God and His Spirit in our lives. All too often when we pray we talk too much and listen too little. Our family comes next. We need to listen to our wives. How else can we know their hopes, dreams, and fears? We need to listen to our children. It's the best way to earn our place in their lives for the rest of our lives. Our wives don't always need to know what we think. Our children don't always need correction or a lecture. Sometimes they just need us to love them enough to let them talk, listen carefully, empathize with their feelings, and show them the dignity and respect every person longs for.

Isn't that what God does for us when we pray?

CONDUCT THAT MATTERS: LAUGH

Our mouths were filled with laughter, our tongues with
songs of joy. Then it was said among the nations,
"The LORD has done great things for them."

PSALM 126:2 NIV

Oh, lighten up!

Life is serious business. But that doesn't mean we can't find joy and laughter in each day if we look for it. All too often men who feel the weight of their responsibilities wear that burden on their faces. Here's the question: Why would our children follow us into the Christian life if we are constantly joyless and unhappy? No one wants that kind of life.

Enjoying life is largely a matter of perspective. For us, a snowy day may mean shoveling the driveway, a slow commute to work, and the frustration of other drivers on slippery streets. To our children, a snowy day is filled with the boundless potential for fun. There's no school! The snow is beautiful. Sledding is great fun, and there's nothing better than pelting your sister with snowballs. It's all a matter of perspective.

We need to learn how to rejoice in the great things God has done and is doing even in the hard times. Let's learn to laugh at ourselves. We all do some amazingly funny things—we don't mean to, but we do! Learn to laugh with others and enjoy being with them. Smile at the silly but annoying things other people do every day. Throw yourself into life and enjoy the trip!

So, lighten up! Have some fun. The Lord has done great things!

CONDUCT THAT MATTERS: WORK HARD

*And then I will be able to boast on the day of
Christ that I did not run or labor in vain.*

PHILIPPIANS 2:16 NIV

There is little to admire in a lazy man. No employer wants to hire one. No woman wants to be married to one, and no child is proud of a lazy father.

We shouldn't be surprised. When God created Adam, He "put him in the garden of Eden to cultivate it and keep it" (Genesis 2:15 NASB). Before God created Eve and gave Adam the responsibilities of a husband and father, God gave him work to do. Work isn't the result of the fall. It just got harder after the fall (Genesis 3:17–19).

Work isn't part of the curse, but was meant as an expression of our nature as beings created in the image of God and in partnership with God's creative work in the world. Successfully completing a task and doing a good job bring a sense of satisfaction and self-esteem to a man that little else can bring. No wonder work is so important to us!

In his admonition to the Philippians, Paul pointed out that his work wasn't in vain and he could boast in the day of Christ. Paul put in the effort and worked hard at what mattered most. Paul did his work so well that he could boast not only in his accomplishment but also in the way he worked. So should we.

CONDUCT THAT MATTERS: BUILD OTHERS

You then, my son, be strong in the grace that is in Christ Jesus. And the things you have heard me say in the presence of many witnesses entrust to reliable people who will also be qualified to teach others. Join with me in suffering, like a good soldier of Christ Jesus.

2 TIMOTHY 2:1–3 NIV

There are plenty of people who are ready to tell our children, our wives, our friends, and our coworkers what's wrong with them. They don't need to hear it from us!

What they need to hear is what's right with them—why we are proud of them, why we love them, and why they are a gift to us and the world. There aren't many people in their lives who can do that for them, but we can.

Paul's adopted son, Timothy, was an outstanding young man who faced unfair criticism. There were plenty of people ready to tell Timothy what was wrong with him. But Paul's place in his life was entirely different. Paul taught Timothy who Jesus was and who Timothy was in Jesus.

First, Paul encouraged Timothy. "Be strong in the grace that is in Christ Jesus."

Second, this letter was part of Paul's long-standing support, instruction, and help. These were things Timothy had heard before.

Third, Paul's praise for Timothy and his teachings were public. He said these things in the "presence of many witnesses."

Fourth, Timothy was responsible to do the same for others.

Finally, Paul invited Timothy to join him as he followed Christ. It's an example worth following.

CONDUCT THAT MATTERS: SACRIFICE

Therefore, I urge you, brothers and sisters, in view of God's mercy, to offer your bodies as a living sacrifice, holy and pleasing to God—this is your true and proper worship.

ROMANS 12:1 NIV

We don't use the word *sacrifice* much, except in baseball and for those who serve in the military. Maybe that's because so few of us ever really sacrifice.

Sacrifice means surrendering something precious for the good of another. Sacrifice is always costly, painful, and challenging. But we should remember that the foundation of our faith is Christ's sacrifice for us. He surrendered heaven to suffer and die as a sacrifice for our sins.

A sacrificial life pleases God. It is true and proper worship. But that sacrifice is taken up in "view of God's mercy." Christ's sacrifice proved His love for us. It changed the world and it changed the future. It brought hope and healing, grace and goodness, joy and peace. So we follow His example.

There is no more powerful demonstration of love and courage than when a man willingly sacrifices his wants and desires for his wife, his children, and the cause of Christ. Sacrifice, not selfishness, is the stuff of heroes. Such loving sacrifice sends a powerful message and leaves a lasting legacy well worth whatever it cost.

A COACH'S WORLD

You have heard me teach things that have been confirmed by many reliable witnesses. Now teach these truths to other trustworthy people who will be able to pass them on to others.

2 TIMOTHY 2:2 NLT

This is the age of executive coaching. Corporations have discovered that coaching or mentoring shouldn't end after a new employee has been on the job for a few months. Individuals are groomed to take advice, take charge, and take risks. Employers don't want you to stop learning new skills.

You may be getting some of your own executive coaching today in church. You may not think of church as coaching, but it can be. It should be.

As Christian men, we start with learning biblical basics, but we never learn it all. Our entire lives can be spent being coached and coaching others.

Barnabas coached Paul. Paul coached Timothy. Timothy coached his own congregation. Great coaching makes great teams.

Because we don't know everything, we need a coach and we need to be a coach. Jesus never had much good to say about spiritual pretenders. Matthew 23:27 (MSG) says, "You're hopeless, you religion scholars and Pharisees! Frauds! You're like manicured grave plots, grass clipped and the flowers bright, but six feet down it's all rotting bones and worm-eaten flesh." Intense? Yeah!

When we think we've learned all there is to learn, we need to think again. God never wants us to stop learning, stop sharing, or stop growing.

Be a coach. Find a coach. Encourage a coach. There's a lot of growing just waiting on your response.

SUPERHERO SUBSTITUTE

*We have seen and testify that the Father has
sent the Son as Savior of the world.*

1 JOHN 4:14 NKJV

More than 125,000 people attend Comic-Con each year. This annual convention is dedicated to comic books and everything developed from those stories. Each month, more than $250,000,000 is spent on the most popular comic books. Worldwide ticket sales for movies that are based on comic books are in the many billions. At least three collectible comic books have sold for more than a million dollars each. Comic book heroes are big business.

Maybe you've been to see a superhero movie. Maybe you have your own collection of comic books. Maybe you even geek out about the backstory of a hero's world.

People love superheroes because they're passionate about identifying with someone with the power to rescue people from bad situations.

First Timothy 1:15 (MSG) says, "Here's a word you can take to heart and depend on: Jesus Christ came into the world to save sinners."

We're born. We sin. We need rescue.

Jesus isn't make-believe. He is more than a compelling story. He's God's champion. He faced the toughest enemy mankind has ever known—and won.

We read comic books because we want a hero. We want to be rescued. We want everything to be all right in the world.

Comic books are a fun substitute, but that's all they are. Spend all the money you want on comic books, but colorful pages can never replace God's living rescue plan.

We need a hero. God gave us Jesus—no charge.

HOMEWORK NEVER ENDS

Parents rejoice when their children turn out well;
wise children become proud parents.

PROVERBS 23:24 MSG

You probably have many labels: man, boss, employee, husband, dad, or coach. Many of the labels we wear involve teaching.

If you're a dad, homework never ends, although some may refuse to accept their assignments.

Being a dad is hard work. Your children look to you as a model. Your behavior can become their behavior. What you accept is what they accept. What you say is, well, you get the idea.

When you're at home, work at being intentional as a parent. When you ask your children to do, be, or say something different than what they see in your life, they can be confused. They may think, "He wants me to be something he isn't?"

Intentional dads understand their legacy comes at a price. Either they pay the price or their kids do. Dads are investors who never gain a return on their investment when they refuse to invest.

The time you spend doing homework is not just an investment in your children, but also in your grandchildren. Leaving our kids without our example and encouragement will ultimately yield a generation with little direction or respect for others.

It's never too late to ask God to be intentional about helping you help your children. They need you, you love them, and God supplies the action plan. Find what you need in His Word.

The good news is you don't have to be perfect to be intentional. Admit mistakes, ask your children for forgiveness, and then return to the plan.

WITHIN THE BOUNDARIES

Keep your minds on whatever is true, pure, right, holy, friendly, and proper. Don't ever stop thinking about what is truly worthwhile and worthy of praise.

PHILIPPIANS 4:8 CEV

Gaze at ranch land and you'll find fences. Ranchers will often say they get along better with their neighbors when there's a good fence between their properties. Why? The property lines are defined by boundaries. When boundaries are clear, the rancher has the freedom to improve, grow, and develop the land within the boundaries.

In our own lives, we have the boundaries of truth, purity, righteousness, holiness, friendliness, and propriety.

Breaking down those boundaries will always make purity less pure, truth less true, and holiness less holy. Broken boundaries allow us to accept bad behavior, participate in poor decision making, and treat others with less respect.

Sometimes we meet people who have no boundaries. When we interact with someone like this, we can run the risk of breaking our own boundaries to be on common ground. Resist this urge.

God wants us to embrace boundaries. We can use boundaries to keep other people out, but maybe God wants us to use boundaries to keep His ideas *in*.

We can be content within the fence when we realize it's for our good, a part of God's plan, and that it reminds us we were born with a purpose.

Why would God want to protect us with boundaries if there was no plan for our good?

Don't resist living in the boundaries. Discover a freedom to improve, grow, and develop the life within the boundaries.

THE INTERSECTION OF INTELLIGENCE AND ENERGY

Jesus said, " 'love the Lord God with all your passion and prayer and intelligence and energy.' "

MARK 12:30 MSG

Transportation moves goods along a specific path. You should know where the freight needs to go and then figure out how to get there. Maps, GPS devices, and conversations with those who have made the trip before are all helpful.

Transportation is usually thought of in terms of highways. However, your blood uses veins to travel throughout your body, your brain sends and receives messages via nerve endings, and phone calls use wires and audio waves.

God has always used transportation to move His message. Often the message God sends reaches our brain first, but for some reason can't quite figure out the map needed to move a few inches from the head to the heart. GPS and maps don't help, and other people may only be able to affirm the heart really is the next stop.

Why is it so hard to take a message that you understand to be true and move it to the place where it can change the way you live?

God's message to us often arrives at four different locations. Our heart is the place where passion lives, and it responds to the message in a way that is different than our soul or prayer life. Our mind is the place where intellect lives, while our strength is a place of energy and activity. Each location is a unique transportation hub.

Stop putting up road blocks, and allow God access to every part of who you are. He's got a message—let Him through.

HOURS: SPENDING THE LEFTOVERS

How can a young person live a clean life? By carefully reading the map of your Word. I'm single-minded in pursuit of you; don't let me miss the road signs you've posted. I've banked your promises in the vault of my heart so I won't sin myself bankrupt.

PSALM 119:9–11 MSG

Each week has 7 days. In those 7 days, 56 hours are dedicated to sleeping. That leaves 112 hours for everything else. If you spend an hour per meal, that removes 21. Now there are 91 hours to use.

Remove the workweek and we're down to 51. Sure, there are commute times and personal hygiene issues, but we're still left with more time than we think.

We might attend a church service on the weekend and read a devotional. So of the 168 hours we have available each week, the grand total of time dedicated to the one thing we say is most important could be less than 2 hours a week. That's 104 hours a year or just over 4 days each year.

Should we be discouraged by this news? Should we feel bad? No. Two hours is a starting point. Add time whenever you can. Place God firmly on your priority list. Pray on the commute. Get connected to a small group. Find a Bible reading plan, and consider reading through the Bible. Use these ideas to improve the quality and quantity of time you spend with God and the people He loves.

"He who began a good work in you will carry it on to completion until the day of Christ Jesus" (Philippians 1:6 NIV).

A COMMUNITY ON THE CORNER

God is love. Whoever lives in love lives in God, and God in them.
1 John 4:16 niv

The barber shop sits at the end of the block. The chairs and décor were installed in 1961, a few years prior to a man landing on the moon. Until recently, the founder of the shop was the first to greet guests. His name was in neon, just to the right of the rotating barber pole.

Inside you'll find men who've made this a regular stop for decades. One conversation with the owner made it clear why they returned.

He was a great barber, but he understood most people just want to be heard. His gentle questions highlighted an unexpected compassion. He remembered what you told him. If a farmer mentioned a struggle, the barber followed up the next visit to see if things had improved. They usually had.

That barber demonstrated what most men look for in friendship. We want friends who are dependable, listen, remember when they need to, and forget when they don't.

Jesus offered that example, but He wants that example to shine through us.

It's easy to get trapped in our own trouble, but other people may need us, and we need them.

That barber shop was a community. It was a place where haircuts were secondary to understanding. It was a throwback to a simpler time and an example of the best of human compassion. Most miss this barber for reasons that have nothing to do with hair.

We don't need to cut hair to learn this barber's skill. Perhaps he learned from someone far more compassionate.

LEAVE THE MUSEUM REJOICING

Jesus Christ is the same yesterday, today, and forever.
HEBREWS 13:8 NLT

Walk into most museums and you find collections inspired by past events. The exhibits depict the best and worst of our past. We can be encouraged, entertained, or thoughtful when we leave a museum. The finest examples of museums engage our memories.

Museums share the narrative of a story that is either cautionary or makes us long for the simplicity we once knew or now long for.

We wouldn't want to *live* in a museum because it only represents something that once was. We *visit* because we want knowledge or entertainment. We leave because there is real life existing in the here and now.

The Bible is filled with *history keepers* who explain what God had done for the people who followed Him. Their role was important and served a great purpose.

When the people remembered a faithful God, they always found a reason to praise Him.

If we look back at our own past, we'll discover that even when we made bad choices, God was faithful to love and forgive. We shouldn't be surprised when gratitude to God is the result of remembering.

While the faithfulness of God doesn't change, neither do His commands. Nor does His willingness to guide, love, forgive, and provide.

God doesn't want His people to only live in His Faithfulness Museum, because as wonderful as that is, His faithfulness reaches into real life for real people right now.

Let God redeem your past by walking with Him today.

GOD'S SPENDING LIMIT?

*"For all the animals of the forest are mine,
and I own the cattle on a thousand hills."*

PSALM 50:10 NLT

Accountants are valuable when it comes to keeping track of expenses. They know what assets have value and which have become liabilities. Budgets are an accountant's playground, and they're really good at making sure all expenses and payments are noted.

God's economy is a bit different. God cares less about numbers and more about people.

If God owns everything then He can use anything to do the most amazing things. God doesn't even get upset at the cost it takes to rescue people. He just keeps relentlessly pursuing with incredible compassion.

He's a lavish God who makes sunsets, forests, stars, and oceans for us to enjoy.

If God did have an accountant, they would probably say, "Why spend another dime? There's a lot of people down there that will never thank You. I'm not sure if You're aware of it or not, but that sunset last night exceeded the budget."

God created everything. He needs nothing. However, He wants each of us to know Him, and He'll keep seeking until He finds us, rescues us, and makes plans for us to live with Him forever.

God never has to worry about running out of resources. In fact, He never worries at all. He just keeps loving real people with real compassion leading to real change. And when He asks you to share what you have, it's all about experiencing a similar sense of joy that He felt when He gave His all for you.

THE BLESSING CONSPIRACY

As God's chosen people, holy and dearly loved, clothe yourselves with compassion, kindness, humility, gentleness and patience.

COLOSSIANS 3:12 NIV

George is a superhero. Those he serves don't know his name and rarely know what he looks like, but they remember what he *does*.

George visits a lot of restaurants. Usually he orders a cup of coffee. He's on a fact-finding mission. He quietly pays attention to what's going on around him. He puts one or two tables on his short list and asks the wait staff for help in his *blessing conspiracy*.

George travels a lot. He doesn't know the people he helps, but his secret efforts always end in personal blessing.

While he sips on coffee, he singles out a table or two for blessing. His *blessing conspiracy* has paid for the meals of elderly couples, single parents, and military veterans (sometimes he leaves an unsigned note). The people try to identify their benefactor, but they don't recognize George and never assume it could be the coffee-drinking stranger.

He leaves a generous tip as a thank-you to the wait staff for helping him.

George doesn't do this with every meal or on every stop, but when he does, people he's never met leave marveling at his kindness, but he simply smiles and wonders how God allows him to be so blessed.

God doesn't ask us to be stingy and self-centered. We're pretty good at that already. He asks us to wear spiritual clothes that encourage us to pay attention to the needs of other people. This is when God does some of His best work—through us.

PRAY FOR THAT PEACE

*[Jesus said,] "I am leaving you with a gift—peace of mind
and heart. And the peace I give is a gift the world
cannot give. So don't be troubled or afraid."*

JOHN 14:27 NLT

We long for peace. We want to experience an absence of war. The desire for this kind of peace seems essential.

God offers peace, but He defines it differently.

Adam and Eve, the first man and woman, disobeyed God's singular request, "Don't eat from this tree." Their disobedience changed how we access peace. It was sin that caused Cain to kill Abel. Wars were common in the Old Testament.

A world without war is not the peace God offers. The peace that God supplies is the assurance that He's in control, trustworthy, and faithful.

Peace is an issue of the heart. Wars can be waged on every continent, and God's people can still have a peace that can't be explained. Philippians 4:6–7 (NLT) says, "Don't worry about anything; instead, pray about everything. Tell God what you need, and thank him for all he has done. Then you will experience God's peace, which exceeds anything we can understand. His peace will guard your hearts and minds as you live in Christ Jesus."

Sin has invaded our world. Wars begin with arguments, broken promises, and disrespect. When mankind refuses to follow God, war is often the result.

On the other hand, God's peace can quiet individual hearts and provide reassurance, and it is compelling enough to encourage individuals to send their fears into exile.

Pray for *that* peace.

HOW TO FOLLOW GOD'S WILL

*[God has] already made it plain how to live, what to do. . .
It's quite simple: Do what is fair and just to your neighbor,
be compassionate and loyal in your love, and don't
take yourself too seriously—take God seriously.*

MICAH 6:8 MSG

Christians want to know God's will because He might have something big for us to do, and we don't want to miss it.

We're confronted with an up-close glimpse at a single verse that tells us exactly what God wants from us, but we tend to dismiss this as nonessential because it doesn't seem to point to a *personalized* plan God might have for us.

Yet we learn God can only trust us with big things when He can trust us with small things. So, God starts small. It's like He's saying, "You want to know My will for you? Treat your neighbor right. Be compassionate to others and show them My love. Take My Word seriously and don't be easily offended."

If you think this is easy, try it sometime. In a world where we don't know our neighbors' names, it can be hard to treat them right. At a time when people don't trust each other, it's hard to show compassion. In a place where God's Word is mocked, it can be difficult to take it seriously. In a world where humans live, it's too easy to be offended.

Therein lies the difficulty of your starting place. God's will starts here. Get to a place of faithfulness with these issues, and God will make sure you know what to do next.

THE SUCCESS OF FAILURE

Commit your actions to the LORD, and your plans will succeed.
PROVERBS 16:3 NLT

We are confronted with innovative products every day. Many show up on infomercials or shopping channels. Some stores have kiosks dedicated to products we've seen on television. Did you know there are plenty of inventions made by mistake?

Penicillin is a remarkable antibiotic, but it wasn't what Sir Alexander Fleming was trying to invent. He had been working on a wonder drug that cured disease. When that failed, he threw everything away, but looking down at his scientific trash, Fleming noticed a petri dish where mold was consuming bacteria. What he thought was failure was actually a success with a refined perspective.

Then there's the creation of chocolate chip cookies. This too was a pretty fantastic failure. The owner of the Toll House Inn needed to make chocolate cookies. Out of baker's chocolate, she used bits of sweetened chocolate thinking they would melt when cooking. Instead she got tan cookies with defined bits of gooey chocolate goodness. Failure? Most would argue for success.

God's plans for us are always *on-purpose* plans, but even if we take a wrong turn somewhere, God can still cause "everything to work together for the good of those who love God and are called according to his purpose for them" (Romans 8:28 NLT).

God never does anything by accident. He loves you intentionally. There's something He planned for you to do. He has made sure you have everything you need to accomplish His plan.

Perspective alters how we define success as well as failure. God can use both.

THINGS WE THINK

*You will keep in perfect peace all who trust in you,
all whose thoughts are fixed on you!*

ISAIAH 26:3 NLT

The things we think often astonish, embarrass, and torture us. We think about things we know are off-limits, and without our permission the thoughts return.

Today we commemorate a holiday called "What You Think upon Grows Day." Chances are you've never acknowledged the day before. When entertaining thoughts that keep us at a distance from God, we may end up acting out in real life what was only supposed to be a private thought.

When we spend time meditating on God's Word, we can have good decisions show up in our lives based on what we *allow* to take up head space.

Hebrews 12:2–3 (MSG) gives some great advice on redirecting and reconnecting your brain to God's plan. "Keep your eyes on Jesus, who both began and finished this race we're in. Study how he did it. Because he never lost sight of where he was headed— that exhilarating finish in and with God—he could put up with anything along the way: Cross, shame, whatever. And now he's there, in the place of honor, right alongside God. When you find yourselves flagging in your faith, go over that story again, item by item, that long litany of hostility he plowed through. That will shoot adrenaline into your souls!"

The story of Jesus is a remedy for bad thinking. We struggle—He helps. We blow it—He forgives. We wander—He encourages focus.

Grow your thought life in God's direction. A full benefits plan is waiting.

HOPE: BEYOND WISHFUL THINKING

The fundamental fact of existence is that this trust in God, this faith, is the firm foundation under everything that makes life worth living. It's our handle on what we can't see. The act of faith is what distinguished our ancestors, set them above the crowd.

HEBREWS 11:1–2 MSG

The Bible uses the word *hope* dozens of times, but did you know that when the Bible uses the word *hope*, it rarely means wishful thinking?

When God tells us to put our hope in Him, He is saying we should have *no doubts*. If we think of hope as wishful thinking, then doubt can creep into our thinking, overpowering what should be confident trust.

If we use a phrase from another era, God is asking us to *put all our eggs in His basket*. In more recent language, we should be *all in*.

Hope is a firm foundation, confident belief, and determined faith.

In our everyday life we can hope an unexpected check comes in the mail, we can hope our boss doubles our salary, and we can hope our car will sell for more than we paid for it. In each case, that is little more than wishful thinking. If we're honest with ourselves, we would admit we have very little confidence that these things will actually happen.

God's hope should be unshakable, fully dependable, and rooted in the promises of a loving God.

It is a brave man who hopes in God the way God wants us to hope. We need to have the intestinal fortitude (guts) to, without doubt, believe that the God who promised *will* come through.

NOTHING ESCAPES HIS ATTENTION

"For all that is secret will eventually be brought into the open, and everything that is concealed will be brought to light and made known to all."

LUKE 8:17 NLT

One of the first things you'll notice if you ever have the opportunity to take a hot air balloon ride is how quiet it can be. Because you're blowing with the wind, you don't typically hear it. Because there's no engine, the only noise is the occasional blast of the propane burner to heat the air. Because you're floating on air currents, there's little turbulence.

Equally remarkable are the clear sounds from the earth below. You can hear dogs barking, the excitement of children when they notice you, and the sounds of people calling to you thinking you can't hear them.

While not a perfect picture, this is a bit like God's relationship with us. Nothing escapes His attention—even when He's not recognized. He sees all. He hears all. He knows who we are.

We can't hide from God. Hiding is a lie our adversary asks us to believe is possible, and when we believe it, he comes back to accuse us of being unfaithful to God.

If you've never been in a hot air balloon, it can be hard to imagine what it is like. If you've never really trusted in God, it can be hard to imagine what it's like for God to know all about you while you continue to ignore His presence.

God knows we *will* break His law. He watches, not as a judge but as one who can compassionately offer forgiveness.

STOOP DOWN—REACH OUT—SHARE BURDENS

Stoop down and reach out to those who are oppressed.
Share their burdens, and so complete Christ's law.

GALATIANS 6:2 MSG

A friend lost his job. A neighbor lost his health. A coworker lost his promotion. What can you do? How should you respond?

Most men aren't especially gifted in emotional encounters. If our children get hurt, we often send them to Mom for comfort. If our teen daughter suffers heartbreak, we're usually ill equipped for the tears.

Maybe we're afraid that if we get too close, the problems we see in the lives of others will become our problems. If things are running smooth in our own lives, we avoid complications.

Following the Golden Rule (see Luke 6:31) will find us doing for others the things they could only hope for. Our actions might involve sweat equity, a listening ear, or perhaps a few dollars.

We give because God gave. We love because He loves. We forgive because we've been forgiven.

When it feels awkward to share the burden of others, just remember God's Son, Jesus, became one of us and saw firsthand how we live. Jesus fed the hungry, healed the sick, and taught those He encountered.

If left to ourselves, we are self-preservationists. We want to make sure we have enough, enjoy enough, and play enough. The problems others face are not our problems. Right?

Stoop down. Reach out. Share burdens.

When you do that, you're living in obedience to the God who has never turned His back on you.

LIFE'S POP QUIZZES

I treasure your word above all else;
it keeps me from sinning against you.

PSALM 119:11 CEV

There's good news: life is an open book test, and you have access to all the information you need to answer life's most important questions. There's bad news: the only book you really need is often overlooked.

We live in a world where access to information is not only available but expected. If we want the latest news, a few deft moves on a smartphone, tablet, or computer and the world is delivered to our screens. We can gain as much information as we want—whenever we want.

We have come to believe that we don't have to be an expert in anything. Why? We can make new discoveries online when needed and then forget them just as quickly—or we store up information that isn't especially important.

God has always wanted us to know what He thinks about the issues that affect us most. We can't act in the way we should if we don't have God's wisdom. We have access to His Word, yet we often stand back and guess when life's pop quizzes show up.

When bad days come and the tests seem the hardest, we should consult God's Word, but our usual response is to complain to the Instructor about the existence of tests.

In school, we review textbooks in preparation for exams, but in real life, we tend to view the Bible as an optional text rather than our primary source of wisdom.

We should keep the Bible handy, but as a *treasure* for consultation not bookshelf ornamentation.

THE LORD'S ARMY?

*No one serving as a soldier gets entangled in civilian affairs,
but rather tries to please his commanding officer.*

2 TIMOTHY 2:4 NIV

There's an old hymn that begins, "Onward Christian soldiers, marching as to war, with the cross of Jesus going on before." This has been sung for more than 150 years.

Ironically, the song was originally written for children, and the Salvation Army accepted the song as identifiable with their ministry, but there's been confusion ever since.

Some wrongly consider the song an anthem for Christians to engage the culture with violence in order to win back peace. Others object to the notion that God would have us engage in war at all.

This hymn is best understood when we consider that it takes dedication, discipleship, and discipline to follow God.

We are God's soldiers when we do what He commands. God's greatest commands are to love God and then everyone else. We only win when we show God's love.

We're to be at peace with people as often as we can (see Romans 12:18), serve others (see Acts 20:35), and give generously (see 2 Corinthians 9:7).

Soldiers are trained, soldiers obey, and soldiers love their commanding officer.

The war Christians wage is for the spiritual health of those we know. We protect our own health, nurture our children's health, and introduce Jesus to those we encounter. We press forward because lives are at stake. We should protect and defend but never attack.

The role of a military soldier and a Christian soldier are unique. Sometimes they overlap, but being a soldier for God means your first choice is love.

SOMETIMES WE FORGET

They traded the true God for a fake god, and worshiped the god they made instead of the God who made them.

ROMANS 1:25 MSG

Men are made to worship, and we will. Worshiping God is important, but most of us make time, room, and effort to worship other things.

When left with a sense of awe and wonder, we can quickly, and far too easily, turn away from God toward whatever inspired the wonder.

This could mean a visit to the mountains finds us thinking more about the mountains than the God who made them. We can watch sports and find ourselves in awe of the player instead of the One who gave the skill. We might taste a food that causes us to believe the cook is more inspired than the God who spoke food into existence.

But the connection doesn't stop there.

We test drive a car, buy a new phone, and can't stop smiling when watching our new home theater system.

All these things can be appreciated, but in each case our sense of awe and wonder can lead us to worship something or someone other than God. We can worship a car, sports, jobs, entertainment, nature, comfort, and even sex.

We replace God with something that doesn't have the ability to rescue lives, forgive sin, or change futures. We reevaluate what's most important and move God from first place.

Faith is important in worship. We have to believe that the God we *do not* see can fill us with more awe and wonder than everything we can see.

Sometimes, we forget.

ANXIETY AWARENESS

[Jesus said,] "Father, if you are willing, please take this cup of suffering away from me. Yet I want your will to be done, not mine."

LUKE 22:42 NLT

Imagine the time drawing close for Jesus to be betrayed, abused, slandered, and crucified. Jesus had never been human before being born in Bethlehem. Jesus had never died before after facing a bogus trial in Jerusalem.

As the *Son of God*, Jesus knew what things were like on the other side of His personal sacrifice. He knew forgiveness would be available to all who sought it. Love and grace? A free gift. As a *human*, he struggled with the weight of His final human act.

Some may want to bypass the words of Jesus when He asked God to remove the assignment of death from Him. The part of Him that was God knew what needed to be done. The part of Him that was human was overwhelmed by the task.

We should all be in awe of Jesus' next words, "Yet I want your will to be done, not mine."

God's plan for the rescue of humanity was ironclad. It was perfect, near completion, and unexpected. God didn't need a backup plan. He needed an obedient Son. When Jesus said, "It is finished," as He hung from the cross, it was clear God's plan was accomplished on a hill of sorrow.

God is aware of the anxiety we feel when things seem out of control. God knows the strength we need to walk through the toughest days—and He walks with us.

He'll even lead if we let Him.

INTERRUPTIONS ENCOURAGED

"So whenever we are in need, we should come bravely before the throne of our merciful God. There we will be treated with undeserved kindness, and we will find help."

HEBREWS 4:16 CEV

When you were in school, the teacher would invite students to ask questions, but at some point you were no longer allowed to ask because you had to take a test, quiz, or complete seat work.

Your parents may have been patient and allowed you to ask questions, but at some point you may have been told, "You have asked enough questions."

In the workplace, your boss may not mind being interrupted for questions that help you learn to do your job without needing to ask so many questions.

Try to think of someone—anyone—who likes being interrupted. Is it hard to identify this superhuman?

God is the only one who doesn't mind His children asking as many questions as they want. He never objects to interruptions. He never asks us to be more considerate. What God actually tells us is to be brave when we come to Him, expect kindness we don't deserve, and find the help we need.

God is more than patient with our interruptions. Why? Maybe it's because when we're willing to be brave enough to come to Him, we are telling Him we are interested in knowing His heart, plan, and purpose for our lives.

Relationships begin with conversation. Interrupt God whenever you need to. The end result is a closeness that will never be found trying to do things on your own—without His help.

SHOW THE GRACE

Be gentle with one another, sensitive. Forgive one another as quickly and thoroughly as God in Christ forgave you.

Ephesians 4:32 MSG

To her, he's just the nice man that helps her. To him, it's heartbreaking to see the woman he fell in love with view him as *the help*.

Confusion is her closest companion. She despises her new best friend as mind and body betray her. Personal dignity left no forwarding address.

The care she requires falls almost entirely on his shoulders. Not fair? Absolutely. Not fun? Who would think such a thought? Perfect reaction in every situation? Humanity prevents it. Yet, he has been put out, called upon, and has become a vivid example of commitment. Perhaps time will remind him that at the worst of times he did his best.

Those who know her sing an internal lamentation song for the woman who's disappeared. It's a song she neither hears nor remembers.

But in those times when recollections sparkle, or a comment reaches her funny bone and she reacts—he is reminded that his commitment has unexpected and precious rewards.

There are over 5 million American men and women currently suffering from Alzheimer's disease. Half a million will die this year from its complications. That's five million families struggling to understand and fight through issues of the disease. They are often overlooked, misunderstood, and in a regular state of distress, and this is only one disease on a very long list.

Everyone's going through something more difficult than you can imagine. Make the choice to show the grace, love, and compassion God has shown to you.

GAME PLAN COMMITMENT

Keep your eyes open, hold tight to your convictions, give it all you've got, be resolute, and love without stopping.

1 CORINTHIANS 16:13–14 MSG

George Mueller once said, "Nine-tenths of the difficulties are overcome when our hearts are ready to do the Lord's will, whatever it may be."

There can be intense anxiety when you believe you're standing alone in your faith. God gave us everything we need to stand for Him, but it can feel like we're in a battle we can't win when loneliness seems to be our only fellow traveler.

Maybe this is why the church in Corinth needed to hear the equivalent of a halftime speech by the apostle Paul in today's verse. Some may have been tired while others were invited back to the role of fulltime soldier.

The Bible is filled with examples of men who thought they were alone in their stand for God and against evil. Many felt alone, betrayed, exhausted, and broken.

Maybe this describes you. Maybe you've been looking for reinforcements. Maybe you want to be reassigned to something less *front line*.

God never intended you to be a sideline Christian. He doesn't ask you to sit in the stands. He doesn't commend armchair Christians, but He will give seasons of rest.

Take courage in Paul's speech—"Keep your eyes open, hold tight to your convictions, give it all you've got, be resolute, and love without stopping."

There's work to do. Even if you feel like you're the only one working. Remember, when you serve God, even the impossible becomes possible. Stand firm—walk on—be brave—serve well.

RESTLESS, AND HATING IT

Why am I discouraged? Why am I restless? I trust you!
And I will praise you again because you help me.

PSALM 42:5 CEV

Have you ever had feelings of restlessness? You feel like you should do something, but you don't know what. You can't sleep well, and you don't know why. You feel like you have a deadline, but you don't know when.

There are two primary reasons why men experience restlessness. The first is because they know they're in a bad place where poor choice or discontent are their best friends. The second is when they recognize they're in the wrong spiritual location.

There is a restlessness that results in a downward spiral, and there is a restlessness that results in a U-turn.

Feelings of unrest can leave us with plenty of room for self-reflection. Identifying the reasons why we're restless can help us determine where we're headed next and why.

Restlessness usually means we're not where we should be and suggests the need to relocate our heads, hearts, and hopes.

God can send unrest into our lives when we get too comfortable in circumstances God doesn't want for us in a place where we've stayed too long.

Restlessness can be God's invitation to a new adventure.

Confusion, apprehension, and depression may all be words that could be used to describe that godly unrest that screams, "*Move*."

God's call can be ignored, but the restlessness will not go away until you answer the call.

When you feel restless, and we all will, it's an incredible opportunity to follow God's plan.

THE THREE INVESTMENTS

"Above all and before all, do this: Get Wisdom!
Write this at the top of your list: Get Understanding!"

PROVERBS 4:7 MSG

Everything we do requires an investment of time, energy, or talents.

Some of our actions might be considered *necessary*. Some are optional. Still others may be thought of as a complete waste, but even that could be debated. For instance, some might consider it a misuse of time, energy, and talent to help someone who has no way to return the favor.

If you believe that the best use of these three investments is for monetary or personal gain, then it becomes easy to believe that helping others is a waste. However, if you believe that God has given you these three investments to use for His purposes, then helping others is not only a good use but perhaps the best use of your personal resources. To put this in perspective, understand that God invests everything He has in *relationships*.

What you believe about the use of these three investments will inform how you manage—or mismanage—their use.

First Timothy 6:17–19 is a pretty good overview of how God looks at our investments. "Tell those rich in this world's wealth to quit being so full of themselves and so obsessed with money, which is here today and gone tomorrow. Tell them to go after God, who piles on all the riches we could ever manage—to do good, to be rich in helping others, to be extravagantly generous. If they do that, they'll build a treasury that will last, gaining life that is truly life."

THE PLAN, GOAL, AND PURPOSE

Keep your eyes on Jesus, who both began and finished this race we're in. Study how he did it. Because he never lost sight of where he was headed—that exhilarating finish in and with God—he could put up with anything along the way: Cross, shame, whatever. And now he's there, in the place of honor, right alongside God. When you find yourselves flagging in your faith, go over that story again, item by item, that long litany of hostility he plowed through. That will shoot adrenaline into your souls!

HEBREWS 12:2–3 MSG

Keep your eye on the prize. Get your head into the game. Press on. Play with purpose.

Every single thing that requires a plan, completes a goal, and captures the purpose of the heart requires focus.

When a runner is *beyond* tired, it's the finish line that inspires him to push forward and finish strong. When a singer has been invited to perform his first solo, it's the audience that inspires courage. When an entrepreneur comes up with a brilliant idea, it's the launch of his product that gives him his first real sense of hope.

There will be days when the Christian life is hard. Our adversary will distract us and offer the equivalent of a recliner, detour, or false promise. He won't care if he's able to totally ruin our lives. All he really wants is to shift our focus.

Keep the focus on Jesus. Learn who He is, how He lived, and what He wants.

Feeling weary? Spend time with His story. Regain your focus, get your second wind, and press on.

DISCRIMINATION ENCOURAGES COMPARISONS

*Faith in Christ Jesus is what makes each of you equal
with each other, whether you are a Jew or a Greek,
a slave or a free person, a man or a woman.*

GALATIANS 3:28 CEV

The Emancipation Proclamation freed slaves during the Civil War. The Civil Rights Act of 1964 fought discrimination. Both were considered landmark moments, but God's thoughts on discrimination predate these watershed moments by centuries.

When the apostle Paul wrote to the church in Galatia, he essentially said, "When you believe in Jesus, the playing field becomes level. Where you come from no longer matters. How much money you make is irrelevant. Men and women are both welcome to accept this message as equals."

Sometimes we compare. We tend to judge ourselves by thinking of someone who doesn't seem to have it all together. *The playing field has become level.*

Sometimes we play favorites and chose our own team while leaving others out. *Where you come from no longer matters.*

Sometimes we feel superior because it doesn't seem we need help. *How much money you make is irrelevant.*

Sometimes we think our spouse would never understand. *Men and women are both welcome to accept this message as equals.*

God accepts everyone who accepts His Son. God loves everyone and some love Him back. God forgives and some accept forgiveness. God doesn't discriminate. He offers His best gifts to everyone. Some choose to refuse His gifts.

If we're distant from God, we need to remember He keeps the line of communication open. Maybe He's just waiting for our call—no matter who we are.

A PLACE TO SIT

And seeing the multitudes, He went up on a mountain,
and when He was seated His disciples came to Him.
Then He opened His mouth and taught them.

MATTHEW 5:1–2 NKJV

When we think of the Sermon on the Mount, we picture Jesus (as Hollywood has coached us) perched on a high rock up in the hills, teaching the multitudes—or walking through tall grass on the mountainside, reciting the Beatitudes as He maneuvers among the masses congregated there. But scripture says He walked *away* from the crowd, headed into the hills, and found a place to sit. When His closest followers came to Him, He taught them. This is a picture of intimate impartation to a few, not a scene with stage lights, microphones, and a megachurch multitude.

Evangelist Billy Graham spent a long life in the spotlight, and millions have responded to his presentation of the gospel. Yet, if he could live his life over, he'd do a few things differently. "For one thing," he said, "I would speak less and study more, and I would spend more time with my family."

Men too often long for the soap box and the spotlight. We want to hear the applause and the "amen." But Jesus looks for faithfulness in little things (Luke 16:10). He calls us to feed our own households and teach our own children first and foremost (Matthew 24:45; Ephesians 6:4; 1 Timothy 5:8). Whether or not we're called to speak to the many, we must often step away from the crowds and find a place to sit with the few in our lives who matter most.

BE BLESSED

"Blessed are. . ."
MATTHEW 5:3 NKJV

Jesus begins the Sermon on the Mount with a list of proverbs that the Church calls the Beatitudes (a Latin word for "blessings"). "Blessed" means "happy." In the pagan Greek culture of Jesus' day, the word *blessed* meant to be as happy as the gods!—to have *their* perks, *their* rights—to be *above* the toils and troubles of earth while enjoying its treasures.

But this isn't Greek mythology we're reading—this is *eternal truth* that Jesus is proclaiming of a joy much fuller than the worldly blessings of health, wealth, pleasure, power, and the pursuit of happiness.

For "mountain men" (those willing to follow Jesus into the mountain to be taught by Him), the Beatitudes are about life in pursuit of a different set of goals. Philippians 2:5–8 tells us to have the same attitude that Jesus had when He gave up heaven's haven to become a man. He humbled Himself, surrendered most of His God-rights, and became obedient to the Father in all things, even death on the cross.

Like Christ, we must give up our own rights and submit to the Father. To be truly, deeply happy (blessed), we must become poor in spirit. We must mourn. We must be meek, merciful, and pure in heart. We must suffer for others in Jesus' name. We must even rejoice in the persecution that comes as we follow Christ.

The Beatitudes (the blessings) aren't about houses, clothes, cars, smartphones, or anything else on this planet. The blessings are about laying up treasures in heaven by living like Jesus here.

THE POVERTY OF PRIDE

"Blessed are the poor in spirit, for theirs is the kingdom of heaven."
MATTHEW 5:3 NKJV

The climb up the mountain with Jesus begins with a descent into the heart—and a commitment to humility. To be poor in spirit is to be humble. Only those who take themselves low will be lifted high enough to inherit heaven (Matthew 23:12). God opposes the proud but gives grace to the humble (James 4:6).

It's hard for men to humble themselves. We've been taught to stand tall, to take the lead, to pull ourselves up by our bootstraps, to never let anybody push us around. Even in the Church we are sometimes encouraged to "claim our rights" as sons of the King— as if God owes us something other than the mercy that Jesus bought for us by His blood. In a religious environment focused on winning the blessings of earth, humility gets stuffed in a closet. In a culture focused on worldly prosperity, spiritual poverty can seem almost heretical!

But wait! Doesn't the Bible tell us that no man can muscle his way into heaven? Doesn't Jesus call us to admit that life is too heavy to carry on our own? Doesn't He tell us to link arms with Him and learn about Him? He said that He is "meek and lowly of heart," and only by embracing those qualities can we find rest for our souls (Matthew 11:29; Romans 8:29). No wonder we are called to be humble and poor in spirit, for this is who Christ Jesus is!

A HUNGRY MAN

"Blessed are those who hunger and thirst for righteousness,
for they shall be filled."

MATTHEW 5:6 NKJV

When Jesus said this, He wasn't peddling burgers and beer to a TV audience munching potato chips. He was addressing men and women who understood hunger and thirst intimately.

In Jesus' day, the daily wage was equivalent to three cents; nobody got fat on that. Israeli working men—never far from the borderline of real hunger or actual starvation—ate meat once a week. And thirst was worse; few besides the Romans had water in their homes.

In reality, this beatitude is a stark challenge: Do you want righteousness as much as a starving man wants food or a parched man needs water? How intense is your desire for God, for His goodness and glory?

To the privileged, hunger and thirst can become idolatrous. Desiring food we don't need, eating when we've had enough (more than enough), we become gluttons. I may be guilty of it too. But hunger and thirst for righteousness is a safe appetite, a holy appetite, a right appetite. We were created for righteousness.

Saint Augustine, in his *Confessions*, wrote, "God, you have made us for yourself, and our hearts are restless till they find their rest in you."

Jesus said, "I am the bread of life. Whoever comes to me will never go hungry, and whoever believes in me will never be thirsty (John 6:35 NIV). 'Man shall not live on bread alone, but on every word that comes from the mouth of God' (Matthew 4:4 NIV)."

Only God and His Word can fill us and refuel us to follow Jesus.

MERCY ME

"Blessed are the merciful, for they shall obtain mercy."
MATTHEW 5:7 NKJV

Second Corinthians 1:3 says that God is the "Father of mercies." Mercy is one of God's attributes, given to us in Christ so that we may extend it to others—even to our enemies. To be like our Father, we must be merciful (Luke 6:35–36).

A criminal is shown mercy when his sentence is shortened. A prisoner of war is shown mercy when he is treated humanely. The fallen gladiator in the Roman Colosseum was shown mercy when the dignitaries in the box seats gave a thumbs-up to let him live.

We extend mercy when we bless those who curse us, pray for those who persecute us, and do good to those who do us wrong (Matthew 5:44). We show our children mercy when we patiently give them another chance at something they've failed (or refused) to do. Mercy, like grace, is undeserved favor; something extended to others who may not merit it but need it.

Though we deserve judgment for our sin, God's great mercy has given us new birth instead and a living hope through the resurrection of Jesus Christ (1 Peter 1:3). Thus we show mercy and forgiveness to others (Ephesians 4:32).

Saint Augustine, an early church father who received the mercy of God through a dramatic conversion experience, wrote: "Two works of mercy set a man free: forgive and you will be forgiven. And give and you will receive." We could call this "the law of divine reciprocity." In other words, "You reap what you sow."

Do you need mercy? Give mercy.

CITY ON A HILL

"You are the light of the world.
A city that is set on a hill cannot be hidden."

MATTHEW 5:14 NKJV

Jesus is the light of the world, and those touched by His torch are set on fire with the same light from heaven. This dark world needs the light of the followers of Christ, but that doesn't mean it wants it. Chrystostom wrote: "Like men with sore eyes, they find the light painful. While darkness, which permits them to see nothing, is restful and agreeable." Jesus put it this way, "Men loved darkness rather than light, because their deeds were evil" (John 3:19).

In the Old West, a gunslinger on the run might take to the desert and pray for nightfall to avoid a determined posse. But in the midst of the midnight sandstorm, the welcome light of another man's campfire always drew him in. At that wild and lonely campfire, coffee and hardtack were offered freely, and no man was an enemy.

The Church, if it is doing the good works it is called to (Ephesians 2:10, John 14:10–12) will not hide the light of life from the fugitive in the desert. We will shine like stars in the night sky (Philippians 2:15), showing the way to life. We will be like a city on the mountaintop, a haven for the lost and weary traveler. Our campfire will signal shelter—eternal shelter—from the storm.

As the old ditty goes (sung around many a church retreat campfire): "This little light of mine, I'm gonna let it shine. Let it shine! Let it shine! Let it shine!"

PHATTER THAN A PHARISEE

*"For I say to you, that unless your righteousness exceeds the
righteousness of the scribes and Pharisees, you will
by no means enter the kingdom of heaven."*

MATTHEW 5:20 NKJV

Phatter than a Pharisee? Anyone could beat them to heaven! Didn't
Jesus say so (Matthew 23)? He called them white-washed tombs.
He said they were blind guides leading blind men, stumbling into a
ditch together. Their lips spouted truths about God, but their hearts
were light-years from heaven. Their evangelism turned converts
into worse "sons of hell" than they were. Jesus called them snakes,
vipers, hypocrites. He said they were blind, dirty, greedy, faithless,
merciless. He called them fools and prophet-killers. He. . .

But wait!

To think we are better than they are is to fall into the same
pit with them. Yes, Jesus called them on their hypocrisy, but the
shocking reality is that the Pharisees were 100 percent committed
to righteousness as they understood it. They dedicated themselves
to the honor of God's Word and the fame of God's name. The
problem was they were so sure of themselves, they couldn't see
that being sure of themselves was their biggest sin. They believed
commitment to right made them right. They thought they had a
patent on truth, and they were blind to their own falsehood—blind
even to God in their midst (John 1:11).

Pride precedes a fall (Proverbs 16:18). Humility precedes wisdom
(Proverbs 11:2). Wisdom says (as John Newton once declared), "I
am a great sinner. Christ is a great savior."

Righteousness greater than the Pharisees' comes by grace,
through faith in the only Righteous One who can save "a wretch
like me."

"YOU FOOL!"

*"But I say to you that whoever is angry with his brother
without a cause shall be in danger of the judgment."*

MATTHEW 5:22 NKJV

Jerry's mother left him when he was young, and now they were separated by four decades and several hundred miles. When Richard asked if Jerry was still in contact with his mother, Jerry replied, "That fool? I hope I never talk to her again!" She was "guilty" according to the anger and judgment in Jerry's heart, and he had never let her out of his interior prison. "I can't forgive her," he said.

"Yes, you can," Richard countered.

"You're right," Jerry admitted, "but I will not!"

Who was really in prison? Jerry was! His mother had long since asked forgiveness for her foolishness, and she was not in her son's prison—he was. Locked up with his anger, it had even eaten away at his body. In his fifties, he was crippled by years of degenerative rheumatoid arthritis. Anger can fester. It can kill. Ecclesiastes 7:9 says, "Do not hasten in your spirit to be angry, for anger rests in the bosom of fools." The Contemporary English Version says, "Only fools. . .hold a grudge." Ephesians 4:26 (CEV) exhorts, "Don't get so angry that you sin. Don't go to bed angry and don't give the devil a chance."

Who is the fool, Jerry or his mother? And who is more in danger of judgment?

What do *you* do with your anger? Have you forgiven others as Christ forgave you? "The hour is coming," wrote Dietrich Bonhoeffer, "when we shall meet the Judge face to face, and then it will be too late."

LOVE YOUR ENEMIES

"Love your enemies, bless those who curse you, do good to those who hate you, and pray for those who spitefully use you and persecute you."

MATTHEW 5:44 NKJV

Most modern translations offer a shortened take of this verse (based on the smallest percentage of the available Greek manuscripts!). But sticking with the New King James Version quoted above, Matthew 5:44 is more than a love portion for our enemies. It's a remarkable summary of the application of love in all relationships: to bless, pray, and do good. We bless with our lips. We pray from our hearts. We do good with our hands. Let's look at the "bless" commandment first.

In the context Jesus is addressing, someone has "cursed" you, someone has intentionally said bad and hurtful things about you. They're mad at you or don't like you, maybe even hate you—so they express ill will toward you vocally. They're not poking voodoo dolls and reciting incantations against you, but they're speaking evil about you. Maybe it's behind your back, maybe to your face.

When cursed, Jesus says, "Bless!" When someone says bad things about us, we say good things to (and about) them. Maybe we'd rather blast than bless. Maybe we even pride ourselves on how fast we can come back with a sarcastic one-liner. But scripture says, "Don't repay evil for evil. Don't retaliate with insults when people insult you. Instead, pay them back with a blessing. That is what God has called you to do, and he will grant you his blessing" (1 Peter 3:9 NLT).

Speak good to others. Bless, and don't curse.

"INSPITEFUL" PRAYER

"Pray for those who spitefully use you and persecute you."
MATTHEW 5:44 NKJV

David prayed, "Break the teeth in their mouths, O God. Lord, tear out the fangs of those lions! Let them vanish like water that flows away. When they draw the bow, let their arrows fall short. May they be like a slug that melts away as it moves along, like a stillborn child that never sees the sun" (Psalm 58:6–8 NIV).

Why can't I pray against my enemies like that? They deserve it, don't they? It's a terribly degrading thing to be bullied, picked on, and singled out for spiteful abuse. It's wrong. It's sin. And we all hate a bully. When we're being abused, we'd like to pay a bit of it back (with interest), but Jesus says, "Don't. That's my job. Your job is to pray that I don't *have* to pay it back."

Jesus prayed from the cross for the men who nailed Him there, for the men gambling for His clothes at his feet, for the men who delivered Him to the Romans and stood gloating, cursing, and mocking Him at His crucifixion. He prayed, "Father, forgive them!"

Stephen, the first Christian martyr, prayed for his executioners when their stones knocked him to his knees, "Lord, do not hold this sin against them!"

When we pray for our enemies, at least two things usually happen: (1) our own hearts change as we become more like Christ, and (2) God hears our prayers! Pray that your enemies will see God's goodness and love, repent of their sin, and be brought near to God (Romans 2:4).

THE GOLDEN RULE

"Whatever you want men to do to you, do also to them."

MATTHEW 7:12 NKJV

These words capture the essence of the Christian life—in every situation, treat others as we ourselves want to be treated. This is indeed the "Golden Rule" of civilized humanity.

Tragically, the human heart is anything but golden. It is, in fact, deceitful above all things (Jeremiah 17:9), and therefore incapable—apart from God—of living by this rule. It rewrites the rule to say: "Do to others *before* they do to you," anticipating the betrayal of other hearts. It says, "Do to others as they *have done* to you," to justify the age-old maxim of retribution: "An eye for an eye, a tooth for a tooth."

But Solomon wrote, "Whoever digs a pit will fall into it; if someone rolls a stone, it will roll back on them" (Proverbs 26:27 NIV). Any act against anyone will have its eventual payback, because "God cannot be mocked. A man reaps what he sows. Whoever sows to please their flesh, from the flesh will reap destruction; whoever sows to please the Spirit, from the Spirit will reap eternal life" (Galatians 6:7–8 NIV).

The Spirit enables us to obey the Golden Rule, so "Let us not become weary in doing good, for at the proper time we will reap a harvest if we do not give up. Therefore, as we have opportunity, let us do good to all people, especially to those who belong to the family of believers" (Galatians 6:9–10 NIV).

How do we define "good"? Apply the Golden Rule: what we think would be good for us, do the same for others.

NARROW-MINDED

"Enter by the narrow gate."

MATTHEW 7:13 NKJV

The world is webbed with highways and byways, but there are only two roads that ultimately matter—the one that leads to destruction and the one that leads to life. The road to destruction is a superhighway; the road to life is a narrow path. They run parallel but in opposite directions. The narrow path is harder to find because it runs down the middle of the wide highway in the face of frenzied traffic.

Most maps don't even mark the narrow path. Many a GPS doesn't have it programmed in. It's too narrow—and our world is increasingly opposed to anything narrow. Those who travel the path are often accused of being narrow-minded, but that's okay, because the One who blazed that trail is narrow-minded. He said, "I am the gate" (John 10:9 NIV). And not the gate only, but "I am the way and the truth and the life. No one comes to the Father except through me" (John 14:6 NIV).

Some call such narrowness "hateful," "exclusive," and "bigoted." Maybe it is: it hates hell, excludes sin, and welcomes only those willing to follow Jesus. But it calls *all* to follow, and it leads to eternal life—there's nothing wider (ultimately) than that!

Each of us was born through a narrow passage out of our mother's womb and into the wide world we now know. The One who created that natural passage (and this wide world) has also marked the one gate and the narrow road that leads to heaven.

Jesus is the Way. And that's the Truth. And that leads to Life.

WHO ARE YOU ENCOURAGING?

"Martha, Martha," the Lord answered, "you are worried and upset about many things, but few things are needed—or indeed only one. Mary has chosen what is better, and it will not be taken away from her."

LUKE 10:41–42 NIV

When Martha asked Jesus to send her sister away from the disciples who were learning at His feet so that she could help prepare food for their guests, Jesus had to choose between the expectations of His culture and the gifts of Mary and Martha. Martha fully expected Jesus to take her side. Why else would she risk a public confrontation in front of their guests?

Surprisingly, the best thing for Martha wasn't necessarily what she wanted. While she wanted Jesus to remove Mary from an opportunity to learn with the disciples, she was actually trying to impose her gifts of hospitality on Mary. At the critical moment when Martha's frustration peaked, Jesus offered encouragement to both sisters, even if Martha received it as a rebuke. Jesus encouraged Mary to continue learning, to sit as His feet as a disciple, and to seek "what is better."

At the same time, Jesus put Martha's many worries into perspective. She was concerned about a lot, but her gift of hospitality didn't have to leave her aggravated or resentful toward others. At a crucial moment, Jesus offered important insights that pointed both women toward fulfilling their callings. Who do you know who needs encouragement to take risks or to find contentment and peace in their present circumstances?

LOVE THAT BREAKS THE RECORD BOOKS

*Love is patient, love is kind. It does not envy, it does not boast,
it is not proud. It does not dishonor others, it is not self-seeking,
it is not easily angered, it keeps no record of wrongs.*

1 CORINTHIANS 13:4–5 NIV

If we believe that God is love, as John assures us (1 John 4:8), and that love keeps no record of wrongs, then we have a staggering revelation on our hands. God's love isn't a conditional, record-keeping kind of love. Our wrongs have been forgiven AND forgotten. Perhaps our greatest barrier to loving others with this kind of generous abandon is our inability to receive God's love.

We may believe that God can only love us if we pray more, live ashamed of our failures, or even hide our faults. This checklist approach to love alienates us from God and robs us from the experience of love that could revolutionize how we interact with our family, friends, and colleagues.

Once we understand that God loves us and isn't keeping track of our wrongs, we'll begin to extend that generous love to others. That isn't to say others can't or won't hurt us. They will. But once we experience the depths of God's love and forgiveness for us, we'll have a solid foundation and assurance of our worth that doesn't require the approval of others.

When we know that we are loved without condition, we become free to extend the same forgiveness to others—a forgiveness that keeps no record of wrongs.

HOW OUR JOURNEYS BEGIN

Then Jesus came from Galilee to the Jordan to be baptized by John. But John tried to deter him, saying, "I need to be baptized by you, and do you come to me?" Jesus replied, "Let it be so now; it is proper for us to do this to fulfill all righteousness." Then John consented.

MATTHEW 3:13–15 NIV

At the start of His ministry, Jesus humbly sought baptism under John in order to fulfill all righteousness, placing Himself alongside the people among whom He planned to minister. Just as death precedes resurrection and new life, the baptism of Jesus was a lowly moment of identifying with repentant people who had gotten far more wrong than they had gotten right.

The muddy waters of the Jordan River were no place for a King to begin His realm. Even a powerful army commander thought these waters were beneath him. For all that Jesus accomplished in His ministry, He didn't begin by rising to the top. He began by descending to the lowest point so that He could reach all people. It's one thing to read about starting small or at the bottom and working your way up, but actually taking a step down at the start of a ministry or new season of life takes a lot of faith.

In fact, Jesus' faith was firmly fixed in the power of God to raise Him up from both the lowly, muddy waters of the Jordan River and the darkness of death so that He could offer new life to all who have faith to follow Him.

THE END OF PAIN

And I heard a loud voice from the throne saying, "Look! God's dwelling place is now among the people, and he will dwell with them. They will be his people, and God himself will be with them and be their God. 'He will wipe every tear from their eyes. There will be no more death' or mourning or crying or pain, for the old order of things has passed away."

REVELATION 21:3–4 NIV

When we hear about tragedy in the news, experience a personal loss, or pass through a difficult season of life, it's tempting to think that our grief and sorrow has no end in sight. It may feel like life is an irredeemable mess that lacks direction or meaning. However, the final revelation of God will end all death, crying, and pain.

As we consider the hope that God offers us, we can find peace in this assurance that our future is leading toward a day when God dwells among us and brings us the comfort we have longed for all our lives.

The Bible points us consistently in this direction: God dwelling among us. From the days of the tabernacle among the Israelites in the wilderness, to the temple in Jerusalem, to the coming of the Spirit at Pentecost, God has consistently moved closer to us, not farther away.

While Revelation assures us that God's coming will bring justice, we do the story of scripture and the hope of the Gospel a great disservice if we overlook the comfort that God will bring to us. In the light of God's presence, darkness can't help but flee.

ARE WE PASSING RULES OR THE STORY OF GOD'S RULE?

We will not hide them from their descendants; we will tell
the next generation the praiseworthy deeds of the
Lord, his power, and the wonders he has done.

Psalm 78:4 niv

It's easy to pass along rules and laws to younger generations and new believers, but the psalmist writes that rules aren't enough. While resolving to pass along the law of the Lord to the next generation, the writer of this psalm points us toward sharing the deeds of the Lord, His power, and the wonders He has done.

This isn't just a matter of leading good Bible studies. The most powerful truth we can pass along is the power of God in our own lives. It's not enough to just pass along stories of God's power based on hearsay or legend. We have to live lives of faith and dependence that result in testimonies of God's presence and power. We need to demonstrate how the words of scripture have come to life in our daily lives. In fact, we are assured by Jesus that His followers can perform the same acts, and the early church in Acts repeatedly called themselves "witnesses" of God's deeds.

If we haven't experienced the power and goodness of God for ourselves, what makes us think the next generation will do any better? If we hope to pass along the stories of God's power and deeds, we should first seek the presence of God so that our stories will be grounded in real-life experiences that we can relate to others.

WHO ARE WE TO TELL GOD WHAT TO DO?

Do not be anxious about anything, but in every situation, by prayer and petition, with thanksgiving, present your requests to God.

PHILIPPIANS 4:6 NIV

While talking with a friend who was brand new to the Christian faith, I learned that her family was experiencing a difficult situation. When I offered to pray for her, she hesitated but then told me to go ahead. After praying for her and her family, she asked me a really good question: "I appreciate you praying for me, but who are we to tell God what to do?"

I agreed with her that we can make that mistake sometimes in prayer. In fact, some people can use prayer to control and manipulate others, to say nothing of trying to do the same with God. However, Paul offers us a helpful path forward. We begin with gratitude for God's present work, lest we forget all of the ways God is working in our lives and those around us. We also let go of anxiety when we pray because anxiety betrays a struggle to control our circumstances.

With our hands off future outcomes, we are in a better position to humbly present our requests to God. These are only requests, not commands. In fact, while praying, we may get a better sense of what to ask for before presenting another request. Lastly, God welcomes our requests and petitions. We may never overcome our anxiety if we don't invite God to intervene in our lives. Until we tell God what we're really thinking, we may never experience His peace.

RESTORATION AFTER WE FAIL

DAY 02 – MORNING

"Give ear, our God, and hear; open your eyes and see the desolation of the city that bears your Name. We do not make requests of you because we are righteous, but because of your great mercy."

DANIEL 9:18 NIV

I suspect that we've all failed in some pretty major ways over the years. Perhaps we failed a spouse, child, relative, or close friend. Perhaps we even went so far as betraying someone. After we've confessed our wrongs and tried to make things right with others, it can be daunting to seek out reconciliation with God. How do you begin again with God after a significant failure? Those who have disregarded the commands of God or inflicted others with pain may not even feel worthy of following a holy God.

The book of Daniel was written after the worst national tragedy that ever befell the people of Israel. After years of religious unfaithfulness and systemic injustice against the poor and vulnerable, the majority of Israel was sent into exile by the Babylonians. In the midst of national failure, the prophet Daniel continued to pray because of God's mercy alone. He knew his people had nothing good to show. They couldn't pretend to have it together. The destroyed city stood as a testimony for everyone to see. Nevertheless, they could still approach God.

It's not up to us to make ourselves righteous before we approach God. Even at our worst, we can count on God's mercy to begin the long process of restoration.

WHAT GETS IN THE WAY OF GOD?

Then Jesus said to his disciples, "Truly I tell you, it is hard for someone who is rich to enter the kingdom of heaven. Again I tell you, it is easier for a camel to go through the eye of a needle than for someone who is rich to enter the kingdom of God."

MATTHEW 19:23–24 NIV

Jesus' words to the rich young ruler can be jarring, especially to readers in the western part of the world who tend to have more wealth. Perhaps we are joining the Philippian jailor in crying out, "What must I do to be saved?"

According to Jesus, wealth is a tremendous obstacle to entering God's kingdom, and so those who want to remove any obstacle to God's kingdom need to ask some hard questions about their attachment to money and physical possessions. Keep in mind that Jesus had wealthy followers. Jesus was supported by women with significant funds who cared for His needs. Wealth itself is not sinful. Rather, wealth can become a substitute for God. The same goes for our possessions. We can rely on our possessions to provide comfort, to define our self-image, and to care for ourselves when we should be caring for the people around us. In other words, wealth can compete with treasuring God's kingdom over anything else.

The best way we can remove the obstacle of wealth is to practice regular generosity so that we learn to rely on God alone and minimize the distractions that could keep us from serving God and others.

HOW DO WE REPENT?

But Zacchaeus stood up and said to the Lord, "Look, Lord! Here and now I give half of my possessions to the poor, and if I have cheated anybody out of anything, I will pay back four times the amount."

LUKE 19:8 NIV

We often hear pastors and teachers say that repentance means turning around and changing course. However, we may struggle to imagine what this could look like in our own lives. The story of Zacchaeus provides one of the most powerful pictures of true repentance in action. Zacchaeus didn't just commit to follow Jesus. He recognized that following Jesus meant he had to completely change his life according to the priorities and standards set by Jesus. He saw the invitation from Jesus as an opportunity to pursue a new course for his life.

At his moment of conversion, Zacchaeus didn't just stop cheating people. He vowed to right the wrongs he had committed. He also pledged to give generously to the poor from his wealth. Zacchaeus recognized that much of his wealth had been acquired dishonestly, and he rightly recognized that following Jesus called for justice to those he'd wronged and the poor in his community whom he'd exploited as a tax collector for Rome.

He signaled his newfound trust in Jesus and allegiance to the kingdom of God by removing the wealth and dishonest tactics that he had relied on for so long. Zacchaeus repented by not only changing his future but by repairing his past.

WE ARE DIRECTED BY OUR DELIGHTS

*Blessed is the one who does not walk in step with the wicked or
stand in the way that sinners take or sit in the company of mockers,
but whose delight is in the law of the LORD, and who meditates
on his law day and night. That person is like a tree planted by
streams of water, which yields its fruit in season and whose
leaf does not wither—whatever they do prospers.*

PSALM 1:1–3 NIV

We often speak of being delighted by a visit with friends or by
spending time with family, but the sources of our delights can
have a far more spiritual significance. Our delights determine the
direction of our lives.

Perhaps we may be shocked to learn that God isn't interested
in shutting down our delights or what gives us joy. Rather, God is
interested in redirecting our delights and joys toward the most
certain sources of both. In fact, these redirections aren't petty
or frivolous. Although it may feel like a sacrifice at first, this is for
our benefit. Those who follow the way of mockers and sinners will
certainly find their own kinds of delights, but those delights will
last only as long as the last punch line.

Those who meditate on scripture and delight in communing with
God will find a deeper, lasting delight that will carry them through
the best and the worst that life has to offer. The delight offered
by God takes time and commitment, but it's assured to last us.

WHEN IS GOD AT WORK AMONG US?

So he replied to the messengers, "Go back and report to John what you have seen and heard: The blind receive sight, the lame walk, those who have leprosy are cleansed, the deaf hear, the dead are raised, and the good news is proclaimed to the poor. Blessed is anyone who does not stumble on account of me."

LUKE 7:22–23 NIV

Perhaps we read the story of Jesus and John the Baptist, and we can't believe that John dared to harbor doubts about Jesus. How could John see the miracles of Jesus and His power over demons and doubt? What more could John have asked of God? If you know the backstory of John, he expected quite a lot more. John expected Jesus at least to destroy the Roman occupiers of Israel with His "winnowing fork."

When Jesus preached a message of repentance for all people, even the Romans, and limited His power to healing the sick and demon-possessed, John was tempted to write Him off. John's story is a powerful reminder of the ways our own agendas can cloud our perspective. Perhaps God is working mightily in our lives or in the lives of those around us, but we've been missing out because we keep expecting God to show up in other ways, in other places, and among different people. Sometimes faith means learning to see where God is working right now in the moment rather than asking God to show up on our terms.

THE BLESSING OF AN ENDING

Teach us to number our days,
that we may gain a heart of wisdom.

PSALM 90:12 NIV

Aging sparks no end of troubling moments and crisis points. There's a quarter-life crisis that hits around twenty-five, the midlife crisis at forty, and then a crisis that typically hits around the sixties as many look into retirement. If anything, we may find less wisdom and more regret and recklessness as yet another year passes by. Each crisis of aging is rooted in the realization that death is a terrifying reality that we will all face one day.

However, the writer of the Psalms assures us that numbering our days with the end in mind can actually lead us to greater wisdom. Perhaps this strikes some as impossible, but consider this—once we view our days as limited, aren't we compelled to consider how to use them best? Doesn't each day become all the more valuable once we see that our days aren't available in an endless supply?

The wisdom that the psalmist talks about will help us ask hard questions about how we spend our time. We may be more driven to prioritize time spent in prayer. We may set aside more time to be with our family. We may change our professional goals or at least measure our success by different means.

As we number our days with an awareness of their limited supply, we'll have greater clarity when discerning our priorities and will find greater peace in the knowledge of God's presence throughout each day.

THE POWER OF SOLITUDE FOR TAKING RISKS

At daybreak, Jesus went out to a solitary place. The people were looking for him and when they came to where he was, they tried to keep him from leaving them. But he said, "I must proclaim the good news of the kingdom of God to the other towns also, because that is why I was sent."

LUKE 4:42–43 NIV

Jesus had just preached a powerful sermon in Nazareth and healed many in the village of Capernaum. His popularity was at an all-time high in the village where He had started to make His home, and the people even begged Him to stick around. Why shouldn't He consolidate His position and continue to perform miracles among His friends and neighbors?

Jesus had very different plans. He had a clear mission that called Him beyond the familiarity of His hometown. Despite the attractiveness of sticking around where He could be comfortable and popular, Jesus saw that His ministry required Him to pursue solitude and to venture beyond His village into many others.

While God may just as likely call others to stay put, this story reminds us that the calling of God often runs against conventional wisdom or at least the "popular vote." In fact, we can assume that Jesus' pursuit of solitude and commitment to His mission were undoubtedly linked. The power and clarity He drew from solitude certainly prepared Him to make the difficult decision to leave what was familiar and to pursue God's calling for His life.

HOPE FOR DOUBTERS

He said to them, "How foolish you are, and how slow to believe all that the prophets have spoken! Did not the Messiah have to suffer these things and then enter his glory?" And beginning with Moses and all the Prophets, he explained to them what was said in all the Scriptures concerning himself.

LUKE 24:25–27 NIV

At one point or another in our lives, we all struggle through situations that test our faith or cause us to question the goodness of God. Perhaps we can't make sense of a profound loss or our faith just wears down gradually as one hard season gives way to another.

In the story of the disciples along the road to Emmaus, we find two "followers" of Jesus who have essentially given up. They're confused and fearful, and they've most certainly left Jerusalem for fear of losing their lives. So far as we can tell, they believe Jesus' movement is finished. If they expected Jesus to rise from the dead, they would have stayed around. Despite their doubts and, as Jesus said, foolishness, Jesus still showed up, explaining the scriptures to them and eventually revealing Himself in the breaking of bread.

While it's true that doubt and unbelief can undermine our ability to follow Jesus, this story reminds us that Jesus won't discard His followers who struggle or who pass through a season of doubts. Whether we're looking for Him or just walking along in confusion, all is not lost. He is more than willing to show up and lead us back to faith.

OUR DAILY BREAD VS. OUR ETERNAL BREAD

"Do not work for food that spoils, but for food that endures to eternal life, which the Son of Man will give you. For on him God the Father has placed his seal of approval."

JOHN 6:27 NIV

When Jesus taught His disciples how to pray, He told them to ask God for the provision of their daily bread. Daily bread isn't something that you can store up for the long term, especially back in Jesus' day. He didn't instruct them to pray for storehouses of grain or even reserves of coins that would give them the ability to manage any crisis. They were welcome to ask God for provision, but only daily provision.

How often are we tempted to pray for a long-term solution to our problems and needs? It's almost maddening to think that a God with limitless resources would instruct us to ask for so small a provision, but then perhaps Jesus knew something of human ambition and our tendency to rely on our possessions and resources rather than God. Ironically, even our best "long-term" solutions are actually quite limited and fleeting.

The presence of Christ in our lives and a long-term faith in Him will never let us down, but our strength, finances, and even relationships may well let us down when we need them the most. The only sure "long-term" bet is the eternal bread of Jesus Himself present in our lives, nourishing us and providing for our needs day by day.

GOD TREATS US AS WE'D TREAT OURSELVES

"If you, then, though you are evil, know how to give good gifts
to your children, how much more will your Father in heaven
give good gifts to those who ask him! So in everything,
do to others what you would have them do to you,
for this sums up the Law and the Prophets."

MATTHEW 7:11–12 NIV

At a time when the religious believed that following God required adhering to a long list of laws and avoiding particular people, Jesus cut through the expectations of His audience with a very simple summary of the Law and Prophets. "Caring for others as we would care for ourselves" forced His audience to stop placing barriers between each other and to treat each other with mercy.

However, Jesus isn't just talking about the way we treat each other in this passage. His focus is much wider than personal interactions. He assured His listeners that God is far more kind and merciful than anticipated. We shouldn't be surprised to find an assurance of God's goodness followed by a command to be kind and merciful to each other. Jesus is asking us to imitate God's mercy and generosity that we've received.

Just as God mercifully gives good gifts to those who ask, we should extend the same kindness to each other. If we're going to be merciful toward anyone, we'll be merciful to ourselves above anyone else. Thankfully, God extends that very same mercy to us when we pray.

WHAT DOES IT MEAN TO LIVE BY FAITH?

Who may ascend the mountain of the Lord? Who may stand in his holy place? The one who has clean hands and a pure heart who does not trust in an idol or swear by a false god.

Psalm 24:3–4 niv

Living by faith each day requires more than believing in the saving work of Christ on the cross. That is just the starting point for our life in Christ! The life of faith is manifested in our day-to-day decisions when we have to choose whether or not we will trust God to provide for us.

When the writer of the Psalms says that those who stand in God's holy place will not trust in an idol or swear by a false god, we would do well to remember that idols and false gods weren't just passing fads or sources of personal fulfillment in Old Testament times. Idols and false gods were trusted to provide essentials for life, such as rain for crops or fertility for future children. Some Israelites surely felt tempted to mix prayers to the Lord with prayers to an idol in order to cover all of their bases.

Those who live by faith in God place their trust in God alone for their daily needs, believing that their obedience will not be in vain. The kind of faith God requires means placing all of our hope in God's provision and deliverance rather than wealth, our personal influence, or relationships with people in power.

WILL JESUS RESTORE US AFTER FAILURE?

The third time he said to him, "Simon son of John, do you love me?"
Peter was hurt because Jesus asked him the third time, "Do you
love me?" He said, "Lord, you know all things; you know
that I love you." Jesus said, "Feed my sheep."

JOHN 21:17 NIV

Perhaps we imagine that Jesus can't do much of anything with us after we've failed. Maybe we believe we've been disqualified or have fallen away because of our misconduct. Maybe we believe that grace only works up to a point, and we've gone too far beyond it. However, Peter committed the grave sin of denying Jesus. He essentially chose to cut himself off from Jesus when his life could have been on the line.

How did Jesus respond to Peter? First, Jesus went to the heart of the matter, "Do you love me?" Despite his failure, Jesus still offered mercy to Peter because He recognized that Peter still loved Him, even if that love was imperfect and prone to fail at times. Second, Jesus restored Peter immediately, tasking him with caring for His followers.

While we can hardly use this as a catchall template for all sins, Jesus was quick to turn Peter from a denier to an affirmer. The point person in teaching others about Jesus was the man who had denied Him. Peter's love for Jesus made the difference when his future hung in the balance, and Jesus restored him even after the most humbling of failures.

THE COURAGE TO RUN AWAY FROM TEMPTATION

One day he went into the house to attend to his duties, and none of the household servants was inside. She caught him by his cloak and said, "Come to bed with me!" But he left his cloak in her hand and ran out of the house.

GENESIS 39:11–12 NIV

We often think of courage and strength in terms of taking a stand and never backing down. We imagine ourselves in situations where we must hold our ground at all costs. However, there are times when the most courageous thing we can do is run away.

In a situation that offered no easy solution, Joseph recognized that his master's wife would continue to pursue him if he remained alone with her. Out of his love for God and loyalty to his master, he had the courage and strength to run away. There are some "battles" that cannot be won by staying put. When temptation threatens to trap us, there are times when our safest move is to retreat by changing our location, seeking help, or starting a new activity.

Resisting temptation can be just as much a matter of where we choose to stay or not stay as it can be a mental battle. Whatever Joseph thought or felt in the moment, his resolve to run away made it possible for him to, in a sense, stand strong.

THE JOY OF GROWING STRONGER

*Consider it pure joy, my brothers and sisters, whenever you face
trials of many kinds, because you know that the testing
of your faith produces perseverance.*

JAMES 1:2–3 NIV

Everyone wants to experience "pure joy," but I don't think many
people would think of a trial or test of faith as an opportunity to
experience it. What could James be thinking?

For starters, James is looking at the big picture for Christians.
He sees the whole of life stretched before him and even into
eternity, where God will reward those who have remained faithful.
All believers will face difficulties in the future as well, so trusting
God in today's trial will prepare them to remain faithful in future
challenges.

James didn't see faith as something that you either have or
don't have. Faith must be developed and grown over time. We can
say that we "have" faith, but our faith becomes stronger the more
we use it. Those who see trials and difficulties as opportunities to
draw near to God and grow their faith will find greater joy in the
most unlikely places.

More than anything else, James is eager for his readers, and
us, to see that our relationship with Christ is more valuable than
our comfort. It is like the pearl of great value that a man sells
everything he has to purchase. If our difficulties help us remain
close to Christ, then we can trust that seeming setbacks will help
our faith leap forward.

WHY WE SHOULD PUT OTHERS FIRST

Do nothing out of selfish ambition or vain conceit. Rather, in humility value others above yourselves, not looking to your own interests but each of you to the interests of the others.

PHILIPPIANS 2:3–4 NIV

Most of the conflict we face in life is rooted in seeking our own interests above those of others. Our ambitions to succeed can be a healthy expression of our talents and gifts, but they can also put us at odds with others if our success becomes linked to prospering at the expense of others. When we place our needs ahead of others, we're bound for conflict with each other, as plenty of other people will also seek their own needs first and foremost.

Paul's solution to conflict is stepping back and seeking out the interests of others above our own. Beyond removing potential points of conflict from our lives, this also forces us to trust God in the same way that Christ trusted God with His life on earth. Rather than seeking our own exaltation at the expense of others, we can trust that God will see and reward our selflessness and generosity.

Jesus assured us that the first will be last and the last shall be first. We can save ourselves from a lot of anger and conflict by choosing to be last, putting the needs of others first, and making ourselves a servant above all else. While we can strive to use our gifts well, servants never seek their own benefit at the expense of others.

LOVE BEGINS WITH FAITH

We love because he first loved us. Whoever claims to love God yet hates a brother or sister is a liar. For whoever does not love their brother and sister, whom they have seen, cannot love God, whom they have not seen. And he has given us this command: Anyone who loves God must also love their brother and sister.

1 John 4:19–21 niv

If we live in fear of God's judgment or condemnation, there's a good chance we'll let that fear define how we treat others. Our image of God will determine how we treat others. Jesus assured us that those who have received mercy will extend the same mercy to others.

When John writes about love, it's from the perspective of someone who sees God's love with tremendous clarity. His worth is determined according to God's love for him. Out of that deep reserve of love and acceptance, John found that he was able to extend that love to others. In fact, the best way to gauge our relationship with God is how we treat others. If we are able to love others, then we have experienced the love and acceptance of God.

If we are fearful, angry, or uncaring toward others, then we are most likely living out of fear, defensiveness, or judgment. Showing love may require some effort on our parts, but it most certainly begins with faith: believing that God loves us. That foundation of love makes it possible to love and accept others regardless of how they have treated us.

THE COURAGE TO SEEK GOD FIRST

The Spirit of God came on Azariah son of Oded. He went out to meet Asa and said to him, "Listen to me, Asa and all Judah and Benjamin. The Lᴏʀᴅ is with you when you are with him. If you seek him, he will be found by you, but if you forsake him, he will forsake you."

2 Cʜʀᴏɴɪᴄʟᴇs 15:1–2 ɴɪᴠ

In a time of turmoil and confusion, King Asa took courage in the promise from the prophet Azariah that he would certainly find the Lord if he sought Him out. He had an enormous task before him. The land was filled with idols and surrounded by threatening armies.

While we wouldn't blame him for focusing on military solutions and building better forts, he prioritized his loyalty to the Lord by removing the idols from the land. He had to trust that putting his allegiance to the Lord first would help solve his many other problems. We can imagine critics who may have said that he was wasting his time with all of his religious reforms. However, he moved forward in the belief that God can be found by all who earnestly seek Him. By the same token, unfaithfulness brought its own consequences. He couldn't hedge his bets by relying on idols and the Lord. Just as Jesus said we cannot serve two masters when referring to God and money, Asa realized that his best "military strategy" rested in trusting God alone.

SUFFERING MAKES US CONFIDENT

The Spirit himself testifies with our spirit that we are God's children. Now if we are children, then we are heirs—heirs of God and co-heirs with Christ, if indeed we share in his sufferings in order that we may also share in his glory.

ROMANS 8:16–17 NIV

Perhaps our first thought in a season of suffering or persecution is that something is terribly wrong. If we are God's children, shouldn't life get easier? We will no doubt pray that our suffering ends soon and that God will bring us relief.

However, Paul encourages us to think of suffering in far different terms. Besides the comforting testimony of the Holy Spirit that we are God's children because we suffer, we also can look to our suffering as an act of solidarity with the sufferings of Christ. If we suffer because of our allegiance to Christ, we'll place ourselves firmly among God's children who can look forward to sharing in glory one day. While we shouldn't hope for our suffering to continue indefinitely, God may give us our greatest confidence and hope of future glory in the midst of our darkest moments today.

Jesus assured us that His own sufferings signaled that the same would surely come to His followers one day. If you're going through a season of suffering or isolation because of your faith, that doesn't mean God has abandoned you. Rather, it means that this world has recognized you belong to a different family and your hope is in a different place.

RECEIVING GOD'S GIFT LIKE A CHILD

But Jesus called the children to him and said, "Let the little children come to me, and do not hinder them, for the kingdom of God belongs to such as these. Truly I tell you, anyone who will not receive the kingdom of God like a little child will never enter it."

LUKE 18:16–17 NIV

We can all recall what it's like to give a gift to a child. She may well cling to it for hours if we let her. Some children may even obsess over keeping the box that the gift came in, re-creating the moment they opened it over and over again.

Children offer their complete attention to gifts, receiving them with joy and focus. There is a simplicity and lack of cynicism among children that allows them to be fully present in the moment. They are brimming over with faith, hope, and joy rather than doubts, fears, and arguments. Perhaps Jesus had grown weary of the latter when He embraced a group of children despite His disciples' efforts to keep them away. Their eagerness to learn and to receive His blessing offers the perfect picture for receiving God's kingdom.

For a kingdom compared to a tiny seed or little flecks of yeast worked through the bread, children are the most likely to perceive its value. Rather than coming up with sophisticated explanations for or against Jesus, they demonstrated that coming to Jesus with open arms is the perfect place to begin.

DO WE BELIEVE GOD ABOUNDS IN LOVE?

But you, Lord, are a compassionate and gracious God, slow to anger, abounding in love and faithfulness. Turn to me and have mercy on me; show your strength in behalf of your servant; save me, because I serve you just as my mother did.

PSALM 86:15–16 NIV

While there's no doubt in the Bible that God is just, the psalmist reminds us that God is abounding in love and faithfulness. Perhaps we are slow to confess our sins and weaknesses because we believe that God is actually abounding in judgment and justice rather than love and faithfulness. Are we slow to confess our faults because we fear we've gone too far this time? Do we believe we are the exception to God's patience and mercy? We could share the same fear as the psalmist that God has turned away from us.

However, we are assured that despite our darkest moments and deepest doubts, the Lord is compassionate and gracious, offering forgiveness to those who turn to Him. In fact, the Lord isn't offering mercy in drips and drops. The Lord's very character is love and faithfulness to His people.

We can trust that the Lord won't just turn to us, but will act in our lives, intervening when we are full of despair. The Lord's people are not cast aside despite failures or seasons of doubt. We can trust that the Lord holds onto us faithfully, not out of duty or obligation, but out of abounding love.

THE SOURCE OF TRUE FREEDOM

Now the Lord is the Spirit, and where the Spirit of the Lord is, there is freedom. And we all, who with unveiled faces contemplate the Lord's glory, are being transformed into his image with ever-increasing glory, which comes from the Lord, who is the Spirit.

2 CORINTHIANS 3:17–18 NIV

As Paul compares the Law of Moses to the new covenant under Christ, he is careful to say that both covenants displayed the glory of God, but Christ has brought a deeper level of intimacy with God. We could say that the picture of God painted by one covenant has been filled in with greater color and detail by the new covenant under Christ.

For instance, while the glory of the old covenant forced Moses to wear a veil and failed to transform minds and hearts, the new covenant under Christ removes the veil between God and humanity. As we turn to the Lord and receive His Spirit, we are transformed into a new kind of freedom that empowers us to follow the lead of the Spirit. We aren't cut off from God's will or struggling to obey laws on our own. God isn't waiting for us to get our acts together.

We are welcome in God's presence through the mediation of the Spirit and are being transformed by the glory of the Lord. While the Law of Moses shared the glory of God with us, the Spirit gives us the freedom to dwell in God's presence and transforms us into the image of Christ.

HOPE IN WHAT GOD HAS SPOKEN

I reach out for your commands, which I love, that I may meditate on your decrees. Remember your word to your servant, for you have given me hope. My comfort in my suffering is this: Your promise preserves my life.

PSALM 119:48–50 NIV

The graduation speaker shuffled forward with the help of his wife. He tapped his stick along the stage with each step. Over the past few years, he had gone completely blind, and he made his blindness the topic of his talk. He shared with unseeing eyes clenched shut, "Never doubt in the darkness what God has shown you in the light."

In this life of peaks and valleys, it's easy to forget the clarity of a mountaintop experience with God when we're mired in a valley of uncertainty and despair. The psalmist reminds us that we find our hope by meditating on the decrees of God, remembering His promises, and finding hope in what God has revealed to us. Just as the Israelites often set up monuments to the great works of God in their history, we will find great hope by remembering the promises and works of God in the past.

We will surely face adversity and discouragement, and the investment we make in remembering God's promises and presence may be the only things that carry us when we have many reasons to doubt and despair. The light we've been given by God will only guide us in the darkness if we resolve to carry it with us.

BOLD LIKE DAD

*According to his eternal purpose that he accomplished in Christ
Jesus our Lord. In him and through faith in him we may
approach God with freedom and confidence.*

EPHESIANS 3:11–12 NIV

God wants His children to share in His personality, to take on His likeness, to live like Him. Boldness is often one of the overlooked traits that He wants us to experience. God is bold, invading history, overturning kingdoms, interrupting our well-crafted plans to have a relationship with us, and by doing so He risks the very opposite— our rejection. His great boldness can only come from His great love. He has not withheld even His own Son (Romans 8:2–3) to bring us into a life-giving relationship with Himself. Writer Francis Chan has coined a name for this kind of relentless pursuit—"Crazy Love." It's the kind of love that makes no excuses for its audacity.

So what does a bold, seeking Father enjoy seeing in His offspring? Reluctance? Hesitance? Or the kind of boldness He Himself demonstrated toward us? What would please Him more than having His children throwing off everything that hinders them (Hebrews 12:1) and approaching Him with freedom and confidence (Ephesians 3:12), knowing He made it possible? In Christ, our boldness pleases the Father, because it tells Him that we are His. Boldness isn't disrespectful as long as we know who made it possible for us to enjoy it. Rather, we are bearing His likeness, showing ourselves to be His children.

If we are to reflect His image, then we must strike out and approach Him with freedom and confidence, just the way Dad likes it.

A FOOL'S GAME

DAY 73 – EVENING

"The king reflected and said, 'Is this not Babylon the great, which I myself have built as a royal residence by the might of my power and for the glory of my majesty?' While the word was in the king's mouth, a voice came from heaven, saying, 'King Nebuchadnezzar, to you it is declared: sovereignty has been removed from you, and you will be driven away from mankind, and your dwelling place will be with the beasts of the field. . .until you recognize that the Most High is ruler over the realm of mankind, and bestows it on whomever He wishes.'"

DANIEL 4:30–32 NASB

Success and achievement are great—unless they lead you to forget basic spiritual truths. Truths like "You cannot really accomplish anything apart from God." He is the *Most High*, and no matter how much we may achieve on earth, our "success" is ultimately His gift, for His purposes.

Another spiritual truth that's easily forgotten in the midst of success is that arrogance always invites correction. As the Apostle Peter says, "God is opposed to the proud, but gives grace to the humble" (1 Peter 5:5 NASB). He doesn't *ignore* the proud, or *work around* them—He actively *opposes* them.

When we are tempted to slap ourselves on the back, we should take note, as Nebuchadnezzar eventually did, that we are playing a fool's game. And you don't have to be some prideful "overachiever" to get God's attention. Anyone who takes credit for what God has done can enjoy His harsh mercy. God rebukes the foolishness of high and low alike, because He is merciful to all.

OPENING YOUR EYES

For since the creation of the world His invisible attributes,
His eternal power and divine nature, have been clearly seen,
being understood through what has been made,
so that they are without excuse.

ROMANS 1:20 NASB

Invisibility doesn't mean inaccessibility. Just because a thing cannot be seen doesn't mean it can't be known or understood in some meaningful way. The air we breathe is an example. So are the inner qualities of people: diligence, intelligence, impatience. When we see a beautiful painting, we see clearly the invisible quality called *talent*.

In the same way, God declares that at least two of His invisible qualities have been "clearly *seen*" from the creation itself. First, His eternal power—outside of time, without beginning and without end. We don't have to wonder who came before Him or who will come after Him. What He promises to mankind will endure since there are no circumstances that can surprise Him. The second invisible quality is His divine nature. He is above the created order and not one of us. He was not born and will not die. He is the first and final authority of all things.

The irony of *seeing* the invisible is resolved in creation itself. The fullest revelation of God in Christ is not required for God to hold mankind accountable for at least the two qualities He has *published* across time and space. As the psalmist writes: "The heavens are telling of the glory of God; and their expanse is declaring the work of His hands. Day to day pours forth speech, and night to night reveals knowledge" (Psalm 19:1–2 NASB).

OVERFLOWING

For we wanted to come to you—I, Paul, more than once—and yet Satan hindered us. For who is our hope or joy or crown of exultation? Is it not even you, in the presence of our Lord Jesus at His coming? For you are our glory and joy.

1 THESSALONIANS 2:18–20 NASB

Paul's enthusiasm for the Thessalonian believers bursts forth in these words, using language usually reserved for God Himself. Imagine! Paul's "hope" and "joy" and "glory" are tied to this small group of people into whom he has poured his life. When Jesus returns, Paul plans on showing them off.

When we come to Christ, we begin our experience as a child of God. We are adopted (Romans 8:15) and begin rethinking our lives as one of His offspring. Then as we share our faith and help people grow in Christ, we begin to see the *other* side of the relationship—the parental side. God's side. This is what Paul is expressing, and why he speaks so joyfully. He's displaying the same excited attitude toward the Thessalonians that God has about all of us—pride and joy!

Paul reflects God's joy toward his own "children" in the faith because God's parental joy is contagious. Like Paul did with the Thessalonians, God rejoices over us, brags about us, dotes on us, and takes pride in us—and the things He's preparing in heaven for those who love Him are beyond imagination (1 Corinthians 2:9). When we see Him face to face, we will truly understand what an extravagant parent God is. We will rejoice in Him, and He will rejoice in us.

THE LIVING AND WORKING WORD

We also constantly thank God that when you received the word of God which you heard from us, you accepted it not as the word of men, but for what it really is, the word of God, which also performs its work in you who believe.

1 THESSALONIANS 2:13 NASB

In the first chapter of the Bible, we see that God's spoken Word was powerful enough to bring all of creation into being. John 1 further explains that the "Word of God" is the person of Jesus Christ Himself, through whom all things were created and find their purpose.

Throughout the Bible, we see that God's Word continues to work since the beginning—giving life, protecting, enlightening, redeeming, effecting change according to God's will. "So will My word be which goes forth from My mouth; it will not return to Me empty, without accomplishing what I desire, and without succeeding in the matter for which I sent it" (Isaiah 55:11 NASB).

God's Word works because it is *alive*. Jesus declares that "the words that I have spoken to you are spirit and are life" (John 6:63 NASB). The writer of Hebrews similarly asserts that "the word of God is living and active" (Hebrews 4:12 NASB). It works because it simply can't sit still!

Paul was delighted with the Thessalonians because they accepted his message as the authoritative, purposeful, and *living* thing that it was, and by doing so, opened up its divine power to work in their lives.

DOWN TO THE TOP

*The LORD came down on Mount Sinai, to the top of the
mountain; and the LORD called Moses to the top
of the mountain, and Moses went up.*

EXODUS 19:20 NASB

Moses received the Law from God in a dramatic face-to-face meeting. And He chose an unusual place to do it considering Moses was about eighty years old—the top of a mountain. God had Moses make the arduous climb to the top of Mount Sinai alone to meet with Him. A truly remarkable feat at his age—it was no doubt painful and exhausting, requiring perseverance and commitment. But even at the top of a mountain, there was yet a distance between Moses and God. Even if Moses had ascended the highest peak on earth, God would still have had to close the gap by coming *down* to meet with him. And this is *Moses*—a central figure in Israel's history—who was called by God at the burning bush, who faced Pharaoh and the power of Egypt, who parted the Red Sea! And even Moses could not completely close the distance between man and God.

In this story lives a beautiful metaphor of man's need to have God fill the space that always remains even after we have done everything we can do to reach Him. No amount of human effort will ever connect us to God—only God's effort will bring us face to face. Thankfully, we do not have to have Moses' résumé or repeat his grueling trip up a mountain; we have perfect access to God through Christ, who forever closes the gap.

THE ODDS ARE IN YOUR FAVOR

The Spirit of the Lord God is upon me, because the Lord has anointed me to bring good news to the afflicted; He has sent me to bind up the brokenhearted, to proclaim liberty to captives, and freedom to prisoners; to proclaim the favorable year of the Lord, and the day of vengeance of our God.

ISAIAH 61:1–2 NASB

Our God is an amazingly giving Person. He sent His Son to bring the good news of a truly amazing opportunity. Christ was sent to proclaim "the favorable *year* of the Lord" and "the *day*" of judgment by God. That's a 365 to 1 ratio in our favor! This propitious arrangement is symbolic of God's great mercy and patience, "not wishing for any to perish but for all to come to repentance" (2 Peter 3:9 NASB). He is interested in us in a way that does not always make sense. Even Jesus' disciples didn't quickly grasp this divine patience, eager to "command fire to come down from heaven and consume" those who rejected Christ (Luke 9:54 NASB). The Lord's response was firm: "But He turned and rebuked them, and said, 'You do not know what kind of spirit you are of; for the Son of Man did not come to destroy men's lives, but to save them' " (Luke 9:55–56 NASB).

God wants *all* to repent. To confuse this time of favor and opportunity is to be of a *different spirit* than the Lord; not "regard[ing] the patience of our Lord as salvation" (2 Peter 3:15 NASB) is to miss God's heart and the chance to be part of it.

NOT SO FAST

*Now when He was in Jerusalem at the Passover, during the feast,
many believed in His name, observing His signs which He was
doing. But Jesus, on His part, was not entrusting Himself to them,
for He knew all men, and because He did not need anyone to
testify concerning man, for He Himself knew what was in man.*

JOHN 2:23–25 NASB

We all know from experience how different we can be from one day
to the next. Everything from the temperature of the room to our
greatest fear can change our moods and influence our decisions.

As history shows, our unstable nature makes certain things
inevitable: conflict, political unrest, war. As an old saying goes,
the only thing constant in life is change. Not that change is bad
in itself. On the contrary, we would never see revival if change
couldn't also be positive. But the very fact that we are creatures
prone to extremes means we must be watched closely. Jesus knew
this better than anyone.

Even though Jesus went through changes while on earth from
birth to resurrection, He was stable in His essential nature and
purpose—unlike those who surrounded Him. Fickle crowds would
follow Him one day awed by His miracles and teachings, and the
next try to throw Him off a cliff (Luke 4:29)! Some in the crowd
that sang "Hosanna" as he rode into Jerusalem would be in the
crowd that cried, "Crucify Him!"

This is why Jesus would not be swayed by popularity. He looked
beyond earthly success to His eternal Father whom He could trust
as the only true unchanging Source.

THE DIVINE PROMISE

God made great and marvelous promises, so that his nature would become part of us. Then we could escape our evil desires and the corrupt influences of this world.

2 PETER 1:4 CEV

Simply avoiding hell isn't the point of salvation. Arguably, that might be enough from a human perspective, but God has something more in mind for us, something far more interesting and exciting.

God's plan, as incredible as it may sound, is that we should partake in and reflect His own divine nature. He wants children that look and sound and act like their Father, free from corruption inside and out. "Therefore, having these promises, beloved, let us cleanse ourselves from all defilement of flesh and spirit, perfecting holiness in the fear of God" (2 Corinthians 7:1 NASB).

What were God's promises? That He would live among His people and be their God, that they would be set apart from the world, even counted as His sons and daughters (2 Corinthians 6). How are those promises fulfilled? Through His Holy Spirit living in us:

"I will give them an undivided heart and put a new spirit in them" (Ezekiel 11:19 NIV).

"When you believed, you were marked in him with a seal, the promised Holy Spirit" (Ephesians 1:13 NIV).

The role of the Holy Spirit is to create a people who could freely and honestly interact with God. Without His working in us, nothing in our experience will ever change, and He won't get the children He wants. Only through the Holy Spirit indwelling and empowering us can we live out the full plan of our salvation.

THE FLIP SIDE OF FAITH

But My righteous one shall live by faith; and if he shrinks back,
My soul has no pleasure in him.
Hebrews 10:38 nasb

People usually assume that *doubt* is the opposite of faith. But in the New Testament (nasb), the words *doubt* or *doubting* appear only a handful of times while *fear* or *afraid* show up over one hundred times. While we can't build theology over a single observation, it's clear that a life of faith is often a battle against fear.

Fear certainly was the synagogue official's test when, in faith, he had begged for Jesus to heal his sick daughter. Then his little girl died. Jesus, knowing the man's heart, comforted him with these words, "Do not be afraid any longer, only believe" (Mark 5:36 nasb).

Later, Jesus, knowing the fear Peter would face after He was arrested, said, "Simon, Simon, behold, Satan has demanded permission to sift you like wheat; but I have prayed for you, that your faith may not fail" (Luke 22:31–32 nasb).

Of course God is not pleased when His people give in to fear, because it means we are shrinking back from *Him*. But the good news is that we have a Father and a Savior who knows our weakness and "has not given us a spirit of timidity, but of power and love and discipline" (2 Timothy 1:7 nasb). We move forward in faith as we keep in step with the Spirit who is our Helper (John 14:16). We may well wrestle with fear, but we are never alone in the struggle.

A GOOD FOUNDATION

*See to it that no one takes you captive through philosophy
and empty deception, according to the tradition of men,
according to the elementary principles of the
world, rather than according to Christ.*

COLOSSIANS 2:8 NASB

The test of every building is in its foundation. No matter how fine in appearance it is, if the foundation is faulty, the whole structure is at risk. Sadly, this is also the way our lives can be if we build our thinking on faulty reasoning and shifting philosophies.

The world offers its perspective and solutions to our problems twenty-four hours a day. The voice of this world rarely lacks confidence, and the advice often seems wise and time tested. The proponents of worldly philosophies may even mean well, but they don't perceive the empty nature of their own beliefs. Why would they? *If it was good enough for Dad*, it's reasoned, *it's good enough for me*. Traditions passed down from one generation to the next carry weight whether they're right or wrong.

Then there are those current worldviews specifically designed for the marketplace—money-making offerings pushed online, in print, and in infomercials. They are easily identified because they are built on the simplest principles of this world: promotion of self, pursuit of pleasure, get-rich-quick schemes, emphasis on appearance, promises of simple solutions to complex problems.

But Christ offers truth, reality, and a future that is eternal rather than fleeting. If we build upon His work and His words, we will avoid the captivity of a dying world and the loss of our opportunity for a solid foundation.

JUST DON'T

The Lord God commanded the man, saying, "From any tree of the garden you may eat freely; but from the tree of the knowledge of good and evil you shall not eat, for in the day that you eat from it you will surely die."

GENESIS 2:16–17 NASB

Adam and Eve were designed to enjoy uninterrupted union with God, and the only "don't" for them was eating the fruit that would end that joy. But of course they went directly against that single commandment, passing on that tendency to all generations that followed. Their one act of disobedience multiplied into all the things we call sin today. No wonder the "don'ts" seem to multiply throughout the Bible. They're just keeping pace with the ways man has invented to disregard God.

Some people dismiss the Bible as a mere collection of rules and restrictions. This misses the original purpose of God to have "a people for His own possession out of all the peoples who are on the face of the earth" (Deuteronomy 7:6 NASB). The Old Testament Law was a gift to set His people apart and increase their joy not end it. It was ultimately designed to lead people to Christ (Galatians 3:24), people who would fulfill God's original purpose when He "gave Himself for us to redeem us from every lawless deed, and to purify for Himself a people for His own possession" (Titus 2:14 NASB).

Now, the things we consider "don'ts" from God do not constitute a law—they provide real freedom and create a holy experience with our Lord. Any "don't" from Him means life for us.

SORRY I ASKED

Then the LORD answered Job out of the storm and said,
"Now gird up your loins like a man; I will ask you,
and you instruct Me. Will you really annul My judgment?
Will you condemn Me that you may be justified?"

JOB 40:6–8 NASB

Sometimes people lament that God doesn't answer them in their suffering. They look at Job and say, *At least God answered Job.* True, but look at the answer! God *rebukes* Job, confronting him with a harshness that seems inappropriate considering his painful circumstances. But God's had enough of being questioned; now it's Job's turn.

Chapter after chapter, Job has complained that he's done nothing to deserve his situation, and he was right. God Himself declared Job "blameless" and "upright" in Job 1:8. Yet Job's friends argued that his suffering was the consequence of sin, though Job knew better. They were rebuked because they condemned him without being able to address his argument.

Job's error wasn't some hidden sin or even a faulty argument, it was in forgetting whom he was addressing. He was demanding that God *justify* Himself, *explain* Himself, even *defend* Himself. "Oh, if only someone would give me a hearing! I've signed my name to my defense—let the Almighty One answer! I want to see my indictment in writing" (Job 31:35–36 MSG).

Job would have the "Almighty One" stand beside him in front of *another* judge and make His case. Job would see God condemned to justify his own understanding.

When we suffer, let us "pour out [our] complaint" to God (Psalm 142:2 NASB), always remembering to whom we are talking.

FREEDOM'S PURPOSE

All things are lawful for me, but not all things are profitable.
All things are lawful for me, but I will not be mastered by anything.

1 CORINTHIANS 6:12 NASB

Grace wouldn't be grace if it didn't allow us room to make mistakes without fear of losing our relationship with God. Grace is God's determination that our sin will not stand between Him and us. As believers, we have come to accept Christ's work alone for our reconciliation to God. In Christ, God fulfills the demands that the Old Testament Law made upon man and eliminates our need to rely on any set of laws to make us acceptable to Him.

But there is always the chance that such a wonderful freedom can be misused. As writer Philip Yancey says, "Grace implies a risk, the risk that we might abuse it." Some Corinthian believers, freed from the arduous burden of legalism, were using their new "freedom" as an excuse to indulge in unprofitable things—a spiritual waste of time. Some had gone further, becoming addicted to activities that, although technically allowable, had replaced God as the focus of their lives. How absurd to think that God's gift of grace would push aside the One who gave it! The whole point of grace was to free us to move *toward* our Father not *away*.

No amount of rationalizing should overrule godly common sense (Hebrews 5:14). God wants preeminence in our lives, and even death will be overcome to achieve this end. So for today, let us use our freedom to become like Him and not test the limits of His patience.

ALWAYS THE BEST POLICY

Truthful lips will be established forever,
but a lying tongue is only for a moment.

PROVERBS 12:19 NASB

If you've ever looked someone in the eye and wondered if they were telling you the truth, then you understand the uneasy feeling it creates. Sometimes, of course, it's easy to tell when a person is lying, like when a child blurts out, "It wasn't me!"

Even if people don't outright lie to you but just "shade the truth," is that any less deceptive? Maybe the consequences are less severe for a child with cookie crumbs on his mouth than a man with blood on his hands, but neither is without deceit. The acorn of deception may not always grow into an oak, but it still has all the same DNA—whether we plan the lie or whether it just pops out when we're caught off guard.

The value God places on truthfulness has always been made plain in the Bible. The power of truth is that it lasts. It's eternal because it comes from the very nature of God. Jesus claimed to be "the Truth" itself (John 14:6 NASB), and promised that "the truth will make you free" (John 8:32 NASB). God wants us to live in truth and the Truth to live in us. "Behold, You desire truth in the innermost being" (Psalm 51:6 NASB), and so God sends the Helper who is "the Spirit of Truth" (John 15:26 NASB) to indwell believers.

We keep pace with the Holy Spirit by living honestly and affirm our connection to God as His children. Truth is our heritage and our birthright as members of God's family.

WELL-SEASONED SPEECH

Conduct yourselves with wisdom toward outsiders, making the most of the opportunity. Let your speech always be with grace, as though seasoned with salt, so that you will know how you should respond to each person.

Colossians 4:5-6 nasb

Biblical wisdom is less about fortune cookie clichés than about instruction for right living. The prophets and disciples of the scriptures weren't like the hermit sages we sometimes envision living on mountaintops dispensing clever sayings. They spoke wisdom that could change lives and were not concerned with answering every philosophical question people raised. They knew that right living makes a person wise by biblical standards and spoke truth to help people understand their choices in all manner of circumstances.

Like the prophets of the Bible, we are surrounded by people who do not see the kingdom of God and need spiritual truths explained. Thus we will always be surrounded by opportunities to share our hope and our faith if we are prepared—not with clever sayings, or a rehearsed speech, or even theological arguments, but with words that are gracious and practical.

"Let no unwholesome word proceed from your mouth, but only such a word as is good for edification according to the need of the moment, so that it will give grace to those who hear" (Ephesians 4:29 nasb).

It's true some people will only be interested in engaging us to debate our faith, but no matter what the reasons, any opportunity to speak of Christ is a good one. Let us just remember to speak as He would, graciously treating each person as an individual created in the image of God.

FLATTERY WILL GET YOU NOWHERE

Now I urge you, brethren, keep your eye on those who cause dissensions and hindrances contrary to the teaching which you learned, and turn away from them. For such men are slaves, not of our Lord Christ but of their own appetites; and by their smooth and flattering speech they deceive the hearts of the unsuspecting.

ROMANS 16:17–18 NASB

Paul was always watchful of his flock. He poured out his life to build the church of Christ on a solid foundation. But he knew others would come who worked only for their own interests and who were slaves "of their own appetites." You can tell who they are, he warns, because they create arguments where there shouldn't be any. They stand out because they teach what is contrary to the truth found in Christ.

Jesus described these same people: "Beware of false prophets, who come to you in sheep's clothing, but inwardly are ravenous wolves. You will know them by their fruits" (Matthew 7:15–16 NASB). What kinds of "fruits"? For one, their "smooth and flattering speech," which never has a place in the body of Christ. Flattery always comes from an ulterior motive, to manipulate the listener. It always serves the flesh.

To heed Paul's warning about such people, we need to be sure we are not one of the "unsuspecting." The *unsuspecting* are those who have never made the effort to mature in Christ. "For everyone who partakes only of milk is not accustomed to the word of righteousness, for he is an infant" (Hebrews 5:13 NASB). Growing in our understanding of Christ is the only way to guard against deception.

WHO IS GOD'S WILL?

"I searched for a man among them who would build up the wall and stand in the gap before Me for the land, so that I would not destroy it; but I found no one."

EZEKIEL 22:30 NASB

When God wanted to do something on the earth to make Himself known or to teach His people, He always started with a person. Think of the history of the Bible—it's the story of people who demonstrated faith. Hebrews 11 provides a type of *Hall of Fame* of such faithful people: Abel, Enoch, Noah, Abraham, Isaac, Jacob, Sarah, Joseph, Moses, Gideon, Barak, Samson, Jephthah, David, Samuel, and all the prophets. These are some of the *Who* of God's will—men and women who became the fulcrum for God to move the world.

God's approach to working His will among mankind hasn't changed. God is still looking for individuals who will stand with Him and answer the call the way Isaiah did: "Then I heard the voice of the Lord, saying, 'Whom shall I send, and who will go for Us?' Then I said, 'Here am I. Send me!'" (Isaiah 6:8 NASB)

Of course, the ultimate *Who* in God's will is His son Jesus of Nazareth—"All things have been created through him and for him. He is before all things, and in him all things hold together" (Colossians 1:16–17 NIV). And He came "to purify for Himself a *people* for His own possession, *zealous for good deeds*" (Titus 2:14 NASB, emphasis added). Through Christ, we have the privilege of becoming the *Who* God is seeking to "build up the wall and stand in the gap."

THE GREATEST TEACHER

"Behold, God is exalted in His power;
who is a teacher like Him?"

JOB 36:22 NASB

God is a gracious and faithful Teacher, and this life is His classroom. Lessons begin with the creation itself: "God's glory is on tour in the skies, God-craft on exhibit across the horizon. Madame Day *holds classes every morning*, Professor Night *lectures each evening*. Their words aren't heard, their voices aren't recorded, but their silence fills the earth: *unspoken truth is spoken everywhere*" (Psalm 19:1–4 MSG, emphasis added).

In addition to creation, God teaches us through His written word: *"All Scripture is inspired by God* and profitable for *teaching*, for reproof, for correction, for training in righteousness (2 Timothy 3:16 NASB, emphasis added). And His Word (specifically the portion known as "the Law") was given for a purpose: "Therefore the Law has become *our tutor to lead us to Christ*, so that we may be justified by faith" (Galatians 3:24 NASB, emphasis added).

Jesus was God in the flesh, and who could make God known more clearly than God speaking face to face? "No one has seen God at any time; the only begotten God who is in the bosom of the Father, *He has explained Him*" (John 1:18 NASB, emphasis added). Peter understood this when he exclaimed, "Lord, to whom shall we go? You have words of eternal life" (John 6:68 NASB).

And as if Christ's earthly appearance wasn't enough, we are given the Spirit of God to be our Teacher forever! "But the Helper, the Holy Spirit, whom the Father will send in My name, He will *teach you all things*, and *bring to your remembrance* all that I said to you" (John 14:26 NASB, emphasis added).

THE RIGHT KIND OF STUDENT

I will instruct you and teach you in the way which you should go;
I will counsel you with My eye upon you. Do not be as the horse
or as the mule which have no understanding, whose trappings
include bit and bridle to hold them in check,
otherwise they will not come near to you.

PSALM 32:8–9 NASB

As a good Father, God provides opportunity after opportunity to learn—about Himself, about ourselves, about the world, and about eternity. He is a faithful Teacher and promises to "counsel" us as we apply His teaching to our daily lives.

As an involved, loving Teacher, what kind of student is God hoping for? What kind of student makes any teacher happy? What kind of child makes their Father's job a delight? Certainly not those who need to be guided like a senseless animal, pulled along day after day. Being resistant to learning is a grief to any teacher and useless to any student. "Obey your leaders and submit to them, for they keep watch over your souls as those who will give an account. Let them do this with joy and not with grief, for this would be *unprofitable for you*" (Hebrews 13:17 NASB, emphasis added).

The goal of all teaching is to pass along new information, resulting in a new perspective, which in turn leads to a new experience. In other words, *growth*. Our Mentor wants to see us imitating Christ, making our own choices, and taking risks. He wants us to grow up in our understanding and see the changes in us, just as any good dad, or coach, or counselor would.

SEVEN QUALITIES OF SPIRITUALLY EFFECTIVE PEOPLE

Do your best to improve your faith. You can do this by adding goodness, understanding, self-control, patience, devotion to God, concern for others, and love. If you keep growing in this way, it will show that what you know about our Lord Jesus Christ has made your lives useful and meaningful.

2 Peter 1:5–8 cev

Most men enjoy being good at something, whether it's a career, a sport, or a hobby. We love the idea of being effective, of pursuing goals and achieving results. It's in us by design. And in order to really stand out at something means acquiring a set of specific skills. Men spend a lot of energy acquiring the right skills for the job.

But in spiritual work—in building the kingdom of God—skills are not the main concern. Certainly they have their place, and God gives each of us spiritual gifts to be used to help others grow (1 Corinthians 12:7 NASB). But effectiveness in the kingdom is tied to the character of the worker. Peter points us to seven "qualities" that make up a foundation for being useful and fruitful in God's plan. The promise is pretty clear—we can't fail if we possess these qualities as growing traits because "no grass will grow under your feet, no day will pass without its reward as you mature in your experience of our Master Jesus" (2 Peter 1:8 MSG).

While we grow in our abilities, talents, and gifts from the Lord, let us remember Peter's admonition to be diligent in adding the qualities that lay a true spiritual foundation for effectiveness.

HAPPY ENDINGS

For I am confident of this very thing, that He who began a good work in you will perfect it until the day of Christ Jesus.

PHILIPPIANS 1:6 NASB

To "perfect" something means to work on it until it's right. Another way to translate "perfect" is to "carry it on to completion" (NIV). Christ does not start something in us only to leave it all in our hands. God already tried that, in a manner of speaking. The Old Testament Law was that very opportunity, but it could not make us right with God (Romans 3:20), and it had no power to make us different from the inside (Romans 8:3). It takes Christ to do those two things. That's why Jesus is the "*author* and *finisher* of our faith" (Hebrews 12:2 KJV, emphasis added). We begin a journey with Christ, who not only promises to walk with us but assures us of a happy ending.

Our journey with Christ is part of a process called *sanctification*. The part we experience in our daily lives is when we begin to think and choose the way Jesus would, approving "the things that are excellent, in order to be sincere and blameless until the day of Christ" (Philippians 1:10 NASB). This is in stark contrast to the Law that didn't require an internal change but still required blamelessness.

The Law was a long and burdensome road, traveled alone. But it was meant to be so we would welcome the help of a Savior (Galatians 3:24). Now, since it's His work *in* us and not our work *for* Him, we can have confidence for a lifetime.

GODLY REBUKE

And they came to Him and woke Him, saying, "Save us, Lord;
we are perishing!" He said to them, "Why are you afraid,
you men of little faith?" Then He got up and rebuked
the winds and the sea, and it became perfectly calm.

MATTHEW 8:25–26 NASB

The disciples were an unlikely mix of educated and uneducated; craftsmen and professionals; strong character and weak. But nothing breaks down barriers like a life-threatening event. When the storm threatened to swamp their boat, the disciples were all in agreement: wake Jesus up!

Of course, Jesus comes through for His fearful men, but the storm wasn't the only thing that got rebuked that day. He wasn't grumpy for being awakened; He was disappointed in their lack of faith. It's ironic to think that calling on Jesus for help could bring a rebuke. In this case, it would have shown more faith for the disciples *not* to cry out for Jesus' help. After all, He was right there with them.

Peter repeats this watery lesson later: "Peter got out of the boat, and walked on the water and came toward Jesus. But seeing the wind, he became frightened, and beginning to sink, he cried out, 'Lord, save me!' Immediately Jesus stretched out His hand and took hold of him, and said to him, 'You of little faith, why did you doubt?'" (Matthew 14:29–31 NASB).

The lesson they seem to keep reviewing is that fear is the most potent form of doubt. Jesus wants us to be free from fear and live like He is truly with us, even in the storm.

CURSES TO BLESSINGS

Shimei was yelling at David, "Get out of here, you murderer!
You good-for-nothing, the Lord is paying you back for killing so
many in Saul's family. You stole his kingdom, but now the Lord has
given it to your son Absalom. You're a murderer, and that's why
you're in such big trouble!" Abishai said, "Your Majesty, this man is
as useless as a dead dog! He shouldn't be allowed to curse you. Let
me go over and chop off his head." David replied. . ."If Shimei
is cursing me because the Lord has told him to,
then who are you to tell him to stop?"

2 Samuel 16:7–10 cev

A willingness to hear from God even when it comes from someone who hates you is the truest form of humility. King David was running for his life from his son Absalom, who had usurped his throne.

Along the way, an embittered old man from Saul's family took the opportunity to ridicule David. "Pay back!" shouted Shimei. Of course he was wrong, since David was God's anointed, but David did not even attempt to correct him. He did not retaliate (though he could have) on the chance that God was using this moment to speak to him. He simply trusted in the Lord's judgment of the situation.

It's hard enough not to defend ourselves when confronted by a friend. But what about someone who honestly doesn't care about us? When we are rebuked, are we willing to look for God's message to us even in the words of those who are ignorant and hurtful? God's voice would be worth the effort.

BEING THE MAN

*[King David to Solomon] "I am going the way of all the earth.
Be strong, therefore, and show yourself a man. Keep the charge
of the LORD your God, to walk in His ways, to keep His statutes,
His commandments, His ordinances, and His testimonies,
according to what is written in the Law of Moses, that you
may succeed in all that you do and wherever you turn."*

1 KINGS 2:2–3 NASB

Solomon had the unique though difficult blessing of being at his father's side as he was dying. Few men get that kind of farewell, and fewer still get the life-directing exhortation that would guide Solomon as the next king of Israel.

David was a warrior and a successful king, leaving Solomon with huge boots to fill—a "man's man" as they say. But at the end of his life, what did he point to as the basis for being a *man*? Keeping "the charge of the Lord"—following wholeheartedly the ways God had revealed. And that, he well knew, would take courage. So David clarified things for Solomon so all the other issues he would potentially wrestle with in life as a man—purpose, success, legacy, leadership—would fall into place. David did not want Solomon to be distracted by what the world says a man is, but to be a man in God's eyes first and foremost.

Solomon's defining moment had come, and with it the weight of a kingdom, but also the blessing of being set on the right course. For all men, in all circumstances, being on the firm foundation of God's will makes a man succeed as a man.

LIFTED LOW

The cords of death encompassed me, and the terrors of Sheol came upon me; I found distress and sorrow. Then I called upon the name of the LORD: "O LORD, I beseech You, save my life!" Gracious is the LORD, and righteous; yes, our God is compassionate. The LORD preserves the simple; I was brought low, and He saved me.

PSALM 116:3–6 NASB

How often we find that being brought low is the only road to rescue! Sometimes it's the only way to see what the psalmist saw: that God is gracious, righteous, and compassionate; that He stands ready to save. We are frequently distracted by our circumstances or by other people or by our own thinking. Sometimes we discover a beseeching heart only when God gets our full attention through difficulty.

It's merciful for God to shake us to the foundations of our faith, to crush our expectations, to allow distress and sorrow to "win" for a while, and thus force from us an earnest cry for His help. The humbling of hardship and suffering is a kindness. "It is never fun to be corrected. In fact, at the time it is always painful. But if we learn to obey by being corrected, we will do right and live at peace" (Hebrews 12:11 CEV).

Humbling ourselves means we stop looking for solutions, for *How* or *What,* and start looking for *Who.* God gives grace to the humble and answers the earnest prayers of His children with the gift of Himself. Being brought to our knees is to be brought into closer communion with our Father.

SEVEN THOUSAND REASONS

*"LORD, THEY HAVE KILLED YOUR PROPHETS, THEY HAVE TORN DOWN
YOUR ALTARS, AND I ALONE AM LEFT, AND THEY ARE SEEKING MY LIFE."
But what is the divine response to him? "I HAVE KEPT FOR MYSELF
SEVEN THOUSAND MEN WHO HAVE NOT BOWED THE KNEE TO BAAL."*

ROMANS 11:3–4 NASB

In 1 Kings 18, the prophet Elijah challenged 450 priests of Baal to a showdown of epic proportions. With all Israel watching, Elijah calls down fire from heaven, devouring a massive, water-soaked offering in divine fashion. The people fall on their faces, confessing God, then dispatch the pagan priests. But Queen Jezebel is furious and swears to kill Elijah. He runs away, hides in a cave, and, completely discouraged, pours out his complaint to God.

What was God's encouragement to Elijah during his spiritual depression? The anonymous men who had resisted the pressure of their times, ordinary men who were faithful day after day. Elijah may have been the star of this epic, but this remnant of unknown men was the story behind the story. And God used them to encourage one of the most powerful prophets of the Bible.

Few of us will ever know anyone who faced the pressures Elijah did, but we all know someone who feels alone in standing for God. That was Lot's experience in Sodom: "For that righteous man, living among them day after day, was tormented in his righteous soul by the lawless deeds he saw and heard" (2 Peter 2:8 NIV). Just remember, in a faithless world, all it takes to be an encouragement to others is to be one of the seven thousand.

GODLY HATE

*"If anyone comes to Me, and does not hate his own father
and mother and wife and children and brothers and sisters,
yes, and even his own life, he cannot be My disciple."*

LUKE 14:26 NASB

It's obvious that Jesus is not instructing us to actively hate our families. That would be absurd since it would contradict just about everything else the Bible says is a man's responsibility to his family. Likewise, despising oneself is not the point since God loves us and has adopted us. *Contrast* is the point—Jesus is illustrating the impossibility of being a true disciple if there is competition for His supremacy.

In the verse, Jesus lists the most likely competitors for His rightful place in our hearts, our minds, and our choices. He doesn't list career or success. Those things can be serious distractions, but they aren't what truly competes for the affection of sincere believers. It's relationships that contend with Him the most—other personalities and desires. Other voices. Choosing a godly "hate" of family is an important philosophical position. It needs to be in place so that when following Christ means alienation from those closest to us, our love for Him is the *only* love that matters. He wins, hands down.

Then there are our own desires, our own voices. If we cling to our vision for ourselves, then that will disqualify us from being His disciple. If what we want matters more than growing in the true knowledge of the One who created us (Colossians 3:10), we won't be *able* to follow Christ. He's not the one who rejects our service—we make ourselves unavailable.

EXPERIENCING GOD, OR THE OTHER WAY AROUND?

Work out your salvation with fear and trembling; for it is God who is at work in you, both to will and to work for His good pleasure.

Philippians 2:12–13 nasb

As a baby only knows his side of things, it's perfectly understandable that new Christians focus on their personal experience of God. It's okay because, like a baby, new believers bring joy and pleasure to their Father by simply existing. But as children grow in their understanding, they are expected to make their parents happy by showing maturity and character—to carry on the family name in an honorable way. Likewise, believers are born to please God by reflecting His divine nature.

Paul consistently connected knowing God with pleasing Him. He prayed that believers "may be filled with the knowledge of His will in all spiritual wisdom and understanding, so that you will walk in a manner worthy of the Lord, to please Him in all respects, bearing fruit in every good work and increasing in the knowledge of God" (Colossians 1:9–10 nasb). Our growing understanding of God gives us new experiences of Him, but it also gives God new experiences of us.

As we mature spiritually, we gain the opportunity not just to receive from our Father, but to give to Him. And the great news is that not only *can* we bring our Father pleasure (1 Thessalonians 4:1), He Himself is so committed to His own experience of us, that He actually works in us to see that it happens. If we want to make Him happy, we have nothing to stop us!

LEARNING WISDOM AND SELF—CONTROL

Proverbs will teach you wisdom and self-control and how to understand sayings with deep meanings.

PROVERBS 1:2 CEV

Do you struggle with self-control? If you have given up hope and given yourself over to one sin or another, Solomon has something to say to you. In the verse above, he says the book of Proverbs will teach you wisdom and self-control. Hope does exist. You just have to access it.

When is the last time you worked your way through the book of Proverbs? There are thirty-one Proverbs, one for each day of the month. Would you be willing to spend some serious time and contemplation in one chapter of Proverbs per day for the next month? Would you be willing to journal about your revelations? How about enlisting another man to go through them with you? Commit to not talking about anything temporal during the month, but instead speak only about the truths you are learning. It might be awkward at first, but awkward is okay. All it will take is one revelation to set you on a new course.

Solomon says that in addition to gaining wisdom and self-control, you will learn how to understand sayings with deep meanings. This doesn't come as a natural gift or even a developed skill. It comes from the Spirit of God as you ingest the wisdom of His Word.

If your soul has been dry during this season of sin, expect a change. Expect deep understanding. Expect deep revelation. Expect victory.

PLEASING THE WEAKER BROTHER

*If our faith is strong, we should be patient with the Lord's
followers whose faith is weak. We should try to
please them instead of ourselves.*

ROMANS 15:1 CEV

If you've ever wondered whether you fall into the "stronger" or "weaker" brother camp as expressed in the scriptures, the truth in Romans 15:1 might help you answer that question.

Generally speaking, stronger brothers have been and continue to be immersed in the Word. They have clarity regarding the precepts of God. They are under authority and accountable. And they treat those who are just starting out in their faith journey with the utmost respect and patience—so much so that they try to please their brother rather than themselves.

When it comes to matters of food and drink and various other issues that fall under the banner of Christian liberty, stronger Christians should never attempt to flaunt such liberties, but rather be sensitive toward the weaker believer who is still formulating his personal theological understanding of such things.

If that means not ordering a glass of wine at dinner with a weaker brother who might object, then the stronger believer gladly does so out of love and concern for how his actions might be perceived by the weaker brother.

As the weaker brother grows, he will find himself in the presence of newer, weaker brothers, and your witness of having loved him right where he was will help him to do the same for others.

PUT OFF ANGER. PUT ON CHRIST.

Don't make friends with anyone who has a bad temper.
PROVERBS 22:24 CEV

The biblical principal of not befriending people who have a bad temper is meant to keep us from becoming just like that person. We are influenced by the people we hang out with and vice versa. There is little room for grace in the life of a hot-tempered man, and wisdom is far from him.

But most of us know this. In fact, we nod our head in agreement when we read this verse, believing it to be good common sense, but have you ever considered it from the opposite point of view? Are fellow believers avoiding friendship with you because you have a bad temper? If you know you have a problem with anger and are currently experiencing isolation as a result, now is the time to ask for help.

Approach your pastor, small group leader, or someone who has known you for a long time and allow him to ask you hard questions that examine your motivation(s). Once they find your triggers, you can begin the work of putting off your spirit of anger and putting on the mercy of Christ.

If anybody ever had a right to be angry, it was Jesus. He was betrayed, falsely accused of blasphemy, beaten beyond recognition, and executed in the most painful of ways. But after conquering death, He was anything but angry. Instead, He was with His apostles for forty more days, speaking about God's kingdom (Acts 1:3)—one that practices love, happiness, peacefulness, patience, kindness, goodness, faithfulness, gentleness, and self-control.

BECOME A GOD PLEASER

*I am not trying to please people. I want to please God.
Do you think I am trying to please people? If I were
doing that, I would not be a servant of Christ.*

GALATIANS 1:10 CEV

The apostle Paul was indeed a people pleaser at one point in his life. As a Pharisee, he studied to show himself approved by men. As a persecutor of those who followed Jesus, he pleased men by holding the coats of the men who stoned Stephen to death (Acts 7:58). He even approached the high priest at one point for permission to persecute Christians (Acts 9:1–2).

Post conversion, Paul became a God pleaser, contending for the Gospel at all cost, no matter what man thought. His letter to the Galatian church was a warning. He heard that they were straying from God and ultimately the Gospel as it had been taught to them by the apostles. His language was sharp, saying, "I pray that God will punish anyone who preaches anything different from our message to you! It doesn't matter if that person is one of us or an angel from heaven" (Galatians 1:8).

As believers, we are called to love one another and our neighbors as ourselves. And we are called to be humble. But when a false gospel is presented, we must speak the truth as lovingly as possible. We cannot afford to be people pleasers when it comes to the Gospel. Souls are at stake. We are not servants of Christ if we compromise in this area.

A LEADER OF HONOR

Every honest leader rules with help from me.
PROVERBS 8:16 CEV

In our modern world in which leaders often try to cover up one scandal or another, it's easy to lose trust in leaders of all stripes—from political to religious to business. But some leaders are indeed honest, and whether they know it not, they are only able to be so because God governs the affairs of men at every level.

He cares about how our presidents, governors, senators, members of congress, and mayors use their power. He wants to see them use their power for good, not for personal gain. He cares about how pastors, elders, and Sunday school teachers shepherd the flock. He wants to see them use their power to bring His people to a deeper understanding of Him, which helps us draw closer to Him. He cares about how CEOs, COOs, CFOs, and the like run the companies they have been entrusted with. He wants them to use honest weights and measures because trusted companies lead to stable economies.

At some level, you are a leader. You are a leader at work, at church, or at home—maybe all three. Do those who are under your authority trust you? Would they say you are honest? If you have made mistakes or committed sins in your leadership role, ask for forgiveness. And then trust God to help you to be the honest leader He spoke about in Proverbs 8:16.

OUR BODIES ARE NOT OUR OWN

The wife does not have authority over her own body but yields it to her husband. In the same way, the husband does not have authority over his own body but yields it to his wife.

1 CORINTHIANS 7:4 NIV

In theory, as men we understand the principle of leaving and cleaving. And we understand that when we marry, we become one flesh with our wives. More than one of us, however, have used the verse above to point out why a wife shouldn't deny her husband in the marriage bed. And we throw a spiritual fit when she uses the marriage bed as a weapon. She belongs to us not herself! She has no right.

While all of this is true, we rarely consider the second part of the verse. If our bodies belong to our wives instead of ourselves, that means we do not have the right to abuse it with fornication, adultery, pornography, or any other type of sexual impurity. Doing so unjustly wrenches control of our bodies from our wives. Our bodies do not belong to us, so we do not have the right to pleasure it outside of the marriage bed.

This is a countercultural message in a sex-crazed society, but the Holy Spirit resides inside of us and stands at the ready to empower us to live as only the followers of Christ are able. We have the same power in us that raised Christ from the dead. Surely that is ample to empower us to obey and embrace the truth of this verse.

MODELING CONSISTENT SELF-CONTROL

Tell the older men to have self-control and to be serious and sensible. Their faith, love, and patience must never fail.

Titus 2:2 cev

The apostle Paul left Titus, one of his charges, behind in Crete to do the difficult work of appointing leaders for the churches in each town (Titus 1:5). Paul gave him instructions about which type of men to choose as leaders, as well as instructed him about the type of people they would be ministering to.

Paul quoted and confirmed what one of the Cretan prophets said: "The people of Crete always tell lies. They are greedy and lazy like wild animals" (Titus 1:12). He wanted Titus to be hard on such people so they could grow strong in their faith (v. 13). This brings us to the verse above regarding older men in Crete. Ordinarily, older men don't need to be told to have self-control and to be serious and sensible, but apparently the older men in Crete were among those who were greedy and lazy and therefore needed to hear this message.

When young Christian men are unable to look up to older men in the faith in matters of appetite control, a sense of hopelessness can set in. If older Christian men cannot temper the flesh, what hope does a young man have? Regardless of where you find yourself on the age spectrum, self-control is not only possible, but followers of Christ are called to exhibit it.

THE BIBLICAL WORK ETHIC

Don't be selfish and eager to get rich—
you will end up worse off than you can imagine.
PROVERBS 28:22 CEV

You don't have to look far to find get-rich-quick schemes. They are never presented as such, but if you listen to the pitch for any length of time, it's hard to conclude otherwise. Often, those who are at the lower levels of these schemes have the best of intentions. They are just trying to make a little money on the side, but when they hear the promises of greater riches if they can sign up more people, they start to see real dollar signs.

The Bible warns against such selfishness, saying you will end up worse off than you can imagine. Commentators say that such a heart leads to envy, dishonesty, and covetousness—grieving over those who have more. Such wealth is gone as quickly as it comes. In the most extreme cases, freedom is lost as well. To make matters worse, when these schemes topple, those who are involved lose their reputation and even friendships among those they take down with them.

The biblical work ethic has always been about slow and steady growth (Proverbs 6:6, Matthew 20:1–16), accomplished with hard work that is performed with the utmost of integrity, as unto the Lord (Colossians 3:23). If you are weighing a business opportunity that isn't in line with either of those principles, run from it. It isn't from God.

KNOWING WHEN TO HIDE

When you see trouble coming, don't be stupid
and walk right into it—be smart and hide.

PROVERBS 22:3 CEV

Sometimes situations call for us to stand boldly against injustice or in favor of the oppressed. The prophet Nathan stood against King David and his sin of adultery (2 Samuel 12). Peter and John stood against Annas, Caiaphas, and other members of the high priest's family when they were told never to teach anything about the name of Jesus again (Acts 4).

Other times we are called to run and hide, as mentioned in the verse above. The New International Version, New Living Translation, New American Standard Bible, the New King James Version, and The Message describe the person in this verse as "prudent." In other words, they are wise—immersed in the scriptures, able to know the difference about when to stand and when to run. And when trouble is on the way—the type of trouble that doesn't need to be confronted—they run. Noah heard God's voice, saw impending trouble, and hid in the ark. Joseph was tempted by Potiphar's wife, and he ran in the opposite direction.

Do you see trouble coming in your own life? What is your first instinct? Whatever it is, how does it compare or contrast with the wisdom of the verse above? If you haven't fully developed your sense of discernment, consider enlisting the help of a godly friend who can help you navigate the situation and maybe avoid one of the biggest mistakes of your life.

HEAVENLY CORRECTION

*Our earthly fathers correct us, and we still respect them.
Isn't it even better to be given true life by letting
our spiritual Father correct us?*

HEBREWS 12:9 CEV

We tend to run at the first hint of correction. Correction is humiliating and pride-crushing even when it's justified. When you were growing up and faced the possibility of corporal punishment, or you expected the loss of certain privileges because you did something that was worthy of correction, you probably not only hid, but you also fretted, begged, and pleaded before finally submitting to your punishment.

But, assuming you weren't physically abused, when you were older, you were thankful that your earthly father cared enough to correct you, because it made you the man you are today. You probably even respect your father for stepping in when the situation warranted it, because now you can see the fruit.

The writer of Hebrews indicates that something much larger is at stake than simply becoming a better person. When we go astray spiritually, our heavenly Father has to step in because *true life* is at stake, meaning eternity in heaven.

Putting the theological debate about eternal security aside and just examining this verse for what it says, God loves us enough to correct us in such a fashion that will keep us from experiencing true death as the result of our wayward actions. If you are experiencing His correction or have done so recently, rejoice! You are being prepared for heaven by our Creator.

WHO, OR WHAT, RULES YOU?

People who are ruled by their desires think only of themselves. Everyone who is ruled by the Holy Spirit thinks about spiritual things.

ROMANS 8:5 CEV

I need coffee. Time for a shower. What should I wear? How am I doing on time? Why doesn't this guy in front of me drive any faster? I wonder how my 10:00 a.m. meeting will go? Who took my parking spot? Why is the receptionist so grumpy every morning? I hope I don't have any difficult problems to solve in my email inbox this morning. I hope Greg doesn't stop by my desk for his typical twenty minute chat. I have too much to do for that. The meeting went better than I thought it would. What's on TV tonight?

If you were to keep a running list today of every major thought you have, what would it reveal? Would your typical day look anything like the paragraph above? None of these concerns are bad or even selfish, necessarily, but for a Christian to go an entire day without contemplating spiritual things is an indication of a spiritual problem because the Holy Spirit naturally directs and guides us as we go about our daily routines.

As we submit to Him, we see otherwise mundane tasks and situations through spiritual eyes—eyes that want to honor and obey God, eyes that earnestly desire to see beyond our own desires, eyes that want to minister to others. We are quicker to forgive and slower to anger. We long for heaven rather than the recliner.

ATTRACTING SINNERS

The Pharisee who had invited Jesus saw this [a sinful woman who washed, kissed, and bathed Jesus' feet with her tears and expensive perfume] and said to himself, "If this man really were a prophet, he would know what kind of woman is touching him! He would know that she is a sinner."

LUKE 7:39 CEV

Simon, a Pharisee, invited Jesus to dine with him and some of his friends. But a sinful woman crashed the party after learning Jesus would be there. She broke down in tears when she saw Him and began washing His feet with her tears, kissing them, and pouring perfume over them, causing Simon to question whether Jesus was a prophet, as many believed Him to be.

Simon expected Jesus to view the woman the way he did. The religious rules he embraced as a Pharisee didn't allow him to interact with notorious sinners, so surely Jesus wouldn't interact with her either. But the woman wasn't bound by any such rules. She simply saw Jesus for who He was, and she was drawn to Him, knowing Him to be full of mercy. She approached Him from behind, perhaps feeling unworthy to be in His presence, and then lovingly displayed her affection for Him. To Simon's amazement, Jesus praised this woman's actions.

Holding to a certain theological bent and then drawing inferences from that theology, as men are wont to do, is of little value if we forget mercy. You will know you have forgotten mercy if the unregenerate are repelled by you and your religious rules rather than attracted to Christ, who lives in you.

KNOWING GOD

Let's do our best to know the LORD. His coming is as certain as the morning sun; he will refresh us like rain renewing the earth in the springtime.

HOSEA 6:3 CEV

In Hosea 6, the prophet is addressing God's people after a period of sin, saying, "He has torn us to shreds, but he will bandage our wounds and make us well" (v. 1). After we have experienced His discipline, Hosea tells us to do our best to know the Lord. This will look different for everybody.

Some of us will turn to what saints of old referred to as the spiritual disciplines. Richard Foster listed twelve such disciplines in His classic, *Celebration of Discipline: The Path to Spiritual Growth*: meditation, prayer, fasting, study, simplicity, solitude, submission, service, confession, guidance, celebration, and worship. Others of us find the disciplines to be too formulaic and opt instead for a more free form of expression, often focusing on one or more of the disciplines outlined by Foster.

Hosea didn't tell us to adhere to one expression or the other as much as he called us to perform some sort of action to know the Lord. You picked up a copy of this book because you want to know Christ in a deeper fashion. That is a great indicator that you are on the right path. What else are you doing to know the Lord? If a new believer came to you looking for help and asked how you draw closer to God, what would you say?

HEAVEN'S REGISTER

*But don't be happy because evil spirits obey you.
Be happy that your names are written in heaven!*

LUKE 10:20 CEV

After Jesus sent out His seventy-two hand-chosen followers to every village and city He planned to visit, they returned to Him and said, "Lord, even the demons obeyed when we spoke in your name!" (v. 17). Jesus acknowledged that fact, but He didn't want their focus to be on the power He had given them. Instead, He wanted it to be on eternity. Their names were written in heaven. That is something to be happy about.

Many of us spend our entire lives trying to get our names known in the business world, hoping to climb the ladder of success as our star rises. And to a degree, there's nothing wrong with this. But if our joy and our satisfaction come from having our nameplate on an office door on the top floor of a tall office building, it will be short-lived. How much better to derive joy and satisfaction over the fact that our names are written in heaven!

In John's Revelation (21:27), he gets a peek inside the New Jerusalem, and he sees the book that will contain our names: "Nothing unworthy will be allowed to enter. No one who is dirty-minded or who tells lies will be there. Only those whose names are written in the Lamb's book of life will be in the city."

If you have been born again, rejoice that your name can be found in heaven's register this very moment.

REJOICE IN HARDSHIP

Dear friends, do not be surprised at the fiery ordeal that has come on you to test you, as though something strange were happening to you. But rejoice inasmuch as you participate in the sufferings of Christ, so that you may be overjoyed when his glory is revealed.

1 PETER 4:12–13 NIV

As Peter wrote these words, Jerusalem was facing impending destruction. Rome considered Christianity a threat, and therefore persecution was heavy. But Peter didn't want believers to lose faith. Instead, he wanted believers to see such hardship as an opportunity to participate in the sufferings of Christ.

Trials and sufferings have a way of causing disillusionment, especially when our expectations include a life of comfort. But one day, our boss or a coworker might see a Bible on our desk and bring sanctions against us. Or we might open a business and the city might force us to honor a sinful practice, and when we resist, we may end up in court or lose our business altogether. When you face fiery ordeals, do you see them as a test or as something strange? Or do you rejoice?

In Acts 5, the apostles were arrested, imprisoned, beaten, and told not to teach about the name of Jesus, but that didn't stop them. It also didn't make them bitter or angry. Verse 41 says, "The apostles left the Sanhedrin, rejoicing because they had been counted worthy of suffering disgrace for the Name."

Rejoicing in the midst of trials is the power of Christ in us, and that is what the world around us needs to see.

GOD'S WILL

It is God's will that you should be sanctified: that you should avoid sexual immorality; that each of you should learn to control your own body in a way that is holy and honorable.

1 THESSALONIANS 4:3–4 NIV

The will of God isn't illusive or hidden. We are to give thanks in all circumstances because this is the will of God for us in Christ Jesus (1 Thessalonians 5:18). It is God's will for us to perform good works so we can silence ignorant talk of foolish people (1 Peter 2:15). And it is God's will that we should be sanctified, or holy, avoiding sexual immorality.

Giving thanks, performing good works, and controlling our sexual urges are not mutually exclusive. When we are thankful and working out our salvation, our sexual urges are better kept in check. On the other hand, when we grumble about our circumstances and are idle and cut off from Christian community, our baser instincts demand attention.

Giving thanks in all circumstances means we are willing to accept the truth of Psalm 16:5: the Lord is our portion; he makes our lot secure. We aren't owed anything more or less than what He has determined ahead of time, including sexual fulfillment. Submitting to this truth is part of the sanctification process.

Performing good works brings a sense of joy that replaces worldly happiness that comes from pleasing the flesh. What good deed has the Holy Spirit been speaking to you about performing— becoming a mentor in your community? Discipling a younger man at church? Visiting the elderly in your neighborhood or taking them on a grocery run?

CHRIST IS YOUR STRENGTH

*And he said to them, "I have eagerly desired to eat this Passover
with you before I suffer. For I tell you, I will not eat it again
until it finds fulfillment in the kingdom of God."*

LUKE 22:15–16 NIV

Jesus spoke these words to men who had failed Him. His disciples
argued over who would be the greatest. They often misunderstood
His teaching. They failed to cast out demons in His name. They fell
asleep when He asked them to stay awake to pray for Him. And
yet Jesus eagerly desired to eat the Passover meal with this band
of misfits before He suffered.

Christ's sacrificial death on the cross led the apostle Paul to
refer to him as Christ, "our Passover lamb" (1 Corinthians 5:7)—
the new had come, the old had passed away. Going forward, Paul
connects Jesus' final Passover meal with the institution of the
Lord's Supper (1 Corinthians 11), in which we proclaim the Lord's
death until He returns.

Do you approach the communion table at your church with
the same vigor and desire as Jesus? Are you eager to settle your
account with God in a corporate worship setting, knowing other
believers around you are doing the same thing? If not, it might
be an indicator that your faith isn't as strong as it should be. The
good news is, He is your strength. The next time communion is
offered at your church, approach the table knowing that grace
awaits you there.

HIDE THE WORD IN YOUR HEART

*I have hidden your word in my heart
that I might not sin against you.*

PSALM 119:11 NIV

We hide things for two reasons. We are either ashamed of something or we treasure something so much that we have to hide it for fear that someone will steal it from us.

David knew great sin, but he also knew great forgiveness. In his experience, hiding the Word of God in his heart was the only way to combat his sinful nature and to keep him from falling even further.

To say that he hid the Word in his heart implies several things. First, he went beyond simply owning a copy of God's Word. Owning a copy isn't transforming. Second, he went beyond hiding the Word in his mind. Our memories can fail us. Third, he went beyond simply reading God's Word on occasion. Reading it is helpful. But possessing it in our hearts is transformative.

If you find your faith lacking the power to overcome sin, consider a Bible memory program. It doesn't have to be elaborate. Index cards will work just fine. Look up verses that speak to the sin you are struggling with, and jot the verses down on the cards. Carry them with, you everywhere, and refer to them throughout the day.

If you meditate, study, and recite the verses often enough, you'll find that they are hidden in your heart—the perfect place for the Holy Spirit to access them for your spiritual breakthrough.

PUTTING ON CHRIST

*Let the Lord Jesus Christ be as near to you as the clothes you
wear. Then you won't try to satisfy your selfish desires.*

ROMANS 13:14 CEV

All of us go through spiritually dry seasons in our Christian walk. Our
desire for Christ and His Word are lacking. Prayer is nonexistent.
We have to make ourselves attend worship, or sometimes we even
give in to the temptation to stay home. Spiritual truths are hard
to digest. And circumstances don't make sense.

One day, our spiritual fog lifts in the form of a word that is
aptly spoken in a song, a book, from a friend, or in a sermon; and
we realize that God was there all along. We were the ones who
strayed not Him. Even in the depths of our despair, we probably
know this to be true, but knowing isn't enough. In the verse above,
Paul tells us we need to let the Lord Jesus Christ be as near to us
as the clothes we wear.

Think about that for a minute. The clothes you are wearing
are touching your skin right now. They are tangible. You can feel
them. Wherever you move, they go with you. You don't have to do
anything to make them go with you other than to move your body.
In fact, you have to remove them intentionally to be free of them.

Can you point to a time in which you intentionally removed Jesus
from your life, chasing after your sinful desires, as the verse above
says? Is it possible that your spiritual dryness began that very day?

SUSTAINING GRACE

*Let us then approach God's throne of grace with confidence,
so that we may receive mercy and find grace to
help us in our time of need.*

HEBREWS 4:16 NIV

Many of us live our entire lives in search of our father's approval. Inherent in his perceived approval is a list of accomplishments he expects us to complete. For some, it's a six-figure income, a seven-figure house, and a beautiful wife. For the more spiritually minded, it could be an expectation to become a pastor, a full-time missionary, or *at least* an elder or deacon.

The problem with all of these expectations is twofold. First, God may not be in any of them. He may have something completely different in mind for us. Second, once we get caught up in seeking our father's approval at the expense of point number one, we end up playing a game of merit. As long as we do what our earthly father wants us to do, we are on track to gain his approval. But the moment we stumble, his approval is withdrawn, and often we become a shell of what we could have been.

God, on the other hand, tells us to approach His throne of grace with confidence. Notice that it is called a "throne of grace," not a throne of rules we have to follow to earn His love or approval. As we approach Him with confidence, we receive even more grace (rather than judgment), and that grace sustains us in time of need.

BECOMING A MAN OF NOBLE CHARACTER

But the noble make noble plans,
and by noble deeds they stand.

ISAIAH 32:8 NIV

Would you consider yourself a man of noble character? If so, you're a man who knows God and His calling on your life. You're a man who is value- and purpose-driven. You're a man with a firm grasp of what's eternal.

Sadly, this world is full of bored men. The truth is, at times every man gets bored. Dr. Harold Dodds, then-president of Princeton University, made this counterintuitive observation: "It is not the fast tempo of modern life that kills but the boredom, a lack of strong interest and failure to grow that destroy. It is the feeling that nothing is worthwhile that makes men ill and unhappy."

During the next few days, you will have the opportunity to strengthen your wish, desire, commitment, and resolve to be a man of noble character. Before saying "yes" to anything, of course, one has to say "no" to other things. True, some of those other things may not *feel* boring, but they lack any connection to or passion for the Lord God, Creator of heaven and earth—and they lack any lasting honor, let alone value for eternity.

The answer isn't to stop everything you're doing. Each established sphere of life is important to God. That includes your continuing education, vocation, marriage, family, church, neighborhood, community, and much more. How do you see God in each sphere? Conversely, how does God see you in each? This would be a great evening for you to resolve to become an even nobler man.

WORKING WITH ALL YOUR HEART

Whatever you do, work at it with all your heart, as working for the Lord, not for human masters, since you know that you will receive an inheritance from the Lord as a reward. It is the Lord Christ you are serving.

COLOSSIANS 3:23–24 NIV

How strange that the all-powerful, omniscient Lord God, Creator of heaven and earth, allows human hands and hearts to do His will. The man of noble character trusts God to work in and through him. Such a man doesn't waste his time longing for a life without God's calling and purpose. He certainly doesn't waste it longing for a life of excitement, dissipation, pleasure, and ease.

A noble man is a God-filled, purpose-driven, and busy man. His hours and minutes are measured and meaningful. "Being busy is not a sin," Max Lucado wisely observes. "Jesus was busy. Paul was busy. Peter was busy. Nothing of significance is achieved without effort and hard work and weariness. That, in and of itself, is not a sin. But being busy in an endless pursuit of things that leave us empty and hollow and broken inside—that cannot be pleasing to God."

Looking back on the past few days and weeks, what is your experience? To what degree were you a noble man? Granted, God designed us to exercise, sleep, eat. He designed us to shave, shower, dress. He designed us to rest, relax, and recreate with family and friends. But that's not all—as we will continue to consider in coming days.

DOING WHAT IS RIGHT NO MATTER WHAT

*[He] who sows to the Spirit will from the Spirit reap eternal life.
Let us not lose heart in doing good, for in due time we will reap
if we do not grow weary. So then, while we have opportunity,
let us do good to all people, and especially to those
who are of the household of faith.*

GALATIANS 6:8–10 NASB

The noble man knows that he can achieve nothing if he doesn't love God with all his heart and love others as himself. He also knows he can achieve nothing without the Holy Spirit's daily cleansing, filling, and fruit-bearing work in his heart and life. Why is it so hard to live such a life? It's difficult, and often impossible, if you are unsure of the eternal value of your goals, if you are overwhelmed by the tasks before you, and if you doubt God's greatness, goodness, and calling on your life.

Today, Phillips Brooks is probably best known for authoring the Christmas carol "O Little Town of Bethlehem." He was arguably one of the best-known and loved American pastors during the latter part of the nineteenth century. He loved the Lord, studied the scriptures, proclaimed the Gospel, lectured and preached at Harvard, published a number of books, and helped create one of the nation's most magnificent church buildings.

His clarion call still echoes after all this time. "Do not pray for easy lives, pray to be stronger men. Do not pray for tasks equal to your powers, pray for power equal to your tasks." As you put this book down for the evening, ask God to strengthen you for the days ahead.

EMBRACING THE ENORMITY OF GOD'S CALLING

So teach us to number our days,
that we may gain a heart of wisdom.

PSALM 90:12 NKJV

Few men know which decade, year, month, or day they will die. Then again, at the very end of his life, Moses knew which day he would die. The same can be said for only a small handful of biblical characters. Yet knowing the day of one's death isn't necessarily good news. Like most people, Moses wanted to live longer. If anyone had good reason, he did. After all, Moses longed to enter the Promised Land and enjoy the "milk and honey" awhile.

Yet God alone appoints the day of one's death. Not even the best of men is exempt. So, it's imperative that we aspire to live nobly before God and others *now* not someday. Why before "God and others"? Because God's calling almost always extends beyond one's lifespan. In other words, we can't expect to fulfill that calling alone or in our own lifetime. The purposes of God are bigger than we can imagine. That's why eternity always must be in view.

A. W. Tozer said it well: "Life is a short and fevered rehearsal for a concert we cannot stay to give. Just when we appear to have attained some proficiency we are forced to lay our instruments down. There is simply not time enough to think, to become, to perform what the constitution of our natures indicates we are capable of."

Only by embracing the eternality of God's calling can we face death with nobility.

LIVING WITH THE END IN MIND

I eagerly expect and hope that I will in no way be ashamed,
but will have sufficient courage so that now as always Christ
will be exalted in my body, whether by life or by death.
For to me, to live is Christ and to die is gain.

PHILIPPIANS 1:20–21 NIV

Thomas à Kempis's first book, *The Imitation of Christ*, especially the closing three chapters, speaks of the importance of beginning with the end in mind. That is, to think deeply and often when alone about the day of your death. In particular: "How do you want to meet God?" To do this, not once, but as a habit of life, in union with several other habits, creates a God-given sense of purpose and mission.

Yet how many people never give serious thought to the end of their life? Oh, they think they do so—they give thought, often excessively, to the way they would like to finish their years in some supposedly blissful retirement. *Then,* they tell themselves, *I'll do what I really want—live in a nice home, travel, write, invest, and do whatever else I please.*

Granted, "We must wait for all good things." Yet why wait until the end of life, when the body is frail and the mind may not be as sharp? Pity the man who never decides to live, whose chief excitement is daydreaming, who never dares to passionately pursue his plans now, today, this month, this next year, the next five years, before it's too late and family and friends lament what might have been.

ASKING GOD FOR EVEN MORE COURAGE

"The thief comes only to steal and kill and destroy;
I came that they may have life, and have it abundantly."

JOHN 10:10 NASB

Life is full of circumstances that test our courage. Winston Churchill once said, "Without courage, all other virtues lose their meaning." It doesn't matter that you're honest, for instance, if you're afraid to tell the truth. Or that you're responsible if you're afraid to try anything new.

It's ironic that our society is bent on the idea of trying to become more rebellious, more risk-taking, less inhibited, more outrageous, less self-controlled. Many blame these trends on the 1960s, but the reality is—people have always been bent away from self-control. This bent against self-control, however, inevitably hurts our community, our family, and our friends. Ultimately, it hurts us.

If you and I lack self-control, who's in control of our thoughts, speech, and actions? One option is we're giving in to the desires of the nature we were born with. That nature's passions and desires are anything but positive, healthy, or life-giving. Another option is we may be manipulated or controlled by the Devil. If we let Satan control us, he will rob us of everything that's good in our lives. He will tempt us to take risky, dangerous, physically destructive, or suicidal actions that could kill us.

So what other option is there? It's the option Jesus calls having "life. . .abundantly." Whatever you do today, choose that option! Specifically, ask God to strengthen you in your inner man, to cleanse and fill you, to cause you to be more self-controlled and courageous than ever.

REMEMBERING GOD'S ANSWERS TO PRAYER

*Though I walk in the midst of trouble, you preserve my life.
You stretch out your hand against the anger of my
foes; with your right hand you save me.*

PSALM 138:7 NIV

In his book *Stories of Faith and Courage from the Korean War,*
retired Marine Corps Lt. Col. Larkin Spivey tells the story of Pvt.
Ed Reeves. "Lord, if the mortar didn't kill me, the shooting didn't
kill me, and the beating didn't kill me, you must want me out of
here. But I can't walk. How can I get outta here?"

As Reeves lay helpless on the frozen ground beside the now-
abandoned and destroyed truck convoy, he continued to pray.
Suddenly, God seemed to answer: "You must crawl before you can
walk." Painfully lifting himself to his hands and wounded knees,
Reeves started crawling over snow-covered fields in the direction
he hoped would take him to friendly lines. He passed more Chinese
troops who somehow made no effort to stop him. Darkness fell,
and he continued his slow, painful journey. He began to sing over
and over, "Yes, Jesus loves me!" Finally, he felt the hardness of ice
underneath him and knew that he was on the Chosen Reservoir.
Exhaustion and the mind-numbing cold were almost overwhelming
day after day. Amazingly, the song of his childhood faith kept
coming back to him: "Jesus loves me, this I know, for the Bible
tells me so." Finally, almost a week after first being wounded, Ed
Reeves was rescued. One of his first comments? "Every time I
asked God, He answered."

FORSAKING WRONG DESIRES AND FEARS

I eagerly expect and hope that I will in no way be ashamed,
but will have sufficient courage so that now as always Christ
will be exalted in my body, whether by life or by death.

PHILIPPIANS 1:20 NIV

When are you most at risk of losing courage and feeling ashamed? First, when you pursue wrong desires. Second, when you give in to fear. Wrong desires often revolve around making more money, amassing power, pursuing illicit sexuality, and pouring endless hours into online multi-user games. All four are terribly damaging. Wrong fears are just as bad. Imminent danger—real or perceived—triggers the strongest of human emotions. Fear is hardwired into your brain. It causes you to shut up, freeze up, give up. The good news: you can rewire your thoughts, beliefs, and automatic responses. If anyone proved that, it was Mother Teresa. One of her most haunting prayers:

> Deliver me, O Jesus, / From the desire of being loved, / From the desire of being extolled, / From the desire of being honored, / From the desire of being praised, / From the desire of being preferred, / From the desire of being consulted, / From the desire of being approved, / From the desire of being popular,
>
> Deliver me, O Jesus, / From the fear of being humiliated, / From the fear of being despised, / From the fear of suffering rebukes, / From the fear of being slandered, / From the fear of being forgotten, / From the fear of being wronged, / From the fear of being ridiculed, / From the fear of being suspected. / Amen.

THE MOST IMPORTANT THING ABOUT YOU

*"You are worthy, O Lord, to receive glory and honor
and power; for You created all things, and by
Your will they exist and were created."*

REVELATION 4:11 NKJV

What is the most important thing about you? Who you are? When you were born? Where you live? What you've done? What you plan to do in the future? What others think of you? What you think of others? Actually, none of these takes top priority. Instead, the most important thing about you is your view of God.

A. W. Tozer put it this way, "Without doubt, the mightiest thought the mind can entertain is the thought of God, and the weightiest word in any language is its word for God." He goes on to say: "The most portentous fact about any man is not what he at a given time may say or do, but what he in his deep heart conceives God to be like. We tend by a secret law of the soul to move toward our mental image of God." Sadly, the images of God prevalent today are "so decadent as to be utterly beneath the dignity of the Most High God and actually to constitute for professed believers something amounting to a moral calamity."

If you say you believe God can do anything, but expect Him to do nothing, is it any wonder you find it hard to pray? Conversely, if you thank God daily for His greatness and goodness, His holiness and love, and His mystery, is it any surprise you like to talk about Him with others? So, what's your view of God today?

REALIZING GOD IS GREATER THAN WE CAN IMAGINE

Oh, how great are God's riches and wisdom and knowledge!
How impossible it is for us to understand his decisions and
his ways! For who can know the LORD's thoughts?
Who knows enough to give him advice?

ROMANS 11:33–34 NLT

How big is God? What does it mean that He is the Creator and Sustainer of humanity, of earth, of the solar system, of the Milky Way galaxy, of the universe? It means that the Lord God is infinitely bigger than human brains and minds can comprehend this side of heaven. So, the foundation of any truths you might state about God is that you don't fully know what He is like. Mere mortals cannot grasp the attributes we ascribe to God, let alone comprehend the total character of God. So many aspects of His nature are mystery to finite man. The thesis of any discussion about theology proper, that is, the study of God, is that He is clothed in both majesty and mystery.

Walter A. Henrichsen is right on the mark when he says, "Every problem a person has is related to his concept of God. If you have a big God, you have small problems. If you have a small God, you have big problems." So, how big are your problems?

You may be struggling with wrong desires, gripping fears, critical health issues, financial problems, employment stressors, marital strains, parental pains, church issues, few meaningful friendships. Whatever your struggles might be, how big is your God? *How* big? Big enough, to be sure!

REMEMBERING WHY WE NEED GOD

Your life is a journey you must travel with a deep consciousness of God. It cost God plenty to get you out of that dead-end, empty-headed life you grew up in. He paid with Christ's sacred blood.

1 Peter 1:18–19 msg

Scores of times the Bible speaks about emptiness. *Void. Nothing. Nothingness. Empty. Empty head. Empty-headed. Empty life. Empty-hearted life. Empty hearts. Empty heart. Soul-empty.* How empty? In *Confessions,* St. Augustine wrote: "Our hearts are restless until they rest in You."

Although Blaise Pascal didn't exactly coin the phrase "God-shaped vacuum," he talked about it extensively. In *Pensées,* Pascal said: "What else does this craving, and this helplessness, proclaim but that there was once in man a true happiness, of which all that now remains is the empty print and trace? This he tries in vain to fill with everything around him, seeking in things that are not there the help he cannot find in those that are, though none can help, since this infinite abyss can be filled only with an infinite and immutable object; in other words by God himself."

C. S. Lewis wrote a great deal about this need as well. He had started his academic and publishing career as an atheist and agnostic, only to be powerfully converted. In *Mere Christianity,* Lewis wrote: "If I find in myself a desire for something which nothing in this world can satisfy, the most probable explanation is that I was made for another world." What is the longing of *your* heart? Ask God to fill it—with Himself—so you can enjoy life, and enjoy it abundantly (John 10:10).

NEVER FORGETTING OUR NEED FOR THE LORD

I am suffering here in prison. But I am not ashamed of it, for I know the one in whom I trust, and I am sure that he is able to guard what I have entrusted to him until the day of his return. Hold on to the pattern of wholesome teaching you learned from me—a pattern shaped by the faith and love that you have in Christ Jesus.

2 TIMOTHY 1:12–13 NLT

The noblest of men are not exempt from abject suffering. They become stellar examples of faith not because of how they stay above the fray, but because their trust in God is tested with fire and proved more valuable than gold. Even in the face of death, they're committed to staying true because their foundation is solid and their convictions deep.

Vance Havner could write: "We find that when Jesus is all we have, He is all we need and all we want. We are shipwrecked on God and stranded on omnipotence." Yet secretly many men dread the day of calamity.

Bishop Westcott gave this frank assessment: "Silently and imperceptibly, as we wake or sleep, we grow strong or we grow weak, and at last some crisis shows us what we have become." Like Havner, Westcott actively sought to be strong in the Lord and to lead others along that same path.

Over the next few months, you can become a stronger man in the Lord. Go for it with everything inside you, in all honesty asking God to search (Psalm 139:23–24), teach (Psalm 86:11), clean (Psalm 51:10) and renew your heart (Psalm 51:12).

WANTING GOD'S BEST FOR YOU

I, Paul, am on special assignment for Christ, carrying out God's plan laid out in the Message of Life by Jesus. I write this to you, Timothy, the son I love so much. All the best from our God and Christ be yours!

2 TIMOTHY 1:1–2 MSG

What does it mean to want and receive God's best for you? First, it means discarding inadequate, insufficient, ignoble thoughts of God. Herman Melville said, "The reason the mass of men fear God, and at bottom dislike Him, is because they rather distrust His heart, and fancy Him all brain like a watch."

Second, wanting God's best means seeing Him as He really is. David Needham writes, "I am convinced that the answers to every problem and issue of life for both time and eternity are resolved through a correct understanding of God."

Third, receiving God's best means shedding your intense desire for temporal pursuits and possessions. George MacDonald observed, "Man finds it hard to get what he wants, because he does not want the best; God finds it hard to give, because He would give the best, and man will not take it."

Fourth, wanting and receiving God's best means desiring His will over and against your own will. C. S. Lewis put it this way: "There are two kinds of people: those who say to God, 'Thy will be done,' and those to whom God says, 'All right, then, have it your way.'" What did you hope to gain over the past 103 days? Have you gained it yet? If yes, is it God's best? If no, again, is it God's best?

WANTING TO EXPERIENCE GOD'S NEARNESS

If you are tired from carrying heavy burdens, come to me and I will
give you rest. Take the yoke I give you. Put it on your shoulders and
learn from me. I am gentle and humble, and you will find rest.
This yoke is easy to bear, and this burden is light.

MATTHEW 11:28–30 CEV

"There is no limit to how close you can get to God." This has been taught for decades, but is it true? Consider what the Bible says keeps you from experiencing God's nearness. Do any ring true? First, unbelief (Psalm 14). Second, not knowing God's Word (Romans 10:17). Third, laziness and carelessness (Hebrews 6:12). Fourth, worry and prayerlessness (Philippians 4:6). Fifth, burdens you haven't cast on the Lord (1 Peter 5:7). Sixth, unconfessed sin (1 John 1:7–2:2).

Next, consider what Scripture says about experiencing God's nearness. First, Psalm 34:18 says, "If your heart is broken, you'll find GOD right there" (MSG) Second, Psalm 145:18 says, "The LORD is close to all who call on him, yes, to all who call on him in truth" (NLT). Third, James 4:8 says, "Draw near to God and he will draw near to you" (NASB). Fourth, Hebrews 7:19 says through hope in Jesus Christ you draw near to God. Fifth, Hebrews 10:22 urges you to draw near to God "with a true heart in full assurance of faith" (NKJV). Finally, Hebrews 11:6 says "without faith it is impossible to please God, because anyone who comes to him must believe that he exists and that he rewards those who earnestly seek him" (NIV).

Jesus is calling. What is your reply?

LOVING JESUS THE CHILDLIKE WAY

Continue in what you have learned and have become convinced of, because you know those from whom you learned it, and how from infancy you have known the Holy Scriptures, which are able to make you wise for salvation through faith in Christ Jesus.

2 TIMOTHY 3:14–15 NIV

Have you ever noticed that some grown-ups love to be around kids and some don't? Even as a grown-up, Jesus loved to be with children. During His three and a half years of ministry as an adult, Jesus gives an amazing amount of priority to ministry to children.

Jesus talks with children, something only parents and grandparents usually did in that culture. Jesus commends the faith of little children, who in that culture were sometimes considered unable to truly embrace religious faith until they were almost teenagers. Not only that, but we see Jesus blessing children. We see Him feeding them. We even see Jesus using a little boy's sack lunch to feed the multitudes and send twelve hefty baskets full of leftovers to help feed others.

Beyond that, we see Jesus healing boys and girls who are demon possessed and curing others who are sick and dying. He even resurrects a twelve-year-old girl who had just died and an older boy who had died a few hours earlier. In His preaching and teaching, Jesus said that children are a strategic, essential part of His kingdom in heaven and on earth. In so many words, Jesus told His disciples, "Listen! My kingdom belongs to kids!"

What's your own view of children and childlike faith?

RECEIVING GOD'S GIFT AS A CHILD

When I was a child, I talked like a child,
I thought like a child, I reasoned like a child.

1 CORINTHIANS 13:11 NIV

Now as in the past, some have the audacity to claim a small child's belief in God doesn't count, but that's not the case. True, children can't understand everything they're taught, yet there is nothing wrong about a child's inadequate concepts of God or of the Christian faith. The Lord and the scriptures certainly don't criticize a child's way of thinking. The One who made us knows us. As we've seen, Jesus loved to be with children. Not only that, but Jesus tells everyone, in essence, "Unless you become like a little kid, you can't even get into My kingdom." What is Jesus talking about? Well, what are kids good at doing? They're good at *receiving.* When you're a small child, your mom and dad give you some food. What do you do? You receive it. Your grandparents send you a birthday card with five shekels in it. What do you do? You receive it. God gives you a sunny day to go outside and play. What do you do? You receive it.

The same thing applies when it comes to God's kingdom. You have to receive something. Or, specifically, Someone: Jesus Christ, God's Son, Creator of heaven and earth, the One who decides how life—real and eternal life—works. And, yes, it works in some amazing, sometimes counterintuitive ways.

MAKING IT EASY FOR A CHILD TO TRUST GOD

*"And anyone who welcomes a little child like
this on my behalf is welcoming me."*

MATTHEW 18:5 NLT

One Sunday a pastor had the opportunity to interview more than a dozen third through sixth graders. Each child sat on a "hot seat" and answered five questions. The first four answers were easy: name, grade, number of siblings, and how many years they have gone to church. The fifth and final answer was a little tougher: talk about when it's hard for you to trust God.

The pastor was amazed at their responses. First, they had a much shorter list of reasons than adults usually do. Second, several of the children honestly and sincerely responded, "It's always been easy for me to trust God." You should have seen the smiles on their faces.

What could possibly ruin such childlike trust in God? Sadly, it's possible for a child to grow up in church, learn many Bible stories, sing wonderful songs, memorize scripture verses, say all the right things, look good—very good—and yet lose his or her faith. Sometimes it's the individual's own choices. Sometimes it is life's harsh realities, which bend and can break a young person. Sometimes it's because of the behaviors of adults the child should have been able to trust.

Any adult can cause a child to begin to lose faith—by hypocrisy, critical attitudes, self-centered living—anything that doesn't truly reflect Christlike, childlike kingdom living. Then again, a child's faith grows, not diminishes, when an adult apologizes to the child for, say, losing his temper. What's your story?

PROTECTING AND BUILDING UP THE FAITH OF THE YOUNG

"But if you cause one of these little ones who trusts in me to [lose faith or] fall into sin, it would be better for you to have a large millstone tied around your neck and be drowned in the depths of the sea."

MATTHEW 18:6 NLT

Scripture couldn't be clearer—anyone who repeatedly or severely harms a boy or girl by sinning against them—physically, psychologically, socially, sexually, or spiritually—is in grave danger of God's judgment.

Ancient Jewish men feared drowning above all else. Even experienced fishermen like Peter and Andrew, James and John were scared to death of drowning. Sure, some like Peter could swim, but that wasn't a given. There was certainly no coast guard at the ready back then. Even if there were, imagine a judge ordering a crew of Roman sailors to take you ten miles out into the Mediterranean Sea, tie a 100-pound millstone around your neck, and send you to the bottom of Davy Jones's locker. Peter and his fellow disciples shuddered at the thought. It should make anyone shudder. Why? Because Jesus warns each and every adult that such a fate would be much better than causing a child to lose his or her faith in Him.

The point Jesus is making is clear: don't let your attitudes, your words, or your actions soil or steal the God-given faith of a child. Like Jesus, the noble man cherishes, protects, nurtures, and builds up the faith of the young. In doing so, he builds up and protects his own heart. What could be better?

WILLINGLY RECEIVING GOD'S COMFORT AND BLESSINGS

He has sent me to tell those who mourn that the time of the Lord's favor has come, and with it, the day of God's anger against their enemies. To all who mourn in Israel, he will give a crown of beauty for ashes, a joyous blessing instead of mourning, festive praise instead of despair. In their righteousness, they will be like great oaks that the Lord has planted for his own glory.

ISAIAH 61:2–3 NLT

What a relevant biblical promise for anyone hurting due to financial pressures, job loss, marital strife, and worse. In biblical times, sorrow, grief, mourning, anguish, and despair were expressed in tangible and physical terms.

What are some specific ways you can demonstrate your trust and submit yourself to God? First, don't forget seven very important words: "Life is a long lesson in humility." Second, don't forget that in time humility bears rich fruit. Because God is near to the humble, God loves to bless them. Third, remember that humility is not denying the strengths, talents, abilities, blessings, and gifts of God at work in and through your life.

Fourth, don't overlook the fact that humility is dependence on Jesus Christ. Fifth, cultivate a strong awareness that God is at work in all His love and power in the other person's life just as much as He is in yours. Sixth, let's not overlook the fact that one of the paths to humility is thankfulness. Seventh, never forget that the Lord promises to comfort those who mourn and provide solace for those who grieve.

JESUS THE CREATOR

*In the beginning was the Word, and the Word was with God,
and the Word was God. He was with God in the beginning.
Through him all things were made; without him nothing was
made that has been made. In him was life, and that life was
the light of all mankind. The light shines in the darkness,
and the darkness has not overcome it.*

JOHN 1:1–5 NIV

Today we begin examining Jesus' presence throughout the Bible.
We'll focus on where Jesus appears in the Old Testament, the
prophecies we read concerning the coming Messiah, and His
incarnation and appearance on earth: Immanuel, God with us.
Literally.

Here the apostle John mirrors Genesis 1: Jesus was the creative
force behind everything that we see, taste, touch, and smell—
including our very own eyes, tongues, hands, and noses. The
very Creator of the universe, as part of His plan to redeem the
creation that had fallen into sin and rebellion against Him (Genesis
3:1–24), *literally put on skin* so that He could advance His plan to
save the human race. As John says in this passage, Jesus came
to bring light into all of the dark places in our world: our hunger,
pain, exhaustion, rejection, intense stress, frustration, anger, and
temptation (Hebrews 2:14–18).

For those of us living in a complex, lightning-fast, and sometimes
frustrating world, this truly is Good News. So as we look for places
where Jesus shows up in the Bible, let's also look together for
places where Jesus shows up, today, in our own lives.

MADE IN THE IMAGE

*Then God said, "Let us make mankind in our image, in our likeness. . ."
So God created mankind in his own image, in the image of God
he created them; male and female he created them.*

GENESIS 1:26–27 NIV

In creation, as an integral part of the Trinity, Jesus formed Adam and Eve into beings that would share the Trinity's likeness and image.

What does being created in the image of God mean to us today? Many thought leaders will say that God's image in us is reflected in our spirituality, creativity, language, relationships, and moral responsibility. Because we are of a higher order than the animals God created, we see the image of God in our own lives whenever we look into the mirror of our intelligence, thoughts, emotions, and spirituality. In other words, there's a big difference between you and Fido based on the way God built His image into you.

So what does that mean for us in practical terms? The Westminster Shorter Catechism simply and beautifully sums up our responsibility in the face of this reality:

Q. What is the chief end of man?

A. Man's chief end is to glorify God [a], and to enjoy Him forever [b].

[a]. Psalm 86:9; Isaiah 60:21; Romans 11:36; 1 Corinthians 6:20; 10:31; Revelation 4:11
[b]. Psalm 16:5–11; 144:15; Isaiah 12:2; Luke 2:10; Philippians 4:4; Revelation 21:3–4

If you have a few minutes, take the time to look through each of these passages. You'll find that our responsibility to act as men created in God's image is powerful, practical, and eternal.

COVENANT PROMISES

Now the earth was corrupt in God's sight and was full of violence. God saw how corrupt the earth had become, for all the people on earth had corrupted their ways. So God said to Noah, "I am going to put an end to all people, for the earth is filled with violence because of them. I am surely going to destroy both them and the earth. So make yourself an ark of cypress wood."

GENESIS 6:11–14 NIV

As we search for Jesus in the Old Testament, today we see a symbol of salvation in the image of the ark. You know the story: God chooses Noah to build an enormous ship that will save only those in Noah's family. This task takes him 120 years, after which time he closes the doors, the deluge comes, and he and his family spend some 370 days on the ship with all kinds of animals, until God gives him the "all clear" (Genesis 8:15–17).

Then God makes a covenant with Noah (Genesis 9:8–11) that resonates with the one He made with Adam and Eve (Genesis 1:22, 28). And as a symbol of this new covenant, God places a rainbow in the sky as a reminder of the promises He has made.

This story foreshadows God's relationship with Israel, His chosen family, a descendant of whom will become another symbol in the sky that symbolizes another new covenant. Jesus' empty cross is that terrible and beautiful symbol.

GOD SHOWS UP

Abram traveled through the land as far as the site of the great tree of Moreh at Shechem. At that time the Canaanites were in the land. The Lord appeared to Abram and said, "To your offspring I will give this land." So he built an altar there to the Lord, who had appeared to him.

GENESIS 12:6–7 NIV

As we search the Old Testament for the ways that God works in our lives, here's an amazing lesson that we learn time and time again: God shows up. He sees us, He knows us, and He wants to be in relationship with us.

This particular appearance came to a man named Abram, whom God had chosen to follow Him. Abram was the first in a long line of broken, sinful, down-to-earth, and very real people who became the ancestors of Jesus (see Matthew 1:1–17). God's appearance to Abram reinforced the promises God had made to this faithful man. And Abram was so grateful that he built an altar to God there so that he would remember this appearance.

In what ways has God shown up in your life? What are the symbols of His faithfulness to His promises: your family, your children, your church, your Bible? How has He provided for you in amazing ways? Like Abram, you can build meaning into specific symbols in your life that will help you remember God's faithfulness to you and your family. Take a moment to think about what one might be, and teach your family about it, as Abram would surely have done with his wife and nephew.

MELCHIZEDEK

Then Melchizedek king of Salem brought out bread and wine.
He was priest of God Most High, and he blessed Abram,
saying, "Blessed be Abram by God Most High,
Creator of heaven and earth."

GENESIS 14:18–19 NIV

While the priest and king of Salem (which later becomes Jerusalem) remains a shadowy figure in history, many commentators point to him as a "type" of Jesus in the Old Testament. We know that he was a priest of God who blessed Abram with words that reflected the words of the covenant promises that God gave Abram (Genesis 12:1–3). His name appears again in the Messianic Psalm 110, where David refers to him as well.

The book of Hebrews gives us further definition: "First, the name Melchizedek means 'king of righteousness'; then also, 'king of Salem' means 'king of peace.' Without father or mother, without genealogy, without beginning of days or end of life, resembling the Son of God, he remains a priest forever" (Hebrews 7:2–3). This incredible description gives rise to the notion that Melchizedek was a Christophany, or a pre-incarnate (meaning prior to His earthly birth) appearance of Jesus, in the Old Testament.

The writer of Hebrews points to Jesus as the great High Priest of a new covenant, a "better way" to salvation than the old Jewish sacrificial system. As our High Priest, He has sacrificed Himself to pay for the sins of humanity. Jesus was always there, even in the Old Testament, and He will always be with us today. How might that reality change your life today?

A LAUGHABLE PROMISE

The Lord appeared to Abraham near the great trees of Mamre
while he was sitting at the entrance to his tent in the heat of the
day. Abraham looked up and saw three men standing nearby.
When he saw them, he hurried from the entrance of his
tent to meet them and bowed low to the ground.

GENESIS 18:1–2 NIV

Many commentators believe that this particular appearance of
the Lord to Abraham is another "Christophany," a pre-incarnate
appearance of Jesus in the Old Testament. Imagine what it must
have been like for Abraham to have seen God again, and this time
in the flesh!

The promise that the Lord made to Abraham in this story is one
that made its hearers laugh—first Sarah, Abraham's wife (see vv.
12–15), and then the billions of people who have heard this story
over the centuries. It's a wonderful example of how God takes
seemingly unqualified—even unable—people and uses them to
accomplish His tasks. When this first descendant of Abraham was
born, the new daddy was one hundred years old, and baby Isaac
said "Ma-ma" to a ninety-year-old woman! Amazing.

If God can use two senior citizens to move His plan of redemption
forward, how can He use you today to expand His kingdom? God
empowers people to do His work. The Bible is full of stories of
God coming through when human effort and qualification were
seriously lacking. Think big, pray hard, and move forward!

INCREDIBLE SACRIFICE

*Some time later God tested Abraham. He said to him,
"Abraham!" "Here I am," he replied. Then God said, "Take your
son, your only son, whom you love—Isaac—and go to the
region of Moriah. Sacrifice him there as a burnt
offering on a mountain I will show you."*

GENESIS 22:1–2 NIV

Abraham was a man who was used to hearing the voice of God. He had followed it closely and lived by faith. God had promised that Abraham's descendants would number more than the stars in the sky (Genesis 15:5), and he'd been given a natural-born son at the impossible age of one hundred. But this time, when Abraham heard the voice, he must have been stunned.

"Kill my son? The one I waited so long to have? The fulfillment of the promise I heard so many years ago?" But he moved forward in faith and passed the test. Please take a moment to read Genesis 22:1–19. It's an incredible story, one that points toward God's sacrifice of His very own Son, Jesus Christ, on the cross. While God provided a ram to be the sacrifice in place of Isaac, the Son Himself would be the full and perfect sacrifice for humanity's sin. No one stayed God's hand when Jesus' time came.

This early picture of the sacrifice of an only son is a vivid foreshadowing of God's plan to redeem the world from sin and brokenness. God's incredible sacrifice of His own Son made it possible for all of humanity to know freedom from sin and eternal life with Him.

Have you accepted that once-for-all sacrifice for your own sin?

WRESTLING WITH GOD

Jacob was left alone, and a man wrestled with him till daybreak. . . .
Then the man said, "Let me go, for it is daybreak." But Jacob
replied, "I will not let you go unless you bless me." The man asked
him, "What is your name?" "Jacob," he answered. Then the man
said, "Your name will no longer be Jacob, but Israel, because you
have struggled with God and with humans and have overcome.". . .
So Jacob called the place Peniel, saying, "It is because I
saw God face to face, and yet my life was spared."

GENESIS 32:24–30 NIV

Here, God, through this earthly manifestation (which some theologians understand to be a pre-incarnation of Jesus), names the leader of the family who will carry the plan of salvation forward. When He changes Jacob's name to "Israel," He sets Jacob on a new path from the meaning of his first name ("supplanter" or "one who grasps the heel," which carries the meaning of "deceiver") to "one who contends with God." This would certainly be true for Israel's descendants—which include Christians in the spiritual sense.

Do you wrestle with God's plan for your life? Do you fight to live in a way that honors Him? Mirror Jacob's determination. Pray that God will bless you as you struggle to be His man with your family, in your workplace, and in your church.

THE PASSOVER LAMB

"Tell the whole community of Israel that on the tenth day of this month each man is to take a lamb for his family. . . . The animals you choose must be year-old males without defect. . . . Then they are to take some of the blood and put it on the sides and tops of the doorframes of the houses where they eat the lambs. . . . On that same night I will pass through Egypt and strike down every firstborn of both people and animals. . . . The blood will be a sign for you on the houses where you are, and when I see the blood, I will pass over you. No destructive plague will touch you when I strike Egypt."

EXODUS 12:3–7, 12–13 NIV

The deliverance of Israel from Egypt is loaded with Messianic symbolism. It's a story and ritual celebrated by Jews for centuries, and for Christians it is full of truths about our living Savior, Jesus Christ.

Through the Passover story we understand that the "lamb without defect" would be killed for the benefit of God's people. Those who acted in faith and placed the blood of the lamb "on the sides and tops of the doorframes" found out that the blood of this lamb did indeed protect them from God's wrath against the Egyptians.

The Israelites ate this Passover meal expectantly, knowing that deliverance was on its way. They acted in faith, waiting for God to stay true to His promise and deliver them from slavery. They did what God demanded, painting the doorframes of their houses with blood, where they couldn't miss it. And they experienced God's delivery.

Was their deliverance easy? No. Was it costly? Yes, moving forward in faith always is. Read Exodus 12:1–30 and marvel at the symbolism in this passage and how it points to the One sinless Lamb.

SACRIFICIAL SYSTEM

*"Sacrifice a bull each day as a sin offering to make atonement.
Purify the altar by making atonement for it, and anoint it to
consecrate it. For seven days make atonement for the altar and
consecrate it. Then the altar will be most holy, and whatever
touches it will be holy. This is what you are to offer on
the altar regularly each day: two lambs a year old."*

EXODUS 29:36–38 NIV

God's commands to the people in Exodus to sacrifice bulls and
lambs comprise another powerful symbol that points to Jesus.
As the people of Israel leave pagan Egypt, God calls them to
be separate from the surrounding countries and to offer costly
sacrifices to Him as a way to atone for their sins.

The root word *atone* appears three times in today's passage.
What does it mean? The dictionary definition is "to make amends or
reparation." The people of Israel were called to atone for their sins
on a daily basis. As they brought their sacrifices to the tabernacle,
the reality of the needed payment for their sins hit home: animals
died, blood was splashed on the altar, smoke rose up into the sky.
For as long as the sacrificial system was in place, the people of
Israel were never without a reminder of their sin.

Now that Jesus has become the perfect, once-for-all sacrifice
for our sins, our responsibility is to turn to Him daily in gratitude
for what He has done for us. He gave His life that we might live; in
exchange, He asks that we give our lives in service to Him, telling
others about the hope that we have through His sinless sacrifice.

THE WARRIOR

Now when Joshua was near Jericho, he looked up and saw a man standing in front of him with a drawn sword in his hand. Joshua went up to him and asked, "Are you for us or for our enemies?" "Neither," he replied, "but as commander of the army of the LORD I have now come." Then Joshua fell facedown to the ground in reverence, and asked him, "What message does my Lord have for his servant?" The commander of the LORD's army replied, "Take off your sandals, for the place where you are standing is holy."

JOSHUA 5:13–15 NIV

Here the commander of the Lord's army surprises Joshua, who is on high alert as he enters enemy territory. He's been called to take the fortified town of Jericho, and he's ready to fight, until the figure identifies himself and Joshua falls on his face in reverence. The fact that this commander accepted this reverent act and called the ground "holy" leads many to surmise that this figure was another Old Testament appearance of Jesus.

God's commands to Joshua form the most bizarre battle plan ever. But they leave no doubt as to who is doing the actual fighting. Again, as we have seen before in the Old Testament, the command is for Joshua to step forward in faith and obedience and watch God claim the victory.

And so it is for us today. When we step forward in faith, we rely on God to win the battles of our lives for us. Those of us who have seen His deliverance can testify, as Joshua did when he saw those walls crumble, that God is indeed the only one who can fight for us, leading us to victory over our sin and bringing us into eternal life.

DAVID POINTS TO JESUS

My God, my God, why have you forsaken me? Why are you so far from saving me, so far from my cries of anguish? . . . All who see me mock me; they hurl insults, shaking their heads. "He trusts in the Lord," they say, "let the Lord rescue him. Let him deliver him, since he delights in him." . . . Dogs surround me, a pack of villains encircles me; they pierce my hands and my feet. All my bones are on display; people stare and gloat over me. They divide my clothes among them and cast lots for my garment.

PSALM 22:1, 7–8, 16–18 NIV

Psalm 22 is quoted from and referred to on numerous occasions in the New Testament. In fact, no psalm is quoted more. It is a psalm, or song, of David, written when he was under pressure from the prolonged attacks of his enemies. It is a picture of the righteous sufferer and, as such, it prefigures the story of Jesus' last days on earth and His crucifixion.

Verse 1 starts out with the words that Jesus used on the cross as He suffered for our sins. Verses 7–8 reflect the derision that passersby heaped on Him as they saw Him hanging on the cross (see Matthew 27:39 and Luke 23:35). Verse 16 points to the nails that would pierce His hands and feet (see Isaiah 53:7 and John 20:27), and verses 17–18 predict the soldiers' gambling for His garments (Matthew 27:35, John 19:23–24).

God gave His people glimpses of what was to come. How does He do the same for you today? Look for ways that He makes His ways known to you in everyday life.

THE CORNERSTONE

The stone the builders rejected has become the cornerstone;
the Lord has done this, and it is marvelous in our eyes.
The Lord has done it this very day; let us rejoice today and
be glad. Blessed is he who comes in the name of the
Lord. From the house of the Lord we bless you.

PSALM 118:22-24, 26 NIV

Here we find another psalm that points to Jesus, this one written in the context of a king giving thanks for victory over his enemies. Verses 22–23 are words that Jesus applied to Himself in the New Testament because He had been rejected by Israel, His own people, yet He was to become the very cornerstone of God's new house, the church (Matthew 21:42; Mark 12:10; Luke 20:17; Acts 4:11; Ephesians 2:20; 1 Peter 2:7).

Verse 26 is the song that the people of Jerusalem sang when Jesus made His entry into the city before His trial and crucifixion. And some scholars believe that this is the very psalm that Jesus and the disciples sang at the conclusion of the Last Supper (Matthew 26:30).

How amazing that we would find such detailed messages about Jesus, the Savior, in these psalms that had been sung centuries before Jesus was even born. It points to the progressive plan of God to save His people that is so carefully laid out in the Bible. Indeed, Jesus is the Cornerstone of our faith, the Rock of our salvation, the only sure footing we have in a world that continues to crumble around us. Turn to Him today and put your feet on solid ground.

THE FIERY FURNACE

He said, "Look! I see four men walking around in the fire,
unbound and unharmed, and the fourth looks
like a son of the gods."

DANIEL 3:25 NIV

The story of Daniel and his three brave friends is a favorite of Sunday school teachers—and students—around the globe. The morals of the stories are so clear, so simple to remember. And in this particular story, we see yet another instance of what many scholars think is a pre-incarnate appearance of Jesus.

Daniel and his friends are captives in a foreign land. Their past is gone, their present is difficult, and their future has also been taken away, for as foreign prisoners they were likely turned into eunuchs, dedicated to the full-time service to the Babylonian king Nebuchadnezzar. Loyalty was demanded of them, yet they remained loyal to their God.

Their story of defiance is well known, and here we see the pagan king looking into the fire, seeing the deliverance of God, which is just as the men had predicted (3:17–18). Having witnessed this miracle, Nebuchadnezzar writes a decree that is simply jaw-dropping. (Please take a moment to read the story in Daniel chapter 3, especially verses 28–30).

If you've believed in the saving power of Jesus, you know what it is like to be delivered from certain death and an eternity in the fire. Do others who may not know Jesus understand from the way you live your life that you have been saved from this fate? Can they see your faithfulness, your trust in this Jesus who stands beside you in the midst of whatever trial you're experiencing?

DESCRIPTION OF THE KING

The people walking in darkness have seen a great light; on those living in the land of deep darkness a light has dawned. . . . For to us a child is born, to us a son is given, and the government will be on his shoulders. And he will be called Wonderful Counselor, Mighty God, Everlasting Father, Prince of Peace. Of the greatness of his government and peace there will be no end. He will reign on David's throne and over his kingdom. . . . The zeal of the LORD Almighty will accomplish this.

ISAIAH 9:2, 6–7 NIV

Up until this point we have been looking for glimpses of Jesus in the Old Testament. Now, we'll marvel at the prophecies of Jesus.

Isaiah prophesied some seven hundred years before the birth of Jesus, and his description of the coming Messiah was jaw dropping. He lived and wrote during a time when Israel was declining and other powers were pressuring the Jewish people. His book points toward the coming defeat and exile of the Jewish people, yet he does not leave them hopeless. God inspired this great prophet to point his listeners toward the coming King that they had been waiting on for centuries.

The coming darkness would indeed be hard as the Jews would have to pay for their disobedience; but, like a candle in a pitch-black room, the King would come. This familiar passage rings through the centuries to inspire us as well—Jesus, the Wonderful Counselor, the Mighty God, the Everlasting Father, the Prince of Peace, is still alive and reigning today in the hearts and lives of those who trust in Him for their salvation. His light chases away the darkness in our lives.

SUFFERING SERVANT PART 1

*He was despised and rejected by mankind, a man of suffering,
and familiar with pain. Like one from whom people hide their faces
he was despised, and we held him in low esteem. Surely he took
up our pain and bore our suffering, yet we considered him
punished by God, stricken by him, and afflicted.*

ISAIAH 53:3–4 NIV

Isaiah 53 continues the amazing description of the suffering Servant
that would come to rescue the people of Israel and to save the
world from sin. Once again, seven hundred years before the birth
of Jesus, we have these promises that describe who and what the
coming Savior would be like.

Despised and rejected—those of us who know the story of the
New Testament know that Jesus would be both loved and hated
by the people that He came to save. How true that is in our lives
today—so many professing their love for the Savior, and so many
adamantly denying that He exists.

Have you been "despised" by those in your circle of influence for
following Jesus? Remember that Jesus understands. He understands
the deepest wounds of our hearts. He knows the ache we feel at the
brokenness we experience. He walked the dark path on our behalf,
and He still lives today to bring healing where we most need it. Jesus
told us, "In this world, you will have trouble. But take heart! I have
overcome the world" (John 16:33).

Living for Jesus in this world may bring pain and difficulty, but
we have a living Source to help us as we stand firm for Him.

SUFFERING SERVANT PART 2

But he was pierced for our transgressions, he was crushed for our iniquities; the punishment that brought us peace was on him, and by his wounds we are healed. We all, like sheep, have gone astray, each of us has turned to our own way; and the LORD has laid on him the iniquity of us all.

ISAIAH 53:5–6 NIV

Have you ever suffered for something that someone else did? Perhaps your wife decided to leave you and you found yourself paying child support for the "privilege" of not seeing your kids. Perhaps a coworker let his deadline slip and now you have to work twice as hard to get the project out on time. Or maybe someone decided to take a quick left in front of you and you smashed the car that you'd just bought a month ago.

Life can be hard, but anything we might be going through because of someone else's poor decisions can hardly compare to the suffering that Isaiah tells us about in this passage. Read the passage again: OUR transgressions. . .OUR iniquities. . .punishment that brought US peace. . .WE are healed. . .all because a perfectly sinless Savior made the choice to cover our sins.

Think of the many ways in which we can be like sheep: stubborn, aimlessly wandering, just following our noses, eating the grass in front of us without looking for danger all around. There's no doubt that we have all "turned to our own way" and rejected the things of God. Then consider how the sin that you stumble into every single day is covered—completely wiped clean—by the sacrifice of Jesus. The incarnation (Christ coming in human form) leads to freedom for us all.

SUFFERING SERVANT PART 3

*Therefore I will give him a portion among the great, and he will
divide the spoils with the strong, because he poured out his life
unto death, and was numbered with the transgressors. For he bore
the sin of many, and made intercession for the transgressors.*

ISAIAH 53:12 NIV

This picture of the Suffering Servant in Isaiah has directed our
thoughts toward Jesus. Today's passage portrays Jesus almost as
an attorney, pleading our case before God, the righteous Judge.
It points toward the victory Jesus experiences today because He
fulfilled the sacrificial system that the Jews had been following
for centuries.

What do you see when you hear the word *transgressors*?
Criminals? Prostitutes? Drug addicts? Sin-sick people who are
so addicted to doing the wrong thing that they can't help but
continue sinning? Maybe, but also think of yourself in this context.

Jesus numbered Himself among us, even though He had no
reason to. As the sinless Son of God, He could have condemned
those who were lost in their sin. And try as we might, we're all
lost in our own sinfulness, which darkens our hearts and makes
our lives difficult.

But, like a lawyer passionately pleading before a judge on
our behalf, Jesus continues to make intercession before God.
He knows we're guilty, and yet He fights for us every single day.
Why? Because He already took our death sentence; He already
did the hard time. And because of this, we can live in freedom
every single day.

ZECHARIAH'S SURPRISE

"Do not be afraid, Zechariah; your prayer has been heard. Your wife Elizabeth will bear you a son, and you are to call him John. . . . He will bring back many of the people of Israel to the Lord their God. And he will go before the Lord, in the spirit and power of Elijah, to turn the hearts of the parents to their children and the disobedient to the wisdom of the righteous— to make ready a people prepared for the Lord."

LUKE 1:13, 16–17 NIV

Here we find Zechariah going about his business as a priest, working in an honored position and burning incense before the Lord. Suddenly an angel appears to him—Gabriel, one who "stand[s] in the presence of God" (v. 19), telling him that his wife, Elizabeth, in her old age would have a son, John, who would prepare the way for the Messiah. Shades of Abraham and Sarah (Genesis 17:19–21)!

Note what a part of John's task would be: calling Israel back to God, but also turning "the hearts of the fathers to the children." This echoes the last words of the Old Testament: "Behold, I am going to send you Elijah the prophet before the coming of the great and terrible day of the LORD. He will restore the hearts of fathers to their children and the hearts of children to their fathers, so that I will not come and smite the land with a curse" (Malachi 4:5–6 NASB).

Are you a father? Reread that passage from Malachi again. Notice that it doesn't talk about mothers here. Have you "turned your heart" toward your children so that they turn their hearts toward you?

GABRIEL COMES TO MARY

In the sixth month of Elizabeth's pregnancy, God sent the angel Gabriel to Nazareth, a town in Galilee. . . . The angel went to her and said, "Greetings, you who are highly favored! The Lord is with you." Mary was greatly troubled at his words and wondered what kind of greeting this might be. But the angel said to her, "Do not be afraid, Mary; you have found favor with God."

LUKE 1:26, 28–30 NIV

The angel Gabriel once again gets called up for duty just a few months after he had appeared to Zechariah. This time, he appears to Mary, who would become the mother of Jesus. As far as we know, Mary was an unknown, normal teenager, perhaps fourteen or fifteen years of age. And the angel came to her as she was in the middle of her daily duties—suddenly before her stood an angel messenger with a shocking, even overwhelming, task for her to accomplish.

Notice his words to her. He called her "highly favored" and told her not to be afraid. Did you know that in the scriptures, whenever an angel appears, the angel tells the people not to be afraid? Here again Gabriel says these words of comfort because his appearance must have scared the living daylights out of her.

We too are "favored" by God because of the saving work of Jesus on our behalf. And the words that Gabriel spoke to Mary are for us as well. God has called us to live and work to build His kingdom, and this passage calls us to fearless service.

Was Mary intimidated? Certainly. And we can be as well. But then Gabriel's words come to us: "Do not be afraid." Where in your life do you need to step out in faith and put fear aside?

AN IMPOSSIBLE CALLING

"You will conceive and give birth to a son, and you are to call him Jesus. He will be great and will be called the Son of the Most High. The Lord God will give him the throne of his father David, and he will reign over Jacob's descendants forever; his kingdom will never end."

LUKE 1:31–33 NIV

If you're a father, you hope for the best for your kids. You do what you can to help them prepare for whatever next phase of life they are approaching, all with the hope that someday they'll be responsible adults who will live successful lives in the world as followers of Jesus.

Mary didn't have to wonder about what her child was going to do when He came of age. She had this word from Jesus that this child, whom she would conceive by the power of the Spirit, would be a king in the line of David. How this young girl must have puzzled about this. . .how any of this could be happening to her? And yet she had this assurance from God that her Son would lead the nation of Israel.

Notice that once again God empowered Mary to do the work. In and of herself, she had no power to do the work. And the same is true for us. Yes, we've been gifted with abilities and love for our kids, but we're far from perfect. Yet we have the same Power Source—the Holy Spirit—who longs to help us raise our kids to follow Mary's Son, our Savior.

Mary's task wasn't easy; ours won't be either. But following God's call means patiently waiting for Him to do the work through us, as unworthy as we may be.

HIS WORD NEVER FAILS

"For no word from God will ever fail." "I am the Lord's servant," Mary answered. "May your word to me be fulfilled." Then the angel left her.

LUKE 1:37–38 NIV

Let's take a moment to consider the words of the angel Gabriel, the messenger who "stand[s] in the presence of God." Listen to his words to Mary: "No word from God will ever fail."

Remember the prophecy of Isaiah, spoken seven hundred years before the birth of Jesus? To a people who were oppressed and crushed, they must have hoped and prayed for this king to come every single day. Generation after generation lived and died under this promise, yet God delayed until the perfect time had come for Jesus to be born.

How long have you been waiting for the promise of God to be fulfilled in your life? What promises are you claiming for your life? Maybe it's a job opportunity that you're hoping will come your way; maybe you and your wife have been struggling to have a child; maybe it's a teenager who has walked away from God and you're waiting for Him to work in your child's life in a powerful way.

The Bible is filled with promises from God. Take it from Gabriel, who knows from personal experience: "No word from God will EVER fail." Waiting can be difficult, but God is faithful. Continue to pray, "I am the Lord's servant," and look for ways that God is working. Perhaps in ways that you would never expect—just as Mary did.

GENERATIONAL MEMORY

*"My soul glorifies the Lord and my spirit rejoices in God my Savior,
for he has been mindful of the humble state of his servant.
From now on all generations will call me blessed, for the Mighty
One has done great things for me—holy is his name."*

LUKE 1:46–49 NIV

Okay, so Mary has been called to a task that none of us men will ever have to do: bear and deliver a child. For most men, this is an enormous relief. We watch our children being born with wonder, pain, and amazement, and for the rest of our lives, we give our wives all kinds of credit for giving up so much of their lives to bear and raise children.

Mary's faithfulness was rewarded, as billions of people have heard her story. Indeed, we do "call her blessed," because she was faithful to God's call. Her prophecy in this song of gratitude did come true.

If you're a father, in a very real sense you are a patriarch, just like Abraham, Isaac, and Jacob. Your children and your children's children will tell stories about you. Are you pointing your children toward Jesus?

Make it your goal to have your children remember you and call *themselves* blessed for having you as a father.

A NEW BAPTISM

The people were waiting expectantly and were all wondering in their hearts if John might possibly be the Messiah. John answered them all, "I baptize you with water. But one who is more powerful than I will come, the straps of whose sandals I am not worthy to untie. He will baptize you with the Holy Spirit and fire."

LUKE 3:15–16 NIV

We read earlier about John the Baptist and how he came to prepare the way for Jesus. This cousin of the Savior never claimed to be the Messiah; he merely pointed the way for people to find Jesus.

John was certainly an odd sight—living in the desert, eating a very strange diet, and passionately urging people to repent from their evil ways and change their hearts. He'd been raised among the Jewish religious elite and represented the ultimate example of a son breaking with his father's occupation with his amazingly countercultural lifestyle.

John was a harbinger of a new era; his appearance signaled a new age, and his message rings through the centuries to those who hope in Jesus for their salvation and who live empowered by the Spirit in the way that God has asked us to live.

John didn't claim to be the Christ; he pointed the way for others to see Him. Does your life point your family, your friends, your neighbors, and your coworkers in the same direction?

EXCELLING AT WORK

Do you see a man who excels in his work? He will stand before kings; he will not stand before unknown men.

PROVERBS 22:29 NKJV

It is easy to get caught up in working for the applause of men—or simply to put food on the table—because both produce tangible results. But a man who excels in his work can do so for other reasons. For the Christian, we are called to work to the glory of God (Colossians 3:17).

A man who excels in his work is diligent. He studies the systems that are in place and tweaks them to make them even better. He knows the needs of his customers and he exceeds them. He keeps his word. He is prompt, accurate, and quick to adjust his course when he sees the need to do so.

Joseph was sold into slavery by his brothers, but he worked hard and found favor with Potiphar, the governor of Egypt, who eventually elevated Joseph to second-in-command. He literally stood before royalty, as the verse above says. But even for those of us who will never meet nobility for our strong work efforts, we will stand before the King of Kings to give account someday.

If you aren't already doing so, what would it look like for you to excel at work for God's glory? Would it mean loving an unlovable boss? Would it mean allowing him or her to take the credit for one of your ideas? Would it mean going above and beyond your work description to benefit your department or company?

STANDING IN THE GAP

*"So I sought for a man among them who would make a wall,
and stand in the gap before Me on behalf of the land,
that I should not destroy it; but I found no one."*

EZEKIEL 22:30 NKJV

When God commissions the prophet Ezekiel to chronicle a long list of sins committed by Jerusalem, Ezekiel covers all his bases: murder, idolatry, mistreatment of parents, oppression of strangers, mistreatment of the fatherless and the widow, profaning the Sabbath, acts of lewdness, bribery, and extortion, as well as her priests violating God's law. In every sense, Jerusalem had become a den of iniquity.

And yet, in the midst of such wickedness, God was looking for a man who would make a wall and stand in the gap before Him on behalf of the land, that He would not destroy it. But sadly, He found no one. As Bible commentators point out, not every man was caught up in debauchery. But one of the few who was—Jeremiah—was forbidden to pray for the city (Jeremiah 11:14). Apparently, the city had crossed the point of no return with God. The righteous had abandoned the gates, His judgment certain.

Nations fall as the righteous stop practicing righteousness. The act of falling away can be so subtle that you almost don't recognize it. A compromise here. A "small" sin there. And before you know it, you have lost your house and then your city—not in the physical sense, generally, but in the moral sense. If God were to look for a man to stand in the gap today, would He find you there?

GODLY PURSUITS

But you, O man of God, flee these things [the love of money and its empty pursuits] and pursue righteousness, godliness, faith, love, patience, gentleness.

1 TIMOTHY 6:11 NKJV

When the Bible tells us to flee certain sins (putting off the old man), it tells us how to do so by pursuing new practices (putting on the new man) (Ephesians 4:21–24). In the verse above, the apostle Paul has just finished warning young Timothy about the perils of loving money, and then he tells him how to fight it: pursue righteousness, godliness, faith, love, patience, and gentleness.

What exactly does that look like? Pursuing righteousness in this context isn't about our eternal standing, according to commentators, but rather it is about dealing with one another justly. In doing so, we are not seeking to unjustly profit from our relationship with them. Pursuing godliness means to do our part in the sanctification process. We can do nothing to purify ourselves of our sin, but we can put ourselves under the preaching and the reading of the Word. Pursuing faith is about taking our eyes off our circumstances and placing them above. Loving God replaces loving money. Pursuing patience means bearing with loss, injury, and persecution. And pursuing gentleness means being content with our lot.

If the love of money is strong in you, the list of pursuits above is the antidote. As you begin to pursue them, your love of money will be loosened, and you will see other spiritual victories in your life as well.

A DIVINE MEETING PLACE

*And Judas, who betrayed Him, also knew the place
[a garden, over the Brook Kidron—also known as the garden
of Gethsemane]; for Jesus often met there with His disciples.*

JOHN 18:2 NKJV

Even though Jesus knew that Judas was about to betray Him, He didn't vary His pattern of meeting with His disciples in the garden of Gethsemane. In fact, He met there with His disciples just after the Last Supper. Judas would have known this pattern well, since he was one of those disciples.

The scriptures don't say why Jesus chose to retire there on this particular occasion, but He typically did so for prayer, reflection, and lodging—away from the craziness of Jerusalem.

Western Protestants seem to minimize the need for an actual meeting place with Jesus since we can worship Him in spirit and in truth from anywhere, but there is something to be said for having a designated place in your home to meet with Him, whether it's on your front porch, on a nearby walking trail, or in a meditative garden. Much like having a dedicated office space helps us to focus better on our work than if we tried to do so from our living room, having a dedicated space to meet with Jesus clears away worldly distractions.

Do you have a place you retire to routinely to meet with Jesus? Do people in your family know that when they see you in this place, you are meeting with Him? Do even your enemies know about this place? If not, find one and begin using it today.

NO MORE PRETENSE

What this adds up to, then, is this: no more lies, no more pretense.
Tell your neighbor the truth. In Christ's body we're all connected
to each other, after all. When you lie to others,
you end up lying to yourself.

EPHESIANS 4:25 MSG

Our natural inclination is to present our best while hiding the rest. We smile even though we are feeling down. We nod our head in agreement during a Bible study or sermon even though we don't understand. We pray in the company of others even when our private prayer life is nonexistent.

In the verse above, the apostle Paul is calling for an end to pretense in the church. He isn't necessarily saying we should wear our heart on our sleeve, or that we should shake our head in disagreement during a Bible study or sermon, or that we should not pray in the company of others if we aren't praying privately. But he is saying that pretense comes with a cost. When we lie to one another openly or subtly, we not only harm the body but we also harm ourselves because we end up lying to ourselves.

Consider your own small group of Christian fellowship. Can you see pretense in others? How has this affected your relationships within the group? How has it affected your ability to minister to one another? If you can see pretense in them, they can probably see it in you too. Resolve to tell them the truth, knowing it will make the ground fertile for ministry.

SUFFERING FOR CHRIST

For to you it has been granted on behalf of Christ,
not only to believe in Him, but also to suffer for His sake.

PHILIPPIANS 1:29 NKJV

Paul knew what it meant to suffer for Christ. He chronicles many of his perils in 2 Corinthians 11:24–27. They include five lashings from the Jews, three beatings with rods, one stoning, and more. He was in constant danger and always in need of food, shelter, and clothing.

Writing from a Roman prison, he wanted the believers in Philippi to understand that they too are called to suffer for Christ. The church in Philippi was known for its generosity, even sending Paul supplies when he was ministering to other churches. They may have been the only church to do so (Philippians 4:15–16). He wanted to hear only good reports about this church, even if he couldn't be with them (Philippians 1:27), so he was preparing them to not fear their adversaries. Suffering for Christ had been granted to them by God; it was a privilege.

How can we see it as any less in our own lives? The American church tends to get caught up in its rights as citizens (and biblically, there is a place for playing the citizen card), hoping to ward off suffering, often forgetting that we are called to suffer for Christ. We aren't called to seek it, but we are called to endure it when it comes. Are you preparing your family accordingly?

NO TURNING BACK

But now after you have known God, or rather are known by God, how is it that you turn again to the weak and beggarly elements, to which you desire again to be in bondage?

GALATIANS 4:9 NKJV

Most of us tend to default to the familiar. The Jews in Galatia were no exception. After hearing the Gospel and responding to it, they knew God in a far more intimate way than when they were trying to keep the ceremonial law by adhering to eating certain foods or observing certain ceremonial holy days, as the law commanded.

None of those practices had any inherent spiritual power. They were shadows of the Gospel to come. Yet Paul is writing to the Galatian church with a heavy heart, knowing they had slipped back into their old ways. "I am afraid for you, lest I have labored for you in vain," he says in verse 11. He goes on to say, "My little children, for whom I labor in birth again until Christ is formed in you, I would like to be present with you now and to change my tone; for I have doubts about you" (vv. 19–20).

Today, we don't struggle with returning to the ceremonial law because most of us didn't come from that background. But we struggle with other empty rituals, such as performance-based Christianity. Formerly, we believed we could earn our way to heaven by good works. Even though we left that behind, we return to it when we believe our performance is a reflection of spiritual strength. Reject that! Return to the power of Christ in you.

BITTER AS WORMWOOD

For the lips of an immoral woman drip honey, and her mouth is smoother than oil; but in the end she is bitter as wormwood.

PROVERBS 5:3–4 NKJV

If we are not on continual guard against sexual immorality, we will be easily swayed away from everything we believe to be true. An immoral woman speaks directly to our carnal nature. She is persuasive and inviting, but in the end, she is bitter as wormwood.

"Wormwood" isn't a word we normally use, but you can also find it in Revelation. When the third angel sounds his trumpet, a great star falls from heaven into a third of the rivers and springs of water (Revelation 8:10). "The name of the star is Wormwood. A third of the waters became wormwood, and many men died from the water, because it was made bitter" (v. 11). In other words, wormwood is poisonous to the point of death.

Sexual immorality is really that serious. If we do not die a physical death from disease, we certainly place ourselves on the edge of spiritual death. In his commentary, Matthew Henry said: "Uncleanness is a sin that does as much as any thing [to] blind the understanding, sear the conscience, and keep people from pondering the path of life. Proverbs 5:5 says the immoral woman's 'feet go down to death.' Proverbs 2:18 says her 'house leads down to death.'"

Are you currently in the clutches of, or being lured by, an immoral woman? Recognize that she is bitter as wormwood. She doesn't have your best interest at heart. Turn from her and embrace life.

FOR KING AND COUNTRY

Therefore I exhort first of all that supplications, prayers, intercessions, and giving of thanks be made for all men, for kings and all who are in authority, that we may lead a quiet and peaceable life in all godliness and reverence.

1 TIMOTHY 2:1–2 NKJV

Throughout history, politics have been divisive. Some Christians are deeply involved; others prefer to steer clear. No matter your natural inclination, we cannot live compartmentalized lives. Politics matter.

Our leaders determine the degree of freedom we enjoy by the laws they pass. They also send our children to war (sometimes justly, sometimes not), set tax rates, choose or confirm judges, and in some sense, they even shape the culture of the generation to follow by the legislation they pass. That's a lot of power.

What is your first reaction when political leaders, or anybody in authority, does something you disagree with? Is it vitriolic criticism? If so, that's probably a good indication that you haven't been praying for them, as Paul advises Timothy in the verses above.

Notice the three types of prayers Paul tells Timothy to pray for all people—including leaders: supplications, intercessions, and giving of thanks. Supplication is an act of asking God to help someone else—to provide for that person's wants and needs. Intercessions are asking God to intervene on somebody else's behalf. And giving thanks is an act of gratitude for that person.

Of course, tyrants and dictators ought to be opposed, and even deposed, but never without praying for them first.

GIVE ME DISCERNMENT, LORD

*Then God said to him: "Because you have asked this thing,
and have not asked long life for yourself, nor have asked riches
for yourself, nor have asked the life of your enemies, but have
asked for yourself understanding to discern justice,
behold, I have done according to your words."*

1 KINGS 3:11–12 NKJV

If the Lord appeared to you in a dream and asked you, "What shall I give you?" how would you respond? If you are young, you might ask for a beautiful wife. If you are middle-aged, you might ask for a larger 401(k). If you are older, you might ask for a longer life.

None of those things are inherently bad, but when the Lord appeared to Solomon in a dream and asked him that very question, Solomon's answer was better:

> *"Now, O LORD my God, You have made Your
> servant king instead of my father David, but I
> am a little child; I do not know how to go out or
> come in. And Your servant is in the midst of Your
> people whom You have chosen, a great people,
> too numerous to be numbered or counted.
> Therefore give to Your servant an understanding
> heart to judge Your people, that I may discern
> between good and evil." (1 Kings 3:7–9)*

Solomon wasn't really a child. He just felt like one because he lacked understanding. So he asked God for discernment, and God was pleased. God may never appear to you in a dream, but He would be just as pleased if you asked Him for discernment today.

GOD'S HERITAGE

Who is a God like You, pardoning iniquity and passing over the transgression of the remnant of His heritage? He does not retain His anger forever, because He delights in mercy.

MICAH 7:18 NKJV

The prophet Micah foresaw Judah's captivity as the nation was drawing to a close during the reigns of Jotham, Ahaz, and Hezekiah (Micah 1:1). Even still, as the prophets often did, Micah warns God's people of the impending judgment for those who had ears to hear.

While judgment and hardship were coming, so was the mercy of God for His remnant. In the verse above, Micah asks, "Who is a God like you?"—a God who delights in mercy and pardons His people's sins? Surely, no false god or idol could make such an offer.

We, as God's people, are His heritage. He was once angry with us for our sins, but He has pardoned us, having passed over our transgressions in the name of Jesus. We are His remnant—the remaining portion of humanity who longs to see God make all things new. He set redemption in progress from the beginning, knowing we would fall short.

As the head of your household, does your family know the relevance of serving a merciful God? Do they know Him to be slow to anger? Do they understand they are part of His heritage—the latest in a long list of generations who have known God and been preserved by Him? Have you made that connection for them?

DEVOUT MEN

*And devout men carried Stephen to his burial,
and made great lamentation over him.*

ACTS 8:2 NKJV

As the Word of God spread in Jerusalem after Pentecost, the number of disciples began to increase, and even a "great many of the priests were obedient to the faith" (Acts 6:7 NKJV). But not all of the religious leaders in the synagogue were happy about it. When Stephen, one of the original seven deacons in the church, was questioned by the high priest, he held nothing back—calling them stiff-necked and uncircumcised in their hearts and ears, as well as resisters of the Holy Spirit (Acts 7:51).

Speaking the truth cost Stephen his life. The religious leaders stoned him to death, leading to a great persecution against the Jerusalem church, forcing many believers (except the apostles) to be scattered throughout Judea and Samaria (Acts 8:1).

The next verse says "devout men carried Stephen to his burial." Commentators vary regarding the identity of these men. At least one believes these men may have been unconverted Jews who didn't like what took place. Others believe these were members of the Jerusalem church. Either way, nobody can doubt their courage after seeing what happened to a man who crossed the authorities. But honoring the fallen at the hands of injustice meant more to them than the possible repercussions.

If persecution of believers were to spread across the country today and believers were scattered, would you be one of the devout men who took risks when the situation called for it the way these men did?

SPIRITUAL GARDENING

Now he who plants and he who waters are one, and each one will receive his own reward according to his own labor.

1 CORINTHIANS 3:8 NKJV

If you've ever been around someone who can turn an ordinary conversation into a spiritual one with thought-provoking, Gospel-laced questions or observations, then you probably feel inadequate in your own evangelization efforts. For most of us, the ground we are planting in seems much drier and less receptive to the Gospel. The next time you encounter such ground, consider the verse above.

Some of us are called to plant seeds in rough terrain, while others are called to pour a little water on those seeds to bring the Gospel to fruition. But the two aren't mutually exclusive. You can be a planter who waters on occasion or a waterer who plants on occasion. The good news is that both will receive his own reward according to his own labor. This should free us to speak Gospel truth no matter whether we are planting or watering. Both are necessary.

But the apostle Paul doesn't leave any room in this verse for not gardening in some fashion. Sitting in the pew while others garden is not an option. So that raises several questions: How are your gardening efforts going? Which role do you naturally gravitate toward? Have you played both roles at some point? Do you seek out the unconverted in your office, at the store, and everywhere else you go so you can plant or water?

WITH JESUS

Now when they saw the boldness of Peter and John, and perceived that they were uneducated and untrained men, they marveled. And they realized that they had been with Jesus.

ACTS 4:13 NKJV

When Peter and John healed the lame man outside the temple, the man did what came naturally to him—he joined Peter and John in the temple, "walking, leaping, and praising God" (Acts 3:8 NKJV). The people inside marveled, giving Peter an opportunity to point out that the man was healed in the name of Jesus—the one this very people had denied.

That landed them in the custody of the Sanhedrin, who weren't all that fond of what Peter and John were saying. As Peter testified at their trial, he accurately portrayed Jesus as the chief cornerstone in whom salvation is found (Acts 4:11–12). That's when the religious leaders began to notice that these two uneducated men who were speaking with such boldness had been in the presence of Jesus. Either they recognized them as having traveled with Jesus, or they recognized something in them that made them realize they had been with Jesus. Either way, spending time with Jesus had changed them—it had given them a boldness they never had before.

Have you been changed by spending time with Jesus? One true test is to evaluate how willing you are to proclaim His truth among people like coworkers or old drinking buddies who might not be open to hearing it. If you've come up short, spend more time with Jesus. He'll make all the difference.

PROVE YOURSELF A MAN

*"I go the way of all the earth; be strong,
therefore, and prove yourself a man."*

1 Kings 2:2 nkjv

At the end of David's life, he charged his son, Solomon, to prove himself a man. Solomon would need to be wise as he assumed the role of king. Even though he was young, he would need to act much older. David explained what that would look like: "And keep the charge of the Lord your God: to walk in His ways, to keep His statutes, His commandments, His judgments, and His testimonies, as it is written in the Law of Moses, that you may prosper in all that you do and wherever you turn" (1 Kings 2:3 nkjv).

Sadly, Solomon wasn't always successful. While he was indeed wise, he "loved many foreign women" (1 Kings 11:1 nkjv), and eventually "his wives turned his heart after other gods; and his heart was not loyal to the Lord his God" (v. 4). He also gathered many possessions (Ecclesiastes 2:7) and indulged in wine (Ecclesiastes 2:3) in search of fulfillment. Eventually, he laments his failures, saying: "Then I looked on all the works that my hands had done and on the labor in which I had toiled; and indeed all was vanity and grasping for the wind. There was no profit under the sun" (Ecclesiastes 2:11 nkjv).

If even the wisest of men can be turned against the Lord by his baser appetites for periods of time in his life, how much more can we? Whatever your struggles, resolve to turn to the Lord today.

LIFTING OTHERS

Therefore let us not judge one another anymore,
but rather resolve this, not to put a stumbling block
or a cause to fall in our brother's way.

ROMANS 14:13 NKJV

It's hard not to play the comparison game with fellow believers. We look at stronger believers and wish we could pray like them or that we had their biblical knowledge. We look at weaker believers and sympathize with them, knowing they lack basic biblical understanding. We even compare ourselves to Christians who appear to be in a similar place we are, spiritually speaking.

The latter two instances can lead to judgment. Pride says we are stronger than the weaker believer because we spend more time in the Bible than he does. And it says that the similar believer's sins might be worse than ours, so maybe we are stronger after all. Paul wanted the Roman church to stop judging one another—to stop looking at spiritual practices like certain dietary restrictions or observing one day instead of another. Instead, he wanted them to put their brothers' spiritual well-being first.

If one believer drinks wine and another doesn't, he didn't want the drinker to flaunt his freedom and perhaps cause the other to fall. The same applies to other spiritual practices. "For the kingdom of God is not eating and drinking, but righteousness and peace and joy in the Holy Spirit," Paul says in Romans 14:17 (NKJV). Rather than comparing yourself to other believers and then judging them, make their spiritual welfare of utmost importance instead. It will lead to joy in the Holy Spirit.

INVESTING IN GOD'S GIFT

Children are a gift from the LORD;
they are a reward from him.

PSALM 127:3 NLT

The idea of an inheritance is God's idea, but His plan for an inheritance may be different than how we view the passing of values to a new generation.

If children are the inheritance we receive from God, then maybe He meant for us to take parenting as a great privilege and awesome responsibility. God doesn't want us to waste our time and opportunities with our kids, but to learn who they are so we can best teach them God's ways and perhaps, eventually, how to accept the role of seeing their children (our grandkids) as their God-given inheritance.

We're to consider our role as dads as one of the most important responsibilities we'll ever have. We can't take money, awards, or our favorite team jersey with us to heaven, but we can create an atmosphere in our homes that extends our faith and its riches to a new generation.

Jesus invited children to come to Him. As dads, we have the opportunity to show our children the way.

God described inheritance as a role of relationship, not a lump-sum cash gift. Why? Maybe our daily investments have a greater impact than an end-of-life monetary award.

Our children have always wanted more meaningful time with us. Let's give it to them.

A CONSUMING UNFORGIVENESS

*Forgive one another as quickly and
thoroughly as God in Christ forgave you.*

EPHESIANS 4:32 MSG

Who do we spend the most time thinking about? Those we love? Maybe, but there's another group of people with equal or greater access to our thinking. Many will think about them every day. Who are they? Those who've hurt us.

We'll replay their misdeeds over and over again. The more we think about them, the angrier we'll get. The angrier we get, the more hurt we feel. The more hurt we feel, the more blame we place on the offender. In some cases, unforgiven offenses will consume the majority of our thoughts.

Forgiveness is something you can give even when there is no apology—even when the offender never asks—but forgiveness can feel like a one-sided gift.

On the other hand, forgiveness doesn't mean an automatic renewal of friendship or trust. You can forgive an offense, but if the offender doesn't change his behavior, he may be forgiven but not trusted. In certain cases, it may be wise to keep your distance from some offenders who may be quick to reapply the hurt.

Humans are incapable of forgetting the hurt inflicted by others. Thankfully, God forgets every sin that we confess and removes it from us "as far as sunrise is from sunset" (Psalm 103:12 MSG). We should forgive as God forgave us so as to prevent a "bitter root" from springing up in our hearts (Hebrews 12:15 NIV), but a renewed relationship will depend on both the forgiver and the forgiven. Are you willing to let go of the offenses you've held on to?

VARIABLE RATE OFFENSE DEBT

"In prayer there is a connection between what God does and what you do. You can't get forgiveness from God, for instance, without also forgiving others. If you refuse to do your part, you cut yourself off from God's part."

MATTHEW 6:14–15 MSG

If you have a variable rate loan, then you know that your rate could go up or down. It could work in your favor, but sometimes it doesn't.

Forgiveness works in a similar way. When others hurt you, it can be easy to think of it in terms of a loan. By offending you, they have taken on a debt you want repaid.

But just like a variable rate loan, there are often changes to the terms. Revenge will increase the total repayment value. It can quickly get out of hand, and there may be no repayment that can satisfy an *offender's* debt.

While we keep track of what the offender owes, he may be unaware (or not even care) that a debt is owed. No matter how much interest you tack on to an *offender's* debt, many offenders will never meet your repayment expectations.

Offenses will happen. When we refuse to forgive, we don't gain anything—we cut ourselves off from God, who expects us to extend the same forgiveness that He's given us. When we're quick to forgive, we'll discover we save a lot of time and emotional energy. . .and we'll stay connected to God too.

LOST AND FOUND

"We must celebrate with a feast, for this son of mine was dead and has now returned to life. He was lost, but now he is found."

LUKE 15:23–24 NLT

He defied tradition. He ruined his father's plans. He misused resources. He lost everything. He was the day's headlines. In the muddy confines of a pigpen, it seemed like he got what he deserved.

If you're familiar with the story of the prodigal son, you know there's more to it. At first glance it would seem the father, who had been ill-used by his son, would have had every justification to disown the boy. He could have treated the wayward youth as an employee—*if* he ever considered allowing the boy to come home at all.

His name could have been repeated with disdain by all who had heard his story, but his father never allowed the negative speech to gain a foothold. The father freed the son from ridicule, humiliation, and shame. The father forgave the son before the son recognized he needed forgiving. Reconciliation began the moment a repentant son came within sight of his father.

Forgiveness offers freedom, reflects God's command to love, inspires restoration, and is the key that unlocks second chances.

AN OPTION WORTH TAKING

*The only thing that counts is faith
expressing itself through love.*

GALATIANS 5:6 NIV

Let's take a look at forgiveness from another angle—love. The greatest commands Jesus gave were very simple: love God and then love everyone else.

The greatest source of teaching about love comes from 1 Corinthians 13. Forgiveness is an essential part of love because love keeps no record of wrongs, is not easily angered, and is not self-seeking (1 Corinthians 13:5). When you can't or won't forgive, you will keep records of the hurts others have done to you, you will be easily provoked to anger, and you will fight for your own self-interests instead of seeking the interests of others.

Does it sound as if you can obey God's command to love while refusing to forgive others?

True love forgives. When faith is expressed through love, bitterness and resentment get an eviction notice. If love is a choice, then forgiveness is also a choice.

You can't blame the past, present, or even negative circumstances for your decisions. Forgiveness is a personal choice that doesn't excuse sin, but it can remove the burden you carry and help to heal old wounds instead of letting them fester.

And finally, forgiveness is the only chance many of us will ever get to restore broken relationships.

So when the choice to forgive presents itself as an option—take it.

NEXT QUESTION

*"Don't bargain with God. Be direct. Ask for what you need.
This isn't a cat-and-mouse, hide-and-seek game we're in."*

MATTHEW 7:7 MSG

It's easy to think that God can ask questions and we can't. However, the Bible is filled with questions, and most come from people who just wanted to understand God a little better. Questions that begin with *how long, who can be saved,* and *would You destroy* may be familiar, but scholars believe there are more than three thousand questions found between the pages of Genesis and Revelation.

Some questions had obvious answers while others were more difficult. Some questions came from a place of great pain while others were used to clarify. Some questions were spoken to try to trap Jesus while He asked questions that made the hearer think.

It's natural to have questions, normal to want to learn, and nice to get an answer. God is not frustrated by the questions you might have. Knowing Jesus isn't just available for some people, but for anyone who draws close to Him (James 4:8). However, once you have your answer, be prepared for changes in how you think, respond, and live.

If prayer and Bible reading is how we talk with God, then questions should be part of the dialogue. Don't be surprised if there are times when He asks the questions. He likes answers too.

HARVEST UNDERSTANDING

*See how the farmer waits for the land to yield its valuable crop,
patiently waiting for the autumn and spring rains.*

JAMES 5:7 NIV

Travel enough and you'll see farms, center pivots, and rows of corn, wheat, and beans. You'll see cattle, sheep, and horses within the confines of barbed wire. There will be trucks, tractors, and all-terrain vehicles on dirt roads and rutted trails. Even in the biggest cities, you'll find farmers' markets where the products farmers grow are on display and on sale.

Because people need to eat, there will always be a need for the farming community. These are the men and women who plant, nourish, and harvest the food we take for granted because the work behind the food is hidden when we find it on the shelf at the grocery store.

The culture of farming was very familiar to Jesus, and He used this culture to help share truth. His agricultural parables and sayings illustrated lessons from spiritual growth to bad influences, from the way we listen to where we place our trust.

Jesus knew farming was a perfect way to help people learn more about the Christian life. Beyond the impact farming has on the economy and our personal well-being, it's good to know that understanding a bit about farming can enhance our understanding of Jesus.

Spend some time in the parables (see Matthew 13), and see what farming can teach you about a lifelong walk with Jesus.

OUR SECOND GREATEST NEED

Make a clean break with all cutting, backbiting, profane talk.
Be gentle with one another, sensitive.

EPHESIANS 4:31 MSG

Moms and dads could have been all-knowing in our eyes, immune from making wrong choices—or they made mistakes that caused us to want to nominate them for World's Worst Parents. Sometimes we can only see their mistakes long after the fact, but other times even as kids we could have written a book on the subject of mistake-prone parenting because we had a front-row seat.

Every parent makes mistakes. There are no college degree programs in perfect parenting. You might wish your parents would have been more understanding, more present, or more caring. You might wish they were more of this, less of that, or just the right amount of something you can't even define.

When you become a parent yourself, you gain some firsthand knowledge of the struggles your parents went through when they were trying to make the right "perfect parent" decisions. . .and then living with their mistakes. Perhaps your own experience has created a new compassion in your heart for your parents, foibles and all.

Love is the greatest need of mankind, but forgiveness is a close second.

Nobody's perfect—that's why God *created* forgiveness. This is as true for parents as it is for children, and this would be a perfect day to think back on your relationship with your parents and try on one of God's *best* creations.

RELATIONSHIPS
BEFORE_____?

"What kind of deal is it to get everything you want but lose yourself? What could you ever trade your soul for?"

MATTHEW 16:26 MSG

One of the easiest responsibilities a man can take on is the financial care of his family.

Easy?

Men are prone to become workaholics. When we're told we need to provide for our families, we tackle that responsibility by focusing our time, talent, and energy into turning our work ethic into a cash equivalent.

David, Samuel, and Eli are biblical men who struggled with their kids because work always came before being a dad.

Making money may be the easy part. Being a dad and husband is much harder because it requires an emotional investment many men struggle to make. It's easier to throw cash at a problem than to be a real and present parent. It's easier to work than listen to the struggles our family goes through. It's even easy to believe that somehow our inattention is directly related to our importance.

Because God is our Father, we can learn a few lessons from Him. He is always accessible, listens, and understands our struggles enough to offer perfect advice.

Never sacrifice your family on the altar of personal achievement. It may be possible to have wealth and a close family, but real relationships need to come before all else.

THE TEAM

You use steel to sharpen steel, and one friend sharpens another.

PROVERBS 27:17 MSG

A lock keeps others out. A hinge opens the way. A door provides a boundary.

An engine provides motivation. A wheel facilitates transportation. Brakes end locomotion.

Everything in life has a purpose, and every purpose needs a team. For instance, if you are playing baseball, you'll need eyes to see the ball, arms to swing the bat, legs to run the bases, and muscles to do everything with precision—and that's only part of the team. We haven't even talked about head and shoulders, knees and toes.

The team Jesus had in the last three years of His life were called *disciples*. This twelve-man team worked together, ate together, and learned together. They would become the core of the first-century church. When they didn't work together, the team suffered.

As a Christian man, you need the encouragement of other Christian men. This can come through Bible study, accountability partners, and acts of service to others.

We each have a place in the body of Christ. We each have a job that we were created to complete. We each need to recognize the contributions of others. Like today's verse says, let's be open to sharpen those around us and to allow ourselves to be sharpened so we can be the most effective team for Christ.

WHO'S LOOKING OUT FOR ME?

I know, GOD, that mere mortals can't run their own lives, that men and women don't have what it takes to take charge of life.

JEREMIAH 10:23 MSG

Humans are prone to wander, make mistakes, and become defeated. Earth's first couple had very simple rules to follow, but they easily became convinced to be lawbreakers.

Adam and Eve had every reason to follow a trustworthy God. However, it seemed easy to believe that God was holding all the best for Himself and that following Him wouldn't be in their best interest.

We're no different. We feel that God doesn't really understand us. We believe He wants to withhold something we want right now.

God designed us to embrace His plan and purpose, but thanks to sin, now our natural bent is to look out for ourselves. We can be convinced that things, fame, and money provide a path to the satisfaction we want, but they can't. Instead, the self-centered pursuit of these things pulls us away from God, the only One who can truly satisfy us.

We're not equipped to do life alone, so God gave us directions to follow, lessons to learn, and the Holy Spirit to lead us.

A self-focused lifestyle often leads us to misunderstanding, misapplication of what we learn, and misguided trips to places God marked KEEP OUT! In what parts of your life have you been only looking out for yourself?

HOME SWEET HOME?

*As long as we are at home in the body
we are away from the Lord.*

2 CORINTHIANS 5:6 NIV

In 2 Corinthians 5:1–10, Paul was speaking about his struggle between life and death. He realized that this physical life in some ways kept him from being "at home" with the Lord.

There is no doubt about it. We are "at home" in this physical world. Our planet is the one place in the universe where life flourishes. We were made for this place. More precisely, this world was created to be our home. Humankind, created in the image of God, was the ultimate purpose of all creation (Genesis 1:26–27).

But this world as it now exists is not our true home. We were never meant for this sin-ravaged and broken planet. We were never meant to experience the suffering and sadness of a cursed world. We were meant to enjoy intimacy with God without any barrier (Genesis 3).

Being "at home" also means being in a place where we feel comfortable, at rest, and at ease. Another way to think about Paul's insight is that the more comfortable we are, the more at home we feel in our sinful culture and society, the farther we are from being at home with Christ and enjoying our walk with Him.

We should not be "at home" with this world's values, lifestyles, and priorities. We should be restless in this world. If we aren't uncomfortable here, we will never be truly "at home" with Christ.

LEAVING HOME

When Jacob learned that there was grain in Egypt, he said to his sons, "Why do you just keep looking at each other?"

GENESIS 42:1 NIV

It's easy to identify with Jacob's frustration. Caught in a great famine, the specter of starvation loomed over his family. But his sons denied the coming crisis and procrastinated. They sat around looking at each other as if they didn't know what to do!

Many of us are more like Jacob's boys than Jacob. We are comfortable where we are, and when faced with a long and difficult journey, we'd rather stay home. We don't move until we have to. But by then it can be too late.

This story sheds light on our spiritual lives. Like Jacob's family, we can't find what we need most where we are now. Our relationship with Christ once nourished our souls but has become as dry as a famine-plagued desert. Second, we are reluctant to move. The status quo is just easier. Third, a crisis is looming. Ultimately we will starve and die if we don't do what must be done. Our wives and families will suffer along with us. Finally, we know where to go to find what we need.

Embarking on a life-giving spiritual journey means leaving comfortable but sinful habits behind, enduring the rigors of a new and different life, overcoming barriers, and dealing with our past failures. But the riches of the kingdom of God wait at the end of the journey.

TROUBLE LETTING GO

"Let me kiss my father and mother goodbye,"
he said, "and then I will come with you."

1 KINGS 19:20 NIV

Elisha had trouble letting go (1 Kings 19:19–21). When the prophet Elijah threw his mantle over Elisha's shoulders, he made Elisha his successor. But Elisha's first reaction was to go home and say goodbye to his parents. He had trouble letting go.

His reaction reminds us of those who made excuses for not following Christ. In His parable of the great banquet (Luke 14:15–23), Jesus recounted three kinds of things people have trouble releasing.

The first man bought land and needed to see it. He couldn't let go of his *place*.

The second man bought oxen and had to see them. He couldn't let go of his *possessions*.

The third man wanted to be with his new wife. He couldn't let go of *people*.

Both Elisha and the characters in Christ's parable had the opportunity for a new life and a tremendous adventure. But the stories end very differently.

Elisha goes back, slaughters his oxen, burns the plow, and (we assume) bids farewell to his parents. He severed the ties to his past and went after his future (1 Kings 19:21).

The characters in Christ's parable clung to their place, possessions, and people. They wouldn't let go. They lost the opportunity, missed the feast, and watched others enjoy what could have been theirs.

It's a simple truth. We need empty hands to take up our cross and follow Him (Mark 8:34–38).

HOLDING ON

Immediately Jesus reached out his hand and caught him.
MATTHEW 14:31 NIV

Following the hero's path means both letting go and holding on.

The story of Peter "walking on water" (Matthew 14:22–36) is a perfect example of this truth. Peter "let go" of the safe confines of the boat. But when he began to sink, Christ caught him, and Peter "held on" with all his strength. It reminds us of Psalm 18:16–17:

> He reached down from on high and took hold
> of me; he drew me out of deep waters. He
> rescued me from my powerful enemy, from my
> foes, who were too strong for me.

Paul wrote in Philippians 3:12 that he pressed "on to take hold of that for which Christ Jesus took hold of me."

Peter at the Temple Gate took hold of the beggar's right hand and saw God do a miracle when the lame man was healed by the power of God (Acts 3:1–9).

Like a trapeze artist, we must let go in order to reach for what can take us to new places and greater heights. Letting go and spinning through the air is an exhilarating, not a terrifying, experience. The performer knows the "catcher" will be there at the right time to catch and hold him in an iron grip and will never let him fall.

We too must hold on with all our strength to the love of God that holds us close. Then we can enjoy soaring free from the limits of our fears and failures.

SECOND THOUGHTS

"We can't attack those people; they are stronger than we are."

NUMBERS 13:31 NIV

Moses sent twelve spies into Canaan in preparation for the coming invasion. All of them had waited a lifetime for the fulfillment of God's promise and the conquest of the land. All of them were delivered from Egypt, crossed the Red Sea, and saw the presence of God at Mt. Sinai and the miracles in the desert.

Ten had second thoughts (Numbers 13:31–33).

On the threshold of their greatest adventure, these ten took a long, hard look at the challenges and decided it wasn't worth it. They preferred the world they knew, even if it was in the wilderness, to the battles before them. It was the defining moment for all twelve spies. Ten died in the wilderness they preferred. Two reached the Promised Land and lived their most cherished dreams.

Every man faces moments when the likelihood of success seems small, the obstacles insurmountable, and the costs immeasurable. Those who turn back never fulfill their wild, wonderful dreams. Those who press on may fail, but they fail daring greatly.

On the threshold of a great spiritual adventure, of leaving behind the wilderness of this world and pursuing a great and glorious life in God, some turn back and refuse to step into that new life. They are afraid. It costs too much. Victory seems impossible.

But those who refuse to retreat press on to live an incredible adventure of faith and follow God into the promised land of a rich, full life.

No one can make that choice for us. Will we live by fear or faith?

MENTOR, PART ONE

Barnabas took Mark and sailed for Cyprus.

ACTS 15:39 NIV

John Mark was fortunate. Barnabas (Mark's cousin, see Colossians 4:10) interceded, took Mark under his wing, and kept a bad decision from becoming disastrous. His decision created a rift with Paul, but Barnabas obviously thought Mark was worth the effort.

We don't know what happened next. What we do know is that years later, Paul asked Timothy to bring John Mark to him because he was "helpful to [him] in [his] ministry" (2 Timothy 4:11 NIV). Clearly, a lot had changed!

All of us need help and guidance to overcome our fears, step into a great future, and grow deep spiritual roots. Barnabas demonstrates the heart of a spiritual mentor.

First, Barnabas believed in Mark and his potential. We all need people who believe the best for us and in us.

Second, he was willing to invest. Barnabas had invested in Paul and saw that investment pay off in the apostle's life and ministry. He was willing to make that investment in Mark.

Third, Barnabas was experienced. Barnabas had been where John Mark needed to go and could show him the way. Mark was a willing follower.

Finally, Barnabas was an encourager. In fact, Barnabas, which means "son of encouragement," was his nickname. He was a Levite from Cyprus named Joseph (Acts 4:36).

We all need someone like Barnabas in our lives who can point us in the right direction and encourage us on the way. And we need to do that for someone else, as we'll see tomorrow morning.

FLOURISHING

The righteous will flourish like a palm tree.

PSALM 92:12 NIV

Most Christians are familiar with the events of Palm Sunday—Jesus Christ's triumphal entry into Jerusalem, the adulation of the crowds as they spread their cloaks in the streets and waved palm fronds. It was a welcome fit for a king, and rightly so! That day began the series of events that led to an upper room, a garden, a mock trial, a cross, and the empty tomb. There is no Easter without Palm Sunday.

In Psalm 92:12–15, the palm tree is a symbol of the spiritual life Christ made possible for all His children. Like the palm, we can grow, flourish, and live a fruitful life.

He made it possible for us to flourish and live joy-filled, exuberant, and meaningful lives.

He made it possible for us to sink our roots deep in the rich spiritual soil of His presence. We are planted in the house of the Lord!

He made it possible for us to have fruitful, productive lives for as long as we live, even bearing fruit in old age.

He made it possible to stay spiritually vital and healthy, to stay green and growing!

He gave us reason to shout with joy and proclaim His righteousness, power, and glory!

But we should remember that we only "flourish in the courts of our God" (Psalm 92:13 NIV). We must draw our life and strength from a deep and nourishing relationship with Him.

An "uprooted" plant doesn't flourish or produce fruit. It dies. Are you rooted in your Savior today?

MENTOR, PART TWO

Elijah and Elisha were on their way from Gilgal.

2 Kings 2:1 niv

Elisha's relationship to his mentor, Elijah, was essential. He could not fulfill God's call on his life without Elijah. From the scripture about the last day they were together, we discover five essential qualities of a spiritual mentor (2 King 2:1–18).

First, Elijah and Elisha were close. Elisha knew that the time had come for them to part, and he put off the final goodbye as long as he could. Three times Elijah tells Elisha to stay behind. Three times Elisha refuses.

Second, Elijah was selfless, willing to give of himself to Elisha even at the last moment. "Tell me, what can I do for you before I am taken from you?" (2 Kings 2:9 niv)

Third, Elijah continued to teach his mentee, demonstrating practices that Elisha needed to complete his journey—parting the Jordan waters by striking it with his rolled-up mantle (2 Kings 2:8, 14).

Fourth, Elijah invested in Elisha. He spent time with Elisha and taught him after Elisha obeyed the call to be his successor (2 Kings 19:19–21).

Fifth, Elijah had what Elisha wanted, the mantle, which represented the power and presence of God. Spiritual mentors must have their own vital spiritual life; mentors cannot give another person what they don't possess. Though the mantle had no power of its own, Elijah's faith helped Elisha know, experience, and operate in the power of God until it was time for Elisha to own it for himself.

Mentors can help us. But they can't do for us what we won't do for ourselves!

THE RISKS OF RETURN

Then Orpah kissed her mother-in-law goodbye.
RUTH 1:14 NIV

Orpah and Ruth faced the same clear choice—go with Naomi to a new land and life or go back to Moab and the life they knew. Orpah refused that new life.

We don't know what happened to Orpah. It seems likely she followed Naomi's advice (Ruth 1:11–13) and went home, married, raised a family, and lived the rest of her life just like everyone else in Moab. She disappeared into the mists of history.

But we do know what happened to Ruth. She lived an incredible life that far surpassed anything she could have imagined. She was David's great-grandmother, an ancestor of the Messiah, and holds an honored place in history. But none of it could have happened without leaving Moab!

Ruth's words to Naomi (Ruth 1:16–18) set the pattern for all who cross the line from the life we have to the life of our dreams.

She committed herself to God, to God's people, and to that future without reservation. It was a long walk into a new land and a new life, but nothing could dissuade her.

Call it what you will—stubbornness, determination, grit. It comes to the same thing, the strength to follow God regardless of what comes our way. We see it in Jesus. "As the time approached for him to be taken up to heaven, Jesus resolutely set out for Jerusalem" (Luke 9:51 NIV).

Pursuing the hero's journey, the great adventure of faith, means crossing the boundary between the life we have and the life we want. It's the only way.

NO ONE SAID IT WOULD BE EASY

As for you, you were dead in your transgressions and sins.

EPHESIANS 2:1 NIV

No one said getting from where we are to where we want to be in God is easy. Anyone who says it's easy is a liar. Anyone who believes it's easy is a fool.

James said we should rejoice in trials because of what they produce in us (James 1:2–4).

Paul compared this life to the harsh discipline of an athlete in training (1 Corinthians 9:24–27).

Jesus warned us that we would have trouble in this world (John 16:33).

The Bible compares our spiritual journey to gold in the refiner's fire or clay on the potter's wheel (Proverbs 17:3; Jeremiah 18:1–5).

In his great work *Summa Theologica*, Thomas Aquinas seemed to echo Ephesians 2:1–2 when he warned against "the world, the flesh and the Devil."

When we pursue Christ with all our hearts, we live a life that challenges the world around us and may prompt an angry, hostile response. They hate Him and all who follow Him.

That pursuit draws us into spiritual warfare. Our enemy uses all his power and influence to deceive us, block our way, and make sure we pay a high price for following God.

But we are our own worst and greatest enemy. We run from, resist, and resent the struggles we inevitably face. We want glory without the cross. It never, ever happens that way.

No one said it would be easy. . .just worth it!

COMMENDATIONS

"I commend to you. . ."

ROMANS 16:1–16 NIV

It's a stunning list.

At the end of his letter to the Romans, Paul takes time to greet, commend, and express gratitude to twenty-five individuals and, in some cases, their congregations. All of them in one way or another were of great value to his life and ministry. It's not an exaggeration to say that Paul's great accomplishments weren't possible without them.

It isn't just more difficult to make this journey alone; it's impossible. All of us need allies who will walk the road to a growing spiritual life with us. We will need help along the way.

Paul's allies were his benefactors, his coworkers, and friends. He even mentions that Rufus's mother had been a mother to him (Romans 16:13). We don't know much about most of the people on this list, but we know he valued and appreciated each of them.

Also, we know that each of them supported and encouraged him on the way. Together they provided a network of material, emotional, relational, and spiritual support. When Paul suffered, they comforted him. When Paul was discouraged, they encouraged him. When Paul wanted to quit, they challenged him. When he didn't have what it took to go on, they gave it to him. Paul accomplished great things and reached great heights standing on their shoulders.

We need to intentionally build this kind of network and work at keeping these relationships healthy and strong. We really can't "go it alone."

FUNDAMENTAL CHOICE

Now choose life.
DEUTERONOMY 30:19 NIV

The children of Israel fled Egypt. They had crossed the Red Sea, camped at the base of Sinai, and spent forty years in the wilderness. Now they stood again at the Jordan, and Moses presented them with a stark choice—life or death.

They were approaching their greatest challenge, conquering the Promised Land. Everything this generation raised in the wilderness knew was going to be different, and they needed to be ready for the cataclysmic challenges and changes they would face on the other side of the Jordan.

All of us face moments like this on our spiritual journey. We stand at the edge of a great transformation and must choose between the future and the past, between spiritual life and death, between what was and what can be.

Moses made clear what was at stake in their decision.

Our spiritual lives are in the balance. If we balk and fail to meet the challenge, we will not experience the deep, rich, and intimate relationship with God we seek.

The future of those we love is in the balance too. "Now choose life so that...your children may live" (Deuteronomy 30:19 NIV). As husbands and fathers, we must be constantly alert to the impact of our lives on those we love. They go with us or stay behind with us. We blaze the trail forward, or we settle for the status quo.

Finally, our future is in the balance. "For the LORD is your life, and he will give you many years in the land" (Deuteronomy 30:20 NIV). Whether or not we inhabit that land is up to us.

GETTING READY

And that you may love the LORD your God,
listen to his voice, and hold fast to him.

DEUTERONOMY 30:20 NIV

The people approached the greatest challenge of their lives, and Moses wanted them to be ready. He knew what we should know—preparation matters.

We too will face great challenges, moments when it feels like life or death on our journey to spiritual growth. Success or failure in the next phase of our journey depends on preparation in this phase.

It's fascinating that his instructions had nothing to do with becoming a conquering army and everything to do with their right relationship with God. Strategies and techniques, no matter how valuable, don't matter if we are not spiritually prepared.

Moses gave four specific instructions (Genesis 30:20):

First, love God. Our affections are at the core of life. We will always follow our greatest love. If He is not our one great love, we will falter when asked to sacrifice what we truly love.

Second, listen to God. God speaks to us through His Word, His Spirit, and His people. He will lead us if we listen and follow His voice.

Third, link your life to His. We must take hold of God in an ironclad grip that will not let go no matter what we face. He won't let go of us, but we must hold on to Him.

Finally, lean on His promises. God has promised greater heights in Him, no matter how difficult the journey. He will keep His promise, but we must keep faith in His promises.

A CLEAR LINE

*As the time approached for him to be taken up to heaven,
Jesus resolutely set out for Jerusalem.*

LUKE 9:51 NIV

Jesus knew false arrest, torture, crucifixion, and death waited for Him in Jerusalem. But He was determined. The word *sterizo* in this verse means "to make firm, to strengthen, or to confirm."

It's an amazing statement that clearly illustrates the great challenge that confronts all who pursue spiritual vitality and growth. There comes a moment when to go forward, to enjoy the life in God we hunger for, we must face a painful challenge, leave something behind, and that something in us must die.

Abraham left family behind in Harran. Moses faced murder charges in Egypt. Paul's self-righteousness died on the road to Damascus. David had his giant, Joseph had a prison, and Peter had his shame. All of them passed through their ordeal and found God waiting on the other side.

It's different for every man. Some face the painful challenge of confessing sin and making amends to those they've harmed. Some have to leave behind a career, friends, or family. Ambition, pride, selfishness, or lust must die in others. It may cost cherished relationships, pleasures we enjoy, or the future we want. It will cost. . .everything. And we know it.

But we must follow Christ, face the challenge, live through the pain, and kill what must die. Like Christ, we must be firm, strong, and resolute! If we aren't, we will fail. But we don't have it in us. We aren't that strong. Remember. . . "I can do all this through him who gives me strength" (Philippians 4:13).

TRANSFORMERS

And we all. . .are being transformed into his image.

2 CORINTHIANS 3:18 NIV

Passing through a great challenge changes us. Peter, the coward of the courtyard, became the lion of Pentecost. Paul, the persecutor, became the great champion of the faith. David, the shepherd boy, became Israel's greatest king. Moses, who ran for his life, faced down Pharaoh and delivered his people.

Paul outlined the process of a great transformation in 2 Corinthians 3:18.

First, we encounter God with *"unveiled faces."* All pretense, self-righteousness, and hubris are stripped away. We see ourselves clearly and know who and what we are—sinners in need of a savior, weaklings in need of great strength, and fools in need of great wisdom.

Second, we *"contemplate the Lord's glory."* Like Moses, we are transformed by confronting the glory of God. We grasp the true majesty and infinite wonder of our Savior and His love. We are humbled and overwhelmed in His presence.

Third, all this *"comes from the Lord."* We can't do any of it! No matter how hard we try, how disciplined, rule-keeping, or religious we are, we remain shameful sinners. We only wash the outside of the cup (Matthew 23:25–26). If God doesn't change us, we can't change.

Fourth, we are *"transformed into his image."* Our destiny is to be like Jesus!

Finally, we are transformed *"with ever-increasing glory."* Transformation is a process, not an event. We keep changing and will never, even in eternity, experience all the transformation or glory we long for or He intends. Hallelujah!

TAKE HOLD OF HIM WHO HAS TAKEN HOLD OF YOU

*I press on to take hold of that for which
Christ Jesus took hold of me.*

PHILIPPIANS 3:12 NIV

Sometimes the prize seems elusive, just out of reach. We shouldn't be surprised. No matter how much we grow in grace, there is always room to grow. And the more we grow in Christ, the more we realize how little we truly know Him.

In Philippians 3:12–14, Paul outlined his strategy for taking hold of more and more of God in his life.

First, don't expect to ever truly reach that goal. Paul didn't.

Second, the more Christ takes hold of us, the more we are captivated by His power and presence in our lives, the more we are motivated to pursue Him.

Third, forget. Let the past, with its mistakes, shortcomings, and failures, stay in the past. Don't long for what you had yesterday. Backward focus prevents forward motion.

Fourth, press on. The word translated "press on" means "to run swiftly in order to catch a person or thing." Just as athletes approaching the finish line lean into the tape, we should exert every effort and lean into God.

Finally, there is a prize! Paul defined this prize in part when he wrote: "I want to know Christ—yes, to know the power of his resurrection" (Philippians 3:10 NIV). That's not all that those who take hold of that for which Christ has taken hold of them can expect. But it is more than enough to keep us in the race!

CHOICE AND CONSEQUENCE

"From everyone who has been given much, much will be demanded."

LUKE 12:48 NIV

The more of God we experience, the more He expects of us. It has always been that way.

Moses had the glory of the burning bush and was expected to set his people free. Paul met Jesus on the Damascus road and was expected to bring the Gospel to the world. Peter had the joy of three years at Jesus' side and was expected to lead the church in the face of great persecution and in a period of incredible expansion.

There is no doubt that this is true. As a matter of fact, one of the barriers to greater spiritual life is knowing that God's call accompanies God's joy. But why? Why are we not free to just enjoy the glory of knowing God without the burden of service?

First, growing in God isn't only about us. It is also about God's glory in the world. It's not about us. It's about Him.

Second, growing in God prepares us to participate in His great work in the world. Surely our relationship with Him is precious. But God wants everyone to know that joy and has chosen us as His emissaries.

Third, growing in God strengthens us for the inevitable challenges we face. We know Him, and we know He will strengthen, sustain, and stay with us.

Finally, it's good for us. We were created to live for a great purpose. We cannot fulfill that destiny or know that satisfaction without a great mission.

What is God expecting of you?

SETTING AN EXAMPLE

Join together in following my example.

PHILIPPIANS 3:17 NIV

Paul realized that he was leading the way and others were following him.

Every man who seeks a great adventure in God is leading the way. The question is: What kind of example are we setting? Are we living up to the life of Christ in us, or are we slipping back into old habits and patterns?

First, Paul knew his life was being watched. His example mattered. Our children, our friends, and the unbelievers who surround us every day are watching us too. We may not think about it, but it's true. Paul took that responsibility seriously.

Second, we ought to follow the example of others who are ahead of us on the path of spiritual growth. Paul wrote, "Keep your eyes on those who live as we do" (Philippians 3:17 NIV). We set an example by following the example of others.

Third, the impact of our example has eternal consequence. In the rest of the paragraph, Paul contrasts those who follow his example and those who are enemies of the cross (Philippians 3:17–21). Setting the wrong example has disastrous consequences.

Finally, our example must have integrity. It isn't about putting our best foot forward or presenting a handsome veneer that hides the truth. How we handle our flaws and failures, how we deal with challenges and difficulties, and how we respond to temptation are part of that example.

The world has plenty of hypocrites. It's men of true integrity that are in short supply.

GLOWING IN THE DARK

All the Israelites saw Moses, his face was radiant.
EXODUS 34:30 NIV

It's one of the Bible's strangest moments. Moses returned from the presence of the Lord glowing (Exodus 34:29–35). Others could observe the changes in his life.

In 2 Corinthians 3:7–18, Paul used this moment to illustrate the transformation believers experience in the presence of God. "And we all, who with unveiled faces contemplate the Lord's glory, are being transformed into his image with ever-increasing glory" (v. 18).

Great spiritual transformation isn't just possible—it's real! God does great work in us to transform us into Christ's image. That is our great and glorious hope!

Great spiritual transformation should be observable. Those around us should notice the difference not because of pious posturing but because we truly are different. It isn't something we put on display. It's something we can't hide!

Great spiritual vitality can fade. Paul is clear: "Moses. . .put a veil over his face to prevent the Israelites from seeing the end of what was passing away" (2 Corinthians 3:13 NIV). Moses put the veil on because his appearance frightened people. He kept the veil on to hide the fact that the glory was fading. Our religious lives can function like that veil and hide the truth that our true spiritual vitality is waning.

Finally, great spiritual vitality can only be renewed in the presence of God. When the glory faded, Moses took off the veil and returned to the source of true transformation (Exodus 34:33–35). When he needed more of God, God was there for him. He's there for us too.

MIDTERM EXAM

*The devil prowls around like a roaring
lion looking for someone to devour.*

1 PETER 5:8 NIV

Sometimes we think growing in grace means we've passed the test, we've overcome, we're victorious! That's true. But it doesn't mean we won't face another test. It won't be the same test, and it may be the most difficult we've ever faced. The stronger we are in God, the more threatening we are to the devil!

Peter compared this test to a roaring, hungry lion looking for prey. In 1 Peter 5:6–9, we find clear instructions on how to deal with the devil.

First, be humble (1 Peter 5:6). Pride really does come before a fall. We are most vulnerable when we think we aren't at risk. We are strongest when we depend on the mighty hand of God for our survival.

Second, don't be anxious (1 Peter 5:7). God is in control. We are secure in Him. Worry and anxiety weaken us. God cares for us, knows what we need, and is there for us.

Third, be sober minded and watchful (1 Peter 5:8). Take the threat seriously. Be on guard against those things the devil knows he can use against you.

Resist him (1 Peter 5:9). Don't give in. Stay strong and stand firm in your faith. No matter how bad it looks, no matter how much it hurts, no matter how enticing the temptation—trust God.

Finally, remember it's a "midterm" exam, not the final. There will be another test.

AFTER...

After you have suffered a little while, [God] will himself restore you and make you strong, firm and steadfast.

1 PETER 5:10 NIV

Peter reminds us that when we are tested, we suffer for "a little while" (1 Peter 4:10 NIV). It doesn't feel that way. Pain stretches time. We feel like it's always been this way, and we fear it will always be this way. It won't.

But we need to understand "a little while" not in terms of this life but in terms of eternity. This life is a quickly evaporating vapor. For those who overcome, who pass the "midterm exam," joy everlasting awaits. We are "called to his eternal glory in Christ" (v. 10).

You and I can rely on God's grace to "restore [us] and make [us] strong, firm and steadfast." Tests purify us, temper us, and make us stronger. Testing won't destroy us. It solidifies those gains and prepares us for the next great step in our spiritual journey.

Perhaps the most comforting words in this passage are found in 1 Peter 5:12 (NIV): "To him be the power for ever and ever. Amen." There has never been and will never be a time when God is not sovereign. His dominion encompasses heaven and earth, spiritual and material, and includes everything that has happened to us or ever will happen!

In times of testing, life feels out of control. It may be out of our control. But it is not out of the control of God who loved us from before time, who only seeks our good, and who has dominion over all things, including our suffering!

SO WHAT?

"Therefore go and make disciples of all nations."
MATTHEW 28:19 NIV

Heroes and adventurers come home. Those who take the journey to a greater, richer spiritual life come back to the reality of day-to-day life. But they are not the same men.

The disciples had completed an incredible journey. They saw Jesus crucified and raised from the dead, and they spent forty days with Him, twice (Matthew 28:16–20; Mark 16:14–20). Jesus called them into the future.

He answered the "so what?" question. What difference does the journey make? Their journey and ours fundamentally changes our relationship with Christ and should result in changes in our place in the world and in us.

"When they saw him, they worshiped him" (Matthew 28:17 NIV). Our spiritual journey should change what we worship, what is of supreme value in our lives. We may enjoy the things of this world, but we no longer worship and slavishly pursue them as the source of life.

"All authority in heaven and on earth has been given to me" (Matthew 28:18 NIV). Christ is the authority not us. We submit to Him, obey His commands, and pursue His purposes.

"Surely I am with you always" (Matthew 28:20 NIV). But the sweetest result is our connection to Christ and His abiding presence with us.

"But some doubted" (Matthew 28:17 NIV). Seeing the resurrected Christ didn't convince all His disciples. We can expect some doubts and struggles to remain. They energize our pursuit for more of God. Doubts are not failures. They are proof of our hunger for another adventure in God!

NOW WHAT?

"Therefore go and make disciples of all nations."
MATTHEW 28:19 NIV

The "now what?" depends on the "so what?"

The call to go and make disciples (Matthew 28:19) and preach the Gospel (Mark 16:15) rests on the "therefore" of Matthew 28:19. Since He has all authority, since He is always with us, and since He alone is of supreme value in our lives, therefore we should. . .

Go proclaim the good news of His coming, His salvation, and the joys of life lived in His power and presence.

Go make disciples and teach others how to know Him, grow in Him, and find their greatest joy in Him. Teach them to obey His word and live for His glory.

Go into all the world. Matthew uses the word for all "peoples," for every ethnic-linguistic group. Mark uses the word for the physical world, the cosmos. There is no place we should not go and no people we should not reach. Most of us are called to go across the street, not around the world. But all of us have the responsibility to go or to send others to the far-flung corners of the earth and the unreached people who live there.

Go because eternity is at stake. Those who don't believe are condemned (Mark 16:16).

Go in His power (Mark 16:17–18). We were never intended to accomplish this great task without His power, protection, and provision.

Our journey ends with a great call to change the world. That is our next great adventure!

GOD'S JEALOUS LOVE FOR YOU

"Do not worship any other god, for the LORD, whose name is Jealous, is a jealous God."

EXODUS 34:14 NIV

Perhaps the thought of a jealous God calls to mind images of a person in a relationship who is pushy or overprotective. However, the full picture of God presented throughout scripture, such as in Hosea, is a heartbroken lover who has been rejected time and time again by His beloved people. This is a jealousy that isn't pushy or overbearing.

When St. Francis of Assisi spoke of God's love, he noted that God has humbly made Himself vulnerable to the point that He allows us to break His heart. This jarring love means an all-powerful God cares deeply enough for us that He is willing to endure the pain of loss and disappointment when we turn away from Him.

God is jealous for our time and attention. When we fail to make God our top priority, He doesn't call us back with anger and obligation. He calls us back as a jealous lover who desires a relationship with us.

The costly love of God that suffered for our sake on the cross is the same jealous love of God that desires us with all of the passion tucked away in the simple message of John 3:16: "God so loved the world. . ."

Perhaps we need to believe that God loves us enough to be jealous, to allow Himself to be moved with grief when we turn away from Him. Perhaps we struggle to love and make space for God because we have yet to know and feel His jealous passion for us.

RESTORATION AFTER GOD'S REBUKE

"The LORD your God is with you, the Mighty Warrior who saves.
He will take great delight in you; in his love he will no longer
rebuke you, but will rejoice over you with singing."

ZEPHANIAH 3:17 NIV

When we fail, and we surely will all fail, we may go through a season of the Lord's discipline or rebuke. Perhaps we dread such seasons. Perhaps we even fear being cut off or losing the Lord's favor forever. Could we ever sin so grievously or repeatedly that God would ever turn us away?

Understandable as these fears may be, a season of discipline is always intended to lead us to restoration with God. In fact, if God merely let us go our own way or spared us the consequences of our disobedience, we could argue that He isn't all that concerned about us. What parent would not reach out in discipline to a beloved child with any other goal than complete restoration? Isn't God's rebuke the ultimate sign that He is truly for us, even if He isn't primarily concerned with our comfort?

And even if we pass through a season of discipline or distance from God, it is never destined to last forever. God longs to rejoice over us with singing and joy. We are His beloved people, the source of His joy and the focus of His song. How surprising it is to pass through a season of failure and discipline only to discover that God remains with us and has never let us go.

THE PROVISION TRAP

For the love of money is a root of all kinds of evil. Some people,
eager for money, have wandered from the faith
and pierced themselves with many griefs.

1 Timothy 6:10 niv

So many men feel a burden to provide for their families, and to a certain degree this is good and responsible. There are, however, lines that can be crossed when it comes to providing—when the drive to "provide" turns into a damaging love for money or a driving ambition that could undermine God's work in your life.

Paul writes about the "love of money," but perhaps we try to disguise it as something else. We justify our financial decisions and commitments, calling them wise investments, good stewardship, or planning for the future.

Isn't it wise to seek out a job that pays better, even if it means longer hours or a longer commute? Isn't it responsible to seek the best possible promotion, even if one's work is rapidly becoming an identity?

Paul hints at the way to determine whether our ambitions and investments are destructive or positive: What do we long for? Do we long for more money? More influence and power? The admiration of others? These are the very things that can undermine and essentially replace our longing for God. Money in particular supplants God's place in our lives because it can provide for our needs, provide security and comfort, and convince us that we are on the right track.

Paul reminds us that the size of the paycheck isn't necessarily the issue; it's about the object of our desires—what we pursue each day above all else.

HOW TO WAIT ON GOD

Let all that I am wait quietly before God, for my hope is in him.
He alone is my rock and my salvation, my fortress
where I will not be shaken.

PSALM 62:5–6 NLT

We are told repeatedly to wait on the Lord throughout the Psalms. However, this particular psalm adds a jarring addition to our waiting: wait *quietly*. The manner in which we wait is very much the test of our faith.

When I wait on God, I'm tempted to make requests, to complain, to suggest solutions, and even to pray for specific outcomes, as if I know the best way for God to act in my life. Most of us can be persuaded into waiting on God, but waiting quietly is a whole other matter. Those who wait quietly have truly surrendered themselves to the direction and provision of God, for they have no other hope than the action of God.

And for the times when we stop waiting and seek our solutions or build our own safety nets and fortresses, it often takes a tragedy, crisis, or difficult situation to shake us loose. Perhaps the quiet waiting leaves us restless and fearful. However, anything that we trust more than God will not last, especially in a time of trouble that shakes our foundations.

Placing our trust completely in God does not guarantee smooth sailing. In fact, the need for God to act as a fortress suggests that we should expect conflict. Trouble is surely coming, and the question is whether we are truly waiting in expectant quiet before God.

HOW TO BLESS OTHERS

*"May the L*ORD* bless you and protect you. May the L*ORD* smile on you and be gracious to you. May the L*ORD* show you his favor and give you his peace."*

NUMBERS 6:24–26 NLT

At an uncertain time in the history of Israel, when the people could scarcely imagine themselves as anything other than slaves and had yet to settle in a land of their own, God provided a priestly blessing for Aaron and his sons. A wandering people in search of a new land certainly needed the protection, gracious favor, and peace of God when there was so little they knew for certain.

The people of Israel rarely had smooth sailing with God. They were disobedient, rebellious, and grumbled even when God blessed them. They were rarely on their best behavior, but God mercifully encouraged them to pray for protection, peace, and the favor of God. In fact, despite their struggles, God encouraged them to imagine Him smiling upon them as He extended His unearned grace to them.

As you think about how to pray for others, consider praying that those in danger will receive God's blessing and protection. Ask God to guide them through uncertain times and to mercifully provide blessings for them. Bless them by interceding for God's favor and peace to be manifested in their lives.

When praying for others, consider asking that God will be present for them in tangible, peaceful ways. As a priesthood of believers, we have inherited the joyful role of intercession, and thankfully, God has shown us how to fill this role.

RETREAT AFTER SUCCESS

Yet the news about him spread all the more, so that crowds of
people came to hear him and to be healed of their sicknesses.
But Jesus often withdrew to lonely places and prayed.

LUKE 5:15–16 NIV

Whenever I experience success, I naturally think of ways to keep it going and build on it. Isn't that "good stewardship"? Jesus had the exact opposite response. As the crowds seeking Him increased, He immediately withdrew to be with God, lest He lose that vital connection with the Father.

This doesn't mean we must leave our work behind in order to set off for a lengthy wilderness retreat. Rather, when Jesus experienced success or His schedule started to fill up, He recognized that was the precise time to retreat. Building on success and influence isn't necessarily the best thing for our souls. We don't have to serve success, but instead we can choose to take measured steps away from our work in pursuit of spiritual renewal. Jesus' first move in the midst of "success" was to step back, and after that, He was able to step forward on firmer footing.

I have learned that whenever I have a free moment, my first move should be toward prayer, reflection on scripture, or just a reflection on my day so that I know how to pray. A full schedule is no excuse to withdraw from God or others. I can find time to pray even for two, five, or twenty minutes throughout my day by making it my first move before doing anything else. Surprisingly, I always find the time I need to get my work done.

FREED TO SERVE

*"I, the L*ORD*, have called you in righteousness; I will take hold of your hand. I will keep you and will make you to be a covenant for the people and a light for the Gentiles, to open eyes that are blind, to free captives from prison and to release from the dungeon those who sit in darkness."*

ISAIAH 42:6–7 NIV

Perhaps we all know quite well that God has made us righteous and freed us from sin's power, but perhaps it's harder to consider what's next. Are we freed from sin only for our own benefit? Today's passage from Isaiah says that we have been freed in order to liberate others from bondage, both spiritual and physical. If this calling strikes you as intimidating, or if you simply don't know where to start, there's good news for you.

God holds you and shapes you. The life of God is taking hold in your life and reshaping your heart, desires, and thoughts. As God brings liberation into your life, you'll start to long to share it with others. You'll even begin to recognize the opportunities to share that light with those who are blind or to bring freedom to those who are trapped.

As God renews our minds, He also says He will take us by the hand, guiding us forward in our calling. Perhaps the thing holding most of us back is doubt that God is reaching out to us. Are you open to God's renewal and guidance? Are you too distracted? Do you need to set aside time today to allow God's renewal to begin taking hold in your life?

THE JOY OF RELYING ON GOD

But I trust in your unfailing love;
my heart rejoices in your salvation.

PSALM 13:5 NIV

We can only approach God because of His mercy, and once again it's His mercy that sustains us. I've found the greatest frustration and discouragement when I've tried to approach God based on my own merits and efforts, as if I could prove myself worthy of God's mercy and saving help.

In light of today's passage, begin by asking what you're trusting in or leaning on today. Are you joyful? Are you feeling fearful or frustrated? Our emotions and thoughts are helpful clues to what we think and practice about God. They provide the evidence of a life of faith or a life attempting to get by on its own.

While following Jesus never assures us of smooth sailing, we are assured of God's presence based on His mercy for us. If you aren't joyful today and even find yourself stuck in despair, it could be that you're trusting in yourself to earn God's mercy or simply relying on your own resources and wisdom to help yourself.

There is great joy and contentment in trusting in God's mercy and falling back on God's saving help. We don't lean on God because we've earned His help or favor. Rather, we start with His mercy that assures us of His saving help and presence whether we are going through good times or bad.

WHO GETS THE CREDIT?

Deliver me, my God, from the hand of the wicked, from the grasp of those who are evil and cruel. For you have been my hope, Sovereign LORD, my confidence since my youth. From birth I have relied on you; you brought me forth from my mother's womb. I will ever praise you.

PSALM 71:4–6 NIV

Today's psalm offers a surefire test for whether we are living by faith, and if I'm honest, it's a test that I don't want to take most days. The psalmist says that his praise shall always be of the Lord, who is his strength.

Who gets the credit in your life?

That's a question I don't want to ask myself. It's easy to get wrapped up in my own plans, talents, and worries each day. Am I offering myself to God and trusting God to guide my steps? Am I depending on God to provide for my needs and to give me the strength to serve others and to accomplish my work?

Alongside this challenging question, we have the encouraging words that God is able to support us and to provide strength for us. We don't have to dive into each day on our own, relying on our own discipline, willpower, or plans to live as faithful disciples.

When trouble comes, we can cry out to God for deliverance and help. Even if we have been distant or dependent on ourselves, we can return to Him because of His mercy. Our God wants us to depend on Him and will not leave us if we turn to Him.

DO YOU WANT TO BE SET FREE?

Therefore confess your sins to each other and pray for each other so that you may be healed. The prayer of a righteous person is powerful and effective.

JAMES 5:16 NIV

Jesus once asked a man if he wanted to be made well, and perhaps we should consider that question for ourselves in light of today's verse. Do you want to be set free from anger, lust, greed, or selfishness? Do you want to experience the freedom and abundant life that Jesus promised us? While we can probably tread water on our own for a while, we may never experience a true breakthrough until we humbly ask a fellow believer to pray for us as we fully confess our sins to them.

James seems to anticipate our potential objections: What if I open up my deepest, darkest secrets to someone and they can't help me? Do I want to risk exposing myself to a fellow Christian if it's not going to do any good?

James assures us that wisely choosing a righteous believer to pray for us will bring the healing we desire for our shortcomings. Whether you feel weak or stuck with a particular issue in your life, consider who you can approach for prayer this week. Your life may not turn around until you openly confess your sin and receive prayer. Do you want to be made well? Then it's time to stop hiding your secret sins and relying on yourself. We may only find true freedom when we finally confess our sins to each other.

ON FIRE IN THE WRONG WAY

When the disciples James and John saw this, they asked, "Lord, do you want us to call fire down from heaven to destroy them?" But Jesus turned and rebuked them.

LUKE 9:54–55 NIV

Zeal and passion can be tremendous assets for followers of Jesus, provided we point our zeal and passion in the right direction. When Jesus and His disciples met opposition from the Samaritans, James and John responded with zeal, asking Jesus if they should ask God to destroy them. Jesus had a different kind of zeal in mind.

Just as Jesus had responded to the Samaritan woman's controversial comments and questions with wisdom and an invitation, He had no desire to exact revenge when someone resisted Him and His message. His disciples had yet to realize that Jesus came as a doctor to heal the sick, not as a judge prepared to bring destruction. Jesus showed patience and mercy, demonstrating that God is far more concerned with changing lives than with condemnation.

We're going to meet people who are negative, insulting, and opposed to Christianity. Jesus challenges us to avoid dehumanizing them. Just as Jesus didn't come to bring judgment but to heal those who were willing, we have a similar calling to respond to criticism and opposition with patience and wisdom.

The "calling down fire" approach is too concerned with the short term. God takes a long-term, big picture view of our world, patiently waiting for people to come to Him. In fact, God's patience isn't just for His opponents. He's also patient with His people who keep trying to call down fire from heaven.

HOW GOD TURNS FAILURE INTO DELIGHT

Who is a God like you, who pardons sin and forgives the transgression. . . . You do not stay angry forever but delight to show mercy.

MICAH 7:18 NIV

What do you imagine about God when you sin? Do you imagine an angry God, eager to turn you away or leave you alone? Do you imagine a disappointed God, incredulous that you've failed yet again?

Whether you are struggling with habitual sin or worry that your transgressions are beyond God's forgiveness, there is a promise for you: God is more merciful than we can imagine. Micah compares our Lord with the false gods of his day—deities that arose from human imagination and demanded offerings in order to be placated. He assures us that our living God is completely unlike these gods.

There is no doubt that sins and transgressions are serious and can alienate us from God, but if we confess our sins, He is all too eager to forgive and restore us. If we imagine God as angry or towering over us to strike us with judgment, the Word assures us that His anger passes quickly and that He delights in showing mercy. In fact, God takes no pleasure in judgment. God's delight is in showing mercy and restoring us. If you want to delight God, stop hiding your sin and failures. Bring them out before God in plain sight so that He can show mercy to you with His pardon and forgiveness.

THANKLESS FAITHFULNESS?

For it seems to me that God has put us apostles on display
at the end of the procession, like those condemned to die
in the arena. We have been made a spectacle to the whole
universe, to angels as well as to human beings.

1 CORINTHIANS 4:9 NIV

What is the sign of God's blessing on a Christian leader? What do we look for in the experts we trust for advice on spiritual living or Bible study? As Paul sought to correct the perceptions of the Corinthian church, he called on graphic images of prisoners being led to die in the arena at the hands of gladiators or wild animals. Paul argues that the apostles who founded the church were not talented speakers or respectable individuals that you'd put on display. Rather, the people doing the essential work of the ministry were the ones you'd toss into the arena for sport and entertainment.

In a single sentence, Paul removes the glamor and notoriety from the work of ministry. However, there is an encouraging aspect to his message. We need not be wise teachers, experienced orators, flashy miracle workers, or skilled writers in order to share the Gospel message. In fact, Paul was criticized for being a boring speaker! Rather than trying to impress the Corinthians with his skill, Paul said that God uses plain, simple people who commit to doing the hard work of ministry day in and day out. They aren't recognized and they don't stand out. While anyone can do the essential work of ministry, there are few, if any, earthly accolades for faithfulness and effectiveness.

THE ONLY WAY TO DEFEAT SIN

So I say, let the Holy Spirit guide your lives.
Then you won't be doing what your sinful nature craves.

GALATIANS 5:16 NLT

Discipline, intentional action, and accountability are all good things that can help us overcome our sinful desires and shortcomings. We won't live as faithful disciples by accident. However, Paul shares the heart of the Gospel with us—the driving force in our lives that both unites us with God and empowers us to live in holiness. The only way we'll definitively and consistently overcome sin is to yield ourselves to the Holy Spirit. With the Holy Spirit as our guide, we'll begin to recognize the power of our own desires and, most importantly, our powerlessness in overcoming them.

The "self" will not fade away if we deny it. Our cravings are too powerful. Our senses of self-preservation and enjoyment are too appealing. We can only educate ourselves so much in the consequences of sin. At a certain point, we need a more powerful guide to show us the way forward and to redirect our desires toward the presence and power of God.

Ironically, the only way to overcome sin is to stop fighting it. We won't be shaped into God's people by what we deny but rather by whom we yield to and who guides us. By yielding our wills to God, we will find new cravings for the presence of God and will discover along the way that we have been shaped into renewed people.

HOW TO CAPTURE GOD'S ATTENTION

But the eyes of the LORD are on those who fear him, on those whose hope is in his unfailing love, to deliver them from death and keep them alive in famine.

PSALM 33:18–19 NIV

God's attention and provision don't hinge on how well we pray or how much we sacrifice. It's all too easy to turn God into a holy slot machine that demands certain practices in order to meet our needs. We run the risk of domesticating God, demanding that God meet our needs and serve our purposes. Who hasn't veered too far toward prayers heavily laden with requests and desires without honoring God's unique, all-powerful qualities?

Those who can expect provision set God apart as holy and powerful, worthy of our reverence and respect. We don't pray for God's presence and power in order to manipulate Him for our purposes. Rather, we yield to God's majestic power because we recognize our place under this awesome God who is rightly feared.

Following quickly on this statement about the reverent fear of God, the psalmist reminds us that God's love is unfailing. We don't fear a monstrous, angry God, but we are reverent before a holy, all-powerful God who loves us deeply and will not fail us even if we have been unfaithful. As we rest in God's love for us and set Him apart as fearsome in His power, we will find the hope of His provision. Those who hope in God will find a constant, unmoving love that is deeply committed to them.

HOW TO SABOTAGE THE GOSPEL

*Do everything without complaining and arguing,
so that no one can criticize you.*

PHILIPPIANS 2:14–15 NLT

There is one certain way to undermine your ability to communicate the Gospel to others: engage in arguments. As we fight to be recognized, to win arguments, to justify our actions, and to make excuses for ourselves, we engage in a practice that is wholly centered upon ourselves and, even worse, has a tendency to cast blame on others. As we fight to justify ourselves, we turn others into our opponents, either blaming them for our problems or eliminating common ground with them as we argue over disagreements.

While communicating the Gospel has the potential to create peace and common ground with others, complaining and arguing will give our listeners cause to criticize us. Even if we're completely convinced that we deserve to complain or have every right to win an argument, we are reminded by Paul that there are unintended consequences that will further separate us from either our fellow Christians or those we are hoping to reach with the Gospel.

As we stop fighting for our rights or to be "right," we remove a major obstacle with others and keep as many doors open as possible for the Gospel to take root and flourish in our relationships.

PEACE IS OURS TODAY

*For God in all his fullness was pleased to live in Christ, and through
him God reconciled everything to himself. He made peace
with everything in heaven and on earth by means
of Christ's blood on the cross.*

COLOSSIANS 1:19–20 NLT

How would you describe your mental state right now? Are you content or discouraged? Do you feel close to God or distant from God? There are many times when I try to answer those questions and struggle with feelings of guilt and inadequacy. I wonder if I'll ever be "good enough," and I worry about where to turn next. I desperately need to read today's passage: God has already reconciled everything to Himself. The path to peace has been made wide open.

God is not distant from us. Jesus has already come to dwell among us and through the cross demonstrated once and for all that God is fully committed to making peace with us. Any barriers between ourselves and God have been finished at the cross. There is nothing we can do to improve on or supplement the cross. There is no way to make ourselves more worthy of the cross. Peace is already here. Reconciliation has been accomplished.

We also have a message with good news to share with others. God has made peace with the rebellious people of the earth. The barriers that divide us from others have been demolished with the cross. The cross is for everyone on earth. We'll only be able to share that message if we first believe that God has made peace with us.

GOD IS COMPASSIONATE TO ALL

The LORD is gracious and compassionate, slow to anger and rich in love. The LORD is good to all; he has compassion on all he has made.

PSALM 145:8-9 NIV

I know all too well what it feels like to lose my temper and to let my anger linger. There's a good chance that you also know what it feels like to be on the receiving end of an angry outburst. Perhaps anger has gotten in the way of an important relationship or caused you to doubt someone's love for you.

Today's psalm teaches us that God is most certainly capable of anger, but that anger is always slow in coming. Even when we experience God's anger, He won't dwell on it because He is so eager to love and forgive us.

This graciousness and compassion begin simply because we are God's beloved creation. God has compassion on all He has made, and the last thing He wants is to be divided from us. Although we may reject Him or go our own way for a season, He is eager to forgive and to restore us. He doesn't want us to dwell on shame or live in fear. There may be no greater tragedy than the people of God believing they could exhaust God's mercy or stray too far from His compassion.

Today's psalm reveals a God who is overflowing in mercy, longing to lavish it on anyone who will turn away from their own way.

THE LIFE-CHANGING PRACTICE OF HOSPITALITY

Dear friend, you are faithful in what you are doing for the brothers and sisters, even though they are strangers to you. They have told the church about your love.

3 JOHN 5–6 NIV

Opening our homes to a missionary, minister, or fellow Christian is a simple but important way to demonstrate the love of God. John notes in his letter that Gaius, the elder he addresses in today's passage, has recognized these unknown ministers as brothers and sisters rather than treating them as strangers. It's likely that Gaius went to great lengths to host these traveling preachers in his home at a time when most people lacked significant resources. When we talk about the cost of discipleship, the ministry of hospitality may be one of the most demanding.

Inviting fellow Christians into our homes, whether for a small group meeting, a family dinner, or lodging for several days, prompts us to change our schedules, to share our resources, and to literally make space for others. More importantly, if we truly believe that we are "brothers and sisters" with fellow Christians, the proof will be in how generously we share our most sacred spaces in our homes with them. Will we invite others into our living rooms and kitchens for rest and refreshment?

Hospitality is a sacrifice, but it is a vital way to encourage and support our fellow believers. Along the way, we'll enjoy deeper relationships with our Christian family and even benefit from the blessings and prayers of those who share our homes.

FAITHFUL TO AN IMPOSSIBLE MISSION

"The people to whom I am sending you are obstinate and stubborn. Say to them, 'This is what the Sovereign LORD says.' And whether they listen or fail to listen—for they are a rebellious people— they will know that a prophet has been among them."

EZEKIEL 2:4–5 NIV

If you serve in a particular ministry or you prayerfully reach out to neighbors or colleagues, there's a trap that is all too easy to fall into when it comes time to measure your success. The Lord warns Ezekiel of this trap: measuring his success based on the responses of others. Ezekiel's calling is only to share the message that God entrusted to him. Whether or not the obstinate and stubborn people respond is well beyond his control.

Ezekiel is responsible only so far as he ensures that he has heard correctly what God has said and then communicated it. He plays the role of a prophet. If people won't listen, he may rightfully wonder if he has shared the correct message. However, in this case he has already received the bracing message from the Lord that his mission is doomed to fail.

Perhaps you aren't facing the same demanding challenges as Ezekiel today in your ministry or relationships. However, much like Ezekiel, you cannot control the thoughts, words, and actions of others. You can only prayerfully consider how God is directing you to live and speak. Sometimes your own faithfulness is the only measure of "success" that you'll have.

KNOW IT ALL NO LONGER

DAY 154 – MORNING

"This is what the LORD says, he who made the earth, the LORD who formed it and established it—the LORD is his name: 'Call to me and I will answer you and tell you great and unsearchable things you do not know.' "

JEREMIAH 33:2–3 NIV

If you aren't in a season of uncertainty, you'll soon experience one. It may reveal itself gradually or come rushing in unexpectedly. When life begins to spin out of control or you find yourself at a bend in a road that remains very uncertain, it's natural to worry about or even obsess over the future. We become attached to certain outcomes and even begin asking God for a particular future. Who hasn't struggled with doubt or at least some hard questions for God when the exact opposite thing happens!

At a time when the prophet Jeremiah confronted uncertainty and the terror of a foreign army invading, the Lord assured him that he could call out and the Lord would answer him. Of course, the Lord didn't guarantee that Jeremiah would like the answer he received. Rather, Jeremiah is assured of deeper mysteries rather than clear-cut answers and resolutions.

Perhaps the answers to our prayers defy our comprehension and could take years or even a lifetime to fully unfold. Even the times when we think we understand God's ways, we'll find that there were mysteries or layers beneath our prayers that simply escaped our attention. Whether or not we want to confront these mysteries from God, the most important thing that this verse promises is the presence of God in uncertain times.

PEACE BEYOND CIRCUMSTANCES

"But the Advocate, the Holy Spirit, whom the Father will send in my name, will teach you all things and will remind you of everything I have said to you. Peace I leave with you; my peace I give you. I do not give to you as the world gives. Do not let your hearts be troubled and do not be afraid."

JOHN 14:26–27 NIV

Mere hours before His arrest and crucifixion, Jesus promised to send His Holy Spirit to comfort and instruct His followers. Even with the relief of Jesus' resurrection in a few days, they would have great need of the Spirit's peace and direction once Jesus ascended into heaven. Perhaps we may think they'd have all the more reason to be alarmed once Jesus ascended to heaven! However, Jesus assures us and them that it's the exact opposite: because Jesus has sent the Spirit, they should not let fear take root in their hearts.

Jesus passes along the assurance that we can seek the direction, wisdom, and peace of the Holy Spirit. We will surely face situations where fear appears to be more than warranted. In Jesus, we can choose to turn to the Holy Spirit. This is not a guarantee that our problems will be resolved or we'll suddenly have incredible wisdom to make the best choices.

Rather, the Spirit will reassure us that we are not alone and that whatever may happen tomorrow, God remains with us. The Spirit guards our souls and keeps us close to Jesus, even when every other measure of peace appears to be far away.

PRAYER THAT'S WORTH THE WAIT

When your words came, I ate them; they were my joy and my heart's delight, for I bear your name, LORD God Almighty.

JEREMIAH 15:16 NIV

The act of eating is often associated with the delight of learning, meditating on, or living out the words of God. In the case of Jeremiah, he actively sought the direction of God and relied on God to speak for his prophetic ministry to Israel. Waiting on God to speak brought him joy and delight, leaving him full and content, as if he had just eaten a full meal.

Just as it can be hard to wait for a meal, it's also quite challenging to wait on God with our prayers. We may imagine someone who has waited for hours on end for an exquisite meal at a restaurant. When the steaming food arrives, it is beyond his wildest expectations, and he carefully savors each bite. Moreover, God's Word to us is abundant and life giving for others as well. As we are nourished by God's Word, we can share what we have received with others so that they can take part in the joy and delight of God.

Waiting on God patiently takes faith and trust that God will eventually bring us the "meal" that we long for so badly. There is no other book, meal, or story that can restore us quite like the presence of God. Are we eagerly awaiting each day, leaving room on our "plates" for God to feed us? May we never settle for any lesser fare for our souls than the words of God for us.

REVEALING GOD'S HEART FOR PRODIGALS

"Say to them, 'As surely as I live, declares the Sovereign LORD,
I take no pleasure in the death of the wicked, but rather that
they turn from their ways and live. Turn! Turn from your
evil ways! Why will you die, people of Israel?' "

EZEKIEL 33:11 NIV

While there's no mistaking the consequences that await those who turn away from God, perhaps our shame and guilt hide the true desires of God from us. If you imagine an angry God eager to judge or to catch you in your sins, let this passage change your mind. Ezekiel shows us a God who pleads with His people and begs them to change their ways. Rather than threatening His people, the Lord shows His people that there are two paths set before them and passionately calls on them to choose the life of God found in obedience.

Each day we face choices and opportunities to move toward God or to shut ourselves off from God. If you've failed or closed yourself off from the Lord today or for as long as you can remember, the same desperate message applies to you: turn from your evil ways! Seeing His beloved people undone by sin devastates the heart of God. The unraveling of our lives under the sway of sin is the absolute last thing He wants.

God stands ready to forgive, to welcome us, and to lead us back to life. His plea for us today is simple and heartfelt: turn back.

THE JOY OF SUFFERING

Dear friends, do not be surprised at the fiery ordeal that has come on you to test you, as though something strange were happening to you. But rejoice inasmuch as you participate in the sufferings of Christ, so that you may be overjoyed when his glory is revealed.

1 PETER 4:12–13 NIV

Suffering and opposition for the sake of Christ isn't just a sign that we have cast our lot with Jesus. Suffering is a way to meet with Christ on a deeper level. As we face opposition, slander, or worse, we create a space in our lives to more fully experience Christ.

By choosing to suffer for Christ, we are denying our own desires and our sinful natures—the very things that come between ourselves and Him. In fact, suffering is guaranteed for us as we take up the cause of Christ. If you are suffering for a season, God can and will meet you and even use that suffering to bring more of His presence and peace into your life.

Most importantly, by choosing to suffer, we are taking a step of faith to believe that God has something better for us. We have the hope of His glory one day as we leave our own wills behind. While our desires promise us joy and fulfillment in the short term, these are fleeting and cannot compare to the joy we can experience today in the presence of the Lord, let alone when we are united with Him one day.

THE SLOW CREEP OF COMPROMISE

King Solomon, however, loved many foreign women besides Pharaoh's daughter—Moabites, Ammonites, Edomites, Sidonians and Hittites. They were from nations about which the Lord had told the Israelites, "You must not intermarry with them, because they will surely turn your hearts after their gods." Nevertheless, Solomon held fast to them in love.

1 Kings 11:1–2 NIV

After King Solomon's wealth and wisdom are presented in striking detail, the author of Kings offers a sobering note that all is not well in the king's heart: he had married many foreign women who turned him away from the Lord. It's likely that Solomon didn't think a few foreign wives could be that much of a threat to his devotion to God. After all, he lived in the epicenter of worship for Yahweh. What harm could a few foreign alliances through marriage do to his heart?

Sure enough, his heart gradually drifted further from God, and he became more tolerant of foreign gods. As he added new wives and allegiances with neighboring kingdoms, Solomon lost sight of Yahweh as he filled his time joining his wives in their idol worship. Even the wisest king was no match for the slow creep of compromise in his devotion to the true God.

As you examine your heart today, ask whether there are places or issues where you're compromising—even if it's just a little. Sin's most powerful trick is convincing us that it's not a big deal and that we can handle ourselves. It's a slow drift away from God, and we'll spare ourselves and our families pain if we recognize it sooner than later.

HONORING DISCIPLINE AND COMMITMENT

*Join with me in suffering, like a good soldier of Christ Jesus.
No one serving as a soldier gets entangled in civilian affairs,
but rather tries to please his commanding officer.*

2 Timothy 2:3–4 NIV

As we honor those who made the ultimate sacrifice for our country, we would do well to remember that Paul looked to soldiers as an ideal of single-minded commitment and devotion to a cause. According to Paul, the model soldier prioritizes the opinion of a commanding officer and avoids the distractions of civilians. A good soldier exists for the single purpose of carrying out the orders of a commanding officer in order to win a battle. Soldiers won't leave their ranks to argue with civilians or to even address their own affairs. Their primary concern is their mission.

While Paul honors the focus and discipline of soldiers, he certainly calls Timothy to a very different kind of combat where the "soldiers of Jesus Christ" endure suffering and slander without striking back. The "soldiers" of Christ win by losing, patiently enduring suffering, and responding to our competitive culture with humility and meekness. There are many "civilian affairs" that can pull us away from the purpose of God, from entertainment to accumulating wealth to engaging in arguments that have nothing to do with sharing the good news of the Gospel.

Our commanding officer has blessed us in order to bless others, and we'll carry out that mission most effectively when we learn from the disciplined focus of soldiers who carry out their orders under even the most demanding circumstances.

STARVING FOR GOD

He humbled you, causing you to hunger and then feeding you with manna, which neither you nor your ancestors had known, to teach you that man does not live on bread alone but on every word that comes from the mouth of the Lord.

DEUTERONOMY 8:3 NIV

As the people of Israel journeyed through the barren wilderness strewn with rocks and sand, we can hardly blame them for worrying about what they would eat, drink, or wear while confined to such a bleak location. Gathering enough food for an entire nation in a land without set-aside fields for agriculture, irrigation, or pasture became a daily struggle for existence. How would such a large people survive forty hours, let alone forty years, in such a hostile wilderness?

While the Israelites surely considered the wilderness the last place they wanted to be, the Lord wasted no time using it for a good purpose. The wilderness was the place to learn complete dependence on God. It's almost counterintuitive for us to read this. Why in the world would God remove their reliable food supply in order to demonstrate that they needed more than bread in order to survive?

In part, the Lord used a difficult situation to teach His people complete and total dependence. They couldn't do anything clever or innovative enough to provide for themselves. Their only way out was prayer, and their only resource was God's timely help. Did God hear their prayers? Would God provide? It took a difficult journey through the wilderness to find out.

ONLY THE UNQUALIFIED NEED APPLY

But the LORD said to Samuel, "Do not consider his appearance or his height, for I have rejected him. The LORD does not look at the things people look at. People look at the outward appearance, but the LORD looks at the heart."

1 SAMUEL 16:7 NIV

What does a king look like? If you had asked that question in the days of Saul and David, you would have heard a lot about personal appearance: height, muscular build, and even tone of voice. Of course, people longed for kings who could lead competently, but the prophet Samuel made the common mistake of confusing a kingly bearing with kingly competence. Don't we all make the same mistake of assuming that the person who looks the part is the best qualified for ministry or leadership?

The Lord turns such thinking over, declaring that He looks on the heart. The heart trumps any other measure of competence or qualification. Perhaps this means that we should change the criteria we have for our leaders, but don't overlook the possibility that this passage applies to you as well. If you sense a potential call to serve in a place or capacity that feels beyond your skill set or abilities, there's a chance that God is still calling you forward in faith.

The heart oriented toward God can accomplish far more than accumulated wisdom and experience. If you feel woefully unqualified for God's call, you're in very good company. In fact, God takes particular delight in using the supposedly "unqualified" to bless others.

KEEP YOUR WORD!

Above all, my brothers and sisters, do not swear—not by heaven or by earth or by anything else. All you need to say is a simple "Yes" or "No." Otherwise you will be condemned.

JAMES 5:12 NIV

Have you ever known someone you knew you could depend on? The kind of guy who always showed up for coffee when he said he would? The kind who you knew would keep his word when he tells you he will help you with those not-too-enjoyable tasks such as moving or painting your house?

That's the kind of friend we'd all like to have, isn't it? But, going a step further, it's the kind of friend we should strive to be.

Some Christians take the words of today's Bible verse quite literally, avoiding making any kinds of promises, taking any kinds of oaths, or entering into contracts with others. But even for someone who doesn't follow this verse by the letter (there are situations in today's world where it's impossible not to take oaths or enter into contractual agreements), there's something about James's words that strongly implies a simple but important principle: *be a man who can be taken at his word.*

In other words, be the kind of man who is so dependable, so true to his word, that no one ever has to ask, "Do you promise?" Be the man whose "yes" can always be taken as "yes" and whose "no" can always be taken as "no."

HE KNOWS WHAT WE'RE THINKING

Finally, brothers and sisters, whatever is true, whatever is noble,
whatever is right, whatever is pure, whatever is lovely,
whatever is admirable—if anything is excellent or
praiseworthy—think about such things.

PHILIPPIANS 4:8 NIV

We've all known those married couples who know each other so well that they seem to know what the other is thinking. In truth, however, no one—not even the ones with whom we share our most intimate relationships—can possibly know everything we think.

And we should be grateful for that.

However, there is one who knows our every thought—our Father in heaven. King David knew this, which is why he wrote, "You have searched me, LORD, and you know me. . .you perceive my thoughts from afar" (Psalm 139:1–2 NIV).

God knows our thoughts—all of them. He knows the things that cross our minds that we'd never share with anyone, even our closest friends.

That's the proverbial two-edged sword, isn't it? On one hand, we're like David, who seemed to welcome his heavenly Father's loving intrusion into his thoughts when he prayed, "Search me, God, and know my heart; test me and know my anxious thoughts" (Psalm 139:23 NIV). On the other hand, we may think, "Oh no! I don't want Him to know I'm thinking about *that*."

This is one of those situations when it's good to speak honestly to our heavenly Father. Since He knows our thoughts anyway, we can bring them all to Him and, like David, pray, "Search my heart and my thoughts, and help me to think on the things You want me to be thinking."

A "HIDDEN" SIN

"You have heard that it was said, 'You shall not commit adultery.'
But I tell you that anyone who looks at a woman lustfully
has already committed adultery with her in his heart."

MATTHEW 5:27–28 NIV

When we read God's seventh commandment—"You shall not commit adultery" (Exodus 20:14 NIV)—it's easy to take comfort in knowing that we've never engaged in "the act" of sex with another man's wife.

But in today's verse, Jesus offered some tough teaching on the subject of adultery, namely that it isn't just about where we take our bodies, but (even more importantly) about the impure places our thoughts can so easily go.

Ouch!

So how do we keep those lust-inducing images from entering through our eyes and into our minds? Job, a godly man who lived thousands of years before Jesus came to earth, offers some practical advice.

Job was committed to keeping his mind from immoral, adulterous thoughts: "I made a covenant with my eyes not to look lustfully at a young woman" (Job 31:1 NIV).

Job was on to something, wasn't he? What we allow to enter our brains through our eyes tends to stay there—as hard as we try to make it just go away. The key, he concluded, was to be very, very careful about what we look at.

That's no easy task, especially in today's world, where seemingly every other image that comes across our field of view can be problematic. But more than anything, it's a matter of commitment...to your spouse, your children, and your Father in heaven.

PEACE AND STRENGTH THROUGH GOD'S WORD

*Great peace have those who love your law,
and nothing can make them stumble.*

PSALM 119:165 NIV

The writer of the epistle to the Hebrews once wrote of scripture, "For the word of God is alive and active. Sharper than any double-edged sword, it penetrates even to dividing soul and spirit, joints and marrow; it judges the thoughts and attitudes of the heart" (Hebrews 4:12 NIV).

That's a great summary of the role the Bible plays in the life of the believer. However, it doesn't mention one great benefit of spending time reading and studying the Word: it brings us peace and strength for our walk.

The writer of Psalm 119 points out that the words in the Bible (he refers to it as God's "law") have an amazing ability not just to bring us that inner peace God wants us to live in, but also to keep us from stumbling and falling into sin.

Have you been lacking peace lately? Does it seem like your life in Christ lacks power? Do you find that you're not walking with Jesus as much as you are stumbling through life? It may be a matter of putting a daily time of reading and studying the Bible higher—maybe *much* higher—on your list of priorities.

Life in the twenty-first century is busy. Once we're finished with our daily work, our family, home projects, and friends all vie for our time. But if we want the peace and strength we need to live the life God calls us to live, we can't afford to miss out on time with Him and His Word.

RADICAL LOVE

*Husbands, love your wives, just as Christ loved
the church and gave himself up for her.*

EPHESIANS 5:25 NIV

Sometimes when we're trying to fully understand what God is communicating through His written Word, it's helpful to look at the context in which it was first written.

The culture at the time when the apostle Paul wrote these words was radically different from ours today. In those days, men ran everything and had total legal and social authority over their wives and children, and women had no choice but to live—submissively and probably without asking a lot of questions—under their husbands' rule.

When Paul enjoined husbands to love their wives "as Christ loved the church," he was suggesting something greatly different from the norms of the day. This was a love that served in the most sacrificial kind of way, a love that looked out for the needs and desires of someone who likely wasn't used to being treated that way by a man.

Though things have changed greatly since the days of the apostle Paul, his instructions to husbands are in many ways still a radical departure for many married men. God calls us men today to love our wives and children—and others in our circle of influence—the same way Jesus loved His people. That's a radical, self-sacrificing kind of love, a kind of love that leads first with a heart toward serving without first being served.

THE RIGHT THING TO BRAG ON

This is what the LORD says: "Let not the wise boast of their wisdom or the strong boast of their strength or the rich boast of their riches, but let the one who boasts boast about this: that they have the understanding to know me."

JEREMIAH 9:23–24 NIV

If you've ever been around someone who spends a lot of time—not to mention his own breath—bragging about his own accomplishments, possessions, or talents, then you probably have a small clue as to why God isn't pleased with human pride and arrogance.

When we boast about our own accomplishments, about our talents and gifts, in essence we communicate a mind-set and heart attitude that what we have and what we can do are a result of our own efforts and not a result of God's blessings.

Indeed, God doesn't want His people carrying around an attitude of braggadocio. He doesn't want us expending our energy letting others know about the great things we've accomplished or about our gifts and skills.

Instead, our God wants us to make sure our words—especially those we speak in relation to our gifts, blessings, and accomplishments—point to Him as our loving benefactor. And, as today's verse instructs us, that should begin with the fact that we know Him as our loving heavenly Father.

SERVING GOD BY SERVING OTHERS

"The King will reply, 'Truly I tell you, whatever you did for one of the least of these brothers and sisters of mine, you did for me.'"

MATTHEW 25:40 NIV

Today's verse—as well as some other passages like James 2:14–26—seem to imply that serving others is a requirement for salvation. That's a real head-scratcher for some Christians, who know that the Bible is clear that salvation is based on faith in Christ alone and not on our good works.

When we step back and take a broader look at the entire biblical message of salvation, we see that Jesus'—as well as James's—words do not contradict or even confuse the message of salvation by faith in Christ alone. Instead, those who by faith have received salvation and therefore have God's Spirit living within them will be motivated to serve out of true love for God and others.

Doing good things for others doesn't make you a Christian, and it won't "earn" you God's eternal salvation. On the other hand, as a follower of Jesus Christ, you'll find yourself motivated to serve others, knowing that when you serve the "least of these," you're serving God Himself.

Do you believe God wants you to have a bigger heart for service? Have you been wondering what kind of service He has in mind for you? Ask Him to first give you the right motivation to serve, and then ask Him to show you ways you can serve others.

The opportunities are all around you, and you'll find them if you just ask and then keep your eyes open.

FORGIVENESS OF OTHERS: GOD REQUIRES IT

*"And when you stand praying, if you hold anything
against anyone, forgive them, so that your Father
in heaven may forgive you your sins."*

MARK 11:25 NIV

If you've ever been around someone who harbors anger and bitterness toward another (for example, a man who hangs on to a wrong his wife committed against him years earlier), you know how uncomfortable it can be. You want to get as far away as possible, as quickly as possible.

Anger and unforgiveness are like love and faith in that they always find outward expressions. You just can't be an angry, bitter person without those around you seeing it in you—or hearing it from you.

God, it turns out, takes our forgiveness of others very seriously, so seriously that Jesus instructed His followers to forgive one another from their hearts. Otherwise, He said, God would not hear their prayers.

Have you ever been in a place with your relationship with God where your prayers seem stale, where it seems like they aren't reaching God's ears? There could be a lot of reasons for that—hidden sin, a particular spiritual struggle, and even those "dry times" we all sometimes experience.

But what about unforgiveness? When you're in that place where you don't feel like God is hearing you, take the time to examine your personal relationships with others and ask yourself if it's possible you're harboring unforgiveness toward someone.

Then forgive. . .from your heart.

JESUS, OUR ADVOCATE

My dear children, I write this to you so that you will not sin.
But if anybody does sin, we have an advocate with
the Father—Jesus Christ, the Righteous One.

1 JOHN 2:1 NIV

It might strike some of us as a bit odd that the apostle John would use the phrase "an advocate with the Father" to describe our Savior. In the context of today's verse, the word *advocate* implies someone who pleads our case before a legal court of justice. In other words, a lawyer.

In today's legal world, a lawyer pleads his client's case—whether or not he believes that client is innocent. Our advocate before God in heaven is different from an earthly lawyer in that He pleads the case before the Father knowing that we're guilty as charged, that we've certainly committed the offense charged against us.

This goes far beyond today's legal standard of "guilty beyond a reasonable doubt."

Jesus knows of our guilt, and so does God the Father. But when Jesus pleads our case, He in effect says, "Father, I know this man is a sinner. But he has come to us and confessed and repented. He has been cleansed and forgiven."

But here's the best part of this arrangement: when Jesus pleads our case, it's not before a stern judge who begrudgingly offers absolution. On the contrary, Jesus pleads our case before a loving, holy God who promises us to "cleanse us from all unrighteousness" when we simply confess our sins (1 John 1:9 NIV).

LOVE GIVES. . .IT HAS TO

"Do not be afraid, little flock, for your Father
has been pleased to give you the kingdom."

LUKE 12:32 NIV

There's something about becoming a father that makes most men great givers. From the time a man first learns that he and his wife are going to be parents, he wants more than anything to give whatever he has to make sure his child has everything it needs—physically, emotionally, and spiritually—to grow and thrive.

In this way, earthly fathers become reflections—imperfect reflections, but reflections nonetheless—of our Father in heaven. The apostle John wrote that "God is love" (1 John 4:8 NIV), and Jesus Himself said that God loved sinful and fallen humankind so much that He gave His most precious gift: His one and only Son (John 3:16).

That's just the nature of love, isn't it? Love, by its very nature, has no choice but to give. Real love can't just be hidden away in the heart; it must find expression through gifts to its object. And the God who identifies Himself as the perfect embodiment of love doesn't just give. . .He gives *joyfully* and He gives *perfectly*.

This perfect, giving love is what the apostle James was pointing to when he wrote, "Every good and perfect gift is from above, coming down from the Father of the heavenly lights, who does not change like shifting shadows" (James 1:17 NIV).

Our God is perfect—perfect in His holiness and perfect in His giving love. He always has been, and He always will be.

SPEAKING OF OTHERS. . .

A gossip betrays a confidence,
but a trustworthy person keeps a secret.

PROVERBS 11:13 NIV

Let's get real with ourselves for a moment. Most of us have a pretty good handle on avoiding the "biggies" where sin is concerned. We don't commit murder or adultery, and we'd never think of taking something that doesn't belong to us.

But many of us—dare we say *most* of us?—aren't always as careful as we need to be when it comes to how we talk about other people. Without giving it much thought, we make less-than-edifying comments about members of our families, people we work with, our spiritual leaders. . .the list goes on and on.

The Bible has plenty to say about someone who somehow finds it necessary to speak ill of other people, and none of it is good. Take a look at these descriptive biblical (King James Version) words for someone who engages in gossip: backbiter (Psalm 15:3), busybody (1 Timothy 5:13), inventors of evil things (Romans 1:30), talebearer (Proverbs 11:13), and whisperer (Proverbs 16:28).

God takes the things we say about others very seriously, and He tells us over and over in His written Word that gossip (even when what we say is factually true) carries with it some very serious consequences—here in this world and in the world to come.

So then, if you don't have something good to say about someone, go out of your way to find something. Otherwise, keep your negative, critical words to yourself.

LITTLE EYES WATCHING

The righteous lead blameless lives;
blessed are their children after them.

PROVERBS 20:7 NIV

Many if not most parents have found themselves red-faced when their little one innocently shares something embarrassing Mom or Dad did or said when they believed it hadn't been seen or heard.

Dads should assume their kids are watching and listening. The things they see and hear shape who they will become.

Make no mistake, your kids are watching and listening to. . .

- How you talk (Is it the same at home as it is in church?)
- How you treat your wife (Do you lead as a servant?)
- Your consumption of various entertainment media (Are you careful to watch movies and television that reflect a heart for godly standards?)
- Your behavior at home (Are you careful not to abuse or overuse alcohol? Is your speech the same everywhere you go?)
- Your walk with the Lord (Do your kids see you praying and reading your Bible?)

Fathers set the examples their children are likely to follow as they grow to adulthood. In other words, parents are making little copies of themselves that grow to be big copies.

The Bible promises us blessing as God's children when we are careful in how we behave, talk, and think. One of those blessings is children who copy our words and deeds.

The greatest gift a father can give his children is to be the kind of man God has called him to be.

TIME FOR SOME HONESTY. . .

*"Come now, let us settle the matter," says the LORD.
"Though your sins are like scarlet, they shall be as white as
snow; though they are red as crimson, they shall be like wool."*

ISAIAH 1:18 NIV

The prophet Isaiah ministered in the kingdom of Judah at a time when the people had fallen into some very grievous sin. They had become both hedonistic in their behavior and complacent toward their God.

In short, they were very much like us today—lost in sin and without hope. . .at least had they been left on their own.

One of the great themes of Isaiah's prophecies—and of the entire Bible—is God's willingness to forgive and restore those who recognize their sin and turn from that sin back toward Him.

The words in today's verse are echoed hundreds of years later by the apostle John, who wrote: "If we claim to be without sin, we deceive ourselves and the truth is not in us. If we confess our sins, he is faithful and just and will forgive us our sins and purify us from all unrighteousness" (1 John 1:8–9 NIV).

We all need God's forgiveness and restoration. He has provided a way for that to happen by sending His Son, Jesus Christ, to die for our sins. Our part in that equation is to acknowledge that we are sinners and that we need to be washed "as white as snow."

AN OFFENSIVE MESSAGE

Just as it is written, "BEHOLD, I LAY IN ZION A STONE OF STUMBLING AND A ROCK OF OFFENSE, AND HE WHO BELIEVES IN HIM WILL NOT BE DISAPPOINTED."

ROMANS 9:33 NASB

We live in a time when many people in our culture seem to have made being offended not just a hobby but a pastime they pursue with passion. It's a time when speaking the truth about the Gospel of Christ and about godly life principles will get you labeled as "intolerant" and a "bigot."

People don't like being told that they need Jesus to save them and change them, and they detest being confronted with their own sins. Being told that there is only one way into the kingdom of God—through Jesus Christ—they probably like even less.

Of course, this shouldn't shock or even surprise those who follow Christ. It also isn't really anything new. In fact, on several occasions, Jesus Himself warned His followers that those who faithfully live and speak for Him would often pay a steep price for their obedience (see Matthew 5:11, 10:22; John 15:18–21).

When we share the Gospel message with others, we should be careful to do it with wisdom, gentleness, and respect (see 1 Peter 3:15). But at the same time, we also need to keep in mind that the truth won't always be well received. In fact, many will find it downright offensive.

OUTWARD APPEARANCES

But the LORD said to Samuel, "Do not consider his appearance or his height, for I have rejected him. The LORD does not look at the things people look at. People look at the outward appearance, but the LORD looks at the heart."

1 SAMUEL 16:7 NIV

Ours is a culture that puts a lot of emphasis on physical appearance. If you don't believe that, just take a look at a good percentage of the advertisements and infomercials that make their way onto television broadcasts on what seems like an hourly basis.

Want to lose weight? Then there's any number of new diets and exercise programs to make it happen, countless companies looking to separate you from your hard-earned cash. Looking to get rid of that wrinkled skin or gray hair? Then there are plenty of companies pushing creams and hair care products.

Most of us would tell others that we're more concerned with what's "inside" another person than we are with his or her physical appearance. For some, that's just a pleasantry they don't really mean when it comes right down to it. But our God says that very thing. . .and He means it.

There's nothing wrong with taking care of yourself, nothing wrong with trying to look better by staying physically fit. But where your relationship with your heavenly Father is concerned, never forget that He's far more interested in the condition of your inner man than He is with the outer man.

WHERE TO TURN WHEN YOU'RE AFRAID

*When I am afraid, I put my trust in you. In God,
whose word I praise—in God I trust and am not afraid.
What can mere mortals do to me?*

PSALM 56:3–4 NIV

You don't need to be an expert in child behavior to know what a small child does when he's afraid, worried, in pain, or just needs comfort. Of course, he runs straight to the arms of his loving parents (more often than not to Mom).

It seems instinctive, doesn't it?

Life is filled with opportunities for us to be overcome by fear and anxiety. And when we enter times in our lives when we feel afraid, worried, and overwhelmed, it can be tempting just to curl up somewhere and try to wait it out alone.

Jesus once told His followers that if they wanted to enter the kingdom of heaven, they needed to do so with the heart attitude like that of a little child (see Matthew 18:2–4). Those moments of fear and worry are good examples of those many times when we need to be like little children.

When life is throwing so much at you that you feel like your fear will overcome you, do the same thing a small child does when he's afraid: run straight to the arms of your heavenly Father, who is more than able to calm your heart. . .and calm the storm that is going on around you.

AN ACCOUNTABILITY BROTHER

Therefore confess your sins to each other and pray for each other so that you may be healed. The prayer of a righteous person is powerful and effective.

JAMES 5:16 NIV

The Bible tells us that we have a spiritual enemy called the devil—or Satan—who works tirelessly to tempt you, weaken you, and discourage you in your life of faith in Jesus Christ. He loves nothing more than to exploit your weaknesses and vulnerabilities and cause you to fall into sin.

And while the Word tells us that God, through His Holy Spirit, will strengthen us for our battle against the devil, it also teaches the importance of having Christian brothers who can hold us accountable, who will pray for us and give us words of encouragement in our battles against sin.

Do you have a friend like that? The kind of brother in Christ in whom you can confide? The kind of friend you are comfortable confessing your sin and your weakness to? The kind of friend who will pray for you and even speak tough truth to you when it's needed?

That's the kind of friend you need when you're struggling with sin.

If you find yourself struggling with some particular sin and you want victory, then first ask God to give you strength to overcome. He will most certainly answer that prayer in the affirmative. Second, try making yourself accountable to a trusted Christian brother or two.

TALKING TO YOURSELF

Why, my soul, are you downcast? Why so disturbed within me? Put your hope in God, for I will yet praise him, my Savior and my God.

PSALM 42:5 NIV

Do you ever look at the difficulties and trials in your life and then start talking to yourself? If you don't, then you're probably in a very small minority. At some point, nearly every one of us has taken stock of our lives—or at least our current situation—and started thinking:

There's no way out of this.

Things aren't going to get better. . .at least not anytime soon.

This is just the way things are going to be for me. . .there's nothing I can do about it.

This just isn't fair!

There are all sorts of voices in our world vying for our attention, especially when life becomes difficult. Among those voices is our own.

Of course, we as believers know to be careful not to listen to the voices of the world and of the enemy of our souls, the devil. But it's also important that we don't allow our own voices to drown out that of our heavenly Father.

So when you find yourself muttering to yourself about the hopelessness or unfairness of your situation, turn your attention instead to the Lord, who is big enough and more than willing to take control of everything going on around you and in you.

As the apostle Peter put it, "Cast all your anxiety on him because he cares for you" (1 Peter 5:7 NIV).

CURB APPEAL

The LORD says, "I will guide you along the best pathway for your life. I will advise you and watch over you."

PSALM 32:8 NLT

Curbs are a very useful, if not underappreciated, invention. They guide water to drains, provide a place for small boys to sit and dream on a warm summer day, provide a shape to streets, and act as a boundary for those who need to park.

Curbs are intended to keep us from going where we shouldn't go while framing the route we should take.

We need curbs. We make better decisions with curbs. We find safety because of curbs. When everyone acknowledges these boundary markers, traffic flows smoothly. Imagine the chaos if people decided it was better to drive across lawns or parks.

We have our own set of internal curbs. These are the boundaries we learned as we grew up. This might include something simple like not touching a hot stove or something more complex like not taking something that doesn't belong to you.

God has given us curbs in the Bible, His good commands that direct us how to live wisely and lovingly as His children. When we refuse to live within these curbs, we find ourselves in trouble while we ruin things that belong to other people.

Cars are perfectly equipped to ride between the curbs on the street—so are we when it comes to God's commands in scripture.

HE NEVER GIVES UP

Finish what you started in me, God.
Your love is eternal—don't quit on me now.

PSALM 138:8 MSG

Do you ever feel panicked, watching the days of your life stretch out before you and not knowing how to use them in the best way to become more like Christ? Or that you see the work ahead and don't know if you're up to the task?

If you've felt anything like that, take comfort in these truths.

- God is the author of your faith; He's writing your story (Hebrews 12:2).
- God is not a God of chaos. He's putting your life in order (1 Corinthians 14:33).
- God began a good work, and He'll complete it in you (Philippians 1:6).
- God saves through His power, grace, and love. When we believe that Jesus was the perfect sacrifice needed to make forgiveness available to all who would ask, we start a new journey that ends with us being called new creations (2 Corinthians 5:17).

You always have access to the God who is reshaping your heart, reordering your direction, and giving purpose to your tomorrow.

There's another benefit. God is faithful, and He won't give up on you. There will be moments when you're stubborn, rebellious, and unwilling to listen. He won't throw up His hands in despair. He will wait, encourage, and put detour signs in your path. You see, He knows your story and He can be trusted to do His part.

While God does the work, life transformation will require your cooperation. Go forward ready to work with Him.

TWICE BORN

Jesus replied, "Very truly I tell you, no one can see the kingdom of God unless they are born again."

JOHN 3:3 NIV

We're born male or female. We're born into a certain family. We're born with a certain ethnicity and skin color.

And we're all born with a will to break God's law.

Since the very beginning, mankind has struggled to trust that God's laws were worth following. We've wondered if perhaps He is withholding good things from us.

God has things for us to do, and we ignore Him. He has things for us to stay away from, and that's what we find ourselves attracted to. God didn't *create us* to defy His law—we do that on our own.

God forgives, offers mercy, extends grace, and loves humanity because Jesus paid the price. God is holy, which means He's perfect, sinless, and set apart. Grace isn't a free pass, forgiveness isn't a green light to sin again, and mercy is a gift not an entitlement.

We are born in sin. We are reborn to follow Jesus. The first birth is into the family of mankind. The second birth is into the family of God. Only one of those families has eternal benefits and life-changing impact. Have you been born again? And if you have, how have you been treating the grace, forgiveness, and mercy that God has extended to you?

TRUST HIM MORE

When I get really afraid I come to you in trust. I'm proud to praise God; fearless now, I trust in God. What can mere mortals do?

PSALM 56:3–4 MSG

We survive in a world of broken promises. Products we buy struggle to exist beyond their warranty. Promises made by family and friends can be broken or forgotten. Something told in confidence becomes the day's gossip.

We often respond to broken promises by putting up walls, keeping things to ourselves, and never really believing anyone who says, "Trust me."

God encourages us to *trust* Him. He's never forgotten to supply the air we breathe or the sunshine we enjoy. He keeps food sources growing. In fact, He holds everything in His creation together (Colossians 1:17), even our very selves—" 'For in him we live and move and have our being' " (Acts 17:28 NIV).

Some of us will still hesitate and say, "I'm not sure I can trust Him."

God is something more and different than humans. He cannot lie or sin, and He always keeps His promises (Numbers 23:19).

The more we trust God, the more trustworthy we find Him. The more we trust His ability, the less we question His authority. The more we trust His love, the less fearful we find ourselves. The more we trust in God, the less ominous life becomes.

When it's hard to trust others, it's the perfect time to trust God.

GRACE HAS A PRICE

Should we keep on sinning so that God can show us more and more of his wonderful grace? Of course not!

ROMANS 6:1–2 NLT

God has freely offered grace to humanity to forgive sin and bring those who believe in Him into His family.

To demonstrate grace and forgiveness, Jesus paid a once and forever price—His life. He became the sacrifice for all who would accept it. Grace costs you nothing. Grace cost God the life of His Son.

While Jesus rose from the dead, the cost of forgiving grace was the most important payment in the history of mankind.

A man of integrity understands grace has a price. It isn't just a concept the mind agrees with. It changes decisions, actions, and motives.

A man of integrity brings God's command to love others into decisions, choosing to do the right thing rather than apologize after the fact. He knows he'll mess up and grace will be freely available, but he decides that sinning to *get* grace is something like abusing God's gift.

The price was high, so receiving the gift should have a life-altering impact. A man of integrity remembers what Jesus said of the sinful woman who anointed Him: that one who has been forgiven much, loves much (Luke 7:47). And this love and integrity sides with discipleship, discipline, and obedience. These are all hard things, but God's children are asked to trust Him and obey His commands. The man of integrity views this as an important, but not burdensome, directive because he understands the immense grace that has been given him.

HE STARTED AND FINISHED WELL

Whoever walks in integrity walks securely.
PROVERBS 10:9 NIV

The Bible is filled with stories of men who started well (like King Saul) with great hopes of doing something big for God. Many of these men ended poorly. Others (like Peter) struggled at the beginning but ended well. Still others started well—and finished well.

Daniel's story fits the last category.

He was born during an era of conflict. He existed in a time of struggling leaders and citizens that often only did what was right in their own eyes. As a teenager, he was taken from his country and taught a new culture. Somehow, in the middle of the crazy world where he found himself, Daniel wholeheartedly attached himself to the God of his people.

As a teenager, he knew God's law, including dietary requirements. He and his godly friends stood up to those who took them from their families by asking for food they knew they could eat in good conscience.

Daniel refused to compromise when he knew it was out of sync with God's will.

This man's life is an open book on what godly integrity looks like. His integrity was noticed by three kings, and Daniel was a trusted adviser for all three.

Be encouraged. No matter where you find yourself in following God, you have the opportunity to finish well.

TIME TO REPRESENT

A sterling reputation is better than striking it rich;
a gracious spirit is better than money in the bank.

PROVERBS 22:1 MSG

At the end of your life, people will talk about you. When your eulogy is given, people learn something about the man you were. How do you wish to be remembered?

One pastor struggled to find something positive to say about the recently departed. The only thing he could find was the guy had been pretty good at bingo.

Most people on their deathbeds focus on what was really important, and they often conclude they did less of the important stuff than they should have. Things like having a better relationship with God, time with loved ones, and the overall value of loving and helping others stand out as either regrets or cherished memories at the end of their lives.

People remember us more for how we helped than how we earned our money. They care more about the acts of kindness than a mantel of awards. They will respond more to a generous spirit than our list of accomplishments.

We represent our most gracious, generous, and giving God. Men of all ethnic groups, economic backgrounds, and nationalities have discovered that being more like Him results in a *sterling reputation* and a *gracious spirit*. Becoming more like Jesus changes how people see us—because it *actually* changes us. In what ways do you want to represent your Savior better? Ask Him; He is more than willing to help you grow.

A TIME OF FAILURE

"It's time to change your ways! Turn to face God so he can wipe away your sins [and] pour out showers of blessing to refresh you."

ACTS 3:19 MSG

Men despise personal failure. We don't want to admit wrongdoing. We even hate asking for directions. Every difficulty becomes our own burden to bear.

Perhaps this is why men tend to spiral out of control when they are caught in sin. They've tried to correct things on their own, personally blamed others for their predicament, and then, when the secret is out, they decide it's no longer worth the effort, spiraling into behaviors they never dreamed possible.

Failure should bring us face to feet with Jesus. We come to Him and bow at His feet in the brokenness of a man finally willing to ask for help. There's no shame in this purifying act—it's exactly what God wants us to do. In fact, He makes a promise that He will heal us from our sin if we confess it: "If we admit our sins—make a clean breast of them—he won't let us down; he'll be true to himself. He'll forgive our sins and purge us of all wrongdoing" (1 John 1:9 MSG).

There is restoration after failure. There is hope after hurt. There is love after rebellion. It's only possible through the God who's all too aware of our failures and chooses to love us anyway.

If this describes the world you live in now, then stop wasting time. Admit your failings and ask God for the help you need.

THE BIG DIFFERENCE

*"My thoughts are nothing like your thoughts," says the Lord.
"And my ways are far beyond anything you could imagine. For just
as the heavens are higher than the earth, so my ways are higher
than your ways and my thoughts higher than your thoughts."*

Isaiah 55:8–9 NLT

The biggest difference between God and man is that God is perfect—man is not.

We let people down—God can be trusted. We destroy—God makes things new. We tell lies—God speaks truth. We're selfish—God gave us everything. We want our way—God knows what's best.

These differences point to a God who's incredibly wise, but He is often thought of as foolish. For instance, His Word says we should lead by serving, find blessings by giving, and discover real life by losing what we thought was most important. In 1 Corinthians 1, the apostle Paul even states that the cross is "foolishness" to those who don't believe, but it is "the power of God" to those who are being saved (1 Corinthians 1:18 NKJV).

Sometimes we want to try to define who God is by what we experience, but God is beyond anything we can explain. He has no beginning or end. He created us and offers us restoration when we blow it. We don't have the credentials to be His children, but He welcomes us to be a part of His family through Jesus.

Thankfully, we don't have to understand everything about God to admit that He's right, trustworthy, and compassionate.

TRY HARDER?

You are not controlled by your sinful nature. You are controlled
by the Spirit if you have the Spirit of God living in you.
(And remember that those who do not have the Spirit
of Christ living in them do not belong to him at all.)

ROMANS 8:9 NLT

When we fail—and we will—we will likely embrace the idea of trying harder. We remind ourselves that we know right from wrong, so all we need to do is police ourselves and double our efforts. After all, God gave us His laws, so shouldn't it be easier to obey them?

Who are we kidding? We tag an extra five miles per hour onto the speed limit and somehow feel law enforcement should allow a little discretion. We've become masters at riding the edge of sin and hoping we don't fall off.

All the self-discipline, extra effort, and good intentions have never been 100 percent successful in keeping us away from sin, because it's never been enough.

God sent a Helper called the Holy Spirit to be both a spiritual companion and a living guide. We tend to ignore His influence and grow deaf to His advice. God wants to help us avoid sin, but we need to be willing to accept the help. Ask for God to open your heart to the Spirit's leading, and ask the Spirit Himself what He would show you today.

WISDOM'S SOURCE

If any of you lacks wisdom, you should ask God, who gives generously to all without finding fault, and it will be given to you.

JAMES 1:5 NIV

Wisdom is often equated with the number of wrinkles on a man's face. What if wisdom comes from a place other than time alone? What if you just have to ask?

The wisdom of God comes from acknowledging Him as the source of wisdom, accepting that wisdom as truth, and living your life according to it. Proverbs 1:7 affirms this: "The fear of the LORD is the beginning of knowledge."

Too often we think of wisdom in terms of our personal experiences. We think we become wise by living through difficulties and learning a lesson afterward. That's a great source of common sense—and part of the reason why older folks have so much good advice to share—but true wisdom from God offers *uncommon* sense, inspired instructions from the Creator Himself on how to best live and honor Him in His world.

Maybe those young people we say are "wise beyond their years" have simply been spending time learning wisdom from its original source.

Don't let age fool you. Wisdom is available to all, and godly wisdom surpasses the earthly wisdom of anyone you know.

The Bible contains hundreds of pages filled with what God can teach about how to be wise. Start exploring them, and learn the ways God's wisdom can change your perspective.

SECURING THE INSECURE

[God said,] My grace is enough; it's all you need.
My strength comes into its own in your weakness.

2 CORINTHIANS 12:9 MSG

He was indecisive, but he wanted people to like him. He was shallow, but he had a lot to hide. He was miserable, but he wore a smile to mask the pain.

There was another man. He was demanding because it stopped any questions. He was aloof because he couldn't allow anyone to get close. He wore his pain proudly and never believed there was relief.

We've all resembled one of these men in their struggle with feelings of insignificance.

Many men believe they'll never live up to the expectations of others or are convinced they are failures.

These two men were attempting to keep others away from their secret place of pain and insecurity. Both were miserable. Both were unsure of their choices.

Only God can secure us from the outside influences and inner conflict in our lives. Our security isn't found in our own ability but in God's. We become sufficient or acceptable because of God's grace, mercy, and peace through Jesus. Though there will be hard days when our feelings sneak up on us, spending time in scripture will remind us of how Jesus loves us and came to rescue us when, in our sin, we couldn't offer Him anything in return, not even love (Romans 5:8).

Feeling insignificant is normal. Knowing we are accepted by God makes us secure, no matter what we are feeling at the moment.

HARDWIRED FOR SUCCESS?

*Earn a reputation for living well in God's
eyes and the eyes of the people.*

PROVERBS 3:4 MSG

Men seem to be hardwired to want to be considered a success. Go to most ten-year high school reunions and men will talk about how successful they are, or they may resort to reliving their high school successes.

Some men will fight for their marriage (and they should), but only to prove they're a success in marriage. They don't want to be viewed as a failure.

Men will do what they feel they have to in order to shore up the appearance of success. However, when failure comes, some men will shift directions completely. These men will embrace failure as an old friend and live as if success is no longer available. They rush to make bad choices, dismiss their wife and children because they view themselves as mistake prone, and move from job to job because they can't find a reason to be passionate about work.

God longs for men to be authentic, transparent fighters for what's right. He longs for us to stop wearing masks and believing that if we just try hard enough, we can move all outside forces to be in our favor.

Our greatest success is to be *forgiven* men of God, to be in right relationship with Him. Let's focus our efforts on knowing and pleasing Him, and then, as we put our attention on what our loving heavenly Father thinks, what others think will not matter so much to us.

HEART PROTECTION

How can a young person stay pure? By obeying your word.
I have tried hard to find you—don't let me wander from
your commands. I have hidden your word in my
heart, that I might not sin against you.

PSALM 119:9–11 NLT

Gloves protect our hands. Shoes protect our feet. Safety goggles protect our eyes. What protects our hearts?

Hearts are where spiritual decisions are made. The heart remains unprotected when we don't know which rules to follow. Accurate spiritual decisions can't be made when we have no idea what God has to say about important life issues.

When we argue that we have no time to read God's Word, we shouldn't be surprised when we break God's law. Christian men lead their families by example. Consuming God's Word is essential to demonstrating how to live a godly life.

Our decisions cannot be made simply because we feel like it's a good decision or because the majority of people we talk to have a strong opinion about it.

The integrity of the heart and the decisions it makes will always be based on the connection between consulting God's Word and a willingness to obey what we read. When we fail in either area, we resemble the heart in Jeremiah 17:9 (NLT), which reads, "The human heart is the most deceitful of all things, and desperately wicked. Who really knows how bad it is?"

CAUTION TAPE CHRISTIANITY

Fix your attention on God. You'll be changed from the inside out.
Readily recognize what he wants from you, and quickly respond to
it. Unlike the culture around you, always dragging you down to
its level of immaturity, God brings the best out of you,
develops well-formed maturity in you.

ROMANS 12:2 MSG

What if there was the equivalent of yellow caution tape when it comes to places, circumstances, and events that we should avoid? Would we pay attention? Would we change direction?

If you go to the theater and the movie doesn't look like it matches God's heart, imagine yellow caution tape warning you to keep out. Imagine the same to be true for individuals the Bible describes as "bad company," or maybe it's arguments you need to stay away from. This visible reminder would solve all kinds of problems, wouldn't it?

God's Holy Spirit came to be that "caution tape." We don't see visible warning signs, but if we pay attention, we'll recognize those warning signs with as much personal impact as seeing bright yellow tape blocking the way to a dangerous area.

God has always provided the warning signs—we just need to recognize them. God gave us the help we need—we just need to stop rejecting it. If we humble ourselves and fix our attention on God and the help He provides in His Spirit, we will see Him "bring[ing] out the best in [us], developing[ing] well-formed maturity in [us]."

THERE WILL BE A FUTURE

"I know the plans I have for you," says the Lᴏʀᴅ. *"They are plans for good and not for disaster, to give you a future and a hope."*

Jᴇʀᴇᴍɪᴀʜ 29:11 ɴʟᴛ

There are no problems God cannot solve, no circumstance that escapes His attention, no future that can't be adapted to His plan.

God is never surprised, never in need of education, and never in doubt.

His way is perfect, precise, and practical.

In the difficult turns of our lives, we struggle, misunderstand, and then blame God. Why? We don't know the end of the story. We think what we face is unfair and that God not only doesn't make sense, but that we can consider Him malicious and untrustworthy.

What He knows—but we don't see—is there is an ending that proves His faithfulness. We just haven't arrived at that part of the story yet.

God doesn't need to recheck His plan to see if it was correct. He doesn't need to ask someone if He should have tried a different plan. What God understands and plans for us *can* be trusted even when we struggle to make sense of it.

We're familiar with the beginning of our story. We're living the present. The future? That's the part God understands, and He promises there will be a future. Hold on. Trust your loving Creator's promise that His plan is perfect and for your good even when it doesn't seem like it.

THE ONE NAME

What marvelous love the Father has extended to us! Just look at it—we're called children of God! That's who we really are.

1 JOHN 3:1 MSG

We are husbands, dads, employees, uncles, nephews, neighbors, plumbers, bakers, farmers, architects, writers, janitors, mechanics, truck drivers, accountants, comedians, gamers, athletes, actors, and a laundry list of other names that can define who we are and what we do.

We can also be called kind, gentle, loving, good, self-controlled, rude, rough, mean, or impulsive.

Of all the names men can be called, the one that should mean the most is *child of God*. This name defines who we are because it defines whom we follow. It indicates God has accepted us and we're part of a family of those accepted by Him. It suggests we're always in a position of learning because a child never knows it all.

It holds within it the promise of being coheirs with Christ, inheriting both eternal life and God's blessing and help in this earthly life: "And we know we are going to get what's coming to us—an unbelievable inheritance! We go through exactly what Christ goes through. If we go through the hard times with him, then we're certainly going to go through the good times with him!" (Romans 8:17 MSG).

Knowing who we are as a child of God helps us put all the other names we may be called into perspective. It also helps us identify with names that describe how a child of God is different from those who aren't God's children.

What's in a name? Perhaps more than you may have thought?

ALL THINGS NEW

Anyone who belongs to Christ has become a new person. The old life is gone; a new life has begun!

2 CORINTHIANS 5:17 NLT

A relationship with Jesus invites us to do things we never thought we could. Somehow impossible reactions become possible. Jesus helps us forgive when we would normally hold a grudge, love when it would be easier to hate, and share when we'd like to withhold. We become people who are generous in love, grace, and gentleness toward those who enter our path, and not because we are expecting anything in return.

God did this by making a new covenant with us. A covenant is a contract that God has bound Himself to fulfill. When we accept Jesus, there's nothing we can offer that would be considered valuable in God's sight—except ourselves.

God brings all the positive attributes, resources, forgiveness, grace, and love. It seems unfair. We get everything, and He doesn't seem to get much, but this is exactly the contract (or covenant) God accepts.

Once we have access to all God offers, we find our perception, attitudes, and thoughts changed. We live life from the perspective of one who doesn't horde time or resources, but instead extends help to others. We remember what it's like to be outside a partnership with God and want to help others discover the new covenant for themselves.

We come to Jesus just as we are, but should never stay the way we came.

THE RIGHT CANDIDATE

Pride lands you flat on your face;
humility prepares you for honors.
PROVERBS 29:23 MSG

If you spend any amount of time in God's Word, you'll notice that the men God used never seemed quite ready for the job they were asked to do. They were fearful, impulsive misfits, oddballs, and sinners, and often the least ideal candidates to do something big for God. In other words, these men were entirely average, normal, and perhaps the last to be picked for a team.

Do you ever feel average or even below average? You just might be the right candidate God can use to do something incredible.

Maybe God never wanted men who *knew* they could do something big. Maybe He likes using men who *know* they need His help.

God seems to need a little more time when He's dealing with the prideful men who know it all and don't mind sharing it. He may set aside those who seem to believe God is fortunate to have them as part of His team. God sees pride as a barrier to usefulness.

So when you feel a little inadequate, a lot out of your element, or lacking in the skills God might need, you shouldn't be surprised when God gives you something only you can do—with His help.

WHAT IS A BLESSING?

All praise to God, the Father of our Lord Jesus Christ,
who has blessed us with every spiritual blessing in the
heavenly realms because we are united with Christ.

EPHESIANS 1:3 NLT

Blessings are prayers at mealtimes and gifts from God. There's another blessing we'll discover over the next four days.

This blessing is a personal gift a father shares with a child. A father's blessing can give a child permission to grow up, offer freedom, and invite the child to dream big dreams and follow God's unique plan.

We *pass* the blessing when we *speak* the blessing. We cannot assume our children understand they're loved and that we want the best for them. They need to hear it from our lips and see it in our actions. A blessing can change futures, strengthen relationships, and provide a vision for their journey.

When a child receives a blessing from her father, it proves he notices her, pays attention to her heart, and knows that by giving her wings she will eventually fly.

Each child needs the blessing, but few receive it. Your children may be grown—it's never too late to bless them.

God has blessed mankind with a future and a hope. He offers a listening ear, a fully developed plan for your life, and forever companionship. He advises, comforts, and He *blesses*.

WHAT THEY NEED THE MOST

LORD Almighty, blessed is the one who trusts in you.
PSALM 84:12 NIV

If you're married, it's possible your family has been waiting for something only you can give. They may not know how to ask. They may not even know they need this, but you have the power to build up or crush your family.

You can change futures by offering your family a *blessing*.

Abraham offered Isaac a blessing. Isaac offered Jacob a blessing. Jacob gave Joseph a blessing.

A blessing speaks life into your family. It lets them know you recognize their importance to you. It indicates you believe they have the ability to make good decisions. It inspires confidence and encourages hope.

Your ability to clearly tell your family they're valued and that you believe in them can go a long way in giving them the courage to face life head-on. Too many families are waiting to be loved unconditionally by their husband or dad.

When we place conditions on our love, our families will still do everything they can to receive a blessing, but they will live with the knowledge that it probably will never happen. Give them a vision for their future that includes your backing.

You can be fifty years old and still be waiting for a father's blessing. Don't make your wife and children wait.

WHEN YOU MISSED THE BLESSING

*"GOD bless you and keep you, GOD smile on you and gift you,
GOD look you full in the face and make you prosper."*

NUMBERS 6:24–26 MSG

What you believed about yourself when you were a small child is likely what you believe today. We were, in many ways, children who believed what we were told by our parents, friends, or schoolhouse bullies. We each carry invisible tattoos reading *last to be picked*, *slow*, *stupid*, or *worthless*.

On bad days, you'll believe what someone said when you were five. It doesn't matter if it's true or not, you'll accept it as true even when the evidence suggests otherwise.

Our future isn't defined by our five-year-old selves, but we'll act the part.

If no one's ever spoken a blessing into your life, consider this. Before you were born, God knew your name, fit you together in your mother's womb, and called you a masterpiece (Psalm 139:13–16). He wants you on His team. He created you for something only you can do. He loved you enough to send His Son, Jesus, to make it possible for you to be a part of His family.

You'll sin, but God can forgive you, and He wants to. He's never abandoned you. He's always loved you. He wants to partner with you on His plan for you.

Don't pay attention to what others called you; pay attention to His call.

REVERSE BLESSING

If you honor your father and mother,
"things will go well for you."

EPHESIANS 6:3 NLT

What if you had one or more parents who just weren't there for you? What if they didn't have what it took to show what love looked like? What if they seemed uncaring and spoke words that couldn't be considered blessings?

Maybe one or both parents were likely never serious candidates for Parent of the Year. They didn't seem to find any joy in *you*.

You may be waiting for a blessing you've never received, validation that never came, an encouraging parent that only seemed the stuff of fairy tales, and you're in conflict. Sure, sharing the blessing with your own children is something you want to do, but giving a blessing to a parent who never blessed you sounds like an awkward impossibility.

Some parents were likely broken by an unspoken blessing that should have come from *their* parents. Even parents may be waiting to be told they're loved.

As much as they may have hurt you, a rebuilt relationship may be possible when *you* give your *parents* a blessing. It may be hard, but it's entirely possible your blessing will put a noticeable crack in the walls they've built around their hearts. If this restored relationship is something you desire but you feel hesitant to try, ask God to increase your love for your parents and to guide you into the right words to say and actions to take.

SAVED ONLY BY GRACE

Christ Jesus came into the world to save sinners,
of whom I am chief.

1 Timothy 1:15 NKJV

Paul wasn't just acting humble when he declared that he was the worst of sinners. He never forgot that, in his blind zeal for Jewish religious traditions, he had arrested and tortured numerous Christians and urged that they be killed. Looking back on his crimes years later, he bluntly stated that any righteousness he once thought he'd had he now realized was "rubbish" (Philippians 3:8 NKJV).

Why did God choose such a violent sinner for one of His leading apostles? Paul explained that God wanted to show by *his* example that there was no person so vile or sinful that He couldn't redeem them (1 Timothy 1:16). You might also ask why God chose Peter as a leading apostle after Peter cursed and swore that he didn't even *know* Jesus (Matthew 26:69–74). Again, the Lord wanted someone presenting His Gospel who knew that he was unworthy, who was convinced that he, and others, could only be saved by God's grace.

However, sometimes after you've been serving the Lord for a few years, have cleaned up your life, and have overcome several bad habits, you can forget what a bad state you were once in. You can begin to think that you're quite righteous and can even start to believe that you're good enough to make it on your own.

But think for a moment about the life Jesus saved you from, and remind yourself that it was by grace you were saved, not by your own goodness (Ephesians 2:8–9).

REPAYING DEBTS

Let no debt remain outstanding,
except the continuing debt to love one another.

Romans 13:8 NIV

Christians are to honor their debts and be faithful to pay them. When you don't have much cash, sometimes the last thing you want to think of is about repaying money you *owe*. You pray that they won't press you to repay immediately. In fact, truth be told, you probably wish that they'd simply forgive the debt.

Jesus said, "Love your enemies, do good, and lend, hoping for nothing in return" (Luke 6:35 NKJV), so you might think, *If they were a true Christian, they wouldn't expect me to repay them. They'd forgive my debt.* But that's missing Jesus' point. He was saying that if you lend money to an *unsaved enemy* because he needs it, do so with the full knowledge that he likely won't repay you. He *is* an unbeliever and an enemy after all.

It's wonderful when someone is in a position to forgive a debt, but they may be unable to or may not feel that they should, so it's your responsibility to repay them—even if you have to do so little by little over an extended period of time. It will teach you discipline and faithfulness.

You can pray that God will supply the money to repay them. And yes, you *can* pray that, if they're in a position to do so, they'll have mercy and forgive the debt. But don't attempt to impose this desire upon them.

The only debt you should never finish paying off is your obligation to love others.

OVERCOMING DESPAIR

He lifted me out of the pit of despair, out of the mud and the mire.
He set my feet on solid ground and steadied me as I walked along.

PSALM 40:2 NLT

The prophet Samuel had anointed David to be the future king of Israel. This was the clear will of God, so obviously God planned to keep David alive so this could happen. At first, David didn't doubt it. But after living like a fugitive in the wilderness for several years, constantly looking over his shoulder, his faith became worn down. "David kept thinking to himself, 'Someday Saul is going to get me. The best thing I can do is escape to the Philistines. Then Saul will stop hunting for me. . .and I will finally be safe' " (1 Samuel 27:1 NLT).

There's no indication that David prayed about this decision. He fled to the land of the Philistines due to his own discouraged reasoning, and this move ended up causing him serious problems.

Perhaps you're in a similar situation. You were convinced that something was God's will for your life, so you stood strong for quite some time, despite severe tests. But perhaps recently you've begun to grow weary and fray around the edges.

God knows this is a human tendency, so He encourages you in the words of Paul, which say, "Let us not grow weary while doing good, for in due season we shall reap if we do not lose heart" (Galatians 6:9 NKJV). The Word also says, "Fight the good fight of faith" (1 Timothy 6:12 KJV), so keep fighting and believing.

KIND TO THE UNGRATEFUL

Love ye your enemies. . .and your reward shall be great,
and ye shall be the children of the Highest: for he
is kind unto the unthankful and to the evil.

Luke 6:35 kjv

One thing that disturbs many Christians is Jesus' command to love their enemies. It just seems so far beyond what they're capable of or willing to do that they write it off as some unrealistic ideal that only the most super-spiritual, mature saints can ever aspire to. But Jesus said that loving your enemies was sure proof that you were a child of the Highest God.

Why is this? Because God is loving and patient by nature. He loves the unthankful and is kind even to evil people. And as His child, you're to emulate your Father and show this same love and kindness.

You may have difficulty even showing kindness to those who don't express due thankfulness, let alone showing love and kindness to people who are evil and show no sign of repenting or changing. Yet Jesus, after explaining God's loving nature in Luke 6:35 above, added, "Be ye therefore merciful, as your Father also is merciful" (v. 36).

He doesn't expect you to be naive about where they're at or deny that they're evil, but He asks you to "overcome evil with good" (Romans 12:21 kjv). And yes, He knows that this is a difficult thing to ask. That's why He promises that "your reward shall be *great*" for obeying Him.

AVOID ARGUMENTS

Refuse to get involved in inane discussions; they always end up in fights. God's servant must not be argumentative, but a gentle listener.

2 TIMOTHY 2:23–24 MSG

If you're often tempted to get drawn into arguments, you might not see it as a fault. You may simply think that you're being honest and "telling it like it is" or setting other people straight. But the fact is most quarrels generate far more heat than light and end up creating hard feelings. Plus, they often descend into emotional exchanges rather than reasoned discussions. This is especially true of political and religious arguments—although it could also describe many marital disagreements.

Ask yourself what you spend the most time doing during a typical argument. Are you patiently listening to the other person, trying to understand his or her point of view, or does "listening" mean impatiently waiting for your turn to speak? The Bible says that God's servant must be "a gentle listener." Does this describe you?

Granted, there *are* times, especially when someone is teaching dangerous false doctrine, when you must "contend earnestly for the faith" (Jude 3 NKJV). But you must contend with facts and solid reasons, not with a raised voice and intimidating emotions and body postures.

Solomon said, "Starting a quarrel is like opening a floodgate, so stop before a dispute breaks out" (Proverbs 17:14 NLT). Know what's actually worth disputing and what's not. Whether you feel you're right or not, often the wisest thing that you can do is to simply avoid getting drawn into an argument in the first place.

PROTECTED IN GOD'S SHADOW

He who dwells in the secret place of the Most High shall abide under the shadow of the Almighty.

PSALM 91:1 NKJV

How do you find rest and calm when there's trouble and rumors all around you—when enemies seek your ruin and the winds of adversity are howling? You must stay close to God. You must dwell (consistently live) in the shelter of the Most High and abide (remain) under His mighty shadow. But what does it mean to remain under God's shadow?

Much of the Negev in southern Israel is one vast, barren, unforgiving desert baking under the heat of the sun and frequently blasted by high winds. Travelers took shelter behind great rocks during windstorms and rested in their shadow during the hottest part of the day. God is just like that to His people. He is "a shelter from the wind and a refuge from the storm. . .and the shadow of a great rock in a thirsty land" (Isaiah 32:2 NIV).

Because you're a Christian, Jesus lives in your heart. The Spirit of God's Son dwells in you. But there is more to the picture. He said, "Abide in Me, and I in you" (John 15:4 NKJV). Jesus lives in you, but you must also live continually in Him. This means seeking Him in prayer and staying close to Him by obeying Him.

God is a great rock in a hostile landscape, and He is more than able to protect you. So stay close to Him, in His shadow.

THE INDWELLING WORD

Let the word of Christ dwell in you richly.
COLOSSIANS 3:16 NKJV

Jeremiah said, "When I discovered your words, I devoured them. They are my joy and my heart's delight" (Jeremiah 15:16 NLT). But what does this mean? How can you *eat* God's Word? You do this by taking His words into your mind and heart, meditating upon them and absorbing them, and allowing them to inspire you and give you life. Just as you must chew, swallow, and digest natural food, so you must take God's Word into your very being.

Paul wrote that you are to be "nourished in the words of faith and of the good doctrine which you have carefully followed" (1 Timothy 4:6 NKJV). You allow the word of Christ to nourish you and dwell in you richly when you make time every day to read it and learn from it. This can be difficult to do in today's busy world, especially if you have a high-demand job that taxes you mentally, physically, and emotionally every day. You may have so much to do that you feel you don't have time to take in God's Word.

But failing to read the Bible is like failing to eat regular meals: you may get away with it for a little while, but eventually this habit will catch up with you. You'll feel weak. And if you do without spiritual nourishment, you won't know right from wrong. So take in a meal of scripture today. "Your word I have hidden in my heart, that I might not sin against You" (Psalm 119:11 NKJV).

LAUGHTER AND WELLNESS

A cheerful heart is good medicine,
but a crushed spirit dries up the bones.

PROVERBS 17:22 NIV

Many modern doctors affirm the truth of this scripture by embracing laughter therapy, which teaches that people who cut loose and laugh will begin to enjoy improved health.

Doctors know that laughter is a natural medicine. It benefits people's physical and emotional beings. It can aid in preventing heart disease by increasing blood flow and improving the way blood vessels work. Laughter has the ability to relax a person's entire body and relieve stress. It can also strengthen the body's immune system and release endorphins to alleviate pain.

Life is often serious business, but it's possible to be sober and serious to the detriment of your health. And definitely if you have a crushed spirit—a discouraged, depressed state of mind—your health is going to suffer. There are quite a number of psychosomatic illnesses caused by little more than negative mental attitudes.

It will do you a world of good to rent a comedy movie and spend a couple hours laughing. You can't live a life of unrelieved seriousness, stress, and worry without suffering for it. And besides the benefits to your physical and emotional health, laughter lightens your mood and causes you to have a more hopeful attitude. A happy, positive attitude will help you face life and rise above difficulties.

"For the happy heart, life is a continual feast" (Proverbs 15:15 NLT). So enjoy laughter as much as you can.

A LIVING SACRIFICE

I plead with you to give your bodies to God because of all he has done for you. Let them be a living and holy sacrifice. . . . This is truly the way to worship him.

ROMANS 12:1 NLT

You might sometimes think that being a disciple of Jesus is nothing but privation and suffering, since several verses talk about dying to self and killing your desires. Romans 12:1 describes laying yourself on God's altar as a "living sacrifice," and that might worry you since another verse says, "Those who are Christ's have crucified the flesh with its passions and desires" (Galatians 5:24 NKJV). You might begin to think that *truly* following Jesus is a life void of pleasure and fun.

Certainly you'll be called upon to make personal sacrifices out of love for God and others, and certainly you must not give in to the *sinful* passions and desires of your flesh—such as hatred, murder, adultery, and greed—but you will have many desires that are perfectly in line with the will of God. That's why He promises, "Delight yourself also in the LORD, and He shall give you the desires of your heart" (Psalm 37:4 NKJV).

So don't be afraid to yield your body as a "living sacrifice." Let His Holy Spirit have His way in your heart. Listen to Him when He tells you to say no to a selfish desire or urges you to crucify hatred, jealousy, and covetousness. He wants what's best for you, and though you'll die to sinful passions and desires, you'll be truly coming alive.

LETTING IT PASS

Overlook an offense and bond a friendship;
fasten on to a slight and—good-bye, friend!

PROVERBS 17:9 MSG

Everyone makes mistakes, but some men are definitely more prone to speak without thinking and cause offense. Other men are always scarfing up the last donut—their third one—without asking whether you'd had one yet. Or they borrow a valuable tool and lose it. . .then inform you that they can't afford to replace it at this time. And you need it for work on Monday. Then the ball is in your court. How do you respond?

Hopefully, you'll be able to let the donut go without too many problems. It is, after all, a rather minor offense. But it may be more difficult to forgive hurtful words or larger losses, especially if this isn't the first time they've happened. But think carefully before you react. Is this really worth losing a friend over? Probably not.

You can still express your disappointment and let him know how this makes you feel, calmly. And you probably should express your emotions. But it's not wise to hold a grudge. Leviticus 19:18 (MSG) says, "Don't. . .carry a grudge against any of your people." It then goes on to say, "Love your neighbor as yourself," which is the whole reason why you shouldn't nurse grudges.

God's commandments about love and forgiveness have practical applications in your everyday life and in the workplace. They may not be easy to implement, but they're guaranteed to work.

DON'T LOSE YOUR CROWN

Hold on to what you have,
so that no one will take away your crown.

REVELATION 3:11 NLT

James said, "Blessed is the man who endures temptation; for. . . he will receive the crown of life which the Lord has promised to those who love Him" (James 1:12 NKJV). This crown symbolizes your salvation and is a gift—free and undeserved—to those who believe in and love Jesus.

Elsewhere, Peter speaks of another crown: "When the Chief Shepherd appears, you will receive the crown of glory that will never fade away" (1 Peter 5:4 NIV). Many Bible scholars believe that when Peter speaks about the "crown of glory," it's *separate* from the crown of life. Can someone have more than one crown in heaven? Jesus does. "On his head were many crowns" (Revelation 19:12 KJV).

When promising "the crown of glory," Peter was talking to older, mature Christians who watched over the church and set an example for other believers. The crown of life is given to *all* believers and cannot be taken from you by any man, but the crown of glory is an award for exceptional service.

Unlike the crown of life, however, it appears that people *can* lose this crown by not fulfilling what God has called them to do, as Revelation 3:11 warns. If God has given you a task to do and you neglect it, He will have to find someone else to do it. . .and they will receive the reward originally intended for you. So be faithful to obey God and fulfill your calling.

AVOID DRIFTING AWAY

We must pay the most careful attention. . .
to what we have heard, so that we do not drift away.

HEBREWS 2:1 NIV

Most people who leave their faith in God behind don't make a sudden, deliberate decision to do so. Rather, they slowly drift away, little by little, day by day. They gradually become colder to the Lord, lose interest in prayer, reading the Word, and fellowshipping with other Christians, and, over time, value their relationship with God less and less.

Hebrews 2:3 (NIV) asks, "How shall we escape if we ignore so great a salvation?" But that's what many people do. They don't dramatically revolt against God. They simply ignore Him for prolonged periods of time. Eventually such people become "nearsighted and blind, forgetting that they have been cleansed from their past sins" (2 Peter 1:9 NIV). First, they become nearsighted, their eyes out of focus. Eventually they completely lose all spiritual sight.

They often still go through the outward motions of being a Christian, but their heart has departed. They question the basic beliefs of the faith and believe it's irrelevant to their life in this modern world.

What is the solution? How can you avoid this happening to you? You must pay careful attention to what you have heard from the Bible. When you hear the Word, ponder it and allow it to change you. "Today, if you hear his voice, do not harden your hearts" (Hebrews 3:7–8 NIV). Pray and ask God to renew your relationship with Him. And determine to truly *live* your faith.

MEDITATE ON GOD

Be still, and know that I am God.
PSALM 46:10 KJV

There's a time to earnestly pray for what you need, and there's a time to praise God for providing all your needs. But there is *also* a time to meditate, to simply think deeply on who God is for an extended period. At times like that, focus entirely on Him and keep your mind from wandering. God will reward you with a deeper knowledge of His nature and His love.

Some Christians shy away from meditation, thinking that Eastern religions have a monopoly on it, but the Bible talked about meditation thousands of years ago, long before any modern fads. God commanded, "Be still, and know that I am God" (Psalm 46:10 KJV). You are to still your heart and focus on knowing Him—that He is almighty God, exalted above all else, supreme, holy, beautiful, and glorious in every way.

You should also meditate on the wonderful things God has done in your life and in the lives of others. Think of His miracles, both great and small. "I meditate on all Your works; I muse on the work of Your hands" (Psalm 143:5 NKJV).

Also, when you read the Bible, don't simply hurry through it. Pause at a verse and meditate deeply on its meaning. "Oh, how I love Your law! It is my meditation all the day" (Psalm 119:97 NKJV). Paul said, "Meditate on these things; give yourself entirely to them" (1 Timothy 4:15 NKJV). Meditate on God and the things of God today.

LOVE DRIVES OUT FEAR

There is no fear in love; but perfect love casts out fear,
because fear involves torment. But he who fears
has not been made perfect in love.

1 John 4:18 NKJV

This is a beautiful scripture, but what exactly does it mean? Well, in the verses leading up to this, John wrote: "We have known and *believed* the love that God has for us. God is love, and he who abides in love abides in God, and God in him. Love has been perfected among us in this: that we may have *boldness* in the day of *judgment*" (1 John 4:16–17 NKJV, emphasis added).

Elsewhere, Paul wrote: "I am convinced that neither death nor life. . .nor anything else in all creation, will be able to separate us from the love of God that is in Christ Jesus our Lord" (Romans 8:38–39 NIV). If you've believed this amazing love God has for you and are convinced that *nothing* can separate you from it, then you know you have nothing to fear from God in the day of judgment.

These are basic Christian truths, but it's good to be reminded of them. Sometimes you may worry that you're not *good* enough to be saved. That's true, by the way. None of us are good enough to deserve salvation. We are all utterly dependent on the mercy of God. That's how you were saved in the first place, and nothing has changed there.

When you know that God loves you more than words can express and that nothing can separate you from His love, this drives out all worry and fear.

DON'T BE COVETOUS

Don't set your heart on anything that is your neighbor's.

Exodus 20:17 msg

In the New King James Version, Exodus 20:17 says, "You shall not covet. . .anything that is your neighbor's." But *covet* is a bit of an archaic word, not in common use today. You might have a vague idea that to be *covetous* means to be greedy or selfish, but what exactly does it mean? *The Message* translates *covet* well: "Don't set your heart on anything that is your neighbor's."

The dictionary defines it this way: "To desire wrongfully, inordinately, or without due regard for the rights of others." Thus, if you covet your neighbor's wife, you'll eventually seek to commit adultery with her—not caring about the pain this causes her, her husband, and their children.

If you covet your neighbor's wealth, you'll seek ways to get it from him—or coveting will cause you to be bitter that you don't have what he has. The Bible advises, "Keep your lives free from the love of money and be content with what you have" (Hebrews 13:5 niv). In fact, you do well if you keep your life free from covetousness of *all* kinds. You spare yourself a lot of trouble if you're just content.

One good way to be content with what you have is to remind yourself of the tremendous rewards that you'll one day have in heaven. God will abundantly compensate you for your lack in the here and now. That's why Jesus said, "Blessed are you who are poor, for yours is the kingdom of God" (Luke 6:20 niv).

BETTER DAYS AHEAD

"You will surely forget your trouble,
recalling it only as waters gone by."

Job 11:16 NIV

Sometimes you're made to pass through a valley of suffering, and more often than not, it has to do with family issues, financial crises, or health problems. At the time, you may not even be certain that you'll survive. It looks like you'll crash. Perhaps you disobeyed God or you acted rashly or inconsiderately to others, and now the consequences of your actions are rising like floodwaters around you. Or perhaps problems have come upon you for no fault of your own.

Yet, difficult as your circumstances may be and difficult as it might be to believe it, soon enough you'll be laughing again and will forget your troubles. They'll be as waters that have evaporated away. David said of God, "For his anger lasts only a moment, but his favor lasts a lifetime; weeping may stay for the night, but rejoicing comes in the morning" (Psalm 30:5 NIV). It's vital to remember when passing through tests that God's favor lasts your entire lifetime; His discipline, by contrast, is usually brief.

God doesn't get any pleasure out of causing His children to suffer, yet some Christians have been led to believe that God is primarily focused on holiness, indignation, and punishment. He does allow suffering, true, but it usually only lasts long enough to bring about good in your life. "The Lord comforts his people and will have compassion on his afflicted ones" (Isaiah 49:13 NIV).

KEEP HIS COMMANDMENTS

"If you love Me, keep My commandments."
JOHN 14:15 NKJV

Jesus made it very clear what it meant to be His follower. It goes without saying that you have to believe in Him, and as a Christian, you do that; but do you wonder at times whether your faith is genuine, if you truly *know* God? Many Christians ask themselves this from time to time. The Bible even advises, "Examine yourselves as to whether you are in the faith. Test yourselves" (2 Corinthians 13:5 NKJV).

And *how* do you test yourself? The apostle John gave a very simple litmus test. He wrote, "By this we know that we know Him, if we keep His commandments" (1 John 2:3 NKJV). It doesn't get much simpler than that.

But which commandments are most important? According to Matthew 22:36–39, the two greatest commands—the ones you must make *certain* to obey—are to love God with all your heart and to love others as you love yourself. John also gave a very simple answer, saying, "This is His commandment: that we should believe on the name of His Son Jesus Christ and love one another" (1 John 3:23 NKJV).

There are a number of other doctrines that you must believe to be sound in the faith, but it's absolutely foundational to love and believe in God and His Son and to genuinely love your neighbor. If you have this foundation in place, you cannot only be assured that your faith is genuine, but you'll be certain to *grow* as a Christian.

ENTERING INTO GOD'S PRESENCE

Let us come before his presence with thanksgiving.
PSALM 95:2 KJV

The book of Psalms commands God's people to come before His presence with thankful hearts and even to "come before his presence with singing" (Psalm 100:2 KJV). In Old Testament times, the temple in Jerusalem was the place where God sometimes manifested Himself as the Shekinah glory in the innermost chamber, the Holy of Holies. Thus, when people entered the temple, they went with an attitude of reverence and awe, offering thanks to God for His goodness and singing songs of praise.

Likewise today, when you worship God, it brings you into His presence. As a Christian, you must remember that you're not praying to a distant deity who may or may not be listening, but you are entering into the very throne room of God. "Let us therefore come boldly unto the throne of grace, that we may obtain mercy, and find grace to help in time of need" (Hebrews 4:16 KJV). You have an audience with your Father, and He's attentive to what you're saying.

But have you ever prayed and, while you were praying, realized that although you were speaking words, you didn't really have faith that you were actually talking to God? You weren't quite sure that He was listening? The problem may have been that you failed to enter His presence *before* you began praying.

Before you begin asking God for things, make sure that you've entered into His presence. And one of the best ways to do that is with a thankful heart and praise.

GETTING DISTRACTED

"While your servant was busy here and there, the man disappeared."

1 KINGS 20:40 NIV

One day a prophet of God called out to King Ahab after a critical campaign and said, "Your servant went into the thick of the battle, and someone came to me with a captive and said, 'Guard this man. If he is missing, it will be your life for his life. . . .' While your servant was busy here and there, the man disappeared" (1 Kings 20:39–40 NIV).

This was a parable to show Ahab that he, king of Israel, was guilty for letting the wicked king of Aram go free after he had defeated him. However, let's focus here on *this* important thought: Many men have, at times, become so busy with a little here and there that they failed to focus on what was truly important. They allowed themselves to get sidetracked in nonessentials, and before they knew it, they'd fiddled away their time. Either they got continually distracted from a task or else they simply kept procrastinating.

The Bible tells you that you must cultivate the virtue of self-control (2 Peter 1:6 NIV). Paul said that men of God must be "self-controlled. . .and disciplined" (Titus 1:8 NIV). Even if you're bored with a task, such as a project at work, you must put forth the effort to focus on it and finish it. Even if you shy away from a responsibility because it's difficult or unpleasant, such as disciplining a child, roll up your sleeves and do it. You'll be glad you did.

CONTROLLING YOUR EYES

"I made a covenant with my eyes not to look with lust at a young woman."

JOB 31:1 NLT

Job lived during an era when polygamy was acceptable, yet he had only one wife. And wealthy men who didn't want the complication of extra marriages could simply take concubines. Job was the richest man in the East, yet he was satisfied with *one* woman. It helped that she was—judging by the beauty their daughters inherited (Job 42:15)—exceptionally lovely. But *most* men's eyes still would've wandered. Why didn't Job's?

Job realized that unless he determined ahead of time not to look lustfully at beautiful women, that his eyes naturally *would* wander—and one thing would lead to another. So he made a covenant (a commitment, a promise) *not* to allow his eyes to linger. Then, when faced with temptation, he refused to lust.

In modern times, men are constantly being bombarded with sexually provocative sights, both in the media and in real life. Even if you don't go looking for it, it can ambush you. If you haven't given thought to the matter ahead of time and determined your reaction, you almost can't help but gawk. But it can be very habit-forming and addictive.

The secret to victory is to gain control of your thoughts *beforehand* and determine not to look in lust, even if a woman deliberately tempts you. "Do not lust in your heart after her beauty or let her captivate you with her eyes" (Proverbs 6:25 NIV). Look away, if necessary. Ask God to help you. And don't give up.

CONFIDENT IN CHRIST

In him and through faith in him we may approach
God with freedom and confidence.

Ephesians 3:12 NIV

So often when men pray to God for a pressing need, a sense of sinfulness rises up to discourage them. The thoughts frequently come in waves: *You're unworthy. God won't answer your prayers. You might as well stop praying.* This is the voice of the enemy. His name, Satan, means "accuser" in Hebrew, and he doesn't just accuse *you* of sin. The Bible calls him "the accuser of our brethren" (Revelation 12:10 NKJV). He accuses *all* believers.

If you've given your heart to Christ, God has forgiven you and made you an heir of His eternal kingdom. If there's current sin that you haven't repented of, however, it will hinder God from blessing you in this life (Isaiah 59:1–2). That's why His Holy Spirit convicts you to repent (John 16:7–8).

But know this also: God *will* forgive you as you confess your failings to Him (1 John 1:9). The devil may try to accuse and condemn you, telling you that God won't forgive you—but don't listen to that lie! God *does* forgive. "Let us therefore come boldly to the throne of grace, that we may obtain mercy and find grace to help in time of need" (Hebrews 4:16 NKJV).

Are you in a time of need? Are you desperate for mercy? Christ's death on the cross, His shed blood, has made the way to His Father's throne open. Your sins are forgiven in Christ. You can come to God's throne with your prayer requests, boldly and with confidence.

GOD CARES ENOUGH TO ACT

Anyone who wants to approach God must believe both that he exists and that he cares enough to respond to those who seek him.

HEBREWS 11:6 MSG

You can believe in God yet lack faith that He cares enough to respond to your heartfelt prayers. Many men believe that God exists and sent His Son to die for their sins; they even concede that He answered prayers in Bible times, but they have little faith that He *still* does. They've been disappointed when past prayers weren't answered, and this has led them to believe that God doesn't involve Himself with people today except in truly unusual circumstances.

They basically believe that God has already done about as much as He is ever *going* to do, and that from here on, it's up to people to work hard, seize opportunities, and take care of themselves. Small wonder that they don't bother to spend much time in prayer! No surprise that they end up thinking that they can pretty much manage life without God's help. They believe that they *have* to.

It's true that God expects you to work hard to provide for yourself and your family and that He expects you to think hard to solve many of your problems, but God is still very active in the world. He still helps the helpless. And He still helps ordinary people who find themselves in unexpected difficulties.

Yes, He cares. And yes, He responds to those who earnestly seek Him. But you have to continually seek Him and not give up easily.

FEELING LIKE A FAILURE

*God is not unjust; he will not forget your work and the love you
have shown him as you have helped his people.*

HEBREWS 6:10 NIV

Sometimes you may feel like a failure, as if your whole life of
attempting to serve God has amounted to nothing. . .or to precious
little. What do you have to show for years of faithfulness? You
haven't even managed to lead your neighbor to the Lord. And
then there's that rebellious child who, despite your admonitions
and prayers, seems determined to go his or her own willful way.

Isaiah expressed his frustration this way: "I said, 'I have labored
in vain; I have spent my strength for nothing at all. Yet what is due
me is in the LORD's hand, and my reward is with my God' " (Isaiah
49:4 NIV). Even though he was despondent, he still couldn't help but
believe that God saw his heart and would reward him accordingly.

Hebrews 6:10 (NIV) says, "God is not unjust; he will not forget
your work and the love you have shown him as you have helped
his people." He sees everything you do, and because He's *not*
unjust, He will surely reward you. After all, by helping His people
you were showing love for God Himself. The same principle is at
play in the following verse: "Whoever is kind to the poor lends
to the LORD, and he will reward them for what they have done"
(Proverbs 19:17 NIV).

It's worth it to serve the Lord. You may feel like you've failed,
but God sees your faithfulness.

PRACTICING HOSPITALITY

When God's people are in need, be ready to help them.
Always be eager to practice hospitality.

ROMANS 12:13 NLT

The ancient Hebrews were urged to show kindness to strangers, to show hospitality by taking them into their homes for the night (Job 31:32). They were expected to feed them and were responsible to protect guests under their roof. Examples of this are Lot taking in two strangers (who turned out to be angels) in Sodom, and the old man in Gibeah taking in the man from Ephraim and his concubine (Genesis 19:1–3; Judges 19:14–21).

These days, such hospitality is rare. With so much crime and users eager to take advantage of soft-hearted people, it's considered dangerous and unadvisable. Granted, you should use wisdom when inviting strangers into your home for the night.

But the Bible still says, "*Always* be *eager* to practice hospitality" (Romans 12:13 NLT, emphasis added). So let's look at other important ways of showing hospitality. What about when a new family comes to your church, doesn't know anyone, and needs friends? Are you eager to practice hospitality? Do you talk with your wife about inviting them over for lunch? Do you help them get settled into your town?

And what about when poor families in your church are struggling without basic needs—without warm clothes, food, or other necessities? Do you simply smile, wave, and say, "Depart in peace, be ye warmed and filled" (James 2:15–16 KJV), or do you reach out in practical ways to help them?

Keep your eyes open. There are many ways to be "a lover of hospitality" today (Titus 1:8 KJV).

AVOID PRIDE OF ACCOMPLISHMENT

By the grace of God I am what I am, and His grace toward me was not in vain; but I labored more abundantly than they all, yet not I, but the grace of God which was with me.

1 CORINTHIANS 15:10 NKJV

After Jesus departed, His apostles began to proclaim the Gospel. Jesus had told them, "You shall be witnesses to Me in Jerusalem, and in all Judea and Samaria, and to the end of the earth" (Acts 1:8 NKJV), and He had commanded, "Go into all the world and preach the gospel" (Mark 16:15 NKJV). However, for the next twenty years, all twelve apostles remained in Jerusalem, content to preach mostly in nearby Judea and Samaria.

Paul, meanwhile, was going "into all the world," to far-flung cities of the Roman Empire. So he wasn't exaggerating when he said, "I labored more abundantly than they all." But those accomplishments didn't make Paul think that he was better than others. He had just finished stating, "I am the least of the apostles. . .not worthy to be called an apostle" (1 Corinthians 15:9 NKJV).

Paul was aware that God was using him to accomplish great things, but he also knew that it was the power of God doing the healing miracles, anointing him to speak, and changing lives—not him. And he was also painfully aware of his own unworthiness.

When you accomplish something great, don't put on false humility and say it's nothing. If it was praiseworthy, acknowledge the fact. Admit that God used you. But be sure to give Him the praise for using you.

CAST YOUR CARES ON GOD

Cast your cares on the LORD and he will sustain you;
he will never let the righteous be shaken.

PSALM 55:22 NIV

This passage of scripture has been a source of great comfort to millions of believers, yet some people protest, "I wish it *were* that simple! When huge problems come, you simply calmly hand them to God and He takes care of everything?" This is a valid question, so let's look at this verse in context.

Earlier in the psalm, David spoke of serious threats, of conspiracies, of battles raging against him, and of the stinging betrayal of friends. (This likely happened during the civil war when Absalom revolted.) David confessed his fear, saying, "My heart is in anguish within me; the terrors of death have fallen on me. Fear and trembling have beset me" (vv. 4–5).

David was eventually able to cast his cares on God and experience peace, but it wasn't a quick or easy process. He also had to plan, strategize, and lead his forces against his enemies' attacks. And he had to pray desperately day after day, several times a day. He said, "Evening, morning and noon I cry out in distress" (v. 17). David *continually* cast his cares and fears upon God, until he finally received assurance that God had heard him and would answer.

Yes, you *can* simply calmly hand small problems over to God, but when huge problems assail you, you may have to desperately and repeatedly cast your cares on Him. And He will answer.

RECOVERING THE LOST

*If you know people who have wandered off from God's truth,
don't write them off. Go after them. Get them back and
you will have rescued precious lives from destruction.*

JAMES 5:20 MSG

It's easy to write off people who have backslid from the faith. You tell yourself that it's a free country, and it's their decision after all. And these things are true. Plus, you tell yourself, they knew full well what they were doing when they went back to their worldly ways. And that too is true. But the question is: Are you *concerned* about them? Do you pray for them and reach out to them?

Jesus said:

> *"What man of you, having a hundred sheep, if he loses one of them, does not leave the ninety-nine in the wilderness, and go after the one which is lost until he finds it? And when he has found it, he lays it on his shoulders, rejoicing. And when he comes home, he calls together his friends and neighbors, saying to them, 'Rejoice with me, for I have found my sheep which was lost!' "*
> (Luke 15:4–6 NKJV)

Jesus took it for granted that *every* person listening would be motivated to scour the desert for a lost sheep, asking, "What man does *not* go after it until he finds it?" And how much more valuable is a person than a sheep?

In the end, the person must make up his own mind whether he'll return to the Lord or not, but you can be a big part of helping restore him.

THE NATURE OF LOVE

*If I have a faith that can move mountains, but do not have love,
I am nothing. If I give all I possess to the poor. . .that I
may boast, but do not have love, I gain nothing.*

1 CORINTHIANS 13:2–3 NIV

You may wonder, "How could I give all that I possess to alleviate the suffering of the poor, and *not* have love? Isn't such giving a clear proof of love?" Besides, Jesus told the rich young ruler, "Sell your possessions and give to the poor, and you will have treasure in heaven" (Matthew 19:21 NIV). But Paul clarifies that even if you give all that you have to the poor, but have selfish motives for doing so ("that I may boast"), you'll gain nothing and receive no reward.

Paul goes on in verses 4–7 to give the definition of love. Love is *not* boastful or easily angered; love is patient, kind, humble, honors others, seeks others' benefit, and keeps no record of wrongs. So even if you go through an outward show of charity but are boastful, easily angered, impatient, envious, proud, self-seeking, or unforgiving, you aren't motivated by God's love.

Jesus also promised that if you have great faith, you can say to a mountain, "Be removed and be cast into the sea," and it will be done (Matthew 21:21 NKJV), but as Paul pointed out, "If I have a faith that can move mountains, but do not have love, I am nothing." So *love*—love God and others—first and foremost, and you'll be greatly rewarded in all you do.

INNER ROOMS

"But when you pray, go into your room, close the door and
pray to your Father, who is unseen. Then your Father,
who sees what is done in secret, will reward you."

MATTHEW 6:6 NIV

When you really want to pray, any place can be a secret place.

Jesus told us not to pray outwardly in ways that draw attention to ourselves. He told us to go into an inner room, where nobody can see us, and trust the One who hears us in that secret place.

But an inner room doesn't have to be an inner room. I've got a hundred inner rooms that I use to hide the fact that I'm praying.

Nobody really believes that you're praying if you're also chewing gum. Chewing gum makes a good prayer room.

Nobody really believes that you're praying if you've got headphones coming from your phone or iPod. This is especially true when you're doing that little rock-and-roll head bob. They don't know that you're emphasizing your prayers, not rocking to the music. Headphones make a good prayer room.

Nobody really believes that you're praying if you've got your nose in a book. . .like this one.

Nobody believes you're praying if you're floating on a lake or the ocean in a water hammock with a baseball cap shielding your face from the sun.

Nobody believes you're praying if you're writing or typing intently on your laptop. . .only you're typing your prayers.

A hundred prayer rooms. Ways to pray "without ceasing" (1 Thessalonians 5:17 NKJV), in secret, to the God who sees in secret.

NERVOUS, NERVOUS, NERVOUS

*For what I received I passed on to you as of first importance:
that Christ died for our sins according to the Scriptures, that he
was buried, that he was raised on the third day according to
the Scriptures. . . . But by the grace of God I am what I am.*

1 CORINTHIANS 15:3–4, 10 NIV

We are God's ambassadors. This means that people will hold God to whatever we say about Him. On top of that, if what we tell people about God is wrong, He isn't going to back it up.

Yet He will hold us accountable for it.

Quite a spot to be on. We'd better explain Him correctly, or God will hold us accountable. As will the world.

We catch it coming, and we catch it going. Who on earth can handle that kind of responsibility? The answer is. . .nobody can. I can't. You can't.

That's why the stories He asks us to tell are so breathtakingly simple. Whether it's the story of Jesus or our own story that we tell the world, they're both almost impossible to get wrong!

Plus we have the Holy Spirit to back us up, to give our words power, and to prod us if we go off on some tangent.

And He has left us His Word, which tells the life of Jesus and what He did to save us four times—in black and white, unmistakable. And surely we know our own testimony! This isn't metaphysics. It isn't some convoluted quest for enlightenment. There is little to be nervous about.

SIN?

Dear friends, if our hearts do not condemn us, we have confidence before God and receive from him anything we ask, because we keep his commands and do what pleases him.

1 JOHN 3:21–22 NIV

Overcoming sin: it's the challenge of every Christian's life. We struggle, we strain, we "put things before the Lord" that we don't like in our lives, we attack one area at a time, and we do a lot of good. We trust God, we ask for the Holy Spirit to help us in practical ways, and He does it. This is all great, but there is a side of this that gets little notice. Most of us overcome sin daily in ways we don't even recognize, ways we can easily build on.

Church. Worshiping God. That's not sin. Shut-in visitation, prison visitation, prayer or devotions with the family, devotional books. No sin there. Relaxation. Recreation. Exercise. Working on the "honey-do" list. Yes, I know it can be overdone. But when I ride my bike, am I sinning? Not likely. I'm staying healthy; I can maybe live and serve the Lord longer. No sin there.

Family barbecues? Sitting on the porch with my wife? Any sin there? No!

When we spend our energy for God's kingdom, when we spend our energy on the good, we don't leave energy or time for sin. That is, indeed, overcoming sin; and we barely even realize it. Then, when we look at all the sins that don't happen in our lives, it gives us momentum to build on, to keep sin out of our lives.

MYSTERY

Now we see only a reflection as in a mirror; then we shall see face to face. Now I know in part; then I shall know fully, even as I am fully known.

1 Corinthians 13:12 NIV

Mystery.

It's a shame it's such a dirty word to so many people.

But if we can't live with some mystery—and some mysteries—we're likely to be uncomfortable in the kingdom of God.

Partly, it's a personality trait. Some of us are just left-brained, mathematically and mechanically inclined, who like to figure out everything to the point of perfection. My dad was like that: an accountant, an amazing mathematician, a bit of a perfectionist. Though we looked very much alike, our minds worked in exactly opposite ways. He was the epitome of a left-brained, mathematical, systematic thinker; I'm the epitome of a right-brained, poetic, emotional thinker. So what surprised me was the degree to which he expressed the wonder, the awe, the mystery of his faith—the degree to which this precise man was willing to admit what he didn't know, what no one can know. . .yet. I think it strongly affected how I came to accept the faith.

It's a principle that's true throughout life: be confident of what you do know; readily admit what you don't know; don't shy away from what you can't know.

I have always been impressed that these are Paul's words—*Paul's* words, the words of the theological genius who wrote *Romans*: "We see but a poor reflection in a mirror. . ."

GOD'S WILL

Do not withhold good from those to whom it is due,
when it is in your power to act. Do not say to your neighbor,
"Come back tomorrow and I'll give it to you"
—when you already have it with you.

PROVERBS 3:27–28 NIV

Some obvious things just plain escaped me for a long, long time.

There are a couple of obvious ideas about God's will that I didn't combine for years. Idea One: "Nobody's here by accident." God knows where we're going to go, therefore He must have prepared things for us. Idea Two: We all need to find out what God wants us to do, and we shouldn't wait any longer than we have to before we find out.

Here's the combination that escaped me for the longest time. I am where I am; and if I come into contact with something that needs to be done for God, and I can do it, I should do it. So I think I've "found God's will." It always seemed such an elusive concept.

But in most cases, God's will isn't elusive, slippery, or unclear at all. The problem for me is that my combination almost makes it too clear. I'd rather be way more "spiritual" about things, more analytical. But Galatians 6:10 (NIV) brings me back to earth: "Therefore, as we have opportunity, let us do good to all people, especially to those who belong to the family of believers."

We are where we are by God's will. The needs we are presented with, we should meet if we can. To me, that's 90 percent of God's will, plain and simple.

GOD'S HONESTY

In those days Hezekiah became ill and was at the point of death. The prophet Isaiah son of Amoz went to him and said, "This is what the LORD says: Put your house in order, because you are going to die."

ISAIAH 38:1 NIV

It was the only time I ever laughed in my wife's face. I had just graduated with a degree in English and journalism. But no job. She said I should get my teaching certificate, that I'd be a great high school teacher. I was way too sophisticated for that. I almost took it as an insult. But I also have this wacky sense of humor. . .

Fourteen years of teaching high school later, I was glad for her honesty.

If we can't handle God's honesty, we will never be able to handle His truth.

Earlier, my wife had made a point that she *didn't* need to make: When I communicated with people, I was either way above their heads or way too blunt. God had already been showing me this as people who I thought were friends would begin shying away as they got to know me.

So later, after teaching, I worked as a hospital chaplain for seven years. If you can't be tactful, you can't be a chaplain.

God's truth is easy; His honesty—truth in the particulars—is hard.

Hezekiah reacted to God's honesty, repented of his attitudes, and lived. He didn't need God's truth; he needed God's honesty.

As do we.

Our lives depend on it.

HOW LONG?

"As in the days when you came out of Egypt,
I will show them my wonders."

MICAH 7:15 NIV

The women have to avert their eyes, cover them, or the pain snaps through their eyes straight into the front of their heads. They know it's the right tomb. It has the same stone, though it's been moved. And that's the cloth that Jesus' body was rolled in, blood and all.

But suddenly two men are there in lightning-bright garments. Such brilliance replacing such gloom throws them to the ground. They're stunned and amazed. Something unimaginable is happening. But the instruction is simple: "Get up, and go tell his disciples."

Later, they follow Jesus north to Galilee. Jesus is speaking, and a low cloud rolls down the slope—they'd seen it happen on these mountains a thousand times—but then this cloud is blowing back up to the sky with Jesus on it, hands outstretched.

Then, suddenly that headache again: the same two men (*men?*) blazingly dressed, and they barely hear what these men say because of the wonder of how they look and their amazement at what just happened. They can't stop staring. But then the two men say, "What are you doing standing here? He told you what to do!"

How long has it been since God's wonders have left us speechless? Have we seen grace in the trust of a child, grandeur in a sunset, a forest, or a tall ship? How long has it been since an angel has had to bring us back down to earth while we were standing open-mouthed with wonder?

STRIPES AND PLAIDS

*However, each one of you also must
love his wife as he loves himself.*

EPHESIANS 5:33 NIV

Dad was the typical retiree. He had his old clothes, and he wore them. Striped and plaid, gray and khaki, he wore them. When he went out with Mom, he always looked great. But at home or just to a store? Striped and plaid. Mismatched everything. The typical retiree.

So I finally concluded something about how I dress. It's important how I look when I'm out with my wife. But something else occurred to me. It's just as important how I look *for* her. When I'm painting or working on the car or the boat or the lawnmower, I get out my junk clothes. But when she has to look at me, I've determined to dress to please her. Nothing fancy; just take a little care.

It isn't any harder to dress in stuff she likes than to dress carelessly. And this attitude bleeds over into other areas too.

This isn't just for wives but for friends, family, the girlfriend, the fiancée. It's an extension of the attitude the Lord wants me to have in every part of my life: I need to do things for others a little better than I have to.

Especially for my wife. More especially: when I don't *have* to.

RAISED FOR OUR FORGIVENESS

*He was delivered over to death for our sins and
was raised to life for our justification.*

ROMANS 4:25 NIV

Peter and John stayed close to Jesus after He was arrested, and John—being "known to the high priest"—was allowed into the high priest's confines, where Jesus was first interrogated. John went back to bring Peter in (John 18:15–16). It was shortly after this that Peter denied, with curses, that he even knew Jesus.

It is a measure of Peter's later honesty and humility that he let the account of his denial be put into writing. But I think I know why. It would explain his extraordinary relief at seeing his Lord alive again.

Peter was the first disciple to enter Jesus' tomb. And in Luke 24:34, reference is made to Jesus appearing to Simon Peter alone, before the famous "closed doors" appearances to the eleven disciples. Why this concentration on Peter?

The denial.

Here's Luke again: When Peter disowned Jesus for the third time, "the Lord turned and looked straight at Peter. . .and [Peter] went outside and wept bitterly" (Luke 22:61–62 NIV).

What an incredible moment. I'm almost surprised it was Judas who committed suicide. Peter had heaped on Jesus His own personal crucifixion. So when Peter met Jesus alive again and found that He would absolve him from his guilt in person *because He had risen*, the relief—mixed with shame at having denied his Lord—must have hit Peter like a tidal wave.

Crucified to forgive our sins, risen to deliver that forgiveness. What a delivery that was for Peter!

And for us.

TOMORROW, AND TOMORROW, AND TOMORROW

*Now listen, you who say, "Today or tomorrow we will go to this or
that city, spend a year there, carry on business and make money."
Why, you do not even know what will happen tomorrow. What is
your life? You are a mist that appears for a little while and then
vanishes. Instead, you ought to say, "If it is the Lord's will,
we will live and do this or that." As it is, you boast in
your arrogant schemes. All such boasting is evil.*

JAMES 4:13–16 NIV

I have this terrible feeling about what God thinks of all our plans.
We express ourselves with a confidence in the future that God
calls pride. The fact that we are accustomed to doing it makes it
no less an offense. It doesn't matter how culturally ingrained our
offenses are; they're still offenses.

I know many, many Christians, including myself when I'm not
careful, who exude confidence in the future and in our plans
for it. "Next year we will implement such and such a program;
these investments will come in at X percent; after five years our
membership will increase to X." This scripture calls such statements
arrogance. That it is culturally ingrained arrogance doesn't help.

It is born of rank self-sufficiency. It's not the healthy self-
sufficiency of doing our best and taking our responsibilities
seriously; it's the self-sufficiency of claiming authority over an
area that is exclusively God's domain: the *future*.

So God says make your plans, but don't trust your plans. Make
your plans with a very light hand, and. . .

Trust Me.

SPIRITUAL DEPENDENCY

Recalling your tears, I long to see you, so that I may be filled with joy. I am reminded of your sincere faith, which first lived in your grandmother Lois and in your mother Eunice and, I am persuaded, now lives in you also.

2 Timothy 1:4–5 niv

It's one of the saddest situations I encounter: spiritual dependency.

Too often Christians let others become their compass, and when the compass is gone, the dependent Christian has no pole to point to. So he or she just spins.

Paul wrote to Timothy, the son of his soul, what Paul probably knew would be his last letter. In it, he gave the key to avoiding spiritual dependency, quoted above.

There are those who feed off others' spiritual dependence on them: some pastors, parents, or just people with dominating personalities. And there are those who make themselves dependent, who might simply be followers or might admire another's supposed spirituality. But here's the key: they can somehow never bring themselves to actually make that spirituality a part of themselves.

Such was not the case with Timothy. The spiritual tradition and maturity that lived in his mother and grandmother, and in Paul himself, now lived in him. It's the opposite of spiritual dependency. Spiritual dependents are empty of faith—and of almost everything else. They depend on someone else's faith.

I simply ask them: Are you walking in your mentor's footsteps, or is he taking all the steps for you?

They need encouragement from those whose walk is steady. . . to start taking their own steps before it's too late.

GUS

*Remember those in prison as if you were together with
them in prison, and those who are mistreated
as if you yourselves were suffering.*

HEBREWS 13:3 NIV

Tenth grade. I had just started at Howe Military School. I needed a friend, and I found one.

Agustin Benitez. I don't remember if we were assigned a room together in the Company B barracks or whether we requested one. I did know that no one wanted to room with little Gus because he ground his teeth when he slept. Didn't bother me. I had grown up in a house less than a hundred yards from the Grand Trunk Western railroad tracks, with only a few trees between. Nothing kept me awake!

We normally switched roommates every three weeks. But Gus and I stayed together through at least three switches. Gus fascinated me, and his life angered me.

Gus's family were refugees from the Castro regime. (His brother was in Company A.) And Gus was intense. They had fled Cuba when Gus was eight. Gus remembered—vividly remembered. Gus's life had a focus—an intense, purposeful, meaningful focus—that my life lacked.

Free Cuba.

Free Cuba.

And his focus helped form my focus: Christians persecuted and murdered by communist regimes.

And a free Cuba.

I've lost contact with Gus, but I haven't lost contact with persecuted Christians. Gus's bulldog tenacity for a free Cuba became the battery powering my prayers and efforts in behalf of Christians—and non-Christians—being persecuted by communists and Muslims.

They need our daily prayers.

So does Gus, and everyone else who works to free them.

A LITTLE PLATO

*"Because you have rejected the word of the Lord,
he has rejected you as king."*

1 Samuel 15:23 NIV

Even God had a hard time finding a decent politician.

The ancient Greek philosopher Plato said many wise things. His "Allegory of the Cave" describes a world where people basically waste their lives on shadows of the real things. It still describes life on this planet quite well.

He gave another allegory, the "Allegory of the Ship." It's simple: There is a struggle over who is going to be captain of a ship. Plato asks the question: Who is likely to win? Someone who is good at running a ship or someone who is good at gaining power?

You know the answer.

We in the United States live in an elective republic. The same question applies: Who is more likely to win an election? Someone who is adept at administering my township/city/county/state/country or someone who is adept at getting my vote? The two skill sets are often mutually exclusive. Plato's point is excellently made. How often do we elect people who have no clue how to represent us? It's because the people who want power the most are generally the ones who get power. These are not generally good public *servants*.

We have to be very discerning with our vote and our support. The first person to want power is the last person we should give power to. I look for candidates—especially believers—who have a history of effective administration and *service* in their backgrounds, and I support them.

If I can find any.

DELIGHTFUL PRAYER

*Take delight in the L*ORD*, and he will give
you the desires of your heart.*

PSALM 37:4 NIV

The last part of that verse is so nice; the first part is so hard!

In this psalm, many prayers are answered, yet the word *prayer* is never mentioned. We are told to "commit," to "wait," to "delight in" the Lord, and then He will give us "the desires of our heart," He will "make your righteous reward shine" (Psalm 37:6 NIV). But the word *pray* is nowhere to be found.

I ask myself how few things there are that I actually "delight in"—not just "like," not "enjoy," but "delight in." There aren't many. And how many other things must I avoid "delighting in" if I am truly to "delight in" the Lord?

All of them. Here's the mystery: Psalm 37 treats this process of shedding all delights other than Yahweh Himself as the process of *prayer*. How do I know? Because it's answered! It's the commitment to the Lord, the delighting in, the waiting for, that is answered.

Prayer is the growing process of the child of the living God, no more and no less. It is the devotion to Jesus that multiplies, differentiates, and strengthens the cells of our reborn spirits. Prayer is the expression of desire for our spirit's Father to work His will in ways His child cannot. But the child does not think of himself: His eyes are on his Father. He loves what his Father loves, delights in what his Father delights in. That process is. . .

Prayer.

And it will be answered.

JOSEPH AND POTIPHAR

When [Joseph's] master [Potiphar] heard the story his wife
told him, saying, "This is how your slave treated me," he burned
with anger. Joseph's master took him and put him in prison,
the place where the king's prisoners were confined.

GENESIS 39:19–20 NIV

Potiphar's wife accused Joseph of trying to seduce her, when it
was actually the other way around. "She caught him by his cloak
and said, 'Come to bed with me!' But he left his cloak in her hand
and ran" (Genesis 39:12 NIV). When I've heard it referred to that
Potiphar "burned with anger," it's always been assumed that he
was angry at Joseph. I looked again; that's not *what it says*. It just
says Potiphar was furious. If he was furious at Joseph—a slave from
parts unknown—his option was clear: kill him.

But he doesn't. I think he knows full well that his wife is lying
(certainly not for the first time!) and that he'll have to take over
the responsibilities that Joseph was handling. But he can't side
with the slave against his wife. So he treats Joseph about as well
as he can, sending him to a prison for the privileged, though that's
still no picnic.

Joseph is forgotten for two years, then begins his rise from the
ashes to vice president of Egypt.

And all because God saw Joseph doing one thing, the one thing
that He longs for from all His people.

He saw Joseph refusing to sin. We should take a hint.

Refuse to sin. It's where everything else begins.

GOD'S LITTLE HELPERS

Now Sarai, Abram's wife, had borne him no children.
But she had an Egyptian slave named Hagar; so she said to Abram,
"The LORD has kept me from having children. Go, sleep with
my slave; perhaps I can build a family through her."

GENESIS 16:1–2 NIV

God promises Abram (Abraham) a son, who will be the beginning of a great nation. This promise of descendants is repeated and repeated. Eventually Sarai (Sarah), who is old and barren, gets the bright idea of giving her servant, Hagar, to Abraham to bear this child of promise. This is not an unusual arrangement for that time. They would of course prefer to have children together, but Sarai thinks she is too old.

So Sarai, God's little helper, decides to give Yahweh's promise a little boost with her own little plan. The first result of this plan is hatred between the mothers and their children. The end result of this plan is the deathly, scorpions-in-a-bottle hatred between Arabs/Muslims and Jews that continues unabated to this day. This hatred continues because, while only the Jews' claim is legitimate, both are true.

Why doesn't God reveal to us the whole timeline of His plans for our lives? Why does He force us to live with day-to-day, one-step-at-a-time trust in His long-range plans?

He remembers Sarai and Abram, and the cost of humans playing God's little helper.

Let's let God be God. Let's do what's at hand with all our heart (Colossians 3:23–24) while we listen for God's leading; then let's trust the God who knows the end from the beginning.

THE BEST THINGS

"His master replied, 'Well done, good and faithful servant! You have been faithful with a few things; I will put you in charge of many things. Come and share your master's happiness!' "

MATTHEW 25:21 NIV

I once had a very wise Bible college professor who said something that has stuck with me. (He also had a name I can't forget: Halton D. Starr. It's the only time I ever encountered the first name "Halton.") There are some things I'll spend a lifetime applying, and this is one of them:

> *You don't get the best things*
> *by going after the best things.*
> *You get the best things*
> *by going after the important things.*

I know what he meant by "best things," because he explained it. "Best things" meant loving relationships, good marriages, good children, spiritual truths and gifts, effective ministry, peace of mind, happiness, even financial security; all the stuff that makes life meaningful. He meant that you don't wind up with all that good stuff by going after it directly.

You get that big stuff by minding the little stuff along the way. Take "happiness," for example. We don't get "happiness" by saying to ourselves, "I'm going to make myself 'happy' today!" Happiness comes almost unconsciously when we get other things right: our relationships, our obedience to God, our daily walk with Him.

Same thing with love. It doesn't come today because I sweat and strain after love. It comes because—and while—I'm doing the little things right with folks, like kindness and concern.

Get the little things right—the *essential* little things—and the big things tend to follow.

REBELLION

But Peter and John replied, "Which is right in God's eyes: to listen to you, or to him? You be the judges! As for us, we cannot help speaking about what we have seen and heard."

ACTS 4:19–20 NIV

I wrote a saying. I want to print it on a T-shirt for my next trip to Cedar Point. On the front, where the pocket would be, I'm going to print *Rebel for Jesus* and on the back *Rebel Against All Social Convention: Do What's **Right***.

When I was a teacher, I was cosponsor of an exchange program among some students at my Christian high school and students from a partner school in Moscow. This was about six years after communism fell in Russia. When the Russian students came here, they split their time between my school and a public high school. Many things surprised them; one thing freaked them out. They were shocked to find that in our "free" country, the Bible couldn't be taught in our public schools. It was the first thing that changed in their schools after communism fell. Bible classes started popping up immediately.

They thought that we Christians were rather cowardly for not rebelling against such limitations. They were probably right. But sometimes we rebel in the ways we can.

Sometimes we rebel for righteousness at a pole.

And then we spread that rebellion with all the power, wit, tact, energy, creativity, and wisdom we can.

Not angry rebels—joyous rebels. Smiling rebels. Rebels for the faith.

Walk tall and straight, rebels, like the pole you meet at. And let your smile wave like the flag that tops it.

DARKNESS ON THE OFFENSE

"If then the light within you is darkness, how great is that darkness!"

MATTHEW 6:23 NIV

I've investigated this for years. It is an investigation that has often brought me to tears, not the least for myself. I have spent my life investigating darkness.

It's a pity, really. People have been looking for the middle ground between darkness and light for generations. They call it "agnosticism" or "humanism" or any number of other names. They live as though some middle ground is there. But then. . .it's lost again. No place to hide from either light or darkness. For anybody.

For I have found—and here is the danger—that Jesus was right when He said that darkness is not the *absence* of something. It is an offensive, spreading, radiating force.

The sad thing that I have seen is that there is no neutral act. There are only radiations of darkness or radiations of light. Jesus spoke here of the "light" that is in us being "darkness." That is, darkness *radiates* from us just as light would: a self-centered woman who has "faith" in miracles—for herself; young men whose dullness of heart and lack of care about their own souls are the tread marks of the tanks of Satan; people thinking they're just "passing time."

Neutrality? Humbug! We're all on the offensive with *something*.

THE MIRACLE OF PSALM TWENTY-TWO

"My God, my God, why have you forsaken me?"
MARK 15:34 NIV

With these words, Jesus quoted the opening phrase of Psalm 22.

Yes, He was expressing His despair. The presence of sin will do that. But when a Jew of that time heard a portion of a psalm quoted, he would remember the whole psalm. Psalms were sung every Sabbath at the synagogue, so it's like any song you've heard since you were a kid: you remember the whole thing.

Psalm 22 was a psalm of shame for those who were crucifying Jesus. It predicted exactly what they were doing ("They hurl insults. . . . 'Let the LORD rescue him.'" Psalm 22:7–8 NIV). After they heard Jesus say this and were thus reminded of the whole psalm, they were gone!

It also predicts the result of this martyrdom: "All the families of the nations will bow down before him" (v. 27).

Not only did Jesus' Jewish hearers remember the whole psalm, but when Jesus quoted the first line, He remembered it too. So when He expresses the first lines, He also expresses the beautiful hope of the whole psalm: "He has. . .listened to his cry for help" (v. 24).

This is not just despair; this is not just torture predicted; it is despair leading to faith in a glorious future. Jesus was in such control that He could use this psalm to declare all of this to those around Him. . .

And to Himself.

God, help us to do the same in our times of despair.

FAMILY

Both the one who makes people holy and those who are made holy are of the same family. So Jesus is not ashamed to call them brothers and sisters. He says, "I will declare your name to my brothers and sisters; in the assembly I will sing your praises."

HEBREWS 2:11–12 NIV

Have you ever been in situations where there was nothing between you and your fellow believers but love, generosity, sharing, sympathy, worship? Even at its best, it doesn't usually last long.

But it reflects what God really wants:

A family.

Acting like a family.

In other words, acting righteously.

We live in a personal universe—by that, I mean this universe and the heavenly one. But how does God enjoy this universe? Is He enthralled with the beauty of the things He has invented? Does He have fun with the powers He has created?

Not so much. He loves the persons—angelic and human—He created it for.

His family: with Himself as our Father, Jesus as our Brother, and the universe as our home. And He wants us to be righteous, but not just living righteously as individuals, not just living in peace as individuals. What He's really after is an atmosphere of righteousness—an atmosphere of *family.*

So that everyone will want to be adopted.

SERENDIPITY

*Have the same mindset as Christ Jesus: Who, being in very nature
God, did not consider equality with God something to be used
to his own advantage; rather, he made himself nothing
by taking the very nature of a servant.*

Philippians 2:5–7 niv

There is a very interesting word in Philippians 2:6. In an earlier edition of the New International Version, translators use the phrase "something to be grasped." The implication is that Jesus didn't think of being God as something He had to hold tightly; He could let it go, lowering Himself to become a man. This is certainly true.

But there is another way this word can be translated: a windfall, a surprise, "serendipity." For Jesus, as He grew and became more aware, realizing that He was God as well as man was not a surprise, a windfall, a shock. His position as the Messiah didn't spring upon Him as an unexpected blessing, as it would have you or me. Equality with God—His existence as God—was a fact to Jesus, not a surprise.

We are to imitate His lack of surprise. We are to have His "attitude": God's presence should be a solid, trustworthy thing to us. Secure in it, we can thus let go of our position, in a sense, in order to relate to unbelievers and to less mature Christians. This was important to me as a teacher, relating to teenagers at all levels of Christian dedication; I was able to "lower myself" and communicate on their level because I was secure in mine.

We can most easily give away what we are most confident about.

COURAGE FOR THE FIGHT

"Have I not commanded you? Be strong and courageous.
Do not be afraid; do not be discouraged, for the LORD
your God will be with you wherever you go."

JOSHUA 1:9 NIV

Over the next few days, we will be examining the encouragement of God as found in the Bible. Nowhere is this illustrated more clearly than in Joshua 1:9, as Joshua's faithfulness is rewarded by his being allowed to enter the Promised Land.

Joshua and Caleb were two of twelve spies sent to reconnoiter the new land that God had promised to give to the people of Israel after the exodus from Egypt. As ten of the twelve spies tried to convince Israel that the enemy was too strong, Joshua and Caleb pleaded with the people instead:

> *"The land we passed through and explored is*
> *exceedingly good. If the LORD is pleased with us,*
> *he will lead us into that land, a land flowing with*
> *milk and honey, and will give it to us. Only do not*
> *rebel against the LORD. And do not be afraid of*
> *the people of the land, because we will devour*
> *them. Their protection is gone, but the LORD is*
> *with us. Do not be afraid of them."*
> (Numbers 14:7–9 NIV)

Now, standing on the precipice of the Promised Land, God gives Joshua a convincing promise of His presence. Hear this word of God to you today: What is God calling you to do for Him? How would you approach it if you heard these words as clearly as Joshua did?

FAITH WHEN IT REALLY COUNTS

"Do not rebel against the LORD. And do not be afraid of the people of the land, because we will devour them. Their protection is gone, but the LORD is with us. Do not be afraid of them."

NUMBERS 14:9 NIV

Joshua and Caleb were the only two men over forty years old who were allowed to enter the Promised Land. After forty years of wandering in the wilderness, these two men carried God's promise to their people as they faced the monumental task of taking the land that God had promised to them. Their courage is exemplified in today's passage as they urge their people to believe in God's presence, blessing, and encouragement.

Their faith in God was a gritty, all-encompassing, as-if-their-lives-depended-on-it kind of faith. Why? Because their lives actually *did* depend on God's promises. If Joshua was to lead Israel into God's promise, he would have to feel God's presence on a second-by-second basis and step out in faith, trusting that God would come through and stand true to His promises.

Understand this: Joshua's job as the leader of Israel was to encourage the people to attack fortified cities in the face of overwhelming odds. Through forty years, his confidence in God's strong arm had not wavered. And God rewarded Joshua's determined faith as He called him to bravery in the face of imminent battle.

Joshua's story of determined, consistent faith is strong encouragement for us today as well.

FORTITUDE IN THE FACE OF BAD NEWS

The Lord gave this command to Joshua son of Nun: "Be strong and courageous, for you will bring the Israelites into the land I promised them on oath, and I myself will be with you."

DEUTERONOMY 31:23 NIV

In Deuteronomy 31, Moses and Joshua have been called to the tent of meeting to hear from God. God tells Moses that the time for Moses' death is near. God Himself predicts the failures of the people of Israel to follow Him once they take possession of the Promised Land:

> *"These people will soon prostitute themselves to the foreign gods of the land they are entering. They will forsake me and break the covenant I made with them. And in that day I will become angry with them and forsake them; I will hide my face from them, and they will be destroyed."* (Deuteronomy 31:16–17 NIV)

Imagine being Joshua in this situation: called to move ahead into battle, knowing that the people he will lead will eventually "be destroyed" because of their unfaithfulness. At that moment, many men might simply ask, "Well then, what's the point?" But there's no sign that Joshua was deterred.

So often in life we find that we can only control how we react in the face of opposition or bad news; there's not much we can do to control the reactions or responses of others to adversity. And we find, as did Joshua, that God rewards our personal faith in Him when the going gets tough.

WE ALL NEED CONTINUED ENCOURAGEMENT

"Be strong and courageous, because you will lead these people to inherit the land I swore to their ancestors to give them."

Joshua 1:6 niv

Today's call to Joshua mirrors almost exactly the one we read in this morning's devotion. If Joshua had stood at the tent of meeting, seen the Lord's physical presence in the pillar of cloud, and heard His audible voice of encouragement, why did God feel it necessary to give Joshua this additional reminder?

That's a great question. Think for a moment about how you might answer that for yourself. In these post–New Testament days, we don't often hear of people being able to see and hear God's presence. Shouldn't this have been enough to encourage Joshua for the rest of his life?

Yet God knew Joshua would need to hear these words again. So often we, like the disciple Peter, move forward in faith and "step out of the boat," out of our comfort zone. But soon the waves of adversity rise around us, and our courage wavers (Matthew 14:22–33). God knew that Joshua would be leading a fearful people into a difficult situation, and that he would need God's continued reassurance.

How often do we find ourselves looking in fear at our surrounding circumstances rather than looking to God and trusting in His strength? Yet we can find that same reassurance by daily searching the scriptures for that guidance and by asking for God's encouragement through the Holy Spirit in our prayers.

PROSPERITY AND SUCCESS— GOD'S DEFINITION, NOT OURS

"Be strong and very courageous. Be careful to obey all the law my servant Moses gave you; do not turn from it to the right or to the left, that you may be successful wherever you go. Keep this Book of the Law always on your lips; meditate on it day and night, so that you may be careful to do everything written in it. Then you will be prosperous and successful."

JOSHUA 1:7–8 NIV

Every man longs to be prosperous and successful in life. We all want to be able to have a meaningful occupation, to provide for our families, and to lead the next generation to God. We want to live a faithful life in front of God and at the end hear the emphatic words, "Well done, good and faithful servant!" (Matthew 25:21 NIV)

Joshua's desire to be prosperous and successful was no different from ours. And the stakes were desperately high. In addition to leading a family, he was also leading a nation into hostile territory. And God gave him the surefire formula for success: an unwavering focus on God's revealed Word, leading to a resolute trust in God's promises.

Do not miss this word to you, *you personally,* today: the *only* sure way to prosperity and success, as God defines it, is by faithfully reading and following God's revealed Word. God has provided the path, with His promise of success, in His Word to you. Follow that template, and rest assured.

LOOKING BACK AT GOD'S FAITHFULNESS

*"Do not be afraid. Stand firm and you will see the deliverance
the Lord will bring you today. The Egyptians you see today
you will never see again. The Lord will fight for
you; you need only to be still."*

Exodus 14:13–14 NIV

As we watch Joshua prepare to lead the people of Israel into the Promised Land, let's look back for a moment at God's work in Joshua's past.

Moses and the Israelites, including Joshua, stood at the edge of the Red Sea. God had delivered them from slavery in Egypt, but Pharaoh, true to form, had changed his mind—he wanted his free slave labor back. So the Egyptian army pursued the nation of Israel as they left Egypt.

Panicked, the nation of Israel despaired at their impending slaughter. But God's reassurance to Moses was, in a word, astounding: "Moses, you don't have to lift a finger. I've got this."

Those of us who know the story know what happened:

> *But the Israelites went through the sea on dry
> ground, with a wall of water on their right and
> on their left. That day the Lord saved Israel from
> the hands of the Egyptians, and Israel saw the
> Egyptians lying dead on the shore. And when
> the Israelites saw the mighty hand of the Lord
> displayed against the Egyptians, the people
> feared the Lord and put their trust in him and in
> Moses his servant.* (Exodus 14:29–31 NIV)

Keep this story in mind today as you face your own adversity.

WORSHIP, NOT WARFARE

Joshua commanded the army, "Shout! For the LORD has given you the city!". . . When the trumpets sounded, the army shouted, and at the sound of the trumpet, when the men gave a loud shout, the wall collapsed; so everyone charged straight in, and they took the city.

JOSHUA 6:16, 20 NIV

Armed with the memory of the defeated Egyptians lying dead on the shore of the Red Sea, Joshua moved to take Jericho in faith, following perhaps the most bizarre battle plan ever executed. God wanted to demonstrate His superiority in the face of Israel's fortified opposition, so He commanded Joshua's army to commit to a ritual of *worship* rather than warfare.

For seven days, Israel's army walked around the locked-tight walled city of Jericho. Instead of army commanders leading the procession, priests were in the front. Instead of troops brandishing their weapons and symbols of strength, the ark of the covenant was the most visible symbol. And instead of scaling the walls and engaging in hand-to-hand combat, the people needed only to wait for God to act and to open the way.

Have you been praying in the face of a seemingly insurmountable circumstance? Have you tried to act to resolve the situation and perhaps experienced failure and frustration? Redouble your trust in God to work on your behalf. He understands the details of your dilemma much more completely than you do, and He knows what's most needed. Remember God's faithful activity in the past. Trust, and then obey.

HAMSTRUNG BY OUR OWN SIN

*Joshua said, "Alas, Sovereign LORD, why did you ever bring
this people across the Jordan to deliver us into the hands of
the Amorites to destroy us? . . . Pardon your servant, Lord.
What can I say, now that Israel has been routed by its enemies?"*

JOSHUA 7:7–8 NIV

This scene, following so closely on the heels of God's resounding
success at Jericho, stands as a strong lesson for us today.

Joshua's efforts to take the small outpost of Ai were hampered
by one man's personal sin. At Jericho, a man named Achan had
taken some of the plunder for himself against God's specific
commands. He had hidden it under his tent.

In the face of being routed by the few troops at Ai, Joshua
despaired and looked for answers. God led him to Achan and
revealed his sin, and after Joshua carried out God's punishment,
Israel was able to move forward in their campaign to take the
Promised Land.

How often does our own personal sin hamper God's work in
our lives? As men, we often keep secrets from our wives, from
our families—even from ourselves. Unconfessed sin in our lives
is a scourge, a cancer that saps our strength and leads to defeat
and despair. Even men who lead high-profile, highly effective
ministries are not immune as greed, pride, sexual sin, and other
evils sometimes hamstring their effectiveness.

Think today about how this may be true for you, and pray about
what God wants from you in the face of this reality.

GOD: OUR DIVINE CHEER KING

Then the LORD said to Joshua, "Do not be afraid; do not be discouraged. Take the whole army with you, and go up and attack Ai. For I have delivered into your hands the king of Ai, his people, his city and his land."

JOSHUA 8:1 NIV

Yesterday evening we looked at how the unconfessed sin of one man stopped the army of Israel in its tracks and how our own unconfessed sin might do the same in our lives.

Yet God's words today show us how God stands eager for us to get past our sin. God's plan for Joshua was to move forward not stand still. Rather than hampering God's plan, God wanted to see the sin removed so that He could continue His work in the lives of the people of Israel. His promises were not taken back because of Israel's sin.

How true this is in our own lives! God has a relentlessly positive inclination toward us. He's cheering for us to move forward in His power; we are encouraged and emboldened by the Holy Spirit He has given to those who believe in Him. Sin is a desperately disastrous reality in our lives, to be sure; however, God desires that we confess that sin and move on in His power and in His strength, for "if we confess our sins, he is faithful and just and will forgive us our sins and purify us from all unrighteousness" (1 John 1:9 NIV).

How will this faithful promise encourage you today?

ENCOURAGING OTHERS IN YOUR CIRCLE

When they had brought these kings to Joshua, he. . .said to the army commanders who had come with him. . ."Do not be afraid; do not be discouraged. Be strong and courageous. This is what the LORD will do to all the enemies you are going to fight."

JOSHUA 10:24–25 NIV

As we leave the story of Joshua today, we see him encouraging his commanding officers. Five Amorite kings had formed an alliance to fight against Israel, and God moved in power to defeat them. Ever eager to follow God's call and continue Israel's campaign, Joshua continued to encourage his commanders as God had consistently encouraged him.

How have you seen God's faithfulness demonstrated in your own life? Perhaps you've seen answers to prayer in the face of disease, marital strife, or financial distress. Perhaps you've felt God's peace and comfort when the answers to your difficult circumstances were long in coming.

If you've felt God's encouragement, how can you mirror Joshua's words today? Can you encourage your coworkers, your spouse, your friends in the face of their own difficult circumstances?

If God has shown Himself faithful to you, commit today to communicate that faithfulness to at least one other person who is experiencing a tough life situation. Your words of empathy may be the ones that reveal God's power in that person's own life.

Nervous about doing this? "Do not be afraid. . . . Be strong and courageous" (v. 25). God can—and will—empower you to encourage others.

ITCHING FOR A FIGHT

From Hebron Caleb drove out the three Anakites—Sheshai,
Ahiman and Talmai, the sons of Anak.

JOSHUA 15:14 NIV

Let's not leave the book of Joshua without looking at the life of Caleb.

In Joshua 14, we learn Caleb followed God "wholeheartedly" (vv. 8, 9, 14). In this, Caleb followed the formula for prosperity and success that we read about in Joshua 1:8.

Joshua 14 tells us of Caleb's desire to take his inheritance (promised to him by Moses) in Hebron, even at eighty-five years old. This octogenarian was still itching for a fight—the same fight he was eager to engage in as a forty-year-old, the first time he encountered these giants. At that time, his confidence in God's power overflowed: "We should go up and take possession of the land, for we can certainly do it" (Numbers 13:30 NIV).

What was Caleb's secret? He still relied—again, wholeheartedly—on God's strength not his own. Even after forty-five years, Caleb believed that God's promises would be fulfilled. He knew his role in this mission, and he was eager to advance against his enemies and prove God's power once again.

This message is for us, whether we're eighty-five, forty, or twenty. Patience, trust, and wholehearted devotion make us ready to take on life's most difficult challenges and pursue God's mission. When we follow God as Caleb did, we're ready to move forward in faith, no matter when God calls us to action.

GOD-INSPIRED OPTIMISM

"On that day Moses swore to me, 'The land. . .will be your inheritance. . .forever, because you have followed the LORD my God wholeheartedly.' . . . The LORD helping me, I will drive them out just as he said."

JOSHUA 14: 9, 12 NIV

A negative spirit is always a mark of self-reliance. To follow God wholeheartedly, as Caleb did, includes an unwavering trust in God's encouragement and empowerment. Along with that comes a confident optimism in God's presence and His power in our lives—an eagerness to engage with God in His mission.

Caleb, forty-five years earlier, exuded this confident optimism. And now, at eighty-five years old, he welcomed the challenge to engage in battle against the Anakites.

"Been there, done that" never entered Caleb's lexicon. He refused to leave the battle for the young men of his clan. Seeing the finish line of the race he started decades earlier, he redoubled his effort and charged into the hill country, confident in *God's* ability not his own. Imagine the Anakites, shaking in their size 25 boots as Caleb approached, weapons drawn. They never stood a chance in the face of Caleb's divinely empowered onslaught.

Are there challenges you've been waiting years to accomplish? Are you ready to reengage, confident that you're accomplishing what God has called you to do?

Caleb's story was still being told years later (Judges 1:20). This is the very definition of "prosperous and successful" that we've been talking about in recent days (Joshua 1:8). Follow Caleb's example of faith, and leave a legacy worthy of God's warriors.

GIDEON: GOD'S STRENGTH, OUR WEAKNESS

The angel of the LORD came and sat down. . .where. . .
Gideon was threshing wheat in a winepress to keep it from
the Midianites. When the angel of the LORD appeared to
Gideon, he said, "The LORD is with you, mighty warrior."

JUDGES 6:11–12 NIV

As we continue to look for God's encouragement, let's focus on Gideon. God's people were oppressed by the Midianites; God's prediction about the people of Israel had come true.

But as we've learned so far, God is always looking for ways to advance His purposes despite our sin. So God sent His angel to Gideon, who was working in secret so that his grain wouldn't be stolen by the regular raids of the Midianite troops.

Does it seem strange to you that the angel would call Gideon a "mighty warrior"? As far as we know, Gideon hadn't done anything to demonstrate courage. So here's the principle for today: deep down, *we truly are who God says we are.*

Perhaps you've been discouraged by a poor performance review at work. Perhaps you've recently gone through a divorce that you didn't want. Perhaps you're facing your retirement years, convinced that your most productive years are behind you.

Be encouraged today! Gideon had no idea that God would use him powerfully to deliver His people, yet God's plan for his life prevailed. Remember, *you are who God says you are.* Pray to be used as Gideon was, no matter what your life circumstances are today.

QUESTIONING GOD'S PROMISES

"Pardon me, my lord," Gideon replied, "but if the Lord is with us, why has all this happened to us? . . . The Lord has abandoned us and given us into the hand of Midian." The Lord. . .said, "Go in the strength you have and save Israel out of Midian's hand. Am I not sending you?" "Pardon me, my lord," Gideon replied, "but how can I save Israel? My clan is the weakest in Manasseh, and I am the least in my family." The Lord answered, "I will be with you, and you will strike down all the Midianites, leaving none alive."

JUDGES 6:13–16 NIV

The reading for today demonstrates one thing: God works out of our weakness, not out of our strength.

Gideon's questions are real. He hasn't seen the promised blessing of the Lord in his own life. His family has been harassed; the food has literally been stolen out of his hands under this Midianite oppression.

When the Lord tells him to defeat the invading army "in his own strength," he objects again. He's the runt of the litter in the smallest family of his Israelite clan.

How like God it is to use our weaknesses to demonstrate His own power. This is why Paul taught, "For Christ's sake, I delight in weaknesses, in insults, in hardships, in persecutions, in difficulties. For when I am weak, then I am strong" (2 Corinthians 12:10 NIV).

When we admit our utter reliance on God, that's when He moves in to do His divinely ordained work.

TESTING GOD'S PROMISES

Then Gideon said to God, "Do not be angry with me. Let me make just one more request. Allow me one more test with the fleece, but this time make the fleece dry and let the ground be covered with dew." That night God did so. Only the fleece was dry; all the ground was covered with dew.

JUDGES 6:39–40 NIV

Gideon's weakness shows through in the face of God's call on his life. Not once but twice he asks God for a visible sign that he will have success in defeating the Midianite army.

Please take a few minutes to read the entire chapter in Judges 6. You'll find God reassured Gideon time and time again that He would do as He had said and work through Gideon to save His people Israel. Yet He also allows Gideon's questions and answers them without showing anger or frustration.

When we're called to move into an unfamiliar or uncomfortable situation where the outcome is in doubt, God allows our questioning. He provides wise counsel from others when we ask; He leads us in answer to our prayers.

Let's look at Gideon not as a doubter, but as a man convinced of his own inability to do what God has asked him to do—utterly reliant on God to be true to His word and act on His promises. Sometimes God allows us to come to the end of our own strength so that He can prove Himself stronger.

GOD-INDUCED PANIC

The three companies blew the trumpets and smashed the jars.
Grasping the torches in their left hands and holding in their right
hands the trumpets they were to blow, they shouted, "A sword for
the LORD and for Gideon!" While each man held his position around
the camp, all the Midianites ran, crying out as they fled.

JUDGES 7:20–21 NIV

Judges 7 details how God worked through weak Gideon and his winnowed-down troops to utterly confuse and defeat the marauding Midianite army. It's well worth the read, so please find a Bible and read the story in Judges chapter 7.

Once again, we see God relentlessly encouraging Gideon, urging him to move forward in power and in faith. God's positivity in urging Gideon encourages us today as well, as He essentially says, "Gideon, with Me running the show, you can't possibly lose. I am faithful; I will do what I have promised." And the rout ensues: the Midianite army is decimated in the confusion.

God's promises to us in Jesus Christ stand in the same power. When we confess our sins, when we follow His Word, when we faithfully pray for the leading of the Holy Spirit, then we will be "prosperous and successful"—as He defines prosperity and success in accordance with His will (Joshua 1:8 NIV).

Using Gideon as an example, surrender your life to God's strength and guidance. Watch Him work powerfully on your behalf to make you the man He wants you to be—at work, in your family, and in your community.

SAMSON'S LAST BATTLE

*Then Samson prayed to the Lord, "Sovereign Lord, remember me.
Please, God, strengthen me just once more, and let me with one
blow get revenge on the Philistines for my two eyes."*

JUDGES 16:28 NIV

Samson was a judge over Israel for twenty years. During the time
of his reign, he demonstrated his great strength time and time
again, routing the Philistines many times and in multiple ways.

Today's passage leads us to Samson's final stand. As with Joshua
and Gideon, Samson's prayer of reliance on God comes at a
critical time—a time during which Samson has the opportunity
to demonstrate God's power and strength and strike a major
blow against God's enemies and their false religion. God, through
Samson, destroys their temple and kills thousands.

Judges chapters 13 through 16 detail the life of Samson, known
throughout history as both a hero and a deeply failed man. Yet we
read one recurring thing about Samson in these chapters. First,
the "Spirit of the Lord began to stir him" (Judges 13:25 NIV) when
he was a young man. Then, three other times in Judges (14:6,
14:19, 15:14) that same Spirit is in evidence right before he marks
another great act of strength.

Samson's strength came from the same Spirit (note the capital
S) that empowers us today. Strength, courage, honor, and the ability
to demonstrate God's power within our circles of influence—all
of this comes from the Holy Spirit living within us as believers in
Christ. How will you move out in faith today?

FINISHING WELL

*Then Samuel left for Ramah, but Saul went up to his home in
Gibeah of Saul. Until the day Samuel died, he did not go to see
Saul again, though Samuel mourned for him. And the LORD
regretted that he had made Saul king over Israel.*

1 SAMUEL 15:34–35 NIV

The prophet Samuel, leader of Israel after the time of the judges,
also presided over the anointing of Saul, the first king over Israel.
He anointed Saul at God's command, and King Saul ruled over
Israel for forty-two years.

By all accounts, God chose and empowered Saul during his reign.
Why then do we read about God's regret at the end of Saul's reign?

Late in his reign, Saul's disobedience dogged him. He relied on
himself against God's specific commands. In Saul's life, we come
to understand a powerful truth—that finishing well is critical to
the legacy we leave in this life.

Pastor James MacDonald writes, "You could decide to destroy
your life by 5:00 tonight. And would God forgive you? Yes. But
would you bear the consequences of that decision for the rest of
your life? Yes, you would! Don't ever mix up God's forgiveness and
[real-life] consequences."

Samuel, who'd invested decades of his life into Saul, mourns
Saul's failure. God even regrets His choice of Saul, despite the
king's multiple decades of faithful leadership. And Saul, frustrated
at his own failures, ends his own life ignobly (1 Samuel 31).

Make no mistake: finishing well matters.

WAITING FOR GOD'S PROMISES

*So Samuel took the horn of oil and anointed him in the presence
of his brothers, and from that day on the Spirit of the
LORD came powerfully upon David.*

1 SAMUEL 16:13 NIV

In the story of Samuel anointing David to be king, we hear an echo of our earlier readings: As with Samson, God's Spirit moved powerfully in this young man; as with Gideon, David was the youngest and the smallest of his family. Yet God told Samuel to anoint Jesse's youngest son, following God's direct command (1 Samuel 16:1, 12).

Notice one important truth at the outset of his story: David had to wait. And wait. God's promise was slow in coming, even though David had been anointed by God's own prophet.

God's timeline is often far from what ours would optimally be. King Saul lived and reigned for a significant amount of time—and David even spent time in his service—before David was eventually crowned king.

Are you waiting for God's promise to you to be fulfilled? Then you stand in a long line of heroes in the Bible: Noah, who built a boat over multiple decades before he ever saw a drop of rain; Abraham, who waited decades for his son Isaac to be born (when he was one hundred years old!); and now David, who waited patiently and faithfully for God's story to develop before he was crowned king over Israel.

Make no mistake: God's timelines are intentional. Faithfulness and patience in the meantime will be rewarded.

WHAT'S YOUR SLING?

"The Lord who rescued me from the paw of the lion and the paw of the bear will rescue me from the hand of this Philistine."

1 Samuel 17:37 niv

When we read of David's anointing, sometimes we wonder what the older brothers were thinking: *This scrawny kid, God's anointed?* Yet we have no indication that David inspired the hatred that an earlier upstart, Joseph, provoked in his older brothers (Genesis 37:5, 12–32).

David's father sent him to the front lines of Israel's battle with the Philistines to resupply his older brothers. There, David heard about Goliath's arrogance in the face of God's people. Evidently his brothers were only too happy to have him engage this giant, and even King Saul saw the fire in David's eyes and gave him his blessing (1 Samuel 17:37).

As this boy approached Goliath in battle, God's Spirit encouraged David's own spirit. As we've seen with other men, David was eager to prove God powerful in the face of God's enemies. He relied wholeheartedly on God to fight for him, trusting in God to engage—and to win.

This kind of practical faith is the hallmark of the man of God. David approached Goliath with what he had, using his God-given talent with the sling to fell the giant. How has God equipped you to face your own circumstances? What's the sling in your hand, and what are the stones in your pouch? God will use what He's given you to accomplish His purposes.

GOD'S SOMETIMES-OBVIOUS BLESSINGS

*When David had fled. . .he went to Samuel at Ramah and told him
all that Saul had done to him. Then he and Samuel went to Naioth
and stayed there. . . . [Saul] sent men to capture him. But when
they saw a group of prophets prophesying, with Samuel standing
there as their leader, the Spirit of God came on Saul's
men, and they also prophesied. Saul was told about it,
and he sent more men, and they prophesied too.*

1 SAMUEL 19:18, 20–21 NIV

Sometimes, as we learn from this amazing passage, God chooses
to deliver His favor and encouragement through very visible signs.

David was on the run from King Saul, who had tried to kill him
not once but twice. Samuel had taken David in and the two of
them hid from Saul together. David must have known that Saul
would send men to come and apprehend him.

How must David have felt when he saw Saul's messengers
overcome by God's Spirit?

How must Saul have felt when he heard about it—not once
but twice?

God's favor, His idea of being "prosperous and successful"
(Joshua 1:8 NIV), manifests itself in different ways for different
men. Some men enjoy material prosperity as they follow God's
plan for their lives. Do you know any such men? Are you one of
them?

David enjoyed God's visible favor even though he was on the
run—a very different kind of success. Let this story help you begin
to redefine what prosperity and success mean in your own life.

ALLOWING GOD TO WRITE THE STORY

[David] said to Saul. . . "This day you have seen with your own eyes how the LORD delivered you into my hands in the cave. Some urged me to kill you, but I spared you; I said, 'I will not lay my hand on my lord, because he is the LORD's anointed.' See, my father. . . . I cut off the corner of your robe but did not kill you."

1 SAMUEL 24:9–11 NIV

Despite having to constantly run from Saul, David's faith remained strong. His commitment to God's will and God's timing was absolute. Finding himself in the back of a cave while Saul sat tantalizingly within his grasp, David exercised almost unbelievable self-control. Even David's troops encouraged him to kill Saul, yet David resisted. He was content to let God be the one writing his story, refusing to take matters into his own hands.

How many men would have acted differently in this situation? How many men act in haste and trust in their own wits and instincts, hastily moving forward into business or personal situations that are fraught with potential consequences?

David wasn't going to usurp the throne of Israel. God had anointed him, and he trusted in God to make him the leader of His people whenever God wanted.

Are you facing a big decision? A major life change? Commit yourself to a time of prayer, of seeking God's face. Search the scriptures for God's leading, and discuss your situation with trusted and godly advisors. Time spent this way is never wasted.

FACING THE BLOODY BATTLES WITH FAITH

Then David and all the men with him took hold of their clothes and tore them. They mourned and wept and fasted till evening for Saul and his son Jonathan.

2 SAMUEL 1:11–12 NIV

David was Israel's anointed king. But after hearing of Saul and Jonathan's deaths, he didn't celebrate; instead, he and all of his men mourned. This is further evidence of a man filled with God's encouragement and empowerment—one who trusted God to write his life story.

David was soon crowned king over the tribe of Judah (2 Samuel 2:4), but he knew that a bitter battle was about to begin, one that would end with him being crowned king over all of Israel. David had been encouraged by God's signs throughout this difficult journey, but he also knew he had more bloody work to do.

Second Samuel chapters 1 through 5 read like a blockbuster thriller movie plot, filled with intrigue, battle, bloodshed, and eventual victory. And David, at the age of thirty, eventually begins a legendary forty-year reign.

After taking Jerusalem, we read this of David: "Then David knew that the LORD had established him as king over Israel and had exalted his kingdom for the sake of his people Israel" (2 Samuel 5:12). Honoring God's work in the past, David now begins the next phase of his life most appropriately: by giving God all of the credit for everything that had happened in the past.

We're wise to share a perspective similar to David's when we look back on our own lives.

A PROMISE OF LEGACY

" 'Your house and your kingdom will endure forever before me;
your throne will be established forever.' "

2 Samuel 7:16 NIV

In our quest to find God's encouragement in the Bible, we'll find no declaration more encouraging than this one, spoken to David through God's prophet, Nathan.

This promise echoes God's lavish promises to other men in the Old Testament—to Adam: "Be fruitful and increase in number; fill the earth and subdue it. Rule over. . .every living creature that moves on the ground" (Genesis 1:28 NIV); to Noah: "I establish my covenant with you: Never again will all life be destroyed by the waters of a flood" (Genesis 9:11 NIV); to Abram: "As for me, this is my covenant with you: You will be the father of many nations" (Genesis 17:4 NIV). These global promises were given by a generous God to His faithful followers.

In the New Testament, Paul makes this critical observation about King David:

> "After removing Saul, [God] made David their king.
> God testified concerning him: 'I have found David
> son of Jesse, a man after my own heart; he will
> do everything I want him to do.' From this man's
> descendants God has brought to Israel the Savior
> Jesus, as he promised." (Acts 13:22–23 NIV)

You and I also stand in this line of promise along with Adam, Noah, Abram, and David. We have the promise of Jesus, the fulfillment of all of the other promises God made in the Bible combined.

Eternal promises given by a grace-filled God to His unworthy followers. Amazing!

GOD MAKES BEAUTY OUT OF BROKEN THINGS

[David, to Bathsheba] "I will surely carry out this very day what I swore to you by the LORD, the God of Israel: Solomon your son shall be king after me, and he will sit on my throne in my place."

1 KINGS 1:30 NIV

Nearly everyone knows the story of David's failure with Bathsheba. Movies have been made about this scandalous story of lust and intrigue. When this man David—whom God called one "after my own heart" (Acts 13:22 NIV)—fell, he fell *hard.*

Yet God is in the business of rebuilding. Indeed, God is always "making everything new" (Revelation 21:5 NIV). In this case, David's repentance after his highly visible failure brings David a son, Solomon, whom the Lord loves. David, in fact, declares that Solomon will be the next king over Israel instead of his eldest son, Adonijah.

Do you remember a time in your own life when you failed, publicly and visibly? A time when you felt caught, dirty, sinful beyond repair? Be encouraged by David's story and the birth of Solomon. Remember, God takes the brokenness of our lives and, when we repent, He makes beautiful things. Like a medieval craftsman, God takes the shattered glass of our lives and makes the pieces into a stained-glass window as beautiful—and as reflective of His light—as any that ever hung in a stately European cathedral.

A TEMPLATE FOR GOD'S MEN

*When the time drew near for David to die, he gave a charge to
Solomon his son. "I am about to go the way of all the earth,"
he said. "So be strong, act like a man, and observe what the
L<small>ORD</small> your God requires: Walk in obedience to him, and keep his
decrees and commands, his laws and regulations, as written in the
Law of Moses. Do this so that you may prosper in all you do and
wherever you go and that the L<small>ORD</small> may keep his promise to me:
'If your descendants watch how they live, and if they walk faithfully
before me with all their heart and soul, you will never fail
to have a successor on the throne of Israel.' "*

1 K<small>INGS</small> 2:1–4 <small>NIV</small>

Today's scripture reading is a little longer than usual. That's because
it gives us as Christian men an important template to follow in
our own lives.

Take note of the components of David's charge to Solomon:
first, encouragement to be strong and take personal responsibility;
second, a call to follow after God's ways; third, a promise of
prosperity and success if the first and second exhortations are
followed; finally, an appeal to look at God's promises via his legacy.

Men, these are critical components of your personal legacy.
The older you get, the more influence you have, whether or not
you have children. Follow David's lead: testify to God's work in
your life and share the encouragement you've received from God
with the next generation.

WISDOM FOR THE ASKING

*God gave Solomon wisdom and very great insight, and a breadth
of understanding as measureless as the sand on the seashore.*

1 KINGS 4:29 NIV

In an earlier reading, we found that God loved Solomon. When he
became king after his father, David, died, God appeared to Solomon
with an enticing proposition: "At Gibeon the LORD appeared to
Solomon during the night in a dream, and God said, 'Ask for
whatever you want me to give you' " (1 Kings 3:5 NIV).

Everyone dreams of being given the chance, just once in life,
to ask for whatever we want. Whether through a lottery ticket or
from a genie in a bottle, we all long for that chance to have the
proverbial "three wishes" that will allow us to fulfill all of our dreams.

Prudently, the newly ascended King Solomon asks for wisdom. Pleased with this request, God delivers with astounding
generosity.

Wouldn't it be amazing to have the same opportunity to be as
wise as Solomon?

The truth is, you have it. Read Jesus' words to His disciples,
and to us, in John 14:26 (NIV): "But the Advocate, the Holy Spirit,
whom the Father will send in my name, will teach you all things
and will remind you of everything I have said to you."

Jesus' Spirit inhabits those who believe. When we're looking
for wisdom, we need look no further than God's Word, sincerely
praying for the Spirit's direction and guidance. Solomon's wisdom
was legendary; with the Spirit's help, yours can be as well.

INSPIRED PEOPLE INSPIRE PEOPLE

[Hezekiah] encouraged them with these words: "Be strong and courageous. Do not be afraid or discouraged because of the king of Assyria and the vast army with him, for there is a greater power with us than with him. With him is only the arm of flesh, but with us is the LORD our God to help us and to fight our battles." And the people gained confidence from what Hezekiah the king of Judah said.

2 CHRONICLES 32:6–8 NIV

King Hezekiah stands in front of the people of Judah as they stare down an imminent siege from the terrifying Assyrian army, a force known for their murderous, grisly, and shocking terror tactics. Assyria's King Sennacherib does his best to terrorize Hezekiah; temporarily, the plan works.

Read what happens next:

> King Hezekiah and the prophet Isaiah son of Amoz cried out in prayer to heaven about this. And the LORD sent an angel, who annihilated all the fighting men and the commanders and officers in the camp of the Assyrian king. So he withdrew to his own land in disgrace. . . . So the LORD saved Hezekiah and the people of Jerusalem from the hand of Sennacherib. . . . He took care of them on every side.
> (2 Chronicles 32:20–22 NIV)

Inspired people inspire people.

Hezekiah, trusting only in God's deliverance, was able to inspire an entire city despite a seemingly hopeless situation. As we've seen, God heard and answered in an overwhelming way.

It's another story of God's action to encourage us today in our own lives.

ISAIAH'S VISION OF GOD'S GLORY

In the year that King Uzziah died, I saw the Lord, high and exalted,
seated on a throne; and the train of his robe filled the temple. . . .
"Woe to me!" I cried. "I am ruined! For I am a man of unclean
lips, and I live among a people of unclean lips, and my
eyes have seen the King, the LORD Almighty."

ISAIAH 6:1, 5 NIV

The prophet Isaiah, who prayed for Jerusalem's deliverance from the king of Assyria, in this passage receives a vision of God Himself, high and exalted and sitting on His throne. At the sight of it, Isaiah is terrified at God's majesty and power.

We know Isaiah as Israel's greatest prophet; Christians understand that God revealed to Isaiah more about God's Messiah than perhaps any other prophet. Indeed, in the very next chapter we find Isaiah's first prophecy about the Christ: "The virgin will conceive and give birth to a son, and will call him Immanuel" (Isaiah 7:14 NIV).

We who follow the Messiah to whom Isaiah pointed have a greater "vision" than the prophet Isaiah could have possibly imagined. We have the totality of the scriptures—the full story of God's intricate and purpose-filled plan to redeem all of humanity, begun in Genesis and ending in Revelation—whenever we hold a Bible in our hands.

God, revealed. How amazing is that?

REASSURANCE

*Among the lampstands was someone like a son of man, dressed in
a robe reaching down to his feet and with a golden sash around
his chest. . . . His voice was like the sound of rushing waters. In his
right hand he held seven stars, and coming out of his mouth was a
sharp, double-edged sword. His face was like the sun shining in all
its brilliance. When I saw him, I fell at his feet as though dead.*

REVELATION 1:13, 15–17 NIV

Here we see a triumphant vision of the resurrected Christ. Like
Isaiah, John's reaction to this glorious vision was dramatic and
immediate.

But Jesus didn't want to leave John, or us, with an intimidating
vision of His power. Rather, He reached down reassuringly to
touch John and delivered an incredible word of encouragement:

> *"Do not be afraid. I am the First and the Last. I
> am the Living One; I was dead, and now look, I
> am alive for ever and ever! And I hold the keys of
> death and Hades." (Revelation 1:17–18 NIV)*

Jesus, both now and forever, is firmly in control of what happens
in our lives and in our world. He sees everything, and nothing
surprises Him. He can be trusted because He is forever all-seeing
and all-powerful.

Have you seen Jesus' glory as revealed in the scriptures? Be
amazed. Be encouraged. Devote your life to Him, and wait faithfully
and patiently for God to work His will—designed just for you, before
the beginning of time—in your life.

A BEAUTIFUL THING

A woman came with an alabaster jar of very expensive perfume, made of pure nard. She broke the jar and poured the perfume on his head. Some of those present were saying indignantly to one another, "Why this waste of perfume? It could have been sold for more than a year's wages and the money given to the poor." And they rebuked her harshly. "Leave her alone," said Jesus. "Why are you bothering her? She has done a beautiful thing to me. The poor you will always have with you, and you can help them any time you want. But you will not always have me. She did what she could. She poured perfume on my body beforehand to prepare for my burial."

MARK 14:3–8 NIV

It is not possible to "waste" anything on Jesus Christ if we are motivated by love. It's not a waste to give up things of value, or our time, or our hopes for the future if He is the One to whom we offer them. Others may scorn our gifts as impractical or impulsive, but Christ sees them as beautiful. Anointing a body that is still alive seems like nonsense, but it's the reason we know of her today (Mark 14:9).

We don't need to have great resources to do beautiful things, either. This woman did not occupy an important or powerful station in life, but as Jesus points out, she did what she could for Him. And she did it when the opportunity came, without hesitation and at the cost of scorn and criticism. May we all have the love and courage of that woman.

A PEOPLE FOR HIMSELF

*"For the sake of his great name the Lord will not reject his people,
because the Lord was pleased to make you his own."*

1 Samuel 12:22 NIV

God has been on a mission since Adam and Eve departed from His will: to gather back to Himself a people of His own—a willing people, eager to be with Him and do His will. But it's been a rough journey for our Father. He hasn't always gotten His way, so to speak. Being a Father committed to our free will, He has done everything to encourage us to respond to Him. Paul described it to the Greek philosophers this way:

> *"From one man he made all the nations, that they should inhabit the whole earth; and he marked out their appointed times in history and the boundaries of their lands. God did this so that they would seek him and perhaps reach out for him and find him, though he is not far from any one of us."* (Acts 17:26–27)

God is so persistent in having a people for Himself that he sacrificed His only begotten Son to make His desire a reality. "[Jesus] gave himself for us to redeem us from all wickedness and to purify for himself a people that are his very own, eager to do what is good" (Titus 2:14 NIV).

Ultimately, a people belonging to God and pleasing to Him will be like Him, eager to do good works and to see others join His family.

EMPTY JARS

Yet you, LORD, are our Father. We are the clay,
you are the potter; we are all the work of your hand.

ISAIAH 64:8 NIV

It's the most natural thing in the world to think we own ourselves, to think that we are the reason we exist. It's the story of human history once mankind "did not think it worthwhile to retain the knowledge of God" (Romans 1:28 NIV). It's an ignorance that has become part of our DNA. But it's not the truth, and God our Father does not want us to struggle under the burden of trying to be fulfilled without Him.

Man was designed to be filled, but not by anything we can devise on our own. A potter makes vessels empty for a purpose. That design feature is what drives man. But it's a vain pursuit without God, as King Solomon—who tested everything to fill the void—declares: " 'Meaningless! Meaningless!' says the Teacher. 'Everything is meaningless!' " (Ecclesiastes 12:8 NIV)

The flesh and the world offer the promise of filling the emptiness inside, but it will always leave us "hardened by sin's deceitfulness" (Hebrews 3:13 NIV). Even good things, apart from God, leave us ultimately unfulfilled. At best, a life of a good, successful, decent man is a life of revolving distractions, if it's done without the Potter's purpose.

Only in God, our Father—God, our Potter—will we ever find the filling we were designed for.

EVERY DAY A BATTLEFIELD

So I say, walk by the Spirit, and you will not gratify the desires of the flesh. For the flesh desires what is contrary to the Spirit, and the Spirit what is contrary to the flesh. They are in conflict with each other, so that you are not to do whatever you want.

GALATIANS 5:16–17 NIV

For the follower of Christ, there is no day without a battle. Some days it rages harder than others, but there's never a truce that lasts between the Spirit and the flesh. They are opposed to each other by their very nature. One is life and peace, the other death (Romans 8:6). From one we will inherit eternal life, from the other only corruption (Galatians 6:8). No wonder they are always in conflict!

We are born into this conflict when we become God's child. So how do we prepare ourselves for this conflict? The Galatians had fallen back into keeping the law, which never did have the power to win this battle. The flesh is always stronger than rules and regulations. The only thing that wins against desire is a stronger desire. To avoid siding with the flesh—which can be a powerful lure at times—means cultivating a *stronger* desire to walk with the Spirit.

Amos 3:3 (MSG) poses the simple question, "Do two people walk hand in hand if they aren't going to the same place?" Walking by the Spirit means we are in agreement, going in the same direction, hand in hand, growing a greater desire for the things of the Spirit every day.

FACING THE FUTURE

*"I will give you every place where you set your foot. . . .
No one will be able to stand against you. . . . I will never
leave you nor forsake you. . . . Be strong and courageous.
Do not be afraid; do not be discouraged, for the LORD
your God will be with you wherever you go."*

JOSHUA 1:3, 5, 9 NIV

Joshua at eighty, with all his life experiences and training, should have been more than prepared to lead the Israelites into the Promised Land, right?

Born into slavery in an empire over a thousand years old before Moses entered the picture, Joshua witnessed the struggle with Pharaoh firsthand, since he "had been Moses' aide since youth" (Numbers 11:28 NIV). He marched out of Egypt through the Red Sea, drank water from the rock, ate manna from heaven, led the first army of Israel, heard Moses read the Ten Commandments, and saw the first tabernacle constructed. At forty, he and eleven others spied on the land of Canaan, but then had to endure the next forty years wandering in the desert with those too fearful to take hold of God's promise. He and Caleb were the only ones over the age of twenty who did not die during that time (Numbers 14:29, 26:65), making them the oldest men in Israel.

So why the big pep talk? Because we are nothing without the presence and the promises of God. No history or résumé can give courage like His presence. We can do nothing without Him, no matter how much we've already achieved with Him.

FROM THE MESS, VALUE

Where no oxen are, the trough is clean;
but much increase comes by the strength of an ox.
PROVERBS 14:4 NKJV

Oxen are messy creatures. But there's no way to take advantage of their strength without having to watch where you step. If you want to produce something of value, you're going to have to deal with the mess it causes.

The work world can be quite messy. It's risky to run a business—people don't always do what you expect, customers demand more than you can provide, and every week you have to clean up something that hits the fan.

Marriage, for all its delights, can generate piles of debris. Sacrificing individual dreams, working through conflict, dealing with in-laws, negotiating finances, serving even when you would prefer to be served—all these make for a messy "trough." For those who persevere, the rewards are well worth it.

Having kids may be literally and figuratively the messiest choice of all. But most parents would tell you they'd do it all over again.

The principle in this verse is that nothing of value comes without work, consequences, and risk. Laziness and fear are our only obstacles. In the parable of the talents (Matthew 25:14–30), two servants risk the money entrusted to them and earn more, while one simply buries it in the ground. He pleads fear; his master calls him a "wicked and lazy servant" (Matthew 25:26 NKJV).

God wants us to work at whatever He's put into our lives, not fearing the consequences, but focusing on creating something of value. He wouldn't assign it if He didn't have a reason.

LET'S MAKE A DEAL

"For the kingdom of heaven is like a landowner who went out early in the morning to hire workers for his vineyard. He agreed to pay them a denarius for the day and sent them into his vineyard."

MATTHEW 20:1–2 NIV

A contract binds two parties to an agreement, each being obligated to the other as long as each upholds his end. In this parable, the workers hired early agreed to a denarius and considered themselves lucky to be hired for a full day. Later, the landowner hires others, but instead of a contract, he promises: "You also go and work in my vineyard, and I will pay you whatever is right" (Matthew 20:4 NIV). Finally, with only one hour left to work, he finds a group of workers whom no one has hired. To these, he simply says: "You also go and work in my vineyard" (Matthew 20:7 NIV).

When the foreman pays the workers, the ones who worked for just one hour, surprisingly, receive a full day's pay! The early workers' complaint sounds justified: "These who were hired last worked only one hour, and you have made them equal to us who have borne the burden of the work and the heat of the day" (Matthew 20:12 NIV). But the landowner reminds them of the contract they happily made that morning.

The first workers were given a legally binding guarantee; the second group received just a promise; the final ones could only hope in the landowner's goodness. Each was rewarded in proportion to the faith it took to go into that vineyard.

LISTENING IS A DANGEROUS ACTIVITY

*Herod feared John [the Baptist] and protected him, knowing him
to be a righteous and holy man. When Herod heard John,
he was greatly puzzled; yet he liked to listen to him.*

MARK 6:20 NIV

John the Baptist was the first prophet to come along after what
has been called the "Four Hundred Silent Years" in Israel's history.
During the time between the last prophet of the Old Testament,
Malachi, and the ministry of John, no prophets spoke to the people
to remind them of God's law and His commandments.

So when John the Baptist showed up, looking and acting like
the greatest prophet in Israel's history (Mark 1:6), preaching "in
the spirit and power of Elijah" (Luke 1:17 NIV), people flocked to
him. He became something of a religious celebrity, so much so
that even tax collectors and soldiers came to ask his advice (Luke
3:12–14). John didn't hold back his message of repentance even
with Herod the tetrarch, publically rebuking him for adultery. That
of course landed John in prison and ultimately cost him his life
(Matthew 14:6–12).

Herod made the worst mistake a person can when it comes
to hearing the Good News—he treated it like entertainment. He
listened without changing. Jesus said bluntly of those people:
"There is a judge for the one who rejects me and does not accept
my words; the very words I have spoken will condemn them at the
last day" (John 12:48 NIV).

Listening is dangerous business, *if* we don't intend to apply what
we hear from God. The very words themselves will testify against us.

MYSTERY TURNED MESSAGE

The mystery that has been kept hidden for ages and generations, but is now disclosed to the Lord's people. To them God has chosen to make known among the Gentiles the glorious riches of this mystery, which is Christ in you, the hope of glory.

COLOSSIANS 1:26–27 NIV

In the Old Testament, God used prophets to reveal mysteries for His purpose. When Daniel interpreted Nebuchadnezzar's dream, the king fell on his face, confessing, "Surely your God is the God of gods and the Lord of kings and a revealer of mysteries" (Daniel 2:47 NIV). Then Daniel was placed in authority over most of Babylon. God reveals mysteries in His own time and His own way—for our benefit and for His own glory.

When the time was right to reveal the mystery of salvation through grace, however, He did not rely on a prophet.

> *But when the set time had fully come, God sent his Son, born of a woman, born under the law, to redeem those under the law, that we might receive adoption to sonship. Because you are his sons, God sent the Spirit of his Son into our hearts, the Spirit who calls out, "Abba, Father."* (Galatians 4:4–6 NIV)

The mystery of mysteries—Jesus Christ living in us—had to be delivered face to face. Jesus revealed it the very night He would pay the price to see it happen: "In that day you will know that I am in My Father, and you in Me, and I in you" (John 14:20 NKJV). In us, Christ turned the mystery of the ages into the message for the world.

NO FORMULAS

*In the course of time Cain brought some of the fruits of the soil
as an offering to the LORD. And Abel also brought an offering—
fat portions from some of the firstborn of his flock. The LORD
looked with favor on Abel and his offering, but on Cain
and his offering he did not look with favor. So Cain
was very angry, and his face was downcast.*

GENESIS 4:3–5 NIV

God doesn't need our "stuff," being the Creator. But the exercise
of sacrificing is the exercise of priorities, of the condition of
our hearts, and the hope for a closer walk with our Father. Abel
approached God in faith (Hebrews 11:4) and was commended. He
offered "firstborn" and "fat portions" because he reverenced God.
But Cain offered his sacrifice reluctantly, not with a whole heart;
he offered it under obligation, not gratitude.

This kind of offering is the beginning of a dead religion built on
formulas and equations. We offer a sacrifice to fulfill a requirement,
and in turn we expect to get blessings. God is not interested in a
"working" relationship with us, and He's certainly not going to be
obligated by anything we do.

God wants us to experience His freedom—the freedom to
be close to Him. Cain's "face was downcast" when his formulaic
approach failed—in other words, he couldn't look God in the eye. If
we insist on formulas rather than a sincere and open heart toward
God, we risk going the way of Cain, angry with our Creator, turning
away to the sin that is "crouching at [our] door" (Genesis 4:7 NIV).

OVERTHINKING AND UNDER-PRAYING

Do not be anxious about anything, but in every situation, by prayer and petition, with thanksgiving, present your requests to God. And the peace of God, which transcends all understanding, will guard your hearts and your minds in Christ Jesus.

PHILIPPIANS 4:6–7 NIV

The Bible is full of stories of some very intelligent men. Joseph was described as discerning and wise (Genesis 41:39); of Daniel and his three companions, it's recorded that "God gave [them] knowledge and understanding of all kinds of literature and learning" (Daniel 1:17 NIV); to Solomon was granted "wisdom and very great insight, and a breadth of understanding as measureless as the sand on the seashore" (1 Kings 4:29).

In their days, these men were renowned for their intellect, and God used all of them to accomplish His will. But their real strength came from knowing the source of their gifts and the absolute necessity of meeting God in prayer.

Prayer does not replace knowledge, wisdom, or discernment—it transcends it. Prayer is borrowing the power of thought that we cannot generate. It's inviting the God of all wisdom to participate in whatever has captured our attention. He delights in trading His peace for the anxiety that has us running in mental circles. Thinking by itself will not get us out of every situation, but He "is able to do immeasurably more than all we ask or imagine" (Ephesians 3:20 NIV).

Let us always ask for wisdom (James 1:5), remembering that we are exercising the highest wisdom by coming to God in prayer.

PUT YOUR GUARD UP

*Then he returned to his disciples and found them sleeping.
"Couldn't you men keep watch with me for one hour?" he asked
Peter. "Watch and pray so that you will not fall into temptation.
The spirit is willing, but the flesh is weak."*

MATTHEW 26:40–41 NIV

Any man in midlife or older who lifts weights, runs, or pursues any
athletic pastime learns one lesson quickly—the heart may be in it,
but the body can't always pull it off. It's also true of other areas
of our lives. We mean to spend more time with our families, but
work keeps us preoccupied. We need to lose weight, but just can't
seem to say no when the burgers are hot off the grill. We plan to
get up earlier to meet with our Father in His Word, but something
always steals that time from us.

Thankfully, Jesus is always gracious with our weaknesses. He
knows we want to do better but that we will need help:

> *"And I will ask the Father, and he will give you
> another advocate to help you and be with you
> forever."* (John 14:16 NIV)

Even in His admonition to watch and pray, He promises to
help us:

> *In the same way, the Spirit helps us in our
> weakness. We do not know what we ought to
> pray for, but the Spirit himself intercedes for us
> through wordless groans.* (Romans 8:26 NIV)

With His promises of help, we can watch and pray with confidence
that He will supply the strength we do not possess within ourselves.

SEEING OURSELVES RIGHTLY

For he knows how we are formed, he remembers that we are dust.
PSALM 103:14 NIV

As our creator, God never needs to be reminded what we are. He knows that we were made from the dust of the earth (Genesis 2:7), that we are "jars of clay" (2 Corinthians 4:7 NIV), a mere "mist that appears for a little while and then vanishes" (James 4:14 NIV). God knows our time is short and our power limited even if we forget.

And we regularly forget. It's easy to think too highly of ourselves and depend on our own strength in a way that "dust" simply wasn't designed for. Pride may tell us we're invincible and powerful, but God knows the truth. Thankfully, He does not look on our frailty with contempt. Instead, He is moved with a Father's compassion when He sees our vulnerability (Psalm 103:13–14). And as a good Father, He patiently disciplines us for our benefit:

> *Moreover, we have all had human fathers who disciplined us and we respected them for it. How much more should we submit to the Father of spirits and live!*
> (Hebrews 12:9 NIV)

God can't afford to have His children taken in by a false sense of strength and power and miss what He has for us. While we may spend our time making great plans, God spends His time making great sons. Whenever the two are in conflict, He will always choose our character over our success. Let us ask Him to open our eyes to our own limitations, not disdaining what we see but allowing it to keep us leaning on Him.

THE BREATH OF LIFE

*Then the LORD God formed a man from the dust of the ground
and breathed into his nostrils the breath of life,
and the man became a living being.*

GENESIS 2:7 NIV

Genesis 1 beautifully describes the origination of everything from a formless, dark void culminating in the creation of man, made in God's likeness and given the purpose of his existence: to use his God-given qualities to complete the picture God had begun painting (Genesis 1:28).

But there's one important element to man's creation that makes him unique: God breathed life into him to make him a "living being [literally, *soul*]." And interestingly, this breath of life was into his "nostrils" rather than his mouth. The natural position of the mouth is closed, but the natural state of the nostrils is open. We "swim" through air, surrounded by our next breaths; oxygen even circulates inside our bodies through the bloodstream, reaching every part of us. There is an inescapable connection and dependence on the God who made us.

In the most literal sense, our natural state of being is one of constant connection to God. Adam was designed to stay in connection with God in order to carry out his mission. Of course, willful disobedience ruined that plan. But hope returns with the promise of the Holy Spirit.

> *And with that he breathed on them and said,
> "Receive the Holy Spirit."* (John 20:22 NIV)

In Christ, our connection to God through the Holy Spirit is as real, as essential, and as satisfying as the next breath we take.

THE SPIRIT OF ADOPTION

The Spirit you received does not make you slaves, so that you live in fear again; rather, the Spirit you received brought about your adoption to sonship. And by him we cry, "Abba, Father."

ROMANS 8:15 NIV

There's nothing more honest than a cry of the heart, one that comes from so deep within that nothing can stop it. That's the powerful affection the Spirit in us has for God the Father.

Of being adopted as sons of God, theologian J.I. Packer notes, "To be right with God the judge is a great thing, but to be loved and cared for by God the father is greater" (*Knowing God*, p. 186–188). Being adopted goes beyond being forgiven, even beyond being made righteous. Adoption brings us into a warm family relationship: "Our fellowship is with the Father and with his Son, Jesus Christ" (1 John 1:3 NIV).

Adoption also bestows on us some specific privileges. First, we are granted immediate, unhindered access to God. "In him and through faith in him we may approach God with freedom and confidence" (Ephesians 3:12 NIV). Nothing can stop us from coming close to our Father. Second, as members of the family, we get to share in His name. "Therefore go and make disciples of all nations, baptizing them in the name of the Father and of the Son and of the Holy Spirit" (Matthew 28:19 NIV). And third, adoption guarantees an inheritance from a Father "who has qualified you to share in the inheritance of his holy people in the kingdom of light" (Colossians 1:12 NIV).

Praise God that He adopted us!

THE FACE OF WISDOM

*The wisdom that comes from heaven is first of all pure;
then peace-loving, considerate, submissive, full of
mercy and good fruit, impartial and sincere.*

JAMES 3:17 NIV

A lot of information these days claims to be "wisdom." Self-help material abounds, consultants and preachers flourish, and think tanks produce opinions on every topic imaginable. How do we recognize what is truly of God?

James gives us a checklist to navigate the many voices claiming to speak wisdom. If a voice fails on one point, it's not wisdom from heaven:

1. *Pure.* Never compromised by sin or contradicting the truth of the Gospel.
2. *Peace-loving.* Does not stir up unnecessary conflict.
3. *Considerate.* Not harsh or divisive but gentle and thoughtful.
4. *Submissive.* Not stubborn, obstinate, or narrow-minded but open to reason as long as truth is not compromised.
5. *Full of mercy.* Gracious to the ignorant, lost, and guilty, ready to forgive and encourage.
6. *Full of good fruit.* Produces real results, inwardly and outwardly, in the lives of those who practice it.
7. *Impartial.* Not swayed by people; doesn't harbor biases; remains true to itself.
8. *Sincere.* Frank, open to all, and has no agenda besides the truth of God.

FRAMEWORK FOR FREEDOM

See to it that no one takes you captive through hollow and deceptive philosophy, which depends on human tradition and the elemental spiritual forces of this world rather than on Christ.

COLOSSIANS 2:8 NIV

Spiritual captivity comes from a mind-set or belief influenced by philosophy originating from this world rather than from God. It may be built on outright deception, cultural bias, false assumptions, or good intentions that don't align with the character of Christ. Worldly thinking can be anything from militant atheism to compassionate humanism. It can be a gospel of self-empowerment or a political message of tolerance. It's anything that promises deliverance without Christ, anything that creates hope without the Messiah, anything that points to a future without the One who created it.

This world has its evangelists looking for converts, so we must be on guard so we are not "spoiled," as the King James Version would say. The framework for our freedom is described in the rest of Colossians 2:

- 2:9—We can know the Father because Christ embodies Him fully.
- 2:10—Christ fills us, and He is the final authority.
- 2:11—Christ marks us as His own by releasing us from the power of the flesh.
- 2:12—Christ gave us a new identity in Himself.
- 2:13–14—God created a "togetherness" with Christ that assures our forgiveness and our permanent release from the debt that the law has the right to demand.
- 2:15—Christ disarmed any authority or power, worldly or spiritual, that stands in opposition to His resurrected life.

THE GOSPEL'S COMPETITION

"But the worries of this life, the deceitfulness of wealth and the desires for other things come in and choke the word, making it unfruitful."

MARK 4:19 NIV

Receiving the word sown by Christ is just the beginning; His goal is to have it grow and become fruitful, but the world pulls against us.

The worries of this life: Getting the right job, finding a wife, buying a house, raising kids, planning for retirement. These can be blessings from God, but they can also engross us to the point that we grow cold in pursuing Christ.

The deceitfulness of wealth: A comfortable life, a nicer house, a more prestigious job, luxuries, and fashionable possessions. "Whoever loves money never has enough; whoever loves wealth is never satisfied with their income. This too is meaningless" (Ecclesiastes 5:10 NIV). Money itself isn't the problem; it's the false promises money makes. If we get on the treadmill of riches, we'll stop running the race we were designed for.

The desires for other things: Success, influence, entertainment, political power, immortality, fame. These idols are just as false as the ones that ensnared ancient Israel when Joshua declared, "Choose for yourselves this day whom you will serve. . . . But as for me and my household, we will serve the LORD" (Joshua 24:15 NIV).

A seed that sprouts is a good start, but fruitfulness is the goal. We need to be alert to the weeds that choke the fruit God wants to produce in our lives.

THE HEART OF FORGIVENESS

Therefore, as God's chosen people, holy and dearly loved, clothe yourselves with compassion, kindness, humility, gentleness and patience. Bear with each other and forgive one another if any of you has a grievance against someone. Forgive as the Lord forgave you. And over all these virtues put on love, which binds them all together in perfect unity.

COLOSSIANS 3:12–14 NIV

The heart has long been the metaphor for the deepest parts of a man's emotions, thoughts, and attitudes. In addition to the Bible, the ancient Greeks and Egyptians credited the heart as the seat of our mind and thoughts and therefore our actions.

Today we can extend that metaphor with what we know about the heart from science. The heart is essentially a pump for the blood, and the blood is a vehicle for oxygen to be taken to every point of the body. Without this pumping of oxygen, the body dies. Perhaps this is why the Bible declares "the blood is the life" of all flesh (Deuteronomy 12:23 NIV).

Importantly, the point of a pump isn't to receive something, but to *push* it along. The heart wouldn't be functioning according to its design if it kept freshly oxygenated blood to itself. In the same way, if we receive forgiveness from the Lord without pushing it along, then our spiritual heart isn't functioning according to its design. A healthy Christian heart is characterized by compassion, kindness, humility, gentleness, and patience; it bears with the shortcomings and offenses of others. The only way to "hear" the beat of that heart is to witness forgiveness in action.

THE LIKENESS OF GOD

*But God disciplines us for our good,
in order that we may share in his holiness.*

HEBREWS 12:10 NIV

Holiness is God's nature and His fondest hope for His children. But the concept of holiness is almost always mired with misconceptions: holiness means no more fun, it's too hard to attain, it's a lot of work, it's boring, it means becoming "too religious."

Holiness is actually freedom. Nothing about it is boring or restrictive *when we are walking in it.* The psalmist described the joy of shared holiness well:

> *You make known to me the path of life; you will
> fill me with joy in your presence, with eternal
> pleasures at your right hand.* (Psalm 16:11 NIV)

And holiness is the only way for us to experience the Lord.

> *Make every effort to live in peace with everyone and
> to be holy; without holiness no one will see the Lord.*
> (Hebrews 12:14 NIV)

Of course, when we deny our new nature in Christ (2 Peter 1:4) and are living according to the flesh, valuing things that God says are worthless, then holiness will most certainly seem burdensome. That's because, even for believers, "the mind governed by the flesh is hostile to God" (Romans 8:7 NIV). When we feel that holiness is growing heavy, we should check our thought life, because "the mind governed by the Spirit is life and peace" (Romans 8:6 NIV).

Let us be on the watch for the discipline God promises so that we embrace it and grow in His likeness. Holiness is our birthright, and He is committed to seeing it in us.

SHARPENING SUCCESS

If the ax is dull, and one does not sharpen the edge,
then he must use more strength; but wisdom brings success.

ECCLESIASTES 10:10 NKJV

If you've ever tried to cut down a tree with an ax instead of a chainsaw, you know how much work it can be. And if you've ever tried to do it with a *dull* ax, you know it's almost impossible. Common sense tells us that it's better to take the time to sharpen the ax beforehand; otherwise, you'll just wear yourself out.

What does this proverb have to say to us today? What areas of life have us exhausted from exerting more and more effort for very little return? Where do we need wisdom to succeed?

Does my work leave me worn out? Do I need more education or training to see results? Am I in the right job to start with?

In relationships, am I constantly frustrated? Does sharpening the ax mean becoming a better listener? Being more patient? Controlling my temper?

What does success look like in my personal life? What goals have I had for years with no real results? Losing weight? Getting on a budget? Sharing my faith?

The challenge of this proverb is to identify where we are exhausting ourselves and to take the time to seek God's wisdom in sharpening the ax for success. Thankfully, He promises to give to those who ask:

If any of you lacks wisdom, you should ask God,
who gives generously to all without finding fault,
and it will be given to you. (James 1:5 NIV)

THE TRUE BATTLE

What causes fights and quarrels among you?
Don't they come from your desires that battle within you?

JAMES 4:1 NIV

The inner life of a man is the real life of a man. Proverb 23:7 (NKJV) puts it this way: "For as he thinks in his heart, so is he." The heart—or inner life—will determine everything that we do and say over time since from it comes our value system. That's why we are warned: "Above all else, guard your heart, for everything you do flows from it" (Proverbs 4:23 NIV).

One of the clear promises of scripture is that the inner life of a man will always come out:

> A good man brings good things out of the good
> stored up in his heart, and an evil man brings evil
> things out of the evil stored up in his heart. For
> the mouth speaks what the heart is full of.
> (Luke 6:45 NIV)

When we experience conflict with others—especially sincere believers—we may be allowing the inner turmoil of our own hearts to express itself in those relationships. Other people may not be "the problem." We may be engaging in the wrong battle. The real battle is saying no to our own desires and wants and humbling ourselves to serve.

> Do nothing out of selfish ambition or vain
> conceit. Rather, in humility value others above
> yourselves, not looking to your own interests but
> each of you to the interests of the others.
> (Philippians 2:3–4)

CULTIVATING GRATITUDE

"Those who sacrifice thank offerings honor me,
and to the blameless I will show my salvation."

PSALM 50:23 NIV

If there was ever a cure for being "hardened by sin's deceitfulness" (Hebrews 3:13 NIV) in a man's life, it's offering thanks to God. It's so easy to let the worries and distractions of this life pull us away from the things that matter; they make us forgetful of the blessings we've received and are daily living in. It takes humility to admit it and direct action to reverse it. And no action softens the heart and encourages the spirit like offering thanks to God.

The scriptures often use the word *sacrifice* in context of thanksgiving. The first instances of sacrificing an offering to God were Cain and Abel. Abel did it well, with a genuinely thankful heart, and Cain did not. The objects offered are not what God receives, but rather the gratitude itself. Consider Jesus' comments to one of ten lepers He had healed:

> *He threw himself at Jesus' feet and thanked him—*
> *and he was a Samaritan.*
> *Jesus asked, "Were not all ten cleansed? Where*
> *are the other nine? Has no one returned to give*
> *praise to God except this foreigner?"*
> (Luke 17:16–18 NIV)

Thanksgiving opens up the relationship God Himself wants. Not giving thanks is the symptom of those who have abandoned truth, as Romans 1:21 (NIV) says, "For although they knew God, they neither glorified him as God nor gave thanks to him, but their thinking became futile and their foolish hearts were darkened."

BREAD FROM HEAVEN

"You are looking for me, not because you saw the signs I performed but because you ate the loaves and had your fill."... So they asked him, "What sign then will you give that we may see it and believe you? What will you do? Our ancestors ate the manna in the wilderness; as it is written: 'He gave them bread from heaven to eat.'"

JOHN 6:26, 30–31 NIV

It's easier to acknowledge Jesus when we've just experienced His power—when our stomachs are full. But our interest in Him often fades as quickly as a good meal.

The five thousand knew a prophet was among them when the baskets of food were being passed around (John 6:14). But as soon as they were hungry again, the gift rather than the Giver became their focus. Though Jesus points this fact out to them, they "cleverly" try to get Him to prove Himself again by providing a daily supply of bread the way Moses had. Wouldn't that be great? No more work, no going hungry, just collect free bread every day.

But they missed the point of the manna. They hungered for an easy solution to this life's hardships, not Jesus Christ filling their souls. So they demanded free bread in exchange for their belief in a Messiah.

Isn't it easy to fall into the trap of trading faith for favors? But it's like being hired to follow—*as long as I'm being paid, I'm on God's side*. Let us all strive not to seek God to be filled only for a day when He offers so much more.

THE VALUE OF BETRAYAL

"Because the patriarchs were jealous of Joseph, they sold him as a slave into Egypt. But God was with him and rescued him from all his troubles. He gave Joseph wisdom and enabled him to gain the goodwill of Pharaoh king of Egypt. So Pharaoh made him ruler over Egypt and all his palace."

Acts 7:9–10 NIV

Betrayal isn't usually part of the recommended route to success. But in Joseph's case it was essential. His brothers hated him because he was their father Israel's favorite (Genesis 37:4). Matters only got worse when he began having dreams of the future in which they all bowed down to him. They considered killing him (Genesis 37:18), then finally settled on selling him into slavery. Of course, in the end, Joseph rescues his entire family from famine because he's been put in charge of all Egypt by Pharaoh.

Betrayal was part of God's plan for Joseph. In His hands, the hardest experiences in life can be tools for His use. Disappointment can clarify our expectations by stripping away false hopes. Tragedy can work its painful service to show us the reality of a world that isn't our home. Pain, as C. S. Lewis once wrote, can be "God's megaphone" to cut through the world and the flesh's noise and temptations.

Joseph remained faithful to God during his afflictions until God's timing was complete and he became the savior, literally, of Israel and the twelve tribes that would come from his brothers and himself. He was a foreshadowing of Jesus, who also endured betrayal as part of God's will in order to save His people eternally.

TRUE RIGHTEOUSNESS

"For I tell you that unless your righteousness surpasses that of the Pharisees and the teachers of the law, you will certainly not enter the kingdom of heaven."

MATTHEW 5:20 NIV

The Pharisees and scribes believed they "earned" righteousness by strictly following the Mosaic law. And, as if that weren't hard enough, they added other rules and traditions—even though sometimes they contradicted the law. Jesus rebuked them about this: "You have a fine way of setting aside the commands of God in order to observe your own traditions!" (Mark 7:9 NIV)

However, before Jesus exposed these groups as hypocrites, they were the top of the line in Jewish righteousness. They were learned, powerful, and influential. They ran the Sanhedrin, passing judgment on all aspects of life. Paul even makes reference to his past as a Pharisee to underscore his religious "pedigree":

> *Circumcised on the eighth day, of the people of Israel, of the tribe of Benjamin, a Hebrew of Hebrews; in regard to the law, a Pharisee; as for zeal, persecuting the church; as for righteousness based on the law, faultless.* (Philippians 3:5–6 NIV)

The Pharisees were an intimidating bunch. There must have been many Jews who said, "If only the law wasn't so hard, we could follow it too!" But Jesus wasn't sympathetic to that argument. The law, Jesus stressed, doesn't change. It's supposed to be hard—in fact, it's impossible if you go beyond outward practices to include the heart's attitudes and intentions. The Pharisees missed this, working instead for a counterfeit righteousness. Only Christ fulfilled the law completely; only He can offer us true righteousness.

WHOLEHEARTEDLY HIS

*[Amaziah] did what was right in the eyes of the Lord,
but not wholeheartedly.*

2 Chronicles 25:2 niv

Religion may ask, "Are you in or are you out?" But God asks, *How far in are you?* His interest is in an active, real relationship. It's the difference between a wedding and a marriage.

Before the wedding, a man is "out" but afterward, he is "in." And once he's married, the question is "How married is he?" Really married or just a little married? Which does his wife expect?

Everything God has done in history is to have His people be "really in"—wholeheartedly with Him. It's possible to do what is right in His eyes, but not in a way that demonstrates a real relationship with Him. Following the rules is never enough for a Father. Character and heart matter more.

No one ever impressed his wife, his boss, his commanding officer, his dad, or anyone else with a halfhearted effort. Why should we expect God to be happy when we just go through the motions? We certainly don't resemble our Father, "who did not spare his own Son, but gave him up for us all" (Romans 8:32 niv) when we hold back in doing His will.

The good news is that in Christ, we are given a whole heart to be His:

> *"I will give them a heart to know me, that I am
> the Lord. They will be my people, and I will be
> their God, for they will return to me with all their
> heart."* (Jeremiah 24:7 niv)

WORDS THAT BURN

They asked each other, "Were not our hearts burning within us while he talked with us on the road and opened the Scriptures to us?"

LUKE 24:32 NIV

On the day of Jesus' resurrection, two of His followers left Jerusalem for Emmaus. They were overwhelmed by the loss of their leader just a few days earlier and disturbed by the report that His body had disappeared from the well-guarded tomb. Then the resurrected Christ joined them on their journey, though "they were kept from recognizing him" (Luke 24:16 NIV). They pour out their anguish and disappointment to Jesus, who gently rebuked their lack of faith (Luke 24:25) and generously opened the scripture to them.

> *And beginning with Moses and all the Prophets, he explained to them what was said in all the Scriptures concerning himself. (Luke 24:27 NIV)*

Imagine the opportunity! Having the Author and Subject of the sacred writings explain everything about how they point to His coming, His suffering, and His resurrection. But even then, they didn't perceive the full truth of things. It wasn't until Christ revealed Himself by breaking bread with them that their eyes were spiritually opened and His teaching became as alive as He was (Luke 24:30–31).

Today we can walk the road to Emmaus whenever we rely on the Holy Spirit to reveal more to us:

> *"But the Advocate, the Holy Spirit, whom the Father will send in my name, will teach you all things and will remind you of everything I have said to you." (John 14:26 NIV)*

WORSHIP LIKE A MAN

*Wearing a linen ephod, David was dancing before the Lord with
all his might, while he and all Israel were bringing up the ark
of the Lord with shouts and the sound of trumpets.*

2 Samuel 6:14–15 NIV

Masculinity is made complete in worship. Where else can a man
open himself so completely without fear of failure, without
pretending to be strong or competent or in control? Where else
can a man be so honest without fear of being taken advantage of?
Where else can a man look into the face of the most Real Man of all?

To worship as a man means to disdain what others think of your
openness. The Complete Jewish Bible says David "danced and spun
around with abandon." When his wife, Michal, daughter of Saul,
rebuked him for this enthusiastic public display, he responded:

> *"It was before the Lord, who chose me rather
> than your father or anyone from his house when
> he appointed me ruler over the Lord's people
> Israel—I will celebrate before the Lord."*
> (2 Samuel 6:21 NIV)

Basically, David didn't give a rip what people thought of him
when he was worshipping. David cared only for God's opinion. As
a king, a warrior, and a shepherd, he had faced death from man
and beast, so public opinion wasn't about to scare him away from
worshipping with all his might.

Humbling yourself in worship, confessing, singing, crying,
dancing with wild abandon before your Maker, your Redeemer,
your Eternal Example is to return to masculinity not to relinquish it.

YOUR WILL BE DONE

*He was near Jerusalem and the people thought that the
kingdom of God was going to appear at once.*

LUKE 19:11 NIV

When God leads, it's easy to get ahead of Him. The *idea* of His
will can become the object of our hopes. We begin to love our
expectations of God's will so that we stop following Him to see
where His will actually takes us.

The disciples sometimes missed Jesus' will spectacularly:

> *[The Samaritans] did not receive Him, because
> His face was set for the journey to Jerusalem.
> And when His disciples James and John saw this,
> they said, "Lord, do You want us to command fire
> to come down from heaven and consume them,
> just as Elijah did?" But He turned and rebuked
> them, and said, "You do not know what manner
> of spirit you are of. For the Son of Man did not
> come to destroy men's lives but to save them."*
> (Luke 9:53–56 NKJV)

Talk about being on the wrong page! Clearly they hadn't been
paying attention to Christ during their time together.

We can learn from the disciples' worldly mind-set and apply
Paul's sound advice so that we stay in step with God's unfolding
will for our lives:

> *And do not be conformed to this world, but be
> transformed by the renewing of your mind, that
> you may prove what is that good and acceptable
> and perfect will of God.* (Romans 12:2 NKJV)

WHO JESUS CHRIST IS IN US

For it pleased the Father that in Him all the fullness
should dwell, and by Him to reconcile all things to Himself,
by Him, whether things on earth or things in heaven,
having made peace through the blood of His cross.

COLOSSIANS 1:19–20 NKJV

In a classic *Peanuts* cartoon, Charlie Brown hears that Snoopy is writing a book of theology and tells him, "I hope you have a good title." Snoopy lifts his hands off the typewriter, closes his eyes, and thinks to himself, *I have the perfect title.* He then types, "Has It Ever Occurred to You That You Might Be Wrong?"

True, we probably haven't thought of even 10 percent of the questions we should be asking, let alone answering, biblically, intellectually, and experientially. Still, we have learned and experienced so much that is true. Truths we can't review too often!

Truly transforming? Reviewing the dozens of "who I am in Christ" statements compiled and popularized by Neil T. Anderson, and more than doubled in size by others. Untold millions have experienced spiritual healing, health, and hope by reading them.

What would happen, however, if we turned the equation around? Specifically, what would happen in our heart and life if we began affirming what's true about "who Jesus Christ is in me"?

When we ponder "who Jesus Christ is in me," what immediately comes to mind? We can thank the Lord daily for His sovereignty (greatness), providence (goodness), holiness (glory), love (graciousness), and mystery (God alone knows).

In the coming days, let's continue to consider majestic truths about our Lord and Savior.

JESUS CHRIST OFFERS FORETASTES OF HEAVEN

"Go back and report to John what you have seen and heard:
The blind receive sight, the lame walk, those who have leprosy
are cleansed, the deaf hear, the dead are raised,
and the good news is proclaimed to the poor."

LUKE 7:22 NIV

Two thousand years ago, Jesus Christ's earthly ministry gave the men, women, youth, and children around Him amazing foretastes of what is eternal for each of His followers. Those foretastes cover a wide horizon. To name but a few: seeing individuals raised from the dead, seeing other individuals healed spiritually, seeing still others healed physically, seeing yet other persons healed psychologically.

Let's not make the mistake, however, of thinking that wonderful foretastes of heaven aren't *ours* to experience *today*. As followers of Jesus Christ, our sins past, present, and future are already all forgiven, yet we experience it anew each time we confess our sins. Immediately afterward, we want to slow down and savor that specific experience of being forgiven. If we do, we enjoy a delicious foretaste of heaven.

Even though our salvation is all-encompassing, it doesn't mean we don't sin—any more than it means we never get sick, never suffer trials, never wrestle with temptation, never fail, never fall, never fear cancer, and never end up dying. Aren't these means, while on this planet, helping us to continue longing for heaven?

What we don't want to miss is the critical need to slow down and savor each specific foretaste experience this side of eternity. In a real sense, these are Jesus Christ's rich and valuable gifts to us.

BEGIN WITH JESUS CHRIST

*God, who at various times and in various ways spoke
in time past to the fathers by the prophets, has
in these last days spoken to us by His Son.*

HEBREWS 1:1–2 NKJV

Let's consider what the opening verses of the New Testament letter to the Hebrews tell us about our majestic Lord and Savior. After all, Hebrews is a passionate appeal urging readers to see a bigger vision of Jesus Christ—and then worship and live accordingly.

In the opening verses, though, the writer of Hebrews doesn't say "Jesus Christ." He waits until partway through chapter 2 before mentioning "Jesus" by name, partway through chapter 3 before using the name "Christ," and all the way to chapter 10 before combining the two names together. Usage of *Jesus*, *Christ*, and *Jesus Christ* is much more prevalent in the latter chapters of Hebrews. From the get-go, however, the writer's preferred name for Jesus Christ is the "Son" of God, as we see in today's scripture passage.

Does it matter which English words we do and do not use to speak of Jesus Christ?

And does it matter how biblically accurate and true those words are?

A. W. Tozer said: "Much of our difficulty. . .stems from our unwillingness to take God as He is and adjust our lives accordingly." Do you agree or disagree?

What's more, how do you think a bigger vision of Jesus Christ could change how you worship and live?

BEGIN AND END WITH JESUS CHRIST

*In the past God spoke to our ancestors through the
prophets at many times and in various ways.*

HEBREWS 1:1 NIV

Hebrews begins as dramatically as a missile launch. It rockets past
the familiar Old Testament scriptures and the terrible cross of Jesus
Christ, following the path of Jesus Christ's ascension, where He reigns
on the throne of heaven.

Looking at Hebrews 1:1: *In the past* refers to the millennia
between Adam and Malachi. *God spoke* means we need to listen!
To our ancestors refers to leaders of the ancient Israelite nation.
Through the prophets refers to the Old Testament writers. *At many
times* understates God's hundreds of revelations over thousands
of years. *And in various ways* makes it clear God doesn't have only
one or two methods of communicating with humanity. Instead,
the Lord uses a wide variety of means:

- Through personal appearances and angels
- Through visions and dreams
- With lightning and fire
- With the voice of a trumpet and a quiet inner voice
- Using dictation and dialogue
- By using laws, institutions, ceremonies, sacrifices
- By issuing warnings and exhortations
- By using types, parables, and proverbs
- By using psalms, laments, histories, sermons,
  prophecies, and direct oracles
- By the perseverance of godly men and women,
  despite severe persecutions—persecutions no
  ordinary human beings could endure

JESUS CHRIST IS GREATER

But in these last days he [God the Father] has spoken to us
by his Son, whom he appointed heir of all things.

HEBREWS 1:2 NIV

The more we worship Jesus Christ with our heart, soul, strength, and mind, the greater He will become in our eyes.

C. S. Lewis portrays the growing Christian's experience of an ever-enlarging Jesus Christ in book 2 of *The Chronicles of Narnia.* One of the four children, Lucy, sees the lion Aslan—a Christ figure in the series—shining white and huge in the moonlight.

> *"Welcome, child," he said.*
> *"Aslan," said Lucy, "you're bigger."*
> *"That is because you are older, little one,"*
> *answered he.*
> *"Not because you are?"*
> *"I am not. But every year you grow, you will find*
> *me bigger."*

In Hebrews 1:2–3, our Lord and Savior Jesus Christ is honored in four distinct ways *in relation to God the Father.* This morning, we will consider the first two ways.

1. As the unique Son of God. This is something that never could be said of angels or other created beings. By putting our faith and trust in Jesus Christ, we become children of God, His sons, part of His family. Then again, Jesus Christ alone is God the Son.

2. As the heir of God. God has "appointed [Jesus Christ the] heir of all things." All things means *we* are part of His inheritance, *now and forever.* For some incredible reason, the Lord values and treasures us. And why is that true? Because He has invited us to join His forever family.

JESUS CHRIST IS FULLY GOD

*The Son is the radiance of God's glory
and the exact representation of his being.*

HEBREWS 1:3 NIV

Only God could script something so unexpected, so radical as sending Jesus Christ to earth.

No, this isn't an earthly king wearing common clothes to secretly visit his people. Instead, this is God Himself entering fully into humanity—supernaturally conceived, naturally formed in His earthly mother's womb, and humbly born into the most austere of circumstances.

In Hebrews 1:2–3, God the Son, Jesus Christ, is honored in four different ways *in relation to God the Father*. This evening, we will consider the third and fourth ways.

3. As the manifestation of God. The phrase "the radiance of God's glory" speaks of a flood of resplendent light. The word *radiance* means an outshining not a reflection. The moon reflects light; the sun radiates it—and so does God the Son.

As the brilliance of the sun is inseparable from the sun itself, so the Son's radiance is inseparable from Deity. No wonder the Nicene Creed describes Jesus Christ as "God of God, Light of Light, Very God of Very God." In Jesus, we see God Himself.

4. As the ultimate revealer of God. The phrase "the exact representation of his being" reiterates the fact that Jesus Christ is fully God—equal to and yet distinct from God the Father and God the Holy Spirit. Scripture calls us to worship Jesus accordingly.

One encounter with God's Son is enough to change someone instantly, forever. What has been your most meaningful experience with Jesus Christ? What was your response?

JESUS CHRIST, CREATOR AND SUSTAINER

In the past God spoke to our ancestors through the prophets at many times and in various ways, but in these last days he has spoken to us by his Son, whom he appointed heir of all things, and through whom also he made the universe. The Son is the radiance of God's glory and the exact representation of his being, sustaining all things by his powerful word.

HEBREWS 1:1–3 NIV

We can never honor Jesus Christ too much. The past two days we saw how Jesus Christ is honored four distinct ways *in relation to God*. This morning, we see two ways Jesus Christ is honored *in relation to all things*.

1. As the creator of the universe. This isn't a new idea. The fact that Jesus Christ is the creator of all things is taught in John 1:3, Colossians 1:16, and other scriptures. The implication is clear: *We* are part of Jesus Christ's creation. No wonder *He values us!*

Sometimes, though, we have a hard time feeling a sense of personal self-worth. Such worth isn't something we strive to obtain. Instead, it's something God has breathed into us from the moment He began creating us.

2. As the sustainer of the universe. The phrase "sustaining all things by his powerful word" means we are sustained not by our own strength but by Jesus Christ. We experience that strengthening as we read the Bible, meditate on it, read devotionally, pray with God, worship Him alone and with others, spend time with other growing Christian men, love our neighbors, and share our faith with them.

JESUS CHRIST, SAVIOR AND LORD

After he [Jesus Christ] had provided purification for sins,
he sat down at the right hand of the Majesty in heaven.

HEBREWS 1:3 NIV

In relation to all things, Jesus Christ is honored four ways. This evening, let's consider the third and fourth.

3. As the Savior of the universe. Romans 8:20–21, Colossians 1:19–20, and other scriptures tell us that Jesus intends to redeem creation itself. The phrase "had provided purification for sins" speaks more particularly of the fact that we are purified, washed, redeemed, and being sanctified because of Jesus Christ's death on the cross.

4. As the Lord of the universe. The phrase "he sat down at the right hand of the Majesty in heaven" spoke powerfully to the original readers, because they knew that priests never sat down. Jesus could sit down, however, because His priestly work of redemption was complete. He is now supremely honored in heaven.

What's more, in His position of authority, Christ intercedes with the Father on our behalf. It's quite astounding to realize that even when we don't feel we can pray, Jesus never stops praying for us.

The healing method of the writer of Hebrews is to lift the Son higher and higher. He is sure that the eloquence of Jesus Christ's person is the most practical thing on earth. Indeed, Jesus, understood and exalted, eloquently informs every area of life.

Does your life sometimes feel stressful and perhaps even overwhelming? If so, the essential answer to each of life's problems is. . .what? *Who Jesus Christ is*—in you. Not in theory. Not in "theology." But—*in you!*

JESUS CHRIST WILL ALWAYS BE FULLY HUMAN

For this reason he had to be made like them, fully human in every way, in order that he might become a merciful and faithful high priest in service to God, and that he might make atonement for the sins of the people. Because he himself suffered when he was tempted, he is able to help those who are being tempted.

HEBREWS 2:17–18 NIV

As we talk with friends about Jesus Christ, mistakes are bound to happen. According to leading pollsters, it's quite astounding how many misconceptions people have about the Bible, about God, and specifically about Jesus Christ.

The one mistake we don't want to make is assuming our friends understand that Jesus Christ is eternal. As God's Son, Jesus has existed for all of eternity past. There is no point at which Jesus Christ didn't exist.

Yet many speak as if Jesus came alive and was created at the point of conception in the virgin Mary's womb. That point simply represents when He went from being fully God to being fully God *and human*.

It sometimes can be hard to imagine Jesus spending nine months "trapped" before birth, let alone spending years "trapped" as an infant, toddler, child, older child, young man, and full-fledged adult before starting His public ministry at age thirty.

Yet Jesus Christ didn't become *barely human*. Instead, He became, is, and for all eternity will be *fully God and fully human.*

Our scripture today mentions three reasons Jesus had become "fully human in every way." They're great reasons to thank Him again today.

HOW WE BRING JOY TO THE LORD

Therefore by Him let us continually offer the sacrifice of praise to God, that is, the fruit of our lips, giving thanks to His name. But do not forget to do good and to share, for with such sacrifices God is well pleased.

HEBREWS 13:15–16 NKJV

Unlike the original cast of characters in the Holy Lands two thousand years ago, we know that the greatest story ever told doesn't begin, let alone end, with the birth of Jesus.

The story of Jesus Christ, as God's eternal Son, has *no beginning*.

The story of Jesus Christ, as fully God *and fully human*, begins with His conception and birth, which we celebrate during Advent and Christmas. Three months later, we celebrate the focal point of His earthly life and ministry during Passion, Good Friday, Easter Resurrection Sunday, and His Ascension six weeks later.

And how do we celebrate these decidedly Christian holidays? We do so by praising and thanking God the Father, God the Son, and God the Holy Spirit. We also do so by doing good and sharing with others, "for with such sacrifices God is well pleased."

Put another way, our words praising who Jesus Christ is in us and our words and actions toward family and friends around us make the Trinity happy!

So, it's okay to decorate our homes, make delicious foods, assemble gifts, offer hospitality, and then give thanks to the Lord during Christianity's most important holidays.

After all, actions speak loudest *with* words.

JOSEPH SAID WHAT?

This is how Jesus the Messiah was born. His mother, Mary, was engaged to be married to Joseph. But before the marriage took place, while she was still a virgin, she became pregnant through the power of the Holy Spirit. Joseph, to whom she was engaged, was a righteous man and did not want to disgrace her publicly, so he decided to break the engagement quietly.

MATTHEW 1:18–19 NLT

What do we know about Joseph? He lived in Nazareth of Galilee. He worked as a carpenter. He was a good, godly man. His fiancée was godly young Mary. He liked to do things "quietly." More remarkable? An angel of the Lord spoke to him in dreams not once or twice but four times.

The first time, the angel told him not to fear God's miraculous plan to visit earth through His Son already conceived by the Holy Spirit in Mary.

Perhaps a few months later, shortly after the visit of the magi, the angel told Joseph to get up immediately and flee to Egypt with Mary and Jesus.

Perhaps a year later, the angel appears to Joseph in a third dream, telling him to return to Israel. In a companion dream a short time later, Joseph is told to take Mary and Jesus farther north back to Galilee. In the end, they return to their hometown, Nazareth.

So, what do we know about Joseph? He is a man of action, immediately getting up in the middle of the night to obey God. More remarkable? Scripture doesn't record a single word Joseph said.

What matters most is being a good, godly man of action!

SEEING LIFE AS JESUS CHRIST SEES IT

Jesus wept.

JOHN 11:35 KJV

During quiet evenings and times of rest, we often like to read great literature, watch a great movie, or hear a great story—and be deeply moved.

Yet what moves us?

Among other things, point of view (POV) strongly affects how we're moved.

To the very finite, limited extent that a story's POV reflects God's POV, we can be moved to a new appreciation of Jesus Christ's unlimited POV in our lives.

POV can be omniscient or all-knowing. It doesn't mean the narrator tells us everything he or she knows. In fact, the best narrators tell us only what we need to know. During His public ministry, Jesus certainly didn't say everything He knew. In fact, most times He refused to answer the direct questions darting His way. He did that on purpose!

POV can be omnipotent or all-powerful. In most stories, the narrator isn't directly making this or that happen. Then again, that sometimes happens. Outside of the days of Moses, the days of Elijah and Elisha, and the days of Jesus Christ and the apostles, God doesn't directly speak to individuals, cast down plagues, blind armies, and bend the laws of nature. Or, does He?

POV can be omnipresent or all-present. Among other places, this is seen in movies with rapidly changing points of view, particularly during epic battle scenes.

Again, any story's POV is only a small inkling of the Lord's unlimited POV. So, don't get too carried away! Still, look for this the next time you sit down to enjoy a great story.

WHY WE DON'T NEED TO FEAR THE FUTURE

"Don't let your hearts be troubled."

JOHN 14:1 NLT

Outside of the Bible, no other sacred writings contain accurate, detailed prophecies of the future. Only God can say what's going to happen! In 125 words, here's what we learn from biblical prophecy.

We should never be surprised by the phenomenal (albeit short-lived) success of evil, Satan-inspired men. Until the climax of history, many evil men will triumph for a time. The twentieth century was no exception. There's no reason to believe the twenty-first century will be an exception either. But we never need fear that evil will triumph completely. Why not? Because God controls the day they ascend to power and the day of their downfall. This will be true of even the most wicked, Satan-inspired man of all, the Antichrist. In the end, God will crush His enemies. Of that we can be sure! No matter what happens this century, we need to keep the end of God's story clearly in view—and never lose faith.

After calling His first disciples, Jesus takes them to Capernaum, where an unseen war became visible momentarily. When a demon-possessed man tries to tell Jesus what to do, He immediate rebukes the evil spirit and tells *him* what to do. To everyone's astonishment, the demon has to obey what Jesus says.

The reality is we all have to obey Jesus. We may shake and scream. We may try to tell Jesus what to do. But in the end, *we* have to obey Him. The question isn't "Is Jesus Lord of your life?" The question is "Have you acknowledged that fact?"

THE FIRST WAY WE BECOME WHOLE MEN

And Jesus grew in wisdom and stature,
and in favor with God and man.

LUKE 2:52 NIV

We live in a broken world. . .full of broken promises, broken dreams, broken lives. Nothing seems "all together" anymore. In the midst of such shatteredness, however, God invites us to experience wholeness, wholeness in our own life and in our relationships.

As a result, growth as whole persons is anything but optional. We see this most concisely in the Bible's description of Jesus as a teenager (quoted above). Though Jesus was the perfect Son of God, He experienced apparent personal growth in four ways.

It is vital that we do the same! Over the next 48 hours, let's consider each way—from the most tangible to the most spiritual.

PHYSICALLY ("and stature")

We need proper exercise physically. How? By playing ball. Golfing. Walking. Jogging. By riding a stationary bike. By working out with light weights. By exercising regularly. . .and feeling better as a result.

We need proper rest physically. How? By not pushing too hard all the time. By getting enough sleep. By taking a nap if needed (even athletes do this). By being consistent in our sleeping patterns (inconsistency makes us even more tired—think "jet lag").

We need proper nourishment physically. How? By eating three well-planned meals daily. By eating plenty of whole grains, vegetables, fruits, and proteins. By enjoying desserts and junk food once in a while, not as a steady diet.

In everything, let's give thanks to God for blessing us with the joys that come from good exercise, sleep, and eating!

THE SECOND WAY WE BECOME WHOLE MEN

Now that we know what we have—Jesus, this great High Priest with ready access to God—let's not let it slip through our fingers. We don't have a priest who is out of touch with our reality. He's been through weakness and testing, experienced it all— all but the sin. So let's walk right up to him and get what he is so ready to give. Take the mercy, accept the help.

HEBREWS 4:14–16 MSG

Though Jesus was the perfect Son of God, He experienced apparent personal growth. This enabled Him to relate fully with others. The same can be true for us.

SOCIALLY ("and man," Luke 2:52 NIV)

We need proper exercise socially. How? By cultivating existing friendships. By sharing a meal with new friends from church. By offering practical assistance to a neighbor. By being a listening ear. By keeping in touch with family. By praying for others by name.

We need proper rest socially. How? By taking breaks. By enjoying the great outdoors. By jettisoning any compulsive need to be with others all the time. By appreciating downtime before an appointment. By listening to a favorite mix of music. By meditating on God's Word. By taking extended time to worship and pray privately.

We need proper nourishment socially. How? By not viewing all friendships the same. By discerning who our good friends and our closest friends are. By cultivating deep friendships. By inviting trusted friends to speak into our lives with truth and grace. In turn, by actively encouraging our best friend to become the man God wants him to be.

THE THIRD WAY WE BECOME WHOLE MEN

May God himself, the God of peace, sanctify you through and through. May your whole spirit, soul and body be kept blameless at the coming of our Lord Jesus Christ. The one who calls you is faithful, and he will do it.

1 THESSALONIANS 5:23–24 NIV

How good that God invites us to experience personal growth and wholeness four ways. The past two days we've looked at good health physically and socially. Today, let's look at a third way.

PSYCHOLOGICALLY ("in wisdom," Luke 2:52 NIV)

We need proper exercise volitionally. How? By our choices. In particular, by consistently exercising our will for good. Each of us faces the problem of "choice overload." Daily we are faced with too many choices. Not only must we decide preferences between viable options, but we also must make healthy moral judgments, especially in so-called gray areas.

We need proper rest emotionally. How? By getting a refreshing night's sleep. By spending time with a godly friend. By reading an edifying book. By listening to uplifting music. By spending quality quiet time with the Lord. By slowing down (if we've been pushing too hard). By doing more (if we've been too lax). By actively seeking to balance life's demands. By making specific plans for another vacation, even if it's simply a quick getaway.

We need proper nourishment intellectually. How? Actually, scripture has a lot to say! By renewing our mind (Romans 12:1–2). By cultivating a discerning mind (Hebrews 5:14). By nurturing an enlightened mind (1 Corinthians 2:12). By protecting our mind (Philippians 4:8). And, by occupying our mind with Christ (Ephesians 4:13).

THE FOURTH WAY WE BECOME WHOLE MEN

*Everyone who heard about it reflected on these events and asked,
"What will this child turn out to be?" For the hand of the Lord was
surely upon him in a special way. . . . John grew up and became
strong in spirit. And he lived in the wilderness until he
began his public ministry to Israel.*

LUKE 1:66, 80 NLT

Thankfully, there's still time to keep growing stronger physically, socially, psychologically and. . .

SPIRITUALLY ("with God," Luke 2:52 NIV)

We need proper exercise spiritually. How? By getting on our knees. By depending on God to meet our needs. By coming alongside a friend who's struggling in his faith. By investing in the life of a friend who isn't a Christian yet.

We need proper rest spiritually. How? If a particular spiritual discipline feels "dry," by taking a short break from it and selecting two or three "rest" verses to memorize and claim as our own. Favorites include: "Be still before the LORD and wait patiently for him" (Psalm 37:7 NIV); "Truly my soul silently waits for God; from Him comes my salvation" (Psalm 62:1 NKJV); and "Those who live in the shelter of the Most High will find rest in the shadow of the Almighty" (Psalm 91:1 NLT).

We need proper nourishment spiritually. How? By reading scripture wholeheartedly, asking God to speak to you. By meeting with a small group that loves God and its members. By attending services at a vibrant local church each Sunday. By inviting a wise, gracious older believer to mentor you. And, finally, by reading edifying Christian books.

LOVING OTHER BELIEVERS

We [Paul and Timothy] always pray for you, and we give thanks to God, the Father of our Lord Jesus Christ. For we have heard of your faith in Christ Jesus and your love for all of God's people.

COLOSSIANS 1:3–4 NLT

As God's people, you are called to exhibit love for everyone, including your enemies, but you have a certain affinity for other believers—an instant bond, no matter how long you've known them. You're united in Christ, and that bond is thicker than blood.

Paul wrote to the Colossian church that he wanted them to know how thankful he was for their reputation of loving all of God's people. We can't be certain how Paul and Timothy heard this information, although some commentators speculate that it was passed on by Epaphras (v. 7). We also don't know how they expressed this love, but it undoubtedly involved acts of kindness and mercy because love includes action, and you build a reputation for things you do consistently.

How is your church viewed by other Christians who have never stepped foot inside one of your worship services? Do other believers see your church at local events, praying and serving alongside fellow believers? Does your church reach out to other churches in your city during their time of need? Does your church celebrate with other Christians? If not, what simple steps can you take to change that?

MORNING MEETINGS WITH GOD

My voice shalt thou hear in the morning, O LORD; in the morning will I direct my prayer unto thee, and will look up.

PSALM 5:3 KJV

DAY 243 – MORNING

When David penned these words, he was probably surrounded by his enemies (see vv. 6, 8)—perhaps during the reign of King Saul. No matter what the circumstances, David made a point to meet with God every morning. He was intentional in turning his face toward heaven and directing his voice toward God, being confident that the Lord would hear him.

On this day, he reminded God about His character—how He didn't take pleasure in wickedness (v. 4). He also reminded God that the foolish would not stand before Him (v. 5). But David knew he wasn't perfect either. David was resolute in communicating with God every morning, not because he was without blemish or fault, but because he knew God was merciful (v. 7). So, he approached Him in the morning time with a healthy dose of fear, knowing he deserved judgment, but trusting in God's mercy.

What does your morning routine look like? Does it include approaching God, knowing He will hear you? Do you come before Him with a proper amount of reverent fear, no matter what the circumstances? Or do difficulties, business, or sloth keep you from meeting with Him? Even if you're surrounded by enemies, God will hear you. You're not alone.

SPIRITUAL PROSPERITY

*Better is the poor who walks in his integrity than
one who is perverse in his lips, and is a fool.*

PROVERBS 19:1 NKJV

The man who walks in his integrity is satisfied at the end of the day. He's done an honest day's worth of work, treated people well, and comes home to a meal that no king would necessarily desire, but it fills his stomach and he's thankful for it. He has nothing to be ashamed about. He's put forth his best effort and tomorrow is another day.

The man who is crooked, however, is foolish. He speaks lies and cuts corners to get ahead. He mistreats people for his own gain. He dines extravagantly and drives fancy vehicles. His conscience bothers him from time to time, but he rationalizes his actions, telling himself that everybody does wrong things. He covers up his sins and falls asleep scheming about the next day.

Not surprisingly, the Hebrew word for *integrity* in today's verse can be translated as "prosperity." So, better is the poor who walks in his spiritual prosperity than the one who is perverse in his lips. That would seem to indicate a spiritual divide between the person who spends time tending to spiritual matters versus the person who spends time scheming to get ahead.

Proverbs 19:1 doesn't really speak about middle ground or about the middle class and its values. So ask yourself which side of the spectrum you're currently on and which values you're cultivating.

A VALUABLE EMPLOYEE

*Be diligent to know the state of your flocks,
and attend to your herds; for riches are not forever,
nor does a crown endure to all generations.*

PROVERBS 27:23–24 NKJV

Shepherds need to be experts in the way their animals are bred, sheltered, fed, jugged (separated with their mother for a period after birth), mixed, weaned, dewormed, and even how they play, if the shepherds want to make sure their animals thrive.

Just as shepherds need to be diligent about the state of their flocks, this scripture calls you to know the ins and outs of your occupation. You ought to know all of your industry terms and their nuances. As you grow and immerse yourself in your occupation, you should develop knowledge about what will work and what won't. This will make you a valuable asset to your employer as well as give you some financial stability.

In so doing, you'll set yourself apart from other employees who are simply punching the clock to earn a living. A few of them might follow your example of diligence. Your boss will certainly take note at least. But most importantly, you'll be fulfilling your calling as set forth in Colossians 3:23–24 (NKJV): "And whatever you do, do it heartily, as to the Lord and not to men, knowing that from the Lord you will receive the reward of the inheritance; for you serve the Lord Christ."

OPEN YOUR HOME

*God has given each of you a gift from his great variety of
spiritual gifts. Use them well to serve one another.*

1 PETER 4:10 NLT

When Peter penned these words, the destruction of the Jewish
temple and nation were at hand (1 Peter 4:7 NLT). With persecution
imminent, Peter wanted believers to maintain their focus. He
wanted them to be earnest and disciplined in their prayers while
loving one another and opening their homes to one another
(vv. 7–9). Finally, they were to serve one another by using the
spiritual gifts that God had given them.

Are you concerned that the end of the church and our nation
may be at hand? Are you angry about it—getting caught up in
heated political exchanges, sometimes even with fellow believers?
Is your bitterness poisoning your heart, affecting your attitude,
and rendering you ineffective in your witness? Listen to Peter's
advice. Open your home to fellow believers. Pray with them. Study
with them. Laugh with them. Weep with them. Serve them using
your spiritual gifts.

If you aren't sure about your spiritual gifting, talk to a leader
at church to help you identify it. And then begin to exercise it.
You'll notice a difference in your attitude as you minister to fellow
saints. And you'll make a greater impact for the kingdom of God
as unbelievers see your love for other believers in action.

HIDE THE WORD

Therefore, putting aside all filthiness and all that remains of wickedness, in humility receive the word implanted, which is able to save your souls.

JAMES 1:21 NASB

James, who was probably writing primarily to Jewish converts to Christianity who were dispersed abroad (James 1:1), wanted them to understand that their trials could produce lasting spiritual results because the testing of their faith would produce endurance (v. 3). He wanted them to be quick to hear, slow to speak, and slow to anger (v. 19).

Building on that thought, he told them to put aside all filthiness and other forms of wickedness as they humbly received the Word of God. Putting off wickedness isn't something you do in your flesh. The flesh cries out for wickedness. Instead, putting it off comes as you hear, read, meditate on, and submit to the Word of God. Receiving it in humility means not arguing with it or justifying your sin when the Word confronts it, but rather recognizing the darkness of your heart, confessing it, and repenting.

You will never fully escape the pull of wickedness in this world, but the degree to which you struggle with it equates to the amount of time you spend interacting with and submitting to the Word of God. If the world's pull is stronger than it should be in your life now, find more time to hide the Word in your heart so you won't sin against God (see Psalm 119:11).

FAMILY MANAGERS

*(If anyone does not know how to manage his own family,
how can he take care of God's church?)*

1 TIMOTHY 3:5 NIV

As Paul spelled out the qualifications for a bishop (or deacon) to Timothy, he included the qualification we find in today's verse. A man must be able to manage his own family before he can take care of God's church.

Note that in 1 Timothy 3:1, Paul sets all of this up by saying, "Whoever aspires to be an overseer"—in other words, this office isn't a calling but an aspiration. Think about the setting for a moment. Who would actually aspire to become a bishop/deacon in the hostile environment the first-century church existed in? Persecution and death would have hung around every corner—especially for leaders. Yet, wanting to shepherd young converts is a work of the Holy Spirit who dwells within believers.

As a man, you're called to be a priest in your home. If you don't desire to lovingly lead your family in devotions, prayer, spiritual discussions, and guidance, especially in a country that *allows* such religious freedom, then something is wrong. Yes, Paul's words refer to aspiring bishops in the context of a church, but in a broader context, this should be the call for every Christian man, no matter what his position.

ACCURATE WEIGHTS

DAY 246 – MORNING

The LORD detests the use of dishonest scales,
but he delights in accurate weights.

PROVERBS 11:1 NLT

One of the ancient practices in commerce that scripture refers to often is the use of stones to keep fair and accurate measures.

Deuteronomy 25:13–14 (NKJV) says, "You shall not have in your bag differing weights, a heavy and a light. You shall not have in your house differing measures, a large and a small." Hosea 12:7 (NKJV) says, "A cunning Canaanite! Deceitful scales are in his hand; he loves to oppress." And Proverbs 16:11 as well as Proverbs 20:10 address this issue of unbalanced scales and using unjust weights.

Today, it would be the equivalent of going to the supermarket and purchasing two pounds of roast beef. You watch the butcher put the meat on the scale, see that it's two pounds, and thank him. But when the person after you places the same order, the butcher switches the scales and places much more meat on the (clearly unjust) scale for the same price you paid.

You would be understandably upset over such a thing. The Lord also detests such business practices. He's just and therefore is on the side of those who are treated unjustly. As you head to your workplace today or slide into your home office chair, consider all *your* business practices. Are they fair and just?

PEACEFUL HOUSEHOLDS

"If the household is worthy, let your peace come upon it.
But if it is not worthy, let your peace return to you."

MATTHEW 10:13 NKJV

When Jesus sent out His twelve apostles, He told them to inquire about those who were worthy (receptive to the Gospel) and to stay with those households (Matthew 10:11–12). Then He told them to let their peace come upon those families.

The Greek word for *peace* here means "by implication prosperity, peace, quietness, rest." The disciples were to seek such peace as they entered a house (Luke 10:5), praying with the occupants, offering instruction, and when they left, leaving a spoken blessing behind. Ultimately, they were seeking to offer peace between those who were receptive and God Himself, through the death of Christ on the cross. But their hosts got a healthy dose of the practical implications of the faith by interacting with the disciples in their homes.

Offering a place for strangers to stay was the custom in the first century, but not so much today, so how can you apply this teaching? You can still inquire about people's receptivity to the Gospel by talking to them in supermarkets, baseball games, and over the backyard fence. And you can also meet receptive people in public places like coffee shops. You might even get invited into their homes to speak peace over their families.

BE COURAGEOUS AND OBEDIENT

*"Only be strong and very courageous; be careful to do according
to all the law which Moses My servant commanded you;
do not turn from it to the right or to the left, so that
you may have success wherever you go."*

Joshua 1:7 NASB

As Israel stood on the edge of the Promised Land, God spoke the words in today's verse to Joshua. Every place Joshua and the Israelites stepped inside the Promised Land would be theirs (v. 3), and no man would be able to stand before Israel because God was with them (v. 5). But His promise was conditional. They were to be strong and courageous, acting according to the Law, so that they'd find success.

Sadly, Israel didn't always follow this instruction, and it cost them dearly. They started off strong, conquering Jericho (Joshua 6). But they stumbled in Ai after Achan sinned against the Lord (Joshua 7), and it cost thirty-six men their lives (Joshua 7:5). They went on to have several more victories and then divided the land among the tribes. After the death of Joshua, the next generation didn't know God and began to serve false gods, forsaking the Lord. He then brought judgment on them (Judges 2:11–15) and let them suffer numerous defeats.

Courage must always be tied to obedience to God. Does this describe your walk with Christ? Have you ever exhibited courage without regard for obedience?

THIRSTING FOR GOD

*You, God, are my God, earnestly I seek you; I thirst for you,
my whole being longs for you, in a dry and parched
land where there is no water.*

PSALM 63:1 NIV

Physical thirst is tangible. Your throat is dry. Your muscles begin to cramp. In extreme cases, confusion or hallucinations will set in. No matter how severe the case, nobody needs to tell you that you're thirsty. You instinctively know all the signs.

You also know all the signs of thirst for the good things of this world. You know the longing to finally watch a movie you've been waiting to see. You know how it feels to thirst for the presence of a spouse. You know the thirst you feel to hit a physical fitness goal when you're getting close.

But do you know the signs of spiritual thirst? David did. His whole being longed for God. Bible commentator John Gill suggests that spiritual longing will include a deep desire for the Bible, for worship, for church ordinances, for communion, for greater knowledge of Him, and for more grace from Him.

If you aren't thirsty for such things, something is lacking. When David penned the words of today's verse, he was in the wilderness of Judah. Even in such extreme circumstances, he knew and experienced all of the signs of spiritual thirst. If you don't experience this, engage with God and He will slake your thirst today.

YOUR HELP

I look up to the mountains—does my help come from there?
My help comes from the LORD, who made heaven and earth!

PSALM 121:1–2 NLT

In the Old Testament, the Hebrews were accustomed to facing Jerusalem—which was built on a mountain—whenever they prayed (see Daniel 6:10). The temple had been built there on Mount Moriah. Judea itself was mountainous. The ark of the covenant once rested on the holy hill of Zion. So, it's understandable why the Israelites looked to the hills for spiritual help. Other nations believed, in fact, that "the LORD is God of the hills" (1 Kings 20:28 KJV).

But Jeremiah 3:23 (NLT) declared, "Our worship of idols on the hills and our religious orgies on the mountains are a delusion. Only in the LORD our God will Israel ever find salvation." Looking to the hills for help was useless.

Modern Christians turn to all sorts of things in search of spiritual help or deliverance: anointed artifacts, crucifixes, a word of knowledge, even statues. Some even elevate pastors, healers, and spiritual gurus. But your power and salvation don't come from any such activity. It comes from the Lord, who made heaven and earth.

Spend some time today taking spiritual inventory. Have you elevated anything or anyone above God? Maybe the better question to ask yourself is, if anything was removed from your life, would you lack spiritual power? If so, you're depending on that particular object or person too much.

HOPE

Now the God of hope fill you with all joy and peace in believing,
that ye may abound in hope, through the power of the Holy Ghost.

ROMANS 15:13 KJV

If you look around at the unbelievers in your life, all of them are lacking one thing: hope, in the eternal sense. Some have earthly hope, finding it in fulfilling work, wealth, or even family. Others have false hope in their good deeds. But most of the people you know outside of the church have no real assurance or peace about their standing before a holy God.

In Romans 15, Paul explains that Christ is the great hope for Jews and Gentiles alike. In fact, in today's verse, Paul calls Him the God of hope—a title no Gentile could have dared believe in days gone by. Jesus is the long-awaited Messiah. And belief in Him leads to joy and peace in the here and now, but it also settles eternity in the heart of the believer.

Notice, in fact, that Paul is talking to believers here in Romans 15. You know that it's possible for even Christians to fall into despair and to feel genuine sadness. Even Jesus, God's Son, felt sorrow on occasion. But beyond the tears and grief is the great hope of heaven. Not hope in the sense of a child wishing for ice cream, but rather an earnest expectation for deliverance from life's problems.

PLANT, NURTURE, AND WATER

He that gathereth in summer is a wise son: but he that sleepeth in harvest is a son that causeth shame.

PROVERBS 10:5 KJV

A farmer who doesn't put in the necessary work in the summer shouldn't expect to see a harvest in the fall. Nor should he expect to simply put in the work during the summer and then sleep during the harvest. Planting, nurturing, and gathering all have natural seasons and rhythms. They are not changed by human whims or bouts of laziness.

When you think of a farmer, do you think of someone who avoids work? No. Farmers understand that isn't an option. Often they don't even attend worship services during the fall because it's the time for harvesting and that window of time is very limited.

From the big-picture perspective, you're to be about the business of planting and nurturing during your prime income-earning years because a time is coming in the fall and winter of your life when you'll no longer be able to gather as much.

Today's verse is written with a family in mind. A son who gathers and harvests at the appropriate times is wise. He puts the needs of his family before his own wants. Does your work life resemble a farmer's? Are you consistent in your planting and nurturing, knowing that fall is on the way?

SLOW, STEADY PROGRESS

*The end of a matter is better than its beginning;
patience of spirit is better than haughtiness of spirit.*

ECCLESIASTES 7:8 NASB

If you've ever been to a rally—spiritual, sports, or business-related—then you know how a great message can fire up a crowd. Everybody plans to go home and implement what they learned, but as soon as they walk through the door, reality hits them.

The sink is backed up, the car needs repairs, their son needs a ride to soccer practice, and the baby is crying. So, they dive into their responsibilities, and the end of the matter (their new goal) fades as quickly as the emotion that swept through the auditorium hours earlier. They're like "the man who hears the word and immediately receives it with joy; yet he has no firm root in himself, but is only temporary" (Matthew 13:20–21 NASB).

In today's verse, Solomon calls you to be patient of spirit as you set your mind on something. If your goal is to read God's Word every day without fail, then tend to your responsibilities, but try getting up a little earlier. If your goal is to walk five miles a day, start with one mile and work your way up. If your goal is to set a new sales record, then study the current leader and carefully implement his strategies.

Slow, steady progress beats quick, emotional commitment every time. The end is better than the beginning.

A GOOD SOLDIER

Thou therefore endure hardness,
as a good soldier of Jesus Christ.

2 Timothy 2:3 kjv

Because of God's grace, Paul wanted Timothy to understand that the Christian can and should endure much hardship as a good soldier of Jesus. Consider the hardship a soldier of your country endures for your sake.

He leaves family and friends behind. He leaves career advancement behind. He leaves his personal dreams behind. In their place, he endures hunger, sleep deprivation, and constant threats and danger. Why would someone put himself through something like that?

Partially because he loves his country—the country that granted him his freedom to have a family, to pursue a career, and to chase his dreams. Partially because he knows that if he doesn't go, someone else might *not* and his nation's borders might be insecure. And partially because he wants to keep his family, friends, and community safe. In all three instances, he's motivated by love and a sense of duty.

This is the life that every Christian man is called to—except that your calling is to advance and preach the Gospel of Christ so the next generation can know His grace. You sacrifice and endure hardship because He sacrificed and endured for you. If you haven't been living the life of a solider of Christ, reenlist in His army and pick up your spiritual weapons.

REORIENTATION

Let everyone see that you are considerate in all you do.
Remember, the Lord is coming soon.

PHILIPPIANS 4:5 NLT

At first glance, it's surprising to see Paul telling believers in Philippi to let everyone see that they're considerate in all they do. Aren't Christians supposed to avoid calling attention to themselves? Elsewhere, scripture says to not let your left hand know what your right hand is doing (Matthew 6:3). A few verses later, Jesus tells His disciples to pray in private (v. 6).

But a closer look at all these verses reveals no contradiction with today's verse. In verse 3, Jesus was talking to His disciples about giving in secret to avoid drawing attention to themselves for the sake of self-glorification. And in verse 6, He was talking about not praying for show. Paul, on the other hand, wants believers to live out loud for God's sake, not their own, because Jesus is coming back soon. Having that sense of urgency reorients the way a person lives and keeps him from becoming self-centered.

If you knew Jesus was coming back today, how would it change the way you lived your faith? You'd probably have a short account with God, making sure that each action you took glorified Him. You'd empty yourself of selfish ambitions and seek the good of those around you.

Wouldn't that be a refreshing way to live? Prayerfully commit yourself to such a vision.

WORDS LIKE MEDICINE

Gentle words are a tree of life;
a deceitful tongue crushes the spirit.

PROVERBS 15:4 NLT

What is the most hurtful thing anybody has ever said to you? Can you recall the circumstances? How long ago was it? Did you embrace it as truth—even if it wasn't true—and allow it to affect your life for more years than you care to admit?

Have you ever said something hurtful to somebody that you wished you could take back a second after it left your lips? You saw the reaction on the other person's face, and it confirmed the devastation you realized it might bring. You can say you're sorry later, and that helps, but you can't unsay those words.

Gentle words are a tree of life. That doesn't mean you can't be truthful, but it does mean you should be gentle. Even tough love can be gentle. Some translations (NIV, NASB) use the word *soothing* in place of *gentle*, and the KJV has *wholesome*. The Hebrew word actually means "medicine, cure, deliverance, and remedy," among other things.

Are your words like medicine? Do they offer deliverance and a cure? Or are they sometimes deceitful or crushing? Consider how the negative words you recalled so easily at the beginning of this devotion affected you, and resolve to not weigh anybody down with such a tone going forward.

GOD STILL SPEAKS

We ourselves heard that voice from heaven
when we were with him on the holy mountain.

2 PETER 1:18 NLT

At the transfiguration, Peter saw something that changed him—giving him a message he wanted people to hear. He says James, John, and he himself saw Christ's majestic splendor with their own eyes as Christ received honor and glory from the Father. Can you imagine what that must have looked like? And if that wasn't enough, they heard the very voice of God say, "This is my dearly loved Son, who brings me great joy" (2 Peter 1:17 NLT).

The apostles went on to pass this truth along to the other disciples and ultimately the Church throughout the ages via the scriptures. The three who climbed the mountain with Jesus had a firsthand account of Christ's majesty. You don't have to wonder about it in the abstract. Jesus is God's dearly loved Son, who brings Him great joy.

God has spoken to His people differently from one generation to the next. He talked from a burning bush, whispered on the wind, and even spoke through a donkey. But when Jesus arrived in the flesh, God spoke audibly.

If you've been seeking proof of God's existence before placing your faith in Christ, here you have it—an eyewitness account. If you have become more trusting because the Spirit bore witness with your spirit, then praise God that you can also experience that.

HEAVENLY THOUGHTS

The mind governed by the flesh is death,
but the mind governed by the Spirit is life and peace.

ROMANS 8:6 NIV

If you've ever wondered how a Christian is supposed to set his mind on what the Spirit desires, Paul's admonition to a Greek church (Philippians 4:8 NIV) is a great place to start: "Finally, brothers and sisters, whatever is true, whatever is noble, whatever is right, whatever is pure, whatever is lovely, whatever is admirable—if anything is excellent or praiseworthy—think about such things."

While you'll never fully achieve success in doing so, when you begin to steadfastly meditate on truth, things that are noble, pure, lovely—and anything praiseworthy—you'll notice a decrease in your fleshly desires. Your actions are in direct response to your thoughts, and pure thoughts result in pure actions. Impure thoughts become impure actions.

Practically speaking, you might begin to change your thinking by finding and meditating on a different Bible verse every day; or you might consider how to overhaul a system at work so everything is aboveboard and transparent; or you could begin discipling a man who needs someone to walk alongside him (which means you'll be praying for him and always thinking about your next meeting).

"Set your minds on things above, not on earthly things," Paul writes to the Christians at Colossae (Colossians 3:2–3 NIV). "For you died, and your life is now hidden with Christ in God."

FULL OF GOODNESS

*And concerning you, my brethren, I myself also am convinced
that you yourselves are full of goodness, filled with all
knowledge and able also to admonish one another.*

ROMANS 15:14 NASB

When a man is converted to Christ, a seismic shift takes place in his soul. He begins the process of being transformed into a new person as the Holy Spirit directs. The Christians in Rome eventually reached a point in which Paul said he was convinced that they were full of goodness, filled with all knowledge, and able to admonish one another. The three go hand in hand.

As your new nature becomes more concerned with pleasing God and helping others, you're filled with knowledge from on high to the point that you're able to teach new converts about putting off the old man. It's a lifelong pursuit, and you'll never arrive. You might even take one step forward and two steps back on occasion, but don't let that stop you.

If your pastor had to describe your level of spiritual maturity, could he say the same thing about you that Paul said about these believers in Rome? Would he be confident in your goodness? Has your pastor witnessed you being filled with godly knowledge? Has that led you to encourage fellow believers in your congregation? You shouldn't merely try to please your pastor, but he's bound to learn about your steady habits.

EXCEED YOUR GRASP

But now they desire a better, that is, a heavenly country.
Therefore God is not ashamed to be called their God,
for He has prepared a city for them.

HEBREWS 11:16 NKJV

Some Christians have been accused of being so heavenly minded that they're no earthly good. While that may be so, without the promise of heaven's peace, justice, and reward to inspire you, putting all your hope in this world does you no eternal good. The poet Robert Browning was onto something when he wrote, "A man's reach should exceed his grasp, or what's a heaven for?"

When Joseph and Mary found their twelve-year-old son in the temple, He told them, "Why did you seek Me? Did you not know that I must be about My Father's business?" (Luke 2:49 NKJV). Through the parable of the minas, Jesus told His followers, "Do business till I come" (Luke 19:13 NKJV). The challenge is clear: do whatever you do with the ultimate goal of building God's kingdom.

The full impact of your work on earth is measured not in material wealth but spiritual. How have you used what God has given you to see souls saved? That effort starts at home, extends through the church, and goes out into the world, always with the objective of seeing as many as possible arrive at the wonderful home God has for them. If you look beyond the cares of this world, you can just see it.

FAITHFUL IS SUCCESSFUL

*Make it your ambition to lead a quiet life and attend
to your own business and work with your hands.*

1 Thessalonians 4:11 nasb

In the parable of the talents (Matthew 25:14–30), Jesus told of three men, each of whom was given a different amount of money, "each according to his ability" (Matthew 25:15 niv). The first two doubled their investment, but the third held onto his money and was condemned for doing nothing with it. That tells you a few things about God's definition of success.

First, success comes when you've done the work in front of you—the work God has "prepared in advance" for you to do (Ephesians 2:10 niv). It also means that God hasn't assigned everyone the same type of work or given everyone the same resources, but it *does* mean that whatever He has given you is enough for you to do your job. So, no matter what you do for a living, do it to honor God.

No amount of money can increase God's kingdom, but one man, whether he's digging ditches or investing stocks, can make the difference for the people he's working with, one at a time, to build the eternal nation. When you're focused on living the life God has for you, "attending to your own business" takes on a fresh attitude—you're minding God's business. In His view, to be faithful is to be successful.

REALITY-CHECK THE PECKING ORDER

But if you show favoritism, you sin.

JAMES 2:9 NIV

It's natural for men to establish a pecking order. Whether it's at work, playing softball, or raking leaves—if other guys are involved, you want to know where you stand. Which guys are stronger, smarter, faster, and which aren't? But while it's fine to get the lay of the land, it can also provide a false standard of a person's worth. What better shows a man's worth—a sports car and a fat stock portfolio or the way he treats those from whom he has nothing to gain?

The message of the Gospel is not about getting in good with the Guy who can get you in the pearly gates—you can't. It's not about impressing heaven with earthly success—you won't. The cross reveals an unsettling truth: we're all on the same footing before God, and the earth is shaking. But Jesus offers a hand up to rich and poor alike; the guy in the penthouse and the one in the gutter matter equally to Him.

That's why James spoke against saving seats up front at church for the wealthy contingent; if anything, Jesus wants you to save a seat for the guy who's lost it all, whose sin has messed up his life and hurt others to boot. Save a special place in your heart for the man with the greatest need. It's what Jesus did for you.

WHAT'S REALLY POSSIBLE?

Behold, I am the LORD, the God of all flesh:
is there any thing too hard for me?

JEREMIAH 32:27 KJV

You've met the man who considers it a mark of his intelligence to try to outsmart the Bible. He's the one who knows you're a Christian and makes it a priority to let you know that there's no way Jonah could've survived three days in a whale's belly, or that there must have been some mass hallucination when Joshua and his army fought under a sun that stood still in the sky.

He conveniently ignores the real miracles—that a resistant prophet's message caused the biggest, most wicked city of his day to repent, from the king down to the kids. Or that God actually let a man call the shots for a day and obliged him with a meteorological wonder. Really, though, if you can believe the first line of the Bible—that God created the heavens and the earth—the rest is easy.

And a God who can speak everything you can see and know into existence—and a whole bunch of things you can't—is a God who can take care of your needs. Take your cares to Him, even the one about the guy at the office who thinks he knows better than his Creator. Maybe he's closer to faith than either of you could ever imagine; after all, God's done bigger miracles than that.

LET GOD AVENGE YOU

*"Is there not still someone of the house of Saul,
to whom I may show the kindness of God?"*

2 SAMUEL 9:3 NKJV

When God's Spirit departed from Israel's first king, Saul hunted his replacement, the young shepherd who had killed a giant and played peaceful harmonies to lull his troubled soul. David lived on the run for years, refusing to fight back against God's anointed, even when presented with two ideal opportunities to end Saul's life.

David not only passed up taking revenge, but after Saul died in battle, he sought out his remaining descendants, not to kill them and consolidate his power but to see if he could do them any good.

In David's day, mercy was seen as weakness. To refuse to retaliate or return a slight to your honor tainted you in most eyes as unreliable. The whole turning-the-other-cheek thing would have been as ridiculous to them as wearing a clown nose to meet your future in-laws would be to you.

But, as David demonstrated, the higher virtue is in being able to avenge yourself but refusing to do so. It takes faith to refrain—a belief that when God said vengeance belonged to Him (Proverbs 25:21–22; Romans 12:19), He meant it. Not only will He hold you accountable for all you've said and done, He'll do the same for everyone else. Have the faith to let Him.

SET YOUR EYES ON GOD

Be sure you know the condition of your flocks,
give careful attention to your herds.

PROVERBS 27:23 NIV

What's your vision for your family? Through all the challenges He faced, Jesus had a single vision: to do the will of the Father. God's will is often clear in Scripture: men are the spiritual leaders of their families, kids are supposed to obey parents, dads aren't supposed to wear kids out with constant criticism, and we are to respect authorities because God put them in charge.

But more than a list of *dos* and *don'ts*, doing God's will means recognizing that you're a part of His greater story, not the other way around. The best thing you can do for your family is be the man He asks you to be—a husband and father committed to following Him. One of the ways you do that is by becoming an expert on each member of your family—their strengths, weaknesses, love languages, and daily challenges. Through it all, listen before you speak, stay calm, pray tons, and do it all with love.

That will move you out of your comfort zone at times, and you will make mistakes. Worry less about goofing up than developing the overall vision. Jesus knows you—all your ups and downs—and still thinks you were worth dying for. How's that for a model of the kind of love you should show your family?

REASON TO REJOICE

We can rejoice, too, when we run into problems and trials,
for we know that they help us develop endurance.

ROMANS 5:3 NLT

At various points in your life, you'll sit on the other side of the table from bad news. Sometimes, you'll see it coming, but more often than not, it'll ambush you, a single shot from a stun gun: *downsizing*, *accident*, *cancer*. Somehow, you press on, working through the immediate details as if from a distance, and it's only later when you have a moment to breathe that the grief comes on. You wrestle with the *whys* and the *what nexts*, and begin to find out what you're made of.

Like a cup that's been filled to the brim with whatever you've poured into your heart over the course of your life, when a hard trial strikes, what's inside spills over. If you've habitually sown to the flesh, bitterness gushes out, blended with hopelessness. All your self-sufficiency comes to nothing, and you let God know how He has disappointed you.

But if you've habitually sown to the Spirit, it's different. Previous trials forced you to your knees, but that's where you found God waiting to comfort and strengthen you. You know that Paul wasn't just spouting some holy-sounding advice about tribulation, because you've seen the truth behind it: God uses trials to produce endurance, building character and producing hope. When hope spills over, you have reason to rejoice: God is with you.

A GREATER VISION

*He made himself nothing by taking the very nature
of a servant, being made in human likeness.*

PHILIPPIANS 2:7 NIV

Today is Presidents' Day, and though George Washington was elected America's first president in 1789, the most remarkable thing he ever did was *give up* his power. So potent were Washington's popularity and leadership that there was a public outcry that he remain president as long as he would.

His guidance of the nation in its infancy, however, was matched only by his desire to see it thrive beyond his life, and to do so, there needed to be a safe, stable transfer of power. It was unheard of to give up power—still true today!—especially when victory had been so hard fought for and won, but Washington had a bigger vision.

God had an even more impressive vision for all of mankind—a way to buy His people back from sin and its deprivations—and He had just the Man for the job. Where Washington gave up his office so that he could enjoy the fruits of his accomplishments (and justifiably so!), Jesus gave up His place in heaven at God's right hand to be bound by the frailty of flesh and blood, to have needs and urges, to face temptation and opposition and betrayal firsthand (unheard of!).

He fought your biggest foes—sin, death, and hell—to be able to adopt you as a son and brother.

PUT OUT FIRES BEFORE THEY START

He that covereth his sins shall not prosper:
but whoso confesseth and forsaketh them shall have mercy.

PROVERBS 28:13 KJV

Tragedy struck a Rhode Island nightclub when pyrotechnics from a rock concert ignited a fire that killed one hundred people. The band Great White insisted in their contract that a certain type of fireworks be used, but the club's safety standards weren't up to the task, and people died as a result.

In contrast, the band Van Halen had a contract rider requiring that no brown M&Ms be found among their green room snacks. Rather than a diva move, it was actually a safeguard: the band knew that if they found brown M&Ms, the venue hadn't reviewed or abided by the contract. They would then go through the hall with a fine-toothed comb, almost inevitably finding potential safety hazards that would have caused disaster had they gone unaddressed.

Sin works like that in your life, a hidden livewire behind the walls of your life, just waiting to set it aflame and burn you down. Sin progresses like a burning fuse: desire tempts you, then drags you away to do its bidding. Once it has conceived, it gives birth to sin, which grows up and gives birth to death (James 1:13–15).

Whatever temptation beckons you—whether women, status, or wealth—root it out at the point of contact, like a brown M&M you know isn't supposed to be there.

THE BIGGER PICTURE

*Do you despise the riches of His goodness, forbearance,
and longsuffering, not knowing that the goodness
of God leads you to repentance?*

ROMANS 2:4 NKJV

Why is patience a virtue? Sometimes, people just need to be corrected—like your kids when they're headed for the wall socket with a fork, or the server when she brings your steak well done instead of medium rare. That guy at work who keeps taking your lunch out of the fridge needs to be stopped, and the committee you're on at church is about to make a bad decision about buying a piano. You sitting back and being "patient" isn't going to help anyone.

In those situations, quick action and uncompromising conversations are needed. You're right to act; there are matters of safety, courtesy, professionalism, and stewardship at stake. But *how* will you do it? There's the rub.

Think of all the times Jesus' disciples messed up—Peter with his ongoing foot-in-mouth disease, or John and James arguing over who should be top dog or calling down fire on entire villages. Sometimes you bluntly share your mind, only to succeed in offending people. So frustrating!

While Jesus did correct His followers' failures, He was gentle, courteous, and polite. He saw a bigger picture—their overarching needs rather than their momentary misdeeds. Patience, then, seems to be made up of other virtues—love, mercy, and humility among them. Consider God's patience when others test yours.

PLUG INTO THE POWER

When I am afraid, I put my trust in you.
PSALM 56:3 NIV

The big choices you make—the woman you marry, the job you take, the place you live—should be guided by your trust in and understanding of God, but the main mark of a son of God is his battle against sin. "For if you live according to the flesh you will die; but if by the Spirit you put to death the deeds of the body, you will live" (Romans 8:13 NKJV).

Fear is a red flag that alerts you to oncoming danger. God's Spirit helps you move past that fear, giving you the strength and will to do what is right. "For as many as are led by the Spirit of God, these are sons of God" (Romans 8:14 NKJV). As an adopted son, you don't have God at your beck and call; rather, you're a tool in His hands. His role isn't limited to responding to your needs; you're being led and moved and shaped by Him.

If your sin doesn't scare you as much as those big decisions you face, you're poised on a precipice. But when you confess your sins to God, you're grabbing a live wire and plugging into hopeful expectation. The results will be initially painful but ultimately empowering. That ruthless approach to being more like Jesus is what conquers fear and confirms you as His son.

WORKING FOR GOD

Whatever you do in word or deed, do all in the name of the Lord Jesus, giving thanks through Him to God the Father.

COLOSSIANS 3:17 NASB

You're an employee of the Most High God. Your work matters to Him. He gave you skills that can be used to serve Him well. No matter where you work, you really work for God. He's paying attention. And He wants your best.

If you want to have the opportunity to share your faith with coworkers, begin by being a dependable, faithful, and exceptional employee. Your work ethic has a strong bearing on the believability of your statement of faith.

Your words should reflect God's heart. Your work should bring honor to His name. Be wise. Bring Jesus to work and let Him instill joy, responsibility, and willingness to work in even toxic environments. You can bring light to a spiritually dark workplace. You can bring your *Life CEO* with you and let Him provide the life coaching you need to do your work well. He can change your attitude and impact others who struggle with their own workplace issues.

Office politics, workplace dramas, and bad attitudes are all small issues to the God who created you and who accepts your work as a gift of gratitude and praise. Work was never meant to be just a way to make a living, but to bring *life* to one more area of influence.

ABSOLUTELY TRUSTWORTHY

Do not be anxious about anything, but in every situation, by prayer and petition, with thanksgiving, present your requests to God.

PHILIPPIANS 4:6 NIV

This is the age of superheroes. They fill comic books, television series, and big-budget movies. They have distinct personalities and impressive abilities. Have you ever wondered why they're so popular?

Confidence is hard to find when life seems uncertain. The result is high anxiety. Superheroes become substitutes for diminished personal confidence. God has always had a better idea. In every circumstance you can pray and ask a loving God for help. He is looking out for you. Be grateful. Above all, refuse every delivery of anxiety. Be confident in the God who rescues and delights in taking care of His family.

You don't need to wear a cape, have a secret cave filled with expensive super toys, or look for help from super-powered friends. Psalm 20:7 (NIV) says, "Some trust in chariots and some in horses, but we trust in the name of the LORD our God."

Anxiety diminishes your ability to trust, fills your mind with scenarios that aren't acquainted with reality, and has an odd way of diminishing your ability to hear others speak truth. Anxiety tells God that you're not convinced He's strong enough to handle your deepest struggles.

Find your greatest confidence in the One who has always been *super* trustworthy.

PERSONAL WORSHIP

How long will they speak with arrogance?
How long will these evil people boast?

PSALM 94:4 NLT

The Bible has its fair share of leading characters who let arrogance bring them to personal ruin. Moses killed a man, David committed adultery, and Paul sought to harm the very people Jesus came to rescue. Each man acted as if God's law didn't apply to him. They justified each decision because it was intended to lead to a desired outcome.

Pride and false humility are two sides of the same coin. One side wants to be noticed and the other wants to be noticed by saying they *don't* want to be noticed. Both shine a light on self. When Jesus points you toward true life, you should expect Him to do two things. The first is to teach you that who you are is all about who *He* is and what *He's* done. Nothing you can do changes who you are to God (see Ephesians 2:9). The second is that when you take credit for something God has done through you, it will be the only credit you receive (see Matthew 6:5).

Arrogance is the source of the downfall of men because it replaces God's perfection with man's misguided intentions, and the resulting self-worship is something others don't want to observe. God led Moses, David, and Paul through arrogance to a humble acceptance of the true source of their success. He can do the same for you.

SET FREE FROM SIN

"If the Son sets you free, you will be free indeed."
JOHN 8:36 NIV

It's tough to argue with the truth that you sin (see Romans 3:23). God wants you to admit your sin so He can forgive you (1 John 1:9). You can't undo what you've done. You can't justify your actions in God's courtroom. You come to Him burdened with sin debt and leave as His adopted and forgiven son.

Unlike those who dredge up your old sin to use as a club against you, God takes an entirely unexpected course. He forgives. He forgets (Psalm 103:12). God offers freedom, but Christians often remain incarcerated by choice. You may not feel ready to forgive yourself, but you can't ignore the truth that God can, and does, forgive you. You can accept His forgiveness and discover the freedom your soul has always craved.

Of course, you need to understand the depth of your sin before you can accept and appreciate the freedom found in Christ. But accepting God's forgiveness is important because He's got an incredible future awaiting you, and you won't experience it by living in the past while clutching the *sin rags* that God has already forgiven.

Jesus shared His plan for your life in John 10:10 (NIV): "I have come that they may have life, and have it to the full." Jesus sets you free. Believe and accept His freedom.

GODLY MEN

*How blessed is the man who does not walk in the counsel of the
wicked, nor stand in the path of sinners, nor sit in the seat
of scoffers! But his delight is in the law of the Lord,
and in His law he meditates day and night.*

PSALM 1:1–2 NASB

Godly men—men who follow God and whose lives are blessed by
Him—pay no heed to wicked advice. They don't identify themselves
with those who mock God. Rather, they draw their inspiration from
God's instruction book. They learn what it says and their actions
reflect what they learn. They take the time to meditate on it. They
want to make sure God's Word gets into their minds, filters down
deep into the core of their being, and changes their motivations.

Godly men recognize there's a battle for their minds. They refuse
to rent head space to their adversary. Second Corinthians 10:5
(NASB) tells them to take "every thought captive to the obedience
of Christ." The world's opinions fluctuate and mean little if they're
not aligned with God's truth. The actions of godly men are always
tied to what they believe.

Godly men recognize that dining at the Lord's Table of Truth
doesn't allow for picky consumerism. There's much to taste, and
spending time completely engaged with God's Word is the best
way to be fully fed and entirely convinced that He has a personal
plan for every new sunrise.

LIFE IS SHORT—CHOOSE GOD

Your life is like the morning fog—
it's here a little while, then it's gone.

JAMES 4:14 NLT

At the end of your life you don't get a mulligan, do-over, or a divine reset in an attempt to get it right. You have one life to make the decisions you need to make to determine your place in eternity. Your time on earth isn't an end game, it's a potent beginning. If you only live for what you can get here, you're missing out on the preparation for what's to come.

Life is like grass—here for a season and gone. Life is like fog—visible and impacting for a short period of time. Life is shorter than you realize, yet long enough that you're sometimes convinced to put off making the kind of decisions that must be made *today*.

You can choose to do things your own way or you can find out what God wants you to do. You can determine your own truth or you can consult the God of *all* truth. You can live as though this life is all there is or you can discover this life is a small step into forever.

The only redeemable promises and guarantees you have in life are *God-made*. He promised to be with you. He guarantees Christians an eternal home with Him. There's no good reason to intentionally separate yourself from God. Life is short, so choose Him.

WISDOM SPEECH

*Sin is not ended by multiplying words,
but the prudent hold their tongues.*

PROVERBS 10:19 NIV

God used words to bring the world into existence (Genesis 1). When He describes His Son, He calls Him the Word (John 1:1). What God has to say with His words must have meaning because God is perfect. God has freely given us the words of spirit and life (John 6:63).

Men fall into a different category. You can't call a world into being by your words. You aren't the one who originated language. You aren't perfect. Your words can bring a sense of life to those who hear you, but they often leave scars on hearts, impaired thinking due to a lack of truth, and may even encourage the hearer to follow a bad example. But you can follow God's lead and speak words that heal, share truths that alter thinking, and send out a trust invitation.

If you can't seem to say things that help, you can at least be prudent by holding your tongue, as today's verse states. Some men aren't able to do this and unnecessarily bring trouble upon themselves.

Some men struggle with speaking important words that positively impact others because positive words weren't spoken to them. That's why your best example is the God who created words. Hold your tongue when you have to, speak when you need to, and gain the wisdom to know the difference.

WHITE-WASHED REBELLION

*"I want to see a mighty flood of justice,
an endless river of righteous living."*

AMOS 5:24 NLT

The people of Israel said the right things, sang great songs, and got together to celebrate their national religion. The prophet Amos wasn't impressed. God showed him where the people were at. He told them in verse 12 (NLT), "I know the vast number of your sins and the depth of your rebellions." So God invited the people to come back to Him and seek His heart once more. He told them to hate evil and love what was good, stop the show and pretense, and cease the meaningless offerings (Amos 5:14–15, 22–23).

Hadn't they done the right things publicly, attended the expected religious services, and sought to show evidence of faithfulness? Yes, but God also saw every moment *out* of the public eye. He saw their divided heart. He was aware that they were engaged in white-washed living, and it was time to confront their rebellion.

He wasn't interested in their diligent spiritual *to-do* list. God wanted the hearts of His people to line up with the desires of His heart. Righteous living and compassion were rarely practiced.

Today, God continues to look for righteous living among His people. He desires to see compassion poured out on behalf of those who need love more than a hearty "Serves you right." God still desires a people whose outer life lines up with His truth.

THE ENCOURAGEMENT SPUR

*If someone is caught in a sin, you who live by the Spirit should
restore that person gently. But watch yourselves,
or you also may be tempted.*

GALATIANS 6:1 NIV

There's a reason the Bible says, "Let us not neglect our meeting
together, as some people do, but encourage one another" (Hebrews
10:25 NLT). Call it a gathering, assembly, fellowship, or church, but
each word carries the idea that the Christian life should be lived in
community. A church is filled with the battle-scarred, the newly
trusting, and those who struggle to follow truth.

A church should be a place where you can experience mercy,
expect grace, and from time to time deal with the darkness in the
heart of all mankind.

God's people are never asked to accept sin, but to lovingly hold
a spiritual mirror to the bad behavior of believers who are caught
up in sin. This isn't an *"I'm better than you"* moment. It's a *"God is
better than all"* revelation. God can use you to restore someone
to righteous living, but you can't treat this lightly because you're
also told these situations can bring personal temptation to follow
the poor choices of those you're called to restore.

God didn't call believers to meet together so they could find
out how much others thought they could get away with, but to
"consider how we may spur one another on toward love and good
deeds" (Hebrews 10:24 NIV).

JUSTIFYING FAVORITISM?

*If you show favoritism, you sin and are
convicted by the law as lawbreakers.*

JAMES 2:9 NIV

Favoritism is a plague and can lead to idol worship. If that seems like a stretch, consider this: God says you're not to show favoritism. You sin when you do. By showing favoritism you may be saying you believe that individuals are more important than God. More honorable than His commands. Anything placed above God becomes an idol.

To make this a little clearer, God instructed His people in Exodus 20:3 (NIV), "You shall have no other gods before me." If God gives a command, you shouldn't redefine His instruction. Favoritism, prejudice, discrimination, and racism are examples of lawbreaking—and they grieve God. Most people rarely consider this sin, but instead consider ways to justify their favoritism.

God sent His Son for the lost. He didn't exclude people with certain addresses, bank statements, ethnic backgrounds, or a large sum total of personal sins. Second Corinthians 5:15 (NIV) adds, "[Jesus] died for all, that those who live should no longer live for themselves but for him who died for them and was raised again."

Any time you shrink the community of God by excluding someone, you tell the world you don't need more friends, that only some should have access to God, and that relatively few people really matter. That message doesn't stand up to God's love letter to *all* mankind.

PUT ON MERCY

*Judgment is without mercy to the one who has shown no mercy.
Mercy triumphs over judgment.*

JAMES 2:13 NKJV

Be harsh with other people and you can expect a substantial return on your investment. Mercy gives birth to mercy, and justice to justice. God offers you mercy and forgiveness, and His desire is for mercy to be your go-to response with others. Colossians 3:12–13 (NKJV) says, "As the elect of God, holy and beloved, put on tender mercies, kindness, humility, meekness, longsuffering; bearing with one another, and forgiving one another, if anyone has a complaint against another; even as Christ forgave you, so you also must do."

God blesses those who show mercy (Matthew 5:7). God wants mercy even more than sacrifice (Matthew 9:13). An understanding of mercy can help you draw close to God (Hebrews 4:16).

Identify sin and keep your distance. Don't ever start to invite sin to spend time with your thinking. Make no mistake, you will sometimes entertain sin, but that's when the God of mercy invites you to come home. You don't have the right or even the ability to excuse sin, but. . .you can meet people in Mercy Place just beyond Justice Junction.

Why? Justice is always closer, but mercy takes the extra steps when the offender can't. Personal justice always accuses and demands payment while mercy understands that restoring relationship is the greater priority. God says mercy triumphs over judgment.

PRAY ON

*You don't have what you want because you don't ask God for it.
And even when you ask, you don't get it because your motives
are all wrong—you want only what will give you pleasure.*

JAMES 4:2-3 NLT

Many say prayers under pressure. These are spontaneously uttered during the worst possible life moments. They're not often part of regular conversations with God, and—for many people—may not even be sent with an understanding of who God is or what He wants.

You can look at the first part of today's verses and conclude that all you have to do is ask and God *has* to give you what you want. However, this passage was actually a response to the way early Christians had been dealing with selfishness: "You want what you don't have, so you scheme and kill to get it. You are jealous of what others have, but you can't get it, so you fight and wage war to take it away from them" (vv. 1–2 NLT).

Prayer can be proof that you're following God's lead. As you draw closer to God you begin to speak prayers that reflect what you're learning. As you grow, you're less likely to ask for something you already know He couldn't answer with a yes.

Your prayer life always reflects your relationship with God. When you know God wants the best for you, you'll begin to ask for His best because you will *want* His best.

THE TRANSFORMED DIFFERENCE

*Do not be conformed to this world, but be transformed by the
renewing of your mind, so that you may prove what the will
of God is, that which is good and acceptable and perfect.*

ROMANS 12:2 NASB

Society is pretty good at churning out cookie-cutter characters. If
you follow the pattern, you'll want what others have, wear clothing
approved by society's elite, and be discontent when nothing you
want satisfies.

Society says only some people are special, and if you want to
be special, you need to do what *those* people do. This may explain
why there are so many websites and television shows dedicated to
telling you who's *in* today and why you need to change everything
about you to be like them.

God wants you to stop looking, acting, and sounding like
society's special people, but it will mean changing your perspective.
God wants to change that old way of dealing with life and transform
everything about you into someone who agrees to pursue God's
good, acceptable, and perfect will. You see, God has always had a
plan for your life, but when you take your eyes off Him and pursue
the approval of others who seem to have more of something you
like, you lose connection with the God who understands your
personal life map.

Keeping up with the Joneses could keep you from following
the life plan God created just for you.

WISDOM'S ROADMAP

Be careful how you live. Don't live like fools, but like those who are wise. Make the most of every opportunity in these evil days. Don't act thoughtlessly, but understand what the Lord wants you to do.

EPHESIANS 5:15–17 NLT

The pursuit of wisdom requires intentional decision-making. The choices you make impact personal wisdom. God's Word says it's better to follow the wise than lament your own poor choices. You've probably heard, "You'll learn from your mistakes." While that may be true, God places a great emphasis on obedience.

Because God wants you to have a good reputation, He says, "Be careful how you live." Because you're to reflect God's character, He says, "Don't act like fools." Because He built you for positive relationships, He says, "Make the most of every opportunity." Because He wants you to love others, He says, "Don't act thoughtlessly."

So, what is godly wisdom? Making an intentional choice to follow knowing God will help you "understand what [He] wants you to do." Wisdom isn't available in any store, can't be inherited, and is nontransferable. God can make you wise as you learn what He's said and do what He's asked.

You'll make mistakes. Sin will inevitably be part of your life experience. Wisdom understands that God gave you a choice and the help you'd need to keep your distance from decisions that keep you at arm's length from the One who loves you most (see 1 Corinthians 10:13).

WISDOM, COUNSEL, AND UNDERSTANDING

"Is not wisdom found among the aged? Does not long life bring understanding? To God belong wisdom and power; counsel and understanding are his."

JOB 12:12–13 NIV

Who do you listen to when you need advice? Is it someone who doesn't have a fully formed picture of life? Or is it someone who's spent time in life's trenches and has lived to gain understanding? There's a reason you might seek the advice of your father or other mature men. Their life experience may help you learn what to avoid and what to pursue.

This idea is linked to finding a mentor or becoming a disciple. You'll need to admit you don't know everything in order to learn something. If it's true that you'll likely seek those older men with more life experience to draw from, then shouldn't it be true that you become doggedly determined to follow the God who possesses *complete* wisdom, power, counsel, and understanding?

God wants you to pay attention and make choices as to whose voice you allow into your thinking. If you're careful whom you listen to among your sphere of friendships, shouldn't the voice of God and the wisdom He's given in His Word take first place as your source of counsel for tomorrow's tough choices?

"Come near to God and he will come near to you" (James 4:8 NIV).

THE COMPANION

[Jesus said,] "The Helper, the Holy Spirit, whom the Father will send in My name, He will teach you all things, and bring to your remembrance all things that I said to you."

JOHN 14:26 NKJV

Friends are important. It can be lonely without them. Proverbs 27:17 (NLT) says, "As iron sharpens iron, so a friend sharpens a friend." Your best friends help keep you focused, honest, and inspired. These traits are also found in the Holy Spirit, the least-discussed member of the Trinity. He takes up residence in the core of who you are.

Every temptation you face can be endured with the help of this friend. Jesus sent the Spirit as a personal companion to help you when you need help. Listen closely and learn what God wants from you. The Spirit can speak to your inner man and remind you of things God has already said. He's the Companion, the One sent to walk beside you, the One who teaches, and the One who helps God's character grow in your heart, mind, and soul.

Saying that the Holy Spirit and your conscience are the same thing doesn't take into account all the things God's Holy Spirit can do. He can and does remind you when you're heading in the wrong direction. He can point you in the right direction. And, if allowed, He can teach, train, and transform you into the man God wants you to be.

CROP FAILURE

All Scripture is inspired by God and is useful to teach us what is true and to make us realize what is wrong in our lives. It corrects us when we are wrong and teaches us to do what is right.

2 TIMOTHY 3:16 NLT

God inspired the writing of scripture, but how *much* of the Bible did He actually inspire? *Every word.* Why is this important? Well, if you think some of the Bible is from God but other parts aren't, then you'll be confused as to what can be trusted.

If only part of the Bible is true, how can you believe *any* of it? If it's not all true, you're left to pick and choose what you believe. If you're like most, you'll end up picking what seems easiest to believe and follow. You might believe in God's grace, but not His command to obey Him. You'd accept His love without acknowledging God is the final authority. You'd accept forgiveness while refusing to forgive others.

You should realign your thinking and actions with God's truth. He never said you could simply accept the parts of His Word that make you feel good. In fact, Galatians 6:7 (NLT) puts this in farming terms: "Don't be misled—you cannot mock the justice of God. You will always harvest what you plant."

Determine to believe and obey God's Word, starting with His *simplest* (but hardest to obey) commands—to love others and forgive those who offend you.

SPIRITUAL INVESTMENTS

*Godliness actually is a means of great gain
when accompanied by contentment.*

1 Timothy 6:6 NASB

Godliness always begins with identifying yourself as a man willing to follow God. This decision can include a profound sense of gratitude to the One you're certain holds the answers to living life well, has a plan for your life, and customized it specifically for you. Godliness seeks to line up personal decision-making within the framework of God's Word.

Instead of being fixated on what you don't own, godly living suggests that being content with what you have is a better option. The reason is simple. This current life is extremely short when compared with the eternal life God has prepared for His children, and some things people invest in have extremely short shelf lives.

Matthew 6:19–20 (NASB) says, "Do not store up for yourselves treasures on earth, where moth and rust destroy, and where thieves break in and steal. But store up for yourselves treasures in heaven, where neither moth nor rust destroys, and where thieves do not break in or steal."

Spending time chasing things you can never take to heaven is a poor use of time and resources. The three greatest investments you'll ever make in life are relationships with God, family, and friends. People are the only investments you have any chance of seeing again in heaven.

Godliness + contentment = God's approved life investment strategy.

MORE THAN AN "ATTA BOY!"

Praise the Lord, all you nations. Praise him, all you people of the earth. For his unfailing love for us is powerful; the Lord's faithfulness endures forever. Praise the Lord!

PSALM 117:1–2 NLT

Christian men demonstrate wisdom every time they praise God. Nations who honor God make the right choices. Every bit of praise and every word of honor should be a response to the God who never fails to love and who demonstrates His faithfulness every moment of each new day.

Some translations say God's love is *steadfast*. This word suggests something unmovable—like a mountain or a house-sized boulder in the middle of a stream. God's love is unfailing, powerful, and guaranteed to last forever. It's not going anywhere.

You can't earn it, make Him love you more, or make Him love you less. You're one of His creations, and His love extends to every human ever born—even the ones you don't like.

This is where the praise should be lavished on a magnificent God. He's good. He's mighty. He loves you. Praise and honor isn't simply an "Atta boy!" shouted out to God. Your praise should take the time to think of the many blessings you've discovered in your walk with God that brought you to this moment. By remembering the past, you're able to see more clearly that God's unfailing love has always been enough to get you to, through, and beyond life's toughest moments.

DEAL WITH IT

*Create in me a pure heart, O God,
and renew a steadfast spirit within me.*

PSALM 51:10 NIV

The Bible is clear; you are to bear with other people who struggle with sin (Galatians 6:2). It requires patience, sacrifice, and love. At some point you've likely received the kindness of strangers and friends. Bearing with others helps you maintain positive relationships. Remember, God puts up with you too.

When *you* sin by disobeying God's commands, you aren't supposed to give yourself a free pass. Grace is God's gift and your example. You're not to bear (put up) with your *own* sin. God wants you to deal with it, and His example is ruthless (see Matthew 5:29–30). There are sins that catch the attention of law enforcement like murder and theft, but there are other sins that are equally offensive to God. A short list of these sins includes gossip, envy, and dishonesty.

The only way you can really deal with sin is with help. Men show the greatest wisdom when they allow God's Holy Spirit to create a new heart and a steadfast spirit in a heart born sinful (Psalm 51:5, 10).

God does what you can't. He helps when you ask for help. You can't defeat sin on your own. Wise men understand the best answer to the problem of sin is new life offered by a good God and accepted by fallen men (see Colossians 3).

AUTHENTIC GRATITUDE

*In everything give thanks; for this is the will
of God in Christ Jesus for you.*

1 THESSALONIANS 5:18 NKJV

Sometimes knowing God's will for your life is as simple as reading His Word. For example, it's always His will for you to express gratitude. Wisdom proclaims thankfulness as a daily exercise matching actions with God's will, but at the end of the day you might discover some gratitude you still need to express.

You might be standing in the way of God's will. Every time you choose self-pity over gratitude, God's plans are set aside and delayed. The same is true whenever you entertain greed, envy, lust, covetousness, hatred, bitterness, selfishness, and cynicism.

The list is longer, but the common reason for setting aside God's will is. . .*self*. When you pay too much attention to what you don't have, what you want, and how others have hurt you, then there's no room for authentic gratitude.

God is good, and He supplies everything you need to live. He sends bonus moments like beautiful sunsets, impressive scenery, and the love of family and friends. Yet it's possible to develop a blindness to the good things because difficulties frequently demand your attention. . .and God's will is set aside for another day.

You can't be thankful when you think you deserve more than you have. When you're grateful for what you have, you not only position yourself to follow God's will, but you also give yourself the greatest chance to enjoy contentment.

FOR EACH NEXT STEP

Let my cry come before You, O Lord;
give me understanding according to Your word.
PSALM 119:169 NASB

The Psalms are more than source material for praise songs. They also express human struggle and personal questioning. Take today's verse, for example. There are three takeaways.

"Let my cry come before You." Even the psalmist wanted to be heard. In moments of anger, frustration, and even joy, men need to believe that when they pray, God listens.

"Give me understanding." God's ways, plans, and truth don't always line up with common thinking. Men need direction and shouldn't be afraid to ask God to make things clear.

"According to Your word." God's answers often come in the form of words on the pages of His book, the Bible.

God explains in Isaiah 55:10–11 (NLT) how His Word does something remarkable in helping you understand what He wants. It also lets you know He's heard you. "The rain and snow come down from the heavens and stay on the ground to water the earth. They cause the grain to grow, producing seed for the farmer and bread for the hungry. It is the same with my word. I send it out, and it always produces fruit. It will accomplish all I want it to, and it will prosper everywhere I send it."

His Word nourishes and causes you to grow, and it can produce something productive in the soil of receptive hearts. Read it for wisdom, life, and for each next step.

NO BARRIER EQUALITY

There is no longer Jew or Gentile, slave or free,
male and female. For you are all one in Christ Jesus.

GALATIANS 3:28 NLT

Jesus came with a radical and unexpected message: God loved all mankind, didn't discriminate; women had equal standing in His plan, and the sick were never considered unacceptable.

A person's social status meant nothing to Jesus. Each person had a gift to share and a role in His plan. Where women and children were once treated as property to be discarded at will, men were told, "Love your wives and never treat them harshly" (Colossians 3:19 NLT). God also taught in Ephesians 6:4 (NLT), "Fathers, do not provoke your children to anger by the way you treat them. Rather, bring them up with the discipline and instruction that comes from the Lord."

Part of Jesus' plan was to equalize humanity. No one was less important to Him than another. He didn't come to save a few. His rescue plan was for all. His love was accessible to everyone.

Jesus introduced a new pledge, and He didn't change His mind. This generous pledge challenged thinking and created new opportunities. God doesn't erect barriers when it comes to a relationship with Him. Christian men should remove every barrier that makes it hard for others to meet Jesus or love people the way Jesus loves.

Jesus brought exceptionally good news. Share it. Live it.

ASK

Wise words bring approval,
but fools are destroyed by their own words.

ECCLESIASTES 10:12 NLT

Wisdom recognizes the importance of every decision. Wisdom understands time should be used well. It seeks advice, makes a house a home, and softens the hardest disposition.

Wisdom knows that personal opinion is less important than God's truth. Wisdom is simply knowledge until it's filtered through God's truth. Get wisdom and find that it guards you. Seek wisdom and discover it in the pages of God's Word. Follow wisdom and meet the Lord. Wisdom has rewards that exceed the possession of gold or silver. The greatest wisdom of man is foolishness when compared to the wisdom of God.

Everything you just read was paraphrased from God's Word. If you want to become a man dedicated to wisdom, you will need to return often to wise words in the book that God wrote. It's an instruction manual and book of encouragement, filled with words of grace, and it's offered to enhance life, improve marriage, and deliver wisdom.

The wisdom you'll discover will bring light to dark places, hope to desperate situations, and a way forward when the way seems blocked.

Make wisdom your pursuit; know and stop guessing; seek God's heart and find that doing His will is the pinnacle of your life purpose. God promised to give wisdom to all who ask, so if what you've read sounds good, ask.

WAVER NO MORE

*Let us hold fast the confession of our hope without wavering,
for He who promised is faithful.*

HEBREWS 10:23 NKJV

Buy a product, and you might waver in your opinion of the purchase. It's possible the product never actually delivered on its promise, or it might have failed along the way. Watch a movie and discover your opinion wavering between a waste of time and something more memorable.

Your opinions can waver about almost everything. You like a certain restaurant, but struggle when it comes time to decide if that's where you really want to eat. When it comes to your relationship with God, you shouldn't waver. Your trust in Him doesn't need to change, and your hope in God will never disappoint.

Wavering means "being prone to a divided opinion." Either God is good or He isn't. He loves or He doesn't. He can rescue or He can't. If God has proven faithful, then wavering in your opinion of Him doesn't make sense. Chances are you've felt some doubt. Perhaps you've wavered. You're not alone. Jesus told a man who came to Him for help that he should believe. The man's reply? "Lord, I believe; help my unbelief!" (Mark 9:24 NKJV).

God doesn't want you to waver in your belief, but He knew this would be an issue for all mankind. Spend time remembering the faithfulness of God, and discover a harmony between what you believe and the God you believe in.

A TRUE PRAYER WARRIOR

Epaphras, who is one of you and a servant of Christ Jesus, sends greetings. He is always wrestling in prayer for you, that you may stand firm in all the will of God, mature and fully assured.

COLOSSIANS 4:12 NIV

If you've ever watched a *real* wrestling match (as opposed to the spectacle that's called professional wrestling), you see two highly trained, well-conditioned athletes trying to impose their wills on each other. You see two opponents applying the techniques they've learned from practice and from prior experience to achieve their goals.

In today's verse, the word *wrestling* implies contending passionately and continuously for something. It means coming to God again and again and requesting that which you're convinced in your heart He wants to do for you. Epaphras engaged in that kind of prayer on behalf of the Colossians. Jacob prayed like that during his encounter with God too (Genesis 32:22–31). And the good news is that God invites you to pray the very same way.

Can you think of someone you know who could benefit from your prayers? Maybe a pastor or other full-time minister who is doing battle with the forces of evil? Or a married man who is working to save his marriage? Or how about a friend whom you know needs Jesus? If so, learn from Epaphras and from Jacob, and don't stop asking until God gives you what you know He wants to give you.

HANDLING ANGER PROPERLY

Fools vent their anger, but the wise quietly hold it back.
PROVERBS 29:11 NLT

This may come as a surprise to some Christian men, but the Bible teaches that the emotion of anger isn't necessarily a sin. God Himself expressed His anger in scripture (see Psalm 7:11; Mark 3:5). And the apostle Paul made a distinction between anger and *sinful* anger when he wrote, " 'In your anger do not sin': do not let the sun go down while you are still angry" (Ephesians 4:26 NIV).

Godly anger—also known as righteous indignation—can motivate men to act in ways that glorify God and further His kingdom. It moves you to defend those who are being wronged or mistreated, or to stand up for a biblical principle you see being violated.

But sinful anger, the kind of anger that moves you to contend for your own selfish desires, can damage relationships, cause unneeded pain to those you love, and hurt your witness for Christ.

Life will afford you many opportunities to feel anger. But when you feel that emotion rising up within you, stop and ask yourself if the way you're considering expressing that anger will hurt others or displease your Father in heaven. If the answer to that question is yes, then patiently hold your words in check, and choose to find a godly, healthy way to express how you feel.

THE IMPORTANCE OF "ONE ANOTHER"

*"A new command I give you: Love one another. As I have loved you,
so you must love one another. By this everyone will know
that you are my disciples, if you love one another."*

JOHN 13:34–35 NIV

During His earthly ministry, Jesus brought to His followers some radical new (*new* to them) teachings about the Law, about the nature of their relationship with God, and about love. He taught that by-the-letter "obedience" to the Law of Moses wasn't nearly as importance as obedience to the spirit of the Law. He gave them a glimpse of the loving nature of their heavenly Father, and taught them the vital importance of loving one another.

The New Testament is filled with references to "one another," starting with Jesus' commandment that His followers love one another in the same way He loved them—selflessly, sacrificially, and compassionately. Here are just a few examples from the pen of the apostle Paul:

- "Be devoted to one another in love. Honor one another above yourselves" (Romans 12:10 NIV).
- "Live in harmony with one another" (Romans 12:16 NIV).
- "Serve one another humbly in love" (Galatians 5:13 NIV).
- "Be kind and compassionate to one another" (Ephesians 4:32 NIV).

Clearly, God never intended for followers of Jesus Christ to live self-focused lives. On the contrary, He has commanded you to be lovingly devoted to your brothers and sisters in the faith.

FIRST IMPRESSIONS

Just then Boaz arrived from Bethlehem and greeted the harvesters,
"The LORD be with you!" "The LORD bless you!" they answered.

RUTH 2:4 NIV

When you're first introduced to Boaz, a key character in the beautiful story of redemption that is the book of Ruth, you get a pretty good idea of what kind of man he is. After he greets his workers with a hearty "The LORD be with you!" they respond with an equally enthusiastic "The LORD bless you!"

These words give you a great first impression of Boaz, don't they? Right away, you know that Boaz is a godly man who apparently treats his servants with kindness and compassion, and you know they know him as a man who loves God and others.

As you make your way through Ruth's story, you find that your first impressions of Boaz are well-founded. He indeed is a man who loves God and cares for the well-being of those who enter his sphere of influence.

Someone has rightly observed that you have only one chance to make a first impression. What kind of first impression do your words and actions make on those you meet? Do you think people who encounter you know right away that you're a man who loves God and loves other people—no matter their position in life—and wants to bless them?

That's a first impression any follower of Jesus should want to make on everyone he meets.

KIND WORDS SPOKEN

Kind words are like honey—
sweet to the soul and healthy for the body.
PROVERBS 16:24 NLT

In recent years, leaders in the modern corporate or business world have made an interesting discovery: many, if not most, workers tend to perform better when the boss or supervisor gives them verbal pats on the back for their good work. This may be old news to you, but it was apparently a revelation to many hard-boiled business leaders.

This challenges you as a Christian to consider something: Would the same principle work on your wife and children, your friends, and your coworkers, or the people you lead in the workplace? Well, if you take today's verse to its logical conclusion. . .yes, it would!

People are just naturally *wired*—or should we say *created*—to need affirming, kind words. And while there is certainly a place for correction and discipline, never forget that everyone needs to hear some kind words coming from those they love and those whom God has placed in authority over them.

Do you want to see the best in your wife and children, in your friends, and in those you work with? Try speaking kind words to them. Verbalize your observations of something they're doing well. Let them know you appreciate them for the things they do and for who they are. Let them know they're valued. The results just might pleasantly surprise you.

GUILT: A USELESS EMOTION

A big part of the fallen human condition is negative, destructive emotions, one of the worst being guilt. You've probably felt guilty over things you've done, or failed to do, in the past. But guilt can be an anchor in your life that can hold you down and keep you from living the abundant life Jesus promised those who follow Him.

As a follower of Jesus Christ, you needn't dwell on guilt over your past mistakes and sins. If you find yourself feeling guilt, you should spend some time dwelling on *these* words directly from the mouth of God: "I—yes, I alone—will blot out your sins for my own sake and will never think of them again" (Isaiah 43:25 NLT).

God didn't save you, forgive you, and set you on a new path in life so that you can spend the rest of your days being eaten alive by guilt over your past sins. Yes, learn from your past mistakes and sins and become a better man of God through what you learn, but don't ever let yourself believe, for even a moment, that God holds that which He has forgotten against you.

A PICTURE OF DEPENDABILITY

As Scripture says, "Anyone who believes
in him will never be put to shame."

ROMANS 10:11 NIV

In modern psychology, those who have a difficult time trusting in or depending upon another person are said to have "trust issues." Sometimes those trust issues come as a result of a father who repeatedly proved himself to be undependable.

While some earthly fathers weren't as dependable as they should have been, you never have to worry about this with your Father in heaven. He always keeps His promises and is always there for you if you simply call out to Him.

Jesus, who knew your heavenly Father better than anyone, said this of Him: "Which of you, if your son asks for bread, will give him a stone? Or if he asks for a fish, will give him a snake? If you, then, though you are evil, know how to give good gifts to your children, how much more will your Father in heaven give good gifts to those who ask him!" (Matthew 7:9–11 NIV).

When you come to God in faith for something—your salvation or some other pressing need—you can trust in Him to generously give you what you ask for. When you place that kind of trust in your heavenly Father, He will never let you down or leave you wondering where He is. Even when it seems He's *not* there, He's still there.

A LIVING FAITH

What good is it, my brothers and sisters, if someone claims to have faith but has no deeds? Can such faith save them? . . . Faith by itself, if it is not accompanied by action, is dead.

JAMES 2:14, 17 NIV

Do you find today's verse a little troubling or, at the very least, confusing? If so, you're not alone. Taken in isolation, these words seem to say that without good works, you can't be saved.

However, this passage is a clear example of how context means everything. When you take these words as part of the bigger picture of New Testament teaching about your salvation, you understand that your good works are not a *means to the end* of your salvation, they are a *result* of that salvation.

The New Testament is clear that you're not saved through your own works, no matter how good they are. But when you have God's Spirit dwelling inside you as a result of coming to Jesus Christ for salvation, your Spirit-inspired attitude will always result in good works.

Are you looking for ways to put your faith into action? Then ask God what good works He'd like you to take part in today. But never forget that your good works here on earth can't save you for eternity, and they can't earn you additional favor with God. What they *can* do, however, is make your faith more real to you and others.

AS YOU MAKE YOUR PLANS. . .

*Commit your works to the LORD and
your plans will be established.*

PROVERBS 16:3 NASB

If you've ever been involved in planning for a new project or a new direction at work, you know that there's one all-important step you need to take before those plans can become a reality: your managers or bosses need to sign off on it. Without their approval, you're likely to run into serious problems.

The same thing can be said for the Christian who wants to launch out into some kind of new ministry or professional or personal endeavor. In today's verse, Solomon offers a great bit of wisdom when it comes to planning. The best kind of planning, he tells you, starts with committing your vision for something to your ultimate Boss, your heavenly Father, and continues as you allow Him to give ongoing direction.

Many seemingly great plans—even plans for what looked like a God-appointed ministry—have failed because those with the vision didn't first submit their work to God.

Planning is an important part, a bedrock, in fact, of all great and important things you do. It's simply not a good idea to launch out on some new endeavor without it. So by all means plan, but as you make your plans, don't forget to submit what you're thinking about doing to God for His approval and His direction.

THE IMPORTANCE OF ACCOUNTABILITY

Confess your sins to each other and pray for each other so that you may be healed. The earnest prayer of a righteous person has great power and produces wonderful results.

JAMES 5:16 NLT

Making yourself accountable to others isn't easy a lot of the time, is it? Most men seem to have a touch of "rugged individualism" in them, and they'd rather handle their struggles on their own. Besides being rugged, if they're honest, most of them have some hidden, personal sins they'd rather not reveal to even their best friends.

Today's verse, however, shows that this is exactly the wrong approach to living an overcoming life for Christ. The apostle James challenges all men to come clean with one another and confess their sins—even those sins they might not be comfortable divulging. This is a great piece of wisdom for Christian men. First of all, life experience can teach you that most men won't be shocked when you confess a sin you feel is holding you back in your walk with Jesus. On the contrary, you just might find that your brothers are struggling with a similar sin.

Even more important, however, is that confessing your sins to your brothers allows them to know how to pray for and with you so that you can find lasting freedom. And it also helps you to become accountable to those who love you and want you to overcome.

THE PRIVILEGE OF PAIN

*For you have been given not only the privilege of trusting
in Christ but also the privilege of suffering for him.*

PHILIPPIANS 1:29 NLT

When the apostle Paul wrote of suffering, he did so with authority. He had suffered threats of death and more severe beatings than he could count. He had suffered through sleeplessness, hunger, thirst, and cold. His life as a servant of Jesus Christ was one of constant danger and great personal suffering (see 2 Corinthians 11:23–28).

But this same man not only wrote of suffering for Christ as a privilege, he also wrote of suffering as a means to grow in his faith: "We also glory in our sufferings, because we know that suffering produces perseverance; perseverance, character; and character, hope. And hope does not put us to shame, because God's love has been poured out into our hearts through the Holy Spirit, who has been given to us" (Romans 5:3–5 NIV).

These days, in our society, Christians don't suffer the way Paul did. This is a time and a place of peace and prosperity. But when you suffer—be it from a personal loss, an illness, a disability, or other difficulties—you can look at it as a privilege and a blessing. And you can live in the assurance that your joy is not based on your suffering or on your *lack* of suffering, but in knowing God intimately and walking with Him every day.

LIVING IN THE PAST

Do not say, "Why were the old days better than these?"
For it is not wise to ask such questions.

ECCLESIASTES 7:10 NIV

Have you ever gotten together with a group of old friends—maybe at some reunion—to catch up with one another and reminisce about your times together many years back? Those kinds of gatherings can be enjoyable because you get to see people you haven't seen in a long time and share laughter and memories.

But they can also be frustrating if they cause you to look at your current experiences through the lenses of days gone by. As many have found out, that's not a good thing.

It can be easy sometimes to find yourself living in the past and longing for what you remember as "better times." That can be especially true when you feel dissatisfaction with the present or when you're going through difficult circumstances. In times like these, you may find yourself feeling a sense of ingratitude for what God is doing in your life at present.

There's nothing wrong with reminiscing, with thinking and talking about great times you've enjoyed in the past. You can remember those days fondly and even thank God for them. But you should never let your great memories of days gone by get in the way of living in what God has for you in the here and now.

HONESTY WITH GOD

"I do believe; help my unbelief."
MARK 9:24 NASB

The words spoken in today's verse came from the mouth of a man who was out of options. He wanted Jesus to heal his demon-possessed son, and he had no doubt heard of this Man who had healed many sick, lame, and demoniacs. But still, he doubted.

At first glance, you may wonder how a man who had heard so much about Jesus could possibly doubt Him. And you may even look at his words as a contradiction. But maybe you shouldn't see his words as a contradiction at all. And maybe you shouldn't assume that he had a hard time believing Jesus could heal people. Maybe you should look at his words as an admission that he wondered if Jesus could and would help *him*.

The thought of speaking to God with this kind of honesty scares many men. There are things, after all, you wish you could hide from Him, things you don't even want to admit to yourself. But when you come to the end of yourself and still need God to do something great *for* you and *within* you, it's just the kind of honesty He wants from you.

Do you sometimes find yourself doubting that God wants to do a miracle for you? If so, then confess your doubt to Him. He can handle it, and He can also open your heart and mind to what He has planned for you.

GOD NOTICES

By faith Enoch was taken from this life, so that he did not experience death: "He could not be found, because God had taken him away." For before he was taken, he was commended as one who pleased God.

HEBREWS 11:5 NIV

If you've ever read the Bible cover to cover, starting with the first verse of Genesis and ending with the last words of Revelation, and you still don't know much about a man named Enoch, don't feel bad.

Enoch is mentioned, seemingly in passing, in only four verses in Genesis 5 (vv. 21–24), in one verse in Hebrews 11, and from a quote in Jude 14–15. Nothing else is written of anything he did or said, and yet this man—whom we know little about other than that he "walked faithfully with God" (Genesis 5:24)—rated mention alongside some of the Bible's greatest people of faith.

Maybe Enoch never did anything of note other than walk faithfully with his God during his 365 years here on earth. Or maybe, just maybe, Enoch's short mention in scripture is there to teach you that your God is concerned first not with what you *do* but with the fact that your life is an example of choosing to walk faithfully with Him.

Either way, while you may read the Bible and barely notice Enoch, God most certainly noticed this man, and He counted him worthy to take him to heaven without experiencing physical death.

RECEIVING WISDOM

Listen to counsel and accept discipline,
that you may be wise the rest of your days.
PROVERBS 19:20 NASB

One of the many amazing things about God is that as long as you're committed to walking with Him, He never allows an experience to go to waste. That is especially true of the difficulties and suffering you're sure to encounter as you make your way through this journey called life.

The apostle James understood this well, so as he closed out a section of his epistle dealing with suffering, he wrote, "If any of you lacks wisdom, you should ask God, who gives generously to all without finding fault, and it will be given to you" (James 1:5 NIV).

James had no doubt observed what many Christian leaders since the first century have seen: that people don't always know how to respond wisely during difficult times. That is why he instructed the first-century believers, who lived during very perilous times, to seek God for wisdom—and to be assured that He would give them what they asked for.

God has promised to give wisdom to anyone who asks for it. And like many of His gifts, He uses many means to provide you with the wisdom you ask for—His written Word, His Holy Spirit, life experiences, and other people. So ask God for wisdom, but be open to the many different ways He can give you what you've asked for.

WHO'S YOUR ENEMY?

Be alert and of sober mind. Your enemy the devil prowls around like a roaring lion looking for someone to devour.

1 PETER 5:8 NIV

If someone were to ask you who or what is the greatest enemy of the church today, how would you answer? Some would answer that the biggest enemy is government institutions, which in many ways are becoming more hostile toward the Christian faith. Others might say that other human institutions seem to work tirelessly to oppose the preaching of the Gospel.

While there's no doubt that some worldly and human institutions want to keep Christianity in a corner, Christian men need to understand that they're in a spiritual battle, not a political or physical one. The apostle Paul put it like this: "Our struggle is not against flesh and blood, but against the rulers, against the authorities, against the powers of this dark world and against the spiritual forces of evil in the heavenly realms" (Ephesians 6:12 NIV).

Yes, you should stand against evil in the secular world today and contend for what is right in God's eyes. But you should never forget that your ultimate enemy is the devil, not the lost and misguided people who oppose God.

And above all, you need to remember to put on the full armor of God (Ephesians 6:10–18) as you do battle against the devil and his minions.

WHAT ARE YOUR CREDENTIALS?

Amos answered Amaziah, "I was neither a prophet nor the son of a prophet, but I was a shepherd, and I also took care of sycamore-fig trees."

AMOS 7:14 NIV

You may have felt challenged to get more involved in outreach or some other ministry at some point, but thought, *I don't know how much help I can be. I don't have any kind of education or credentials.*

Men tend to put a lot of stock in credentials, don't they? They see those with high levels of education or impressive accomplishments as somehow more qualified or trustworthy. But God doesn't necessarily see it that way. As someone once wisely said, "God doesn't call the qualified; He qualifies the called."

God doesn't look first at your credentials, and He doesn't focus first on your training and natural abilities. He's concerned, first and foremost, with your willingness to obediently step out and be used of Him to influence your part of the world for His kingdom. When He finds you willing, He enables you to do what He's called you to do.

You don't need a doctorate in theology or a PhD in biblical studies for God to use you in your own sphere of influence. You need just one thing: willingness. So if you'd like to know what you can do to expand the kingdom of God, just ask Him! He'll never answer by first asking about your credentials.

WALKING WITH GOD

*The LORD has told you what is good, and this is what he
requires of you: to do what is right, to love mercy,
and to walk humbly with your God.*

MICAH 6:8 NLT

Sometime during the course of human history, going for walks with
one another became an occasion not just to get some exercise (as
beneficial as that was), but also to enjoy one another's company.
Many a friendship has been enhanced and many a marriage has
been strengthened just through going for walks—or for hikes in
the case of the more athletic, more motivated crowd.

The Bible contains two examples of people it says "walked with
God," using those exact words: Enoch (Genesis 5:21–24) and Noah
(Genesis 6:9). Of course, many other men "walked with God" in
the sense that they remained in close relationship with Him and
obeyed His commands.

But it's probably not much of a stretch to see the use of that
exact phrase in reference to Enoch and Noah as word pictures of
men who walked with God in the sense that they could fellowship
with Him as closely as if they literally went for a stroll with Him,
sharing their hearts with Him and allowing Him to share His heart
with them.

What about you today? Maybe going for a walk and taking
God with you through prayer—talking and listening to Him—could
enhance and strengthen your relationship with Him.

REPULSED BY PRIDE

Human pride will be brought down, and human arrogance will be humbled. Only the LORD will be exalted on that day of judgment.

ISAIAH 2:11 NLT

Have you ever been forced, through a set of circumstances beyond your control, to spend time around a proud, boastful person? You know, the kind of person who never seems to have anything to say unless it's about himself and his accomplishments?

Being around that kind of man for any length of time can be draining, can't it? Pride is a sin each man struggles with in one way or another. But most men find those who seem ruled by pride and arrogance difficult to handle. In a very real way, most of us find excessive pride. . .well, kind of repulsive.

Think about it, though. If you find pride repulsive, then how much more so is it for a God who lists humility as a high virtue and pride as a detestable sin? So much so that He tells you, "God opposes the proud but gives grace to the humble" (James 4:6 NLT).

James's use of the word *opposes* in this verse carries with it an ominous meaning. It connotes a God who doesn't just let the prideful man go about his way, but who actually works against him in every way.

Pride is a serious sin that leads you nowhere good. On the other hand, God gives this promise to those who choose humility: "Humble yourselves, therefore, under God's mighty hand, that he may lift you up in due time" (1 Peter 5:6 NIV).

A BIBLICAL ANATOMY LESSON

Just as a body, though one, has many parts,
but all its many parts form one body, so it is with Christ.

1 CORINTHIANS 12:12 NIV

In 1 Corinthians 12, the apostle Paul likens the church (not the building but the believers who gather there to worship God and fellowship with one another) to the human body, which consists of many individual parts that work wonderfully together for one purpose: to keep you alive and moving.

Paul wanted the believers in Corinth to understand that they all had a role to play within the local church—some bigger and others smaller, some more up front and others more behind the scenes—but all important to the church as a whole. "Now you are the body of Christ, and each one of you is a part of it," he wrote (v. 27).

If Paul were writing to the different church bodies today, he'd tell them the same thing. Each member has a part to play for the greater good of the church.

God doesn't intend for you to attend church services every week just to warm a pew. On the contrary, He has given you special gifts and abilities so that you can serve this wonderful organism called the Body of Christ. Your part in this bargain is to seek out and discover your gifts so that you can begin serving.

A LEGACY OF FAITH

All these people earned a good reputation because of their faith,
yet none of them received all that God had promised.
For God had something better in mind for us, so that
they would not reach perfection without us.

HEBREWS 11:39–40 NLT

The eleventh chapter of Hebrews is an amazing New Testament passage that gives you a pretty good idea of what kind of legacy God calls you to leave behind when your days on this earth are over.

As you read through this chapter, you may recall that the people listed by the writer of this epistle weren't perfect. Far from it! Noah got drunk, Abraham lied because he was afraid, Jacob was a deceiver, Moses doubted God, and David. . .well, his many failings as a man, as a king, and as a father are well chronicled in the Bible.

Yet the writer of Hebrews goes out of his way to tell you that all the people listed in this chapter played their own important parts in making God's plan of redemption a reality for men today—not because they were perfect, but simply because they believed God when He spoke.

As you read Hebrews 11, let it challenge you. Let it bring you to a place of asking yourself what kind of legacy you'll leave behind—for your friends, for your family, and for people whose lives you may touch without even knowing it.

SHOWING RESPECT

*Show proper respect to everyone, love the family of believers,
fear God, honor the emperor.*

1 PETER 2:17 NIV

Today's culture puts great value on respect. But while not everyone practices respect for their fellow human beings, nearly everyone feels entitled to it.

It may come as a surprise to many Christian men, but all people feel an innate need for respect. Even more surprising to some is that God calls each of His people to show respect for others, no matter their beliefs or lifestyles. It's not always easy to show proper respect to others, and it's especially difficult with people whose attitudes and actions show disregard for the truths revealed in God's Word. But the actions and words of others who don't know God don't relieve you who *do* know Him of the responsibility to treat them with respect.

Respect doesn't mean giving approval or acceptance to lifestyles and actions you know God disapproves of. It means simply seeing and treating those you meet—no matter how much you disagree with their views and lifestyle choices—as valued creations made in the image of God.

Your role as a Christian living in a fallen world full of imperfect people is to be an example of God's love and grace. You move yourself closer to that goal when you show love and respect for others, both in how you speak to them and how you treat them.

TELLING YOUR OWN STORY

Give praise to the Lord, proclaim his name;
make known among the nations what he has done.

Psalm 105:1 NIV

Each Christian has his own story about how he came to know Jesus. Not all of these stories may seem like a bona fide water-turned-to-wine miracle—at least not to the people hearing them—but they're all amazing in that they give an account of how Jesus came onto the scene, took what was once dead, and made it alive.

That's just the nature of salvation, isn't it?

The Bible tells you that you're to always be ready "to give an answer to everyone who asks you to give the reason for the hope that you have" (1 Peter 3:15 NIV). Among other things, that can mean being ready to tell others about how Jesus, through the Holy Spirit, brought you to a point of responding to God's love and receiving forgiveness and eternal life. It can also include your story of healing and deliverance from what you once were.

When you begin talking to a friend or family member who needs Jesus, very often the best place to start is not by talking about how that *person* needs Him but instead by telling your *own* story of what He has done for you and how He has impacted your life.

Always remember, your story of salvation is an amazing story people around you need to hear.

LONE RANGER CHRISTIANITY

*All the believers devoted themselves to the apostles' teaching,
and to fellowship, and to sharing in meals (including
the Lord's Supper), and to prayer.*

ACTS 2:42 NLT

In several polls in recent years, more and more people—including many professing Christians—say they don't go to church services regularly, if at all.

One of the most common alibis for consistently skipping church is, "I don't have to go to church to be a Christian." While it may technically be true that you don't have to attend church to be a believer, it's also true that in order to *grow* in your faith, you need the teaching and fellowship you receive when you gather for worship and Bible study.

You receive these things when you attend services at church. That's why the writer of Hebrews admonishes followers of Jesus Christ to not neglect "our own assembling together, as is the habit of some" (Hebrews 10:25 NASB).

Today's verse gives a list of great reasons to attend church regularly, starting with receiving sound biblical teaching. It's also at church that you fellowship with other Christians, which the Bible teaches is important for your spiritual growth.

God never intended for you to be a Lone Ranger Christian. He established the church to provide believers a means to receive teaching and fellowship. That's why it's a good plan for you to find a church that provides sound teaching and then commit yourself to going there on a regular basis.

PRAYING THROUGH THE PAIN

*He touched the socket of his hip; and the socket of Jacob's hip
was out of joint as He wrestled with him. And He said,
"Let Me go, for the day breaks." But he said, "I will
not let You go unless You bless me!"*

GENESIS 32:25–26 NKJV

Today's passage is part of an account in which the patriarch Jacob
became involved in an extended wrestling match with. . .God! It
sounds odd to think of a mere man wrestling with the Almighty.
Certainly, the Creator of the universe not only could have ended
such an encounter in an instant, with but a thought. But your
Father in heaven had a lesson to teach Jacob—and you today too.

God wanted to bless Jacob, but He also wanted him to
understand that prayer isn't always easy, that it means persistent,
sometimes painful, times of pleading with God until he receives
an answer.

If you've ever suffered through a dislocated joint, then you
have some understanding of what Jacob went through in that hour
before dawn. A dislocated toe or finger can be agonizing enough,
but just think of the pain Jacob felt when God dislocated his *hip*!

When a nearly incapacitated Jacob still refused to let his God
go that night, he set an example for believers to follow. Prayer
hurts sometimes, but in the midst of your pain, you should keep
praying and cling to your God with everything you have.

GODLY PAYBACK

*Do not repay evil with evil or insult with insult. On the contrary,
repay evil with blessing, because to this you were
called so that you may inherit a blessing.*

1 PETER 3:9 NIV

How do you respond when someone, intentionally or unintentionally, does you wrong or insults you? It's a rare man who doesn't feel anger and a desire for some payback when someone has done or said something that insults him. But while the anger may sometimes be justified, God tells you that your response to those who do you wrong is to. . .well, *bless* that person.

Your fallen human nature being what it is, you're prone to think that you're entitled to a little vengeance when you've been wronged or to a few sharp, biting comebacks when someone speaks unkind words to you. But God tells you that your responses to evil should be compassionate, kind, and understanding.

On a purely practical level, you need to remember that you can't know what's going on inside the mind of the person who does unkind things and speaks unkind words to you. But God does, and that's one of the reasons He tells you to repay evil and insults with blessings.

No one likes being hurt or insulted. But as a Christian, you must see those unpleasant moments not as negatives but as opportunities to bless those who need God's touch in their lives and to receive God's blessings on yourself.

WHAT GOD CAN'T DO

Why do you look the other way? Why do you ignore our suffering and oppression? We collapse in the dust, lying face down in the dirt. Rise up! Help us! Ransom us because of your unfailing love.

PSALM 44:24–26 NLT

Can God truly hide from you or turn away from His own people? Could God actually ignore what is happening in the world?

Your perceptions of God and reality can appear difficult to reconcile when life begins to fall apart. Whether you're going through a tragedy, a struggle, or a season of spiritual darkness, God isn't hiding, ignoring you, or looking away from you. But God's presence doesn't always mean your problems will be solved, life will go smoothly, or that all of your doubts and uncertainties will disappear.

This tension of suffering or doubt of God's presence goes back centuries, and there's no reason to expect that you'll be part of the generation that finally figures it out. The psalmist leads you to the only place where you can find rest. Even as you feel beaten down by life and struggle to rise up from where you have fallen, place your hope in God's unfailing love.

Even if you have your doubts and come to the end of your faith, because of His unfailing love, God can't turn away from you or ignore you. Even at your lowest point, you are always loved.

IS TRUSTING GOD A "RISK"?

Those who live in the shelter of the Most High will find rest in the shadow of the Almighty. This I declare about the LORD: He alone is my refuge, my place of safety; he is my God, and I trust him.

PSALM 91:1–2 NLT

What would make you feel secure? For some it's a particular place. For others it may mean a certain amount of money in the bank or a particular position at work. Everyone craves security and assurances that they'll be safe from the storms of life that are sure to come.

What does it look like to dwell in God's shelter today and to have God's shadow over you? Perhaps it means releasing control over a specific life circumstance. For others, it may be a step of faith that feels more like a risk than a place of safety or security under God. The irony of living by faith and trusting God as your sole refuge and stronghold can feel risky and even a little chaotic as you perfect your faith in God.

As you grapple with your desires for security and safety, the words of this psalm challenge you to rethink your place under the protection of God. How does it feel to have God as your refuge and stronghold? Does it feel like a risk right now? Are there ways you can learn to grow deeper in your trust in God today?

WHY JESUS IS MERCIFUL

This High Priest of ours understands our weaknesses, for he faced all of the same testings we do, yet he did not sin. So let us come boldly to the throne of our gracious God. There we will receive his mercy, and we will find grace to help us when we need it most.

HEBREWS 4:15–16 NLT

Sometimes it's hard to acknowledge your weaknesses or your need for help. You live in a self-sufficient culture, and so it may come as a shock to read that Jesus spent time on earth in order to feel your weaknesses and to show mercy to you.

If you struggle with sin or don't think you can set your life right, know this: Jesus felt your fears, inadequacies, and even weakness. He knows that you're tempted, that you struggle, and that you won't always make the best choices.

Jesus was tested in all of the ways you have been tested, and while that may be hard to believe, it's even harder to believe that He then is merciful to you. But He is. And He wants you to come to Him in your weakness and failure.

Do you need to know today that Jesus is merciful and ready to help you? He desires that you have no fear when you approach His throne of grace. And take note that this throne is one of grace, not judgment. Acknowledging your weaknesses and failures is the key to restoration.

HOW YOU'RE SAVED FROM SHAME

For I fully expect and hope that I will never be ashamed, but that I will continue to be bold for Christ, as I have been in the past. And I trust that my life will bring honor to Christ, whether I live or die.

PHILIPPIANS 1:20 NLT

What do you fear?

Paul speaks of his fear of being put to shame, and shame is different for each person. Shame could come from the rejection of your peers or community. It could also result from a personal failure or the revelation that you've been inauthentic or fraudulent in some way. However, by identifying what you fear, you can begin to move toward the freedom that prompted Paul to speak with boldness.

If you fear what will become of you and your reputation, then you're in need of the freedom that comes through union with Christ. Your hope and glory are united with Him as you aim to bring God glory with your life.

This approach to glorifying God isn't always high profile or may not appear to be successful. Just as Jesus glorified God through His suffering and death, Paul reminds you that glorifying God looks like faithfulness amid the highs and lows of life. Whether in life or death, you need not fear the potential of shame and failure so long as you've drawn near to Christ and His glory becomes your own.

GOD IS YOUR STRENGTH

Though we are overwhelmed by our sins, you forgive them all.

PSALM 65:3 NLT

How often do you mistake being strong in the Lord with simply being strong on your own?

There are no caveats in this psalm about being stronger than your sins. There are no special exceptions for people who are especially determined when it comes to their weaknesses and imperfections. Sin may overpower you, no matter how much you may want to choose obedience. This is not to excuse sinning. The Bible says, after all, that one of the fruits of the Spirit is self-control (Galatians 5:22–23). So God does expect you to resist sin.

But you can't make yourself more determined or more focused on your own. Your one and only recourse is the mercy and grace of a loving God. If you want to find your strength each day, you must find God, even if that requires beginning with a confession of your failures and weaknesses.

Whether you feel overwhelmed and powerless or you're gritting your teeth in determination, you'll never advance to a point that you'll be able to blot out your own sins. If you rely on your strength and willpower, you'll most assuredly lose eventually. But God's mercy and strength will be there to meet you and deliver you. So cry out to God for His strength.

Once you rest in God, your strength will be endless.

HOW WE GROW

So get rid of all evil behavior. Be done with all deceit, hypocrisy, jealousy, and all unkind speech. Like newborn babies, you must crave pure spiritual milk so that you will grow into a full experience of salvation. Cry out for this nourishment, now that you have had a taste of the Lord's kindness.

1 PETER 2:1–3 NLT

Jesus told His followers to become like children in order to enter the kingdom of God (Matthew 18:3), but Peter seems to take things a step further, telling his readers to become like infants.

Imagining infants who have a simple, single-minded dependence on their mothers for milk, you can catch a glimpse of what Peter has in mind. Perhaps his readers struggled with many serious sins such as envy, hypocrisy, criticism, and deceit because they had turned their faith into something complex. They wondered if they could work harder in order to overcome these many spiritual struggles.

Peter assured them that trying harder wouldn't cut it. They had to become all the *more* dependent on God's nurturing care for them. There's no hope outside of God's spiritual provision for His children.

You may long to stop envying or to become more spiritual, but these are merely dead ends. Your longing should be for the presence of the Lord instead. When you have tasted the goodness of the Lord, you'll find deliverance from your greatest struggles.

WHERE DOES DESPERATION LEAD YOU?

*As the deer longs for streams of water, so I long
for you, O God. I thirst for God, the living God.
When can I go and stand before him?*

PSALM 42:1–2 NLT

Streams can be few and far between in the land of Israel. That's why so many stories of the Old Testament include details about wells and major problems stemming from droughts that drained cisterns. A reliance on wells in the time of Jesus meant He had conversations with people around wells quite often.

With limited water sources, the deer of the land could be hard-pressed sometimes to find water. Perhaps in a season of drought it may have seemed nearly impossible to find a stream.

This intense thirst for a scarce water supply captures the spirit of desperation and longing that the writer of this psalm shares while waiting on God's deliverance. Although you have the assurance that God is alive and well, a season of doubt or isolation can leave you desperate.

Then again, you could just as well become distracted by something else, spending your days longing for things other than God. Perhaps the question you could ask yourself is: *What am I desperate for today?* Your seasons of searching and thirsting for God won't last forever, but that doesn't mean you won't have your times of trial, uncertainty, and longing for God's presence.

WISDOM PUTS YOU IN YOUR PLACE

Fear of the LORD is the foundation of true wisdom. All who obey his commandments will grow in wisdom. Praise him forever!

PSALM 111:10 NLT

Everyone wants to be wise, but fear is rarely valued as a positive virtue. Fear is typically associated with running away, living in paranoia, or lacking any kind of stability. Jesus repeatedly told His disciples to *not* be afraid, so why would the writer of this psalm note that "fear of the Lord" is the foundation of wisdom? Isn't fear the opposite of faith?

What if this "fear" isn't quaking at the thought of God but is a humbling, unsettling grasp of God's holiness and power? The accounts of God showing up among the people in the Old Testament are truly fear-inspiring, but God was also very careful to avoid terrifying people. Even when Moses reflected the glory of God, he veiled his face. God doesn't use His glory and power in order to terrify you into submission. Jesus reaches out to you in love, saying, "Do not fear" (Luke 12:32 NKJV).

However, if you begin to imagine that you're wiser than God, capable of controlling your life, or free to do as you please, the fear of God's power and holiness can offer a helpful correction. Should God choose to show up, you'll have a fearful reminder of how unwise your life choices have been.

YOU SHARE FROM GOD'S GENEROSITY

"But when you give to someone in need, don't let your left hand know what your right hand is doing. Give your gifts in private, and your Father, who sees everything, will reward you."

Matthew 6:3–4 NLT

Everything you have is a gift from God, and so Jesus challenges your desire to gain the praise of fellow men and church leaders when you give generously from your possessions. Giving as freely as you have received without the hope of recognition saves you from the illusion of self-sufficiency and pride in your own abilities. If you're depending on God for your provision, then your generosity to others is between you and God as you give as freely as you have received.

Think about it: the more attached you become to your money and possessions, the less likely you are to see God as your provider and sustainer. Most importantly, the less you live by faith, the more dependent you will become on the opinions of others. Without seeking God's praise first and foremost, you run the risk of building your life on the unstable foundations of what others think and say.

Giving from your possessions also ensures that you won't become dependent on them for your security. Privately giving to others may be one of the purest acts of faith possible.

LETTING GO OF GRUDGES

"So if you are presenting a sacrifice at the altar in the Temple and you suddenly remember that someone has something against you, leave your sacrifice there at the altar. Go and be reconciled to that person. Then come and offer your sacrifice to God."

MATTHEW 5:23–24 NLT

Your worship and your treatment of others are linked. Broken fellowship with a neighbor or colleague can get in the way of your worship of God, and your only path to freedom is through confession and forgiveness.

Perhaps your own pride has offended someone or a grudge has poisoned your relationship. If you give in to anger, you then demand your rights and this can cause divisions or alienate you from others. Whatever you are holding on to, your ability to pray and to worship freely will be damaged by the same things that damage your relationships.

Pride is always destructive, whether before God or before others. A grudge could point to a self-righteousness that keeps you from receiving God's mercy, let alone showing mercy to others. Anger counteracts the humility that keeps you in your place before God.

If you want to know where you stand before God, one of the first places to look should be in your relationships with others. Do your interactions or relationships indicate that you think too highly of yourself? What steps can you take to remedy that?

WHAT MOTIVATES YOU TO PRAY?

Enter his gates with thanksgiving; go into his courts with praise.
Give thanks to him and praise his name. For the LORD is
good. His unfailing love continues forever, and his
faithfulness continues to each generation.

PSALM 100:4–5 NLT

You may be most likely to pray in a time of need, but your own circumstances shouldn't be the first thing on your mind when you enter a time of worship or prayer. In fact, you may struggle to pray if you don't approach God with thanksgiving and praise. Thanksgiving and praise keep your circumstances in proper perspective.

Why do you turn to God in prayer? Is it because of something you want? Or are you moved toward God because of His goodness, unfailing love, and faithfulness throughout the generations? Without a reality check into the love, goodness, and faithfulness of God, who knows which direction your prayers will go?

You come to God because you're His beloved child. You come to God in prayer because He could never forget His own or leave His children behind. You come to God in prayer because you can trust His goodness, even if you can't understand His place in your circumstances.

You have every reason to praise God as you enter into prayer. Skipping the praise that He is due could result in some very self-centered prayers that miss an understanding of how deeply God cares for you.

GOD BUILDS YOU UP FROM THE DUST

The LORD is like a father to his children, tender and compassionate to those who fear him. For he knows how weak we are; he remembers we are only dust.

PSALM 103:13–14 NLT

Do you feel pressure to appear capable, strong, or holy? Have you ever feared being "found out" as a fraud because you struggle either privately or publicly?

Your masks always fall off in God's presence, and while that may be devastating or humiliating for you, God knows full well that it is for your benefit. You will only find freedom from your weaknesses and the false sense of self that you fight to maintain when you see with clarity that although you're little more than dust, God still cares for you like a father cares for his children. You are His child. This is the only identity you have to claim.

When you wish to appear strong or capable, your admission of weakness and dependence opens you to God's strength. You will finally tap into God's greater compassion and mercy for you, and you will then be able to share the same with those around you. God is rebuilding you from the dust on the ground on up.

THE ULTIMATE PAYBACK

Don't repay evil for evil. Don't retaliate with insults when people insult you. Instead, pay them back with a blessing. That is what God has called you to do, and he will grant you his blessing.

1 PETER 3:9 NLT

In the heat of an argument or as you encounter a frustrating situation, it's hard to resist trading insults or giving someone a piece of your mind. As social media and email make it possible to argue without seeing someone face to face, you often experience the worst parts of your anger and discord without the filter of empathy or understanding.

Peter challenges you to bless those who insult you and to avoid any kind of retaliation. While he was writing to Christians who were being actively marginalized and persecuted for their faith, his message remains powerful as you seek to infuse your world with God's hope.

You gain very little from insulting others, and even the act of receiving an insult can be good for you. Perhaps you need reminders that you define yourself as part of God's people and His beloved child. Although an insult may tend to undermine your fragile ego, as you release hurt or anger and hand over a blessing, you bring the other person one step closer to God while reminding yourself of where you find your identity.

WHEN GOD'S MERCY INCREASES

Our ancestors in Egypt were not impressed by the LORD's miraculous deeds. They soon forgot his many acts of kindness to them. Instead, they rebelled against him at the Red Sea. Even so, he saved them—to defend the honor of his name and to demonstrate his mighty power.

PSALM 106:7–8 NLT

Unfaithfulness toward God often begins when you forget how God has acted in the past. As the people of Israel lost sight of God's miracles and kindness, they began to seek other gods and even openly rebelled against God.

The stories in scripture about unfaithfulness, worshipping other gods, or failing to trust God could just as easily be your own stories. It's possible that the fantastic details of these historical accounts cause you to forget that the daily worries of life, the threats of political turmoil, and selfish desires or ambition caused God's own people to forget even the wonder of seeing the sea split before them.

The sins of those who went before you are most likely part of your story as well. If those who witnessed the greatest miracles could forget them, how much more should you be aware of your own weaknesses?

Even during these repeated acts of unfaithfulness and forgetfulness, God's mercy didn't cease. In fact, God's mercy increased in order to save His people. God didn't stop revealing His power.

SEEING GOD BY LOOKING BACK

*The godly will see these things and be glad, while the wicked are
struck silent. Those who are wise will take all this to heart;
they will see in our history the faithful love of the Lord.*

PSALM 107:42–43 NLT

What is filling your mind today? What have you pondered so far?

You're probably surrounded by entertainment, news reports, and commercials that can easily fill your thoughts. Your work and family surely occupy important spots in your mind as well. But how often do you pause to remember the ways that God has been at work in the past week, month, or even year? It's possible that His love may appear far off simply because you need to spend a little time today considering His faithful love.

Whether you're entertaining doubts or uncertain about the future, your faith can be bolstered by taking a moment to notice the ways that God has offered comfort, reassurance, guidance, or the peace of His presence. Just as God's people are expected to learn from their mistakes, there's also great benefit in remembering His provision.

As you consider your next steps, whether at home, work, or in your church community, you can take comfort in remembering God's past actions on your behalf. Sometimes you don't need Him to perform another miracle. You just need to notice what He has already done for you.

FINDING GOD EACH DAY

Praise the LORD! I will thank the LORD with all my heart as I meet with his godly people. How amazing are the deeds of the LORD! All who delight in him should ponder them.

PSALM 111:1–2 NLT

Today's psalm should encourage you to pause and to ponder the works of God around you. How is He present with you today? Can you see how the good and perfect gifts around you are from the Lord? You can see this moment today as an invitation to draw near to God and to become aware of His presence.

It's easy to run from one task to another, and by evening you may wonder where God was throughout the day. Perhaps you even feel abandoned by Him at the end of a busy day. While scripture assures you that He's always with you, you can surely overlook His presence and gifts for you. Unless you take time to see the Lord's works around you, you'll miss out on the delight and joy that belong to you.

You'll also see more of God's works if you spend time with His people. As you see the ways that He has blessed your friends and family, you'll become more aware of Him.

It's also likely that just as you hit a place of stability, someone in your circle will need a reminder of God's care. Your enjoyment of God isn't just for your own benefit after all.

DELIVER US FROM SEEKING RICHES

The disciples were astounded. "Then who in the world can be saved?" they asked. Jesus looked at them intently and said, "Humanly speaking, it is impossible. But not with God. Everything is possible with God."

MARK 10:26–27 NLT

What is it about money that obstructs the way into God's kingdom?

Perhaps for you, money may be a source of security, while others may see their wealth and status as personal validation. But the pursuit of wealth itself can take up your time, pulling you away from family, worship, and service to others. The accumulation of wealth can prompt you to buy things that require more time spent earning money so that you can afford them.

The more you're loaded down with the pursuit and management of money, the harder it becomes to free yourself to be present for God. Wealth can gradually take you captive, and the more you're surrounded by people who pursue it, the easier it becomes to justify the pursuit of "just a little more."

Jesus assures you that while wealth can wreck your soul, God can save you. Your only recourse is to fall on God's mercy and to trust Him fully for the salvation of your soul. Tempting as it is to say that wealth is a blessing from God, it may just as easily become your downfall if you aren't living by faith.

YOU ARE CALLED TO STOP

"Be still, and know that I am God! I will be honored by every nation. I will be honored throughout the world."

PSALM 46:10 NLT

You can wear yourself out trying to bring glory to God. Ministry burnout is common, and many who attend church on Sunday feel like they can't add one more thing to their schedules. The idea of "being still" seems like a nice thought in theory, but who can truly be still?

Perhaps you struggle with being still and knowing that God is present because you believe that your world will fall apart if you stop working. You may have an exaggerated sense of your own importance or you may underestimate the power of God. Either way, being still before God puts you in your place, and, more importantly, acknowledges God's place over you.

Without your efforts and energy, God will still be honored throughout the earth. There is nothing you can give Him that He can't obtain without you. In fact, your ministry to others is merely an outflowing of God through you.

As you become still before God, you can see that He is *already* honored and exalted throughout the earth. The Lord is more than capable of handling your problems and concerns. You'll only see that with clarity if you learn to be still before Him (see Hebrews 4:9–11).

ADMIT YOUR DISAPPOINTMENT WITH GOD

Martha said to Jesus, "Lord, if only you had been here, my brother would not have died. But even now I know that God will give you whatever you ask."

JOHN 11:21–22 NLT

When have you felt hopeless or disappointed in God? Were you afraid to speak exactly what you were thinking? Perhaps you didn't feel God would ever listen to your prayers again if you really told Him what you were thinking.

At her lowest point, Martha spoke her mind to Jesus. She didn't hold back. Her faith held the tension of Jesus' power and her disappointment. She could still believe in His care for her and His healing power, even if He hadn't shown up when she had requested.

Of course, Martha's story ends with a greater display of Jesus' power as He raised her brother Lazarus, but you don't always experience God's deliverance in such dramatic ways. Regardless of the results, Martha's faith after experiencing tremendous loss and grief shows that you can surrender your circumstances to God in faith, hope, and, most importantly, honesty.

Your honesty doesn't have to undermine your faith. Martha's spirit of surrender placed her future in Jesus' hands even as she faced her disappointment about the past. What do you need to speak to God about with complete transparency today? Is it possible that speaking about your disappointment in God could be a greater act of faith than holding yourself back from saying what you really think?

RECEIVING GOD'S MERCY

"I entered this world to render judgment—to give sight to the blind and to show those who think they see that they are blind."

JOHN 9:39 NLT

If you feel like you can't figure out how to draw near to God or if you struggle with particular sins, then you're right where Jesus can help you. In fact, the bigger problem is if you think you have your act together and have no need of His mercy.

Jesus came to reveal your true spiritual state. You can either resist His offer of mercy or you can fight it, claiming that you're good enough on your own and have no need for Him and His help. Ironically, the more you insist on your wisdom and holiness, the less hope you have!

Your only hope is to stop pretending that you can see spiritually and fully admit your need for God's mercy. Jesus knows fully well how blind and lost you are. He came to seek you out, to reveal that He's not interested in people putting on a brave face and acting as if they have things together.

If you come to Him with honesty and a complete dependence on His mercy, you're in the best position to receive His help and to experience true restoration.

TRANSFORMATION ISN'T UP TO YOU

But I will come—and soon—if the Lord lets me, and then I'll find out whether these arrogant people just give pretentious speeches or whether they really have God's power. For the Kingdom of God is not just a lot of talk; it is living by God's power.

1 CORINTHIANS 4:19–20 NLT

Division and discord among Christians is nothing new, but perhaps Paul's approach to resolving it may surprise you. When facing a divisive and contentious church, Paul reminded them that their words held very little power for spiritual transformation. Whether relying on your own words or the teachings of others, the true power of God's kingdom is in the way His power takes hold in you.

Even your best attempts at encouragement may well fall flat if you aren't empowered by God. This puts the responsibility for your spiritual transformation on Him, so the pressure is off you.

You can't make people change and you can't change yourself. You can only submit to the power of God, and that process of surrender and submission will feel like a lot of work at times! However, the end result of seeking God's direction and influence is that you'll change into the kind of person who has something worthwhile to share with others.

GOD'S LIGHT ERASES YOUR DARKNESS

Remember, O LORD, your compassion and unfailing love,
which you have shown from long ages past. Do not remember
the rebellious sins of my youth. Remember me in the light
of your unfailing love, for you are merciful, O LORD.

PSALM 25:6–7 NLT

God's character defines how He interacts with you, not the other way around. If you had to be on your best behavior in order to receive God's mercy, you'd have no hope in the face of His holiness.

You can't hide your sins from God, but you can still approach Him with confidence because of His unfailing love and mercy. Today's psalm notes that in light of God's mercy, you have access to Him. You've never been able to be good enough, but He has always been good enough to receive you.

When God remembers you, He doesn't look at your failures, hypocrisies, and faults. He sees you with compassion as His beloved child. It's this love that changes and transforms you, renewing you and drawing you near to Him on the merits of His unfailing love.

You don't have to bring anything to God because He desires to show mercy and compassion to you. In the warm glow of His light, your darkness is gone and you're free to be loved by Him.

YOU ARE GOD'S BELOVED CREATION

"What is the price of five sparrows—two copper coins? Yet God does not forget a single one of them. And the very hairs on your head are all numbered. So don't be afraid; you are more valuable to God than a whole flock of sparrows."

LUKE 12:6–7 NLT

Do you fear that God sees you as expendable? Are you worried that you could be on the brink of being cast away by the Lord? Perhaps you've gone through some season of life where you've felt abandoned by God and you aren't able to pinpoint what has gone wrong.

God is intimately aware of you and your needs. Most importantly, this intimate knowledge of you doesn't turn Him away or result in your expulsion from His presence. In fact, this is a reason for you to have confidence that your Creator remains near to you and desires to be with you. The Lord is deeply invested in knowing you and in caring for you.

That isn't to say that you'll be spared hardships. Rather, you're assured of God's presence and comfort day after day. Just as the birds He created can never escape His notice, you can also take comfort in His ongoing awareness of you. If even the most common, seemingly inconsequential creature is known by God, how much more will He hold on to you?

WHAT'S THE RESULT OF FAITH?

Let your unfailing love surround us, Lord,
for our hope is in you alone.

PSALM 33:22 NLT

You can feel burdens of stress, of strained relationships, and of crammed schedules each day. You speak of feeling "weighed down" at times as challenges pile up, and as you're weighed down by fear, worries, and obligations, you may lose sight of God's provision for you.

While experiencing stress, fear, and aimlessness, you'll always grasp for answers, solutions, and anything that you can control. If you feel like you can't remove those burdens on your own, that's because you truly are hopeless on your own. Turning to God throughout the day gives you your only lasting relief from these burdens.

As you learn to trust in the Lord alone, you'll begin to see His lovingkindness for you with greater clarity. But being weighed down with your worries and cares may make it almost impossible to find God's concern for you. Your worries will become larger and larger the more you focus on them.

However, when you begin to place your trust in God, you'll see His patience and love for you with greater clarity, freeing you to see His love that has remained unchanged regardless of your circumstances.

SILENCE IS GOOD FOR YOUR SOUL

Lᴏʀᴅ, my heart is not proud; my eyes are not haughty. I don't concern myself with matters too great or too awesome for me to grasp. Instead, I have calmed and quieted myself, like a weaned child who no longer cries for its mother's milk. Yes, like a weaned child is my soul within me.

Psᴀʟᴍ 131:1–2 ɴʟᴛ

Today's psalm reminds you that God nurtures and cares for you the way that a mother cares for her child. Perhaps you have a "tough love" picture of the Lord—you see Him as a God who demands much of you.

If you make the mistake of seeing Him this way, you may well become proud of your holiness, your commitment to Him, or your spiritual accomplishments. You may attempt to master "great matters" that distinguish you from others. The pride that comes with performing for God inevitably results in haughty glances at others. You imagine that they either don't measure up or are a threat to your own pursuit of false holiness.

However, if you see God as infinitely loving like a mother caring for a child, you can respond to Him with silence and rest. Your striving may cease, and you can truly trust in His protection and acceptance.

Then you can move into your days knowing the Lord's love that silences your doubts and striving. You will be humble and care for others since you have nothing to prove or to guard.

GOD IS ALWAYS GENEROUS

"Is it against the law for me to do what I want with my money? Should you be jealous because I am kind to others?"

MATTHEW 20:15 NLT

It's tempting sometimes to imagine that God is holding Himself back from you. You go through spiritual darkness or dry seasons, and *generosity* may be the last word that comes to mind. In fact, you may become so preoccupied with your own needs that you forget just how badly others need God's generous provision as well.

In the parable of the vineyard workers, some labored all day, while others only worked a few hours. Both received what they needed. As your own needs grow, you may not even be able to imagine that anyone else could need God's provision more. Perhaps you may be in a season of waiting for what you need from God, and it's particularly hard to see His blessings go to others. But remember, God is always generous—but not *just* to you.

Envy will dismantle the patience that God is growing within you, robbing you of the joy of His blessings when they finally come to you. The Lord is generous, but everyone experiences that generosity in different ways and at different times.

God's generosity won't spare you seasons of darkness and doubt. It's possible, however, that waiting will help you view His generosity with greater clarity.

LESS TIME THAN YOU THINK

"Watch therefore, for you do not know when the master of the house is coming—in the evening, at midnight, at the crowing of the rooster, or in the morning—lest, coming suddenly, he find you sleeping. And what I say to you I say to all: Watch!"

MARK 13:35–37 NKJV

Jesus gives a rather stern warning that your time on earth could be far shorter than you expect. Whether He returns during your lifetime or your life is cut short unexpectedly, you can't take your time for granted.

You may have plans that fill your schedule each week and prompt you to put off the things that truly matter. Perhaps you hope to get around to spending more time with your kids. You may be waiting on getting involved in a service opportunity in the community. There could be a spiritual growth meeting at church that should be a top priority.

Whatever you're putting off, your time on earth isn't unlimited. You may be surprised to see your carefully laid plans fall to pieces one day when a sudden change happens.

While Jesus isn't saying that you should never rest, there's a spirit of awareness and watchfulness that He wants His followers to adopt. You could well have less time than you expect, and that should change how you approach each day and make plans for the future.

CONQUERING EVERY POWER

No power in the sky above or in the earth below—indeed, nothing in all creation will ever be able to separate us from the love of God that is revealed in Christ Jesus our Lord.

ROMANS 8:39 NLT

You can't stop God's love for you. Nothing created on earth can alter His love. No spiritual power or authority can undermine the Lord's steadfast devotion to you. The ministry of Jesus reveals God's perfect love in its fullness, reaching out to you with healing, compassion, and sacrifice.

How often are you tempted to begin measuring this love by your difficult circumstances or deflated sense of security? How often have you believed that you've failed one too many times?

Your desires and failures lead you astray from within, and enemies constantly assail you from without. Paul saw the powers of this world aligning themselves against believers, with demons and rulers straining themselves to pry you away from the love of God.

Still, this love of God has been bonded to you in Christ Jesus, who has forever linked you to God the Father. You are His child, and there's no force in this world that can change that. You can remain confident that your security in God is rooted in His unshakable love, not in your own circumstances or personal failures.

STABILITY IN UNCERTAIN TIMES

But you, O Lord, will sit on your throne forever.
Your fame will endure to every generation.

PSALM 102:12 NLT

When everything else appears to be shaking around you, you can still deal rightly with fear, anger, and uncertainty about the future. You can't control what tomorrow brings, but you can return to the one certainty that will endure from one generation to another and has remained from the very beginning of time: God will be with you.

Whatever else you may lose, the Lord can't be taken away. As despair sets in during a time of suffering or loss, you have a powerful opportunity to consider what you have placed your trust in. Have you placed your confidence in your health, your finances, your career, or some other material thing?

God is merciful and compassionate, empathizing with you when you're at your lowest point. However, your circumstances don't change the presence of the Lord; rather, your despair and grief can become opportunities to discover His never-changing mercy. While you aren't guaranteed the desires of your heart, you're given something far better: a loving God who will not abandon you and can never be moved.

There surely have been worse times, and tragedies are certain to come in the future, but none of this can disrupt God's presence.

SHOWING KINDNESS

And they [the men of Judah] told David, saying, "It was the men
of Jabesh-gilead who buried Saul." David sent messengers to the
men of Jabesh-gilead, and said to them, "May you be blessed
of the Lord because you have shown this kindness
to Saul your lord, and have buried him."

2 Samuel 2:4–5 nasb

After David was anointed king of Israel in Hebron, he learned that the men of Jabesh-gilead had buried King Saul. Very likely David inquired about Saul's body because he wanted to honor him with a proper burial, or maybe the men of Judah wanted to point the finger at the men of Jabesh-gilead, thinking David might be displeased by their actions. But either way, David sent a blessing back to them.

Regardless of how far Saul ended up going astray, he was the Lord's anointed and was worthy of respect. David always had a firm understanding of this concept, even when he was on the run from Saul, fearing for his life. This is consistent with what the Bible says about how God's people are to respect authority and treat their enemies.

Proverbs 24:17–18 (nasb) says, "Do not rejoice when your enemy falls, and do not let your heart be glad when he stumbles; or the Lord will see it and be displeased, and turn His anger away from him."

How do you respond when one of your enemies falls—either literally or figuratively? How does that compare with today's verse?

COVENANT–KEEPING GOD

"Obey what I command you today. I will drive out before you the Amorites, Canaanites, Hittites, Perizzites, Hivites and Jebusites."

Exodus 34:11 NIV

At this point in Israel's history, the Lord was establishing a covenant with His people, promising to "do wonders never before done in any nation in all the world" (Exodus 34:10 NIV). And He wasn't just promising to do such wonders in front of Moses, but rather, before *all* the people. This was a foreshadowing of God drying up the Jordan River (Joshua 3), His destruction of the walls of Jericho (Joshua 6), and more.

As if that wasn't enough, commentators point out that God listed the six enemies that He would drive out before Israel if they would obey what He commanded them that day. He then went on to list His terms, what He expected of them: they were to cut down the Asherah poles (v. 13), not worship any other god (v. 14), not make idols (v. 17), faithfully celebrate His festivals (vv. 18, 22), honor the Sabbath (v. 21), and more. They could only expect to receive the promises of God if they were faithful to Him.

What sort of enemies are you facing today? If you haven't seen any progress against them, take inventory of your obedience to God. While you won't always be able to understand His ways, He's still a God who covenants with His people and therefore expects obedience.

EXPECT HARDSHIP

*Can anything ever separate us from Christ's love? Does it mean he
no longer loves us if we have trouble or calamity, or are persecuted,
or hungry, or destitute, or in danger, or threatened with death?
(As the Scriptures say, "For your sake we are killed every
day; we are being slaughtered like sheep.")*

ROMANS 8:35–36 NLT

When hardship comes, and it will, you'll find out how strong your
faith is. But how can God allow His own children to be persecuted,
or starve, or be threatened with death? Doesn't He promise to
protect His followers?

After all, Job 5:11 (NLT) says, "He gives prosperity to the poor
and protects those who suffer." And Psalm 12:7 (NLT) tells you,
"Therefore, LORD, we know you will protect the oppressed,
preserving them forever from this lying generation." And Proverbs
19:23 (NLT) promises, "Fear of the LORD leads to life, bringing security
and protection from harm."

In some instances, God does intervene—offering physical
protection to advance His kingdom. In other cases, He offers
spiritual protection against the advances of the enemy. And
sometimes, He allows hardship, while preserving your soul.

Today's verse quotes Psalm 44:22, and one aspect of it that's
hard to miss is this: Christians face death every day for the sake
of the kingdom. But hardship never separates you from the love
of Christ.

DOCTRINAL INTEGRITY

*Likewise, exhort the young men to be sober-minded, in all things
showing yourself to be a pattern of good works; in doctrine
showing integrity, reverence, incorruptibility, sound speech that
cannot be condemned, that one who is an opponent may
be ashamed, having nothing evil to say of you.*

TITUS 2:6–8 NKJV

In today's verses, Paul addressed Titus, his partner and fellow
worker (2 Corinthians 8:23), telling him about the importance of
the older generation teaching the younger one. But they were
to go beyond teaching. They were to display a pattern of good
works, showing integrity, reverence, and incorruptibility in their
doctrine—so much so that even an opponent might not have
anything to say against them.

Doctrinal integrity doesn't mean perfection. It simply means
living out truth as best you understand it, without walking in
contradiction. If you know anger to be a sin, and you teach it as
such, but everybody knows you as a hothead, that's the type of
inconsistency that signals to the next generation that you don't
really believe what you're saying. It also shows that your doctrine
lacks power.

If you're older, say forty-five years of age or more, are you
teaching younger men in the faith? Do they see inconsistencies
in your life, or do they see a repentant heart? If you're younger,
how quick are you to accept the teaching of the older generation
while acknowledging your own weaknesses?

WORK, REST, AND PRAY

*Be still in the presence of the LORD, and wait patiently for him
to act. Don't worry about evil people who prosper
or fret about their wicked schemes.*

PSALM 37:7 NLT

Bible commentators point out that being *still* in the Lord's presence is about more than simply not moving. They say it's about silencing the tongue from all murmuring and complaint. It means to be resigned, content in Him. That doesn't mean you can't ask Him to act, but it *does* mean there should be times when you meet with Him without making requests.

The real test comes when evil people appear to prosper. Shouldn't a Christian fret then? Doesn't God call Christians to speak for the voiceless? Indeed, He does. But not always. Solomon said this in Ecclesiastes 3:1 and 7 (NLT), "For everything there is a season. . .a time to be quiet and a time to speak." If you're always speaking, or if you're always quiet, you haven't found the proper balance.

Either way, today's verse says don't worry about evil people. Instead, wait patiently for the Lord to act. That looks different in every circumstance, but isn't it nice to know that the success of His kingdom doesn't rest in your hands? Neither does toppling evil. You're called to work, rest, and pray—always trusting in Him.

STAY ALERT

Watch out that you do not lose what we have worked so hard to achieve. Be diligent so that you receive your full reward.

2 JOHN 1:8 NLT

Deception has been an issue in every church age. At the heart of one deception was the denial that Jesus came in an actual physical body (2 John 1:7); this was, ultimately, a rejection of Christ. Jesus is always the sticking point with those who come in the spirit of antichrist.

In this epistle, the apostle John warned the church to be on guard—to be diligent against such people. Otherwise, the Christian is in danger of losing his heavenly reward. John went on to say that anyone who wanders from this teaching has no relationship with God (v. 9). With such consequences, it's no wonder that he called the church to be so diligent.

If you knew your car might veer off the road and cause you to plummet off a mountainside at any moment, leading to your certain death, you'd be on heightened alert. Your radio would be off. Your hands would have a firm grip on the steering wheel. And your eyes would be giving the road their full attention.

Spiritual diligence works in a similar fashion. It includes keeping an eye out for deceivers, praying for discernment, and staying close to the Body of Christ so you can experience the process of iron sharpening iron (Proverbs 27:17).

SPIRITUAL EYES

"The LORD will repay each man for his righteousness and his faithfulness; for the LORD delivered you into my hand today, but I refused to stretch out my hand against the LORD's anointed."

1 SAMUEL 26:23 NASB

Sometimes, faithfulness means inaction.

That was the case in today's verse when Saul got wind of the fact that David was hiding from him in the wilderness of Ziph (1 Samuel 26:2–3). Saul took three thousand men in search of him, but David outfoxed him. Then he showed up at Saul's camp early one morning while everybody was sleeping. His cousin Abishai wanted to kill Saul on the spot, but David recognized that Saul was God's anointed, and restrained Abishai.

David's faithfulness to the Lord outweighed an opportunity to kill his oppressor. The Hebrew word for *faithfulness* in this verse means "moral fidelity." To kill Saul would have been the equivalent of being unfaithful to God, and David wouldn't do that. He had other moral failings over the course of his life, but here he saw his situation through spiritual eyes and it made all the difference.

Are you on the cusp of making a decision you'd feel justified in making, yet you know deep down inside that it would mean being unfaithful to God? Put off the flesh and look at the situation through spiritual eyes.

FEAR GOD

"We have been rescued from our enemies so we can serve God without fear, in holiness and righteousness for as long as we live."

Luke 1:74–75 nlt

You're in daily battles with three enemies: the world, the flesh, and the devil (Ephesians 2:1–3). All three are formidable, but in the eternal sense, you have already been rescued from all three. In the here and now, though, the battles will continue. And those battles can weigh you down, throw you off track, and cripple you with fear.

In today's verse, Luke mentions Zechariah's prophecy about the coming Messiah who descended from the royal line of David, just as God promised (Luke 1:69–70). He would be merciful and rescue God's people from their enemies. While Zechariah looked forward to the coming Messiah, you look backward, knowing He has already arrived. Your salvation has been secured. And even now, He's in the process of conquering your earthly enemies while preparing a heavenly place for you.

But for now, live out your salvation. Don't fear persecution or even death for Christ's sake. Instead, fear God. Serve Him faithfully in the spheres of influence where He has placed you, being confident that His work will continue, no matter what His enemies do. Yes, they may prevail in some battles, but the war has already been won.

BOASTING COULD COST YOU

Do not boast about tomorrow,
for you do not know what a day may bring.

PROVERBS 27:1 NIV

In Luke 12:16–20, Jesus shared a parable about a rich man who had an abundant harvest. Presuming upon tomorrow, he decided to tear down his barns and build bigger ones to store his surplus grain. And he said to himself, "You have plenty of grain laid up for many years. Take life easy; eat, drink and be merry." Making such a presumption was a critical mistake because God said to him, "You fool! This very night your life will be demanded from you. Then who will get what you have prepared for yourself?"

The rich man's error wasn't in planning for the future or saving for a rainy day. It was in his boasting of having plenty of provisions and living a life of ease—but not caring about spiritual riches.

James 4:15–17 addressed the same problem. James instructed believers to say, "If it is the Lord's will, we will live and do this or that." He added, "As it is, you boast in your arrogant schemes. All such boasting is evil."

When you talk and plan for the future, do your words include anything that could be construed as boasting? If so, be careful. All your hard work and effort might be for naught.

A GENTLE DEFENSE

But sanctify Christ as Lord in your hearts, always being ready to make a defense to everyone who asks you to give an account for the hope that is in you, yet with gentleness and reverence.

1 PETER 3:15 NASB

You probably live for instances when someone genuinely inquires about your faith, asking you to give an account for the hope they see in you. But even during genuine inquiries, conversations can sometimes become heated—or become focused on one-upping the other person. Has this ever happened to you?

Peter says to give an account, but to do so with gentleness and reverence. This is much more difficult. But in Spurgeon's commentary, he explained why it's so important: "If they wish to know why you believe that you're saved, have your answer all ready in a few plain, simple sentences; and in the gentlest and most modest spirit make your confession of faith to the praise and glory of God. Who knows but what such good seed will bring forth an abundant harvest?"

A gentle, reverent response does a work that has the potential to bring forth great results. It's good seed because it isn't tainted by pride and arrogance. And it's good because the planter is seen as being in just as much need as the receiver. If this describes your evangelism, then carry on. If not, take Peter's words to heart.

FEED THE SPIRIT

Therefore put to death your members which are on the earth:
fornication, uncleanness, passion, evil desire,
and covetousness, which is idolatry.

COLOSSIANS 3:5 NKJV

If you have been raised with Christ, then you are to seek the things that are above (Colossians 3:1). One of the primary ways you can seek the heavenly is by putting the earthly to death. Jesus called His disciples to a life of self-denial. Matthew 16:24 (NKJV) records one instance: "If anyone desires to come after Me, let him deny himself, and take up his cross, and follow Me."

Easier said than done, though, right? What does self-denial and putting your earthly members to death actually entail? Romans 8:5 (NKJV) is the key: "For those who live according to the flesh set their minds on the things of the flesh, but those who live according to the Spirit, the things of the Spirit."

Your spiritual power will increase or decrease based on which aspect of yourself you feed the most. If you feed the flesh, you should expect your earthly appetites to get stronger. If you feed the spirit, your spiritual appetites will increase. Once your flesh's power source is cut off (or starved), it will decrease.

So, the obvious question is: Are you feeding the flesh or the spirit? What can you do to feed the spirit even more?

INTERNAL BATTLES

He that is slow to anger is better than the mighty;
and he that ruleth his spirit than he that taketh a city.

PROVERBS 16:32 KJV

For a split second, just before you either act or react to an event that might make you angry, you have the wherewithal to be measured and restrained, rather than erupt in anger. You might blow right past that internal check, feeling justified, but in so doing, you'll be showing an inability to rule your own spirit.

Being slow to answer shows the emotional fortitude it would have required to take a city back in the day. How so? The person who conquered a city overcame serious obstacles—the weather, a multitude of weapons, snares, and defenders. But the person who rules his spirit in the heat of the moment overcomes an internal battle—one in which the flesh makes demands but is vanquished by the spirit.

Are you quick to anger? If so, then you have some work to do, and that's okay. The Holy Spirit is at work in you. The next time you're tempted to display anger, view that internal check you feel as a gift from God and obey it. Use a soft answer to turn away wrath and the situation will become much less volatile.

GENUINE REPENTANCE

That is why the LORD says, "Turn to me now, while there is time.
Give me your hearts. Come with fasting, weeping, and mourning.
Don't tear your clothing in your grief, but tear your hearts instead."

JOEL 2:12–13 NLT

In Joel 2:1–11, the prophet speaks about a coming day of judgment when everyone should tremble in fear. Nothing will escape. "Who can possibly survive?" asks Joel (v. 11 NLT). And then the Lord provides the answer above.

Anybody who turns to Him now while there is still time can escape judgment. But this is serious business. God calls those who wish to escape the judgment to come with fasting, weeping, and mourning. When is the last time you took your sin that seriously?

But God goes even further, saying that He's not interested in the kind of repentance that is expressed outwardly. Instead, He wants godly sorrow to seep inside, all the way to the heart. David spoke about this in Psalm 51:17 (NLT): "The sacrifice you desire is a broken spirit. You will not reject a broken and repentant heart, O God."

If your heart is broken over your sin, then you've fully grasped what Joel and David are saying. Rejoice in your salvation. If you have never experienced such a broken heart over your sin, ask God to help you repent and find forgiveness.

WHAT THE HEART WANTS

"But the things that proceed out of the mouth come from the heart, and those defile the man. For out of the heart come evil thoughts, murders, adulteries, fornications, thefts, false witness, slanders."

MATTHEW 15:18–19 NASB

Many a man has gotten himself into trouble by embracing "the heart wants what the heart wants" mentality—as if Christians are to be slaves to their hearts' desires. The problem with this thinking is that out of the heart come evil thoughts, murders, adulteries, fornications, thefts, false witness, and slanders.

Genesis 6:5 says that every intent of the thoughts of a man's heart is only evil continually. And Jeremiah 17:9 says the heart is more deceitful than all else and is desperately sick. The heart does want what the heart wants, but that's the *problem*. You can't trust your heart. It only wants all sorts of evil. But that doesn't mean that all is lost.

In the parable of the sower (Luke 8:15 NASB), Jesus explains that "the seed in the good soil, these are the ones who have heard the word in an honest and good heart, and hold it fast, and bear fruit with perseverance." When your heart has the Word in it, it's honest and good. Have you fallen victim to obeying your heart without first bringing it under the authority of the Word?

GOD IS WITH YOU

*David also said to Solomon his son, "Be strong and courageous,
and do the work. Do not be afraid or discouraged, for the LORD
God, my God, is with you. He will not fail you or forsake you until
all the work for the service of the temple of the LORD is finished."*

1 CHRONICLES 28:20 NIV

While Solomon seemed to experience little external opposition
while carrying out his father's wishes to build the temple, he must
have faced *some* sort of opposition, otherwise David wouldn't have
encouraged him to be strong and courageous in doing the work.
In fact, doing God's work *always* requires strength and courage.

Have you been called to start a Bible study at work or maybe
among your friends? Are you sensing that God wants you to start
volunteering at your local homeless shelter or maybe even to
start one? Maybe He's calling you into full-time Christian work of
some sort. Whatever the case, your primary opposition is probably
mostly internal.

Who are you to start a Bible study, or work in a homeless
shelter, or join the mission field, or become a pastor? You are
God's chosen—His anointed for this very task. And if He's telling
you to do something, don't be afraid or discouraged. Do the work.
God is with you.

PURSUING GODLY AMBITIONS

My ambition has always been to preach the Good News where the name of Christ has never been heard, rather than where a church has already been started by someone else.

ROMANS 15:20 NLT

You probably have several ambitions. Professionally, you have your eyes set on a prize—maybe a promotion or ownership of your own business. Personally, you're striving to become a better leader in your home and working on taking care of yourself. What about your spiritual ambitions? Where do your spiritual passions lie?

After his conversion, the apostle Paul had his sights set on preaching the Gospel in places where the name of Jesus had never been heard, and he spent the rest of his life doing so. He wasn't disrespecting the work done in churches started by others. He just left that work to someone else who had a godly zeal for it.

Do you have such clarity of thought? You don't need a "calling" to pursue most of your godly ambitions. You simply need to acknowledge that it exists deep inside your heart and then prayerfully seek ways to live it out.

Maybe your ambition is outside of the box—like starting an online Christian news site in your city, or giving away everything you own to the poor, or starting a ministry to mentally ill men who have fallen through the cracks of society. Whatever it is, jump into it.

WISDOM FROM ABOVE

But the wisdom from above is first of all pure. It is also peace loving, gentle at all times, and willing to yield to others. It is full of mercy and the fruit of good deeds. It shows no favoritism and is always sincere.

JAMES 3:17 NLT

In today's verse, the apostle James provides a filter for understanding whether the wisdom you follow is actually from God or not. Is the message pure? (Will it purify the heart?) Is it peace loving rather than contentious? Is it gentle at all times? Is it willing to yield to others? Is it full of mercy and the fruit of good deeds? Does it show favoritism, or is it sincere?

Compare the characteristics of wisdom that's from above to earthly wisdom, which is at times helpful, but often tainted. Earthly wisdom says to look out for number one, to stand up for yourself, to get what you have coming. That's not to say you shouldn't stand up for yourself, but don't do it because you're motivated by pride or anger.

Jesus spoke only on the Father's authority. He was in constant communication with Him. The two go hand in hand. God does offer us guidance sometimes without being prompted, but even then, it usually happens as a result of being in close relationship with Him.

COMPASSION FOR THE LOST

Seeing the people, He felt compassion for them, because they were distressed and dispirited like sheep without a shepherd.

MATTHEW 9:36 NASB

As Jesus traveled, He encountered people in the synagogues who were sick, diseased, distressed (because of the yoke the Pharisees had placed on them), and helpless—wandering like sheep without a shepherd. The religious leaders of the day ought to have been guiding them properly, but instead, they were caught up in rules and regulations as a means for achieving righteousness. When Jesus saw that, He felt compassion for the people.

Does this describe the way you feel as you look around at work or in your personal life? Do you feel compassion for those who are trapped in religion rather than being in a relationship with Christ? Most of those people probably grew up in faith traditions that taught them that if their good deeds outweighed their bad deeds, then God would accept them.

In essence, they grew up without true Christian leadership, so they embraced the false doctrine, believing heaven could be earned. Have compassion on them. Unless you grew up in a Christian household, you were once just like them.

As you exhibit compassion toward them, you might earn an opportunity to present the true Gospel of mercy and grace—one that no man can earn.

DON'T WAIT

Then Caleb quieted the people before Moses, and said, "Let us go up at once and take possession, for we are well able to overcome it." But the men who had gone up with him said, "We are not able to go up against the people, for they are stronger than we."

NUMBERS 13:30–31 NKJV

The land of Canaan belonged to Israel. God had already promised it to them. But they still had to take possession of it. So, in obedience to God, they sent twelve spies—one from each tribe—who saw that it was indeed a land flowing with milk and honey (Numbers 13:27), just as God had promised (Exodus 3:8). But they also saw descendants of Anak there—people who were strong and tall—so they hesitated and issued an unfavorable report.

Caleb, however, wanted to go up at once to take possession of the land. His eyes weren't on the circumstances, but on the Lord and His promises. The Lord was with the Israelites, but they only trusted in their own might. Sadly, their fear led to disobedience, even though they didn't see things that way. They believed they were being astute and practical.

How often have you allowed fear to lead you astray? To procrastinate? To put off the very thing God leads you to do? Today is the day to throw off excuses.

DETERMINED TO STAY OBEDIENT

But Daniel purposed in his heart that he would not defile himself with the portion of the king's meat, nor with the wine which he drank: therefore he requested of the prince of the eunuchs that he might not defile himself.

DANIEL 1:8 KJV

As one of the gifted Jewish youth taken by Nebuchadnezzar from Jerusalem to Babylon, Daniel had certain privileges, including a daily supply of meat and wine from the king's provisions (Daniel 1:5). But Daniel objected, purposing in his heart that he wouldn't defile himself in such a manner.

Commentators point to three probable reasons why he objected. The Babylonians had no regard for the Law of God and therefore would have eaten ritually unclean animals, as well as animals that had been strangled, and animals that had been offered to Babylon's false gods. Even in captivity, Daniel wanted to be obedient to God's dietary laws, and he was determined to remain as pure as possible—even going so far as to request a dietary change while in captivity. This surely came with a risk.

How would you have responded if you had been in Daniel's position? How determined are you to obey God's Word and ultimately God? Is it your highest priority? What lengths will you go to in order to remain obedient?

PRESUMPTUOUS SINS

Keep back thy servant also from presumptuous sins; let them not have dominion over me: then shall I be upright, and I shall be innocent from the great transgression.

Psalm 19:13 KJV

In today's verse, David asked God to keep him from presumptuous sins—that is, deliberate, intentional sins, what the NIV calls "willful sins." He knew that when he indulged in disobedient acts willfully, they'd end up becoming habits that ruled over him. It's not that unintentional sins cause any less harm than intentional ones, but they don't flow as readily from a person's heart and mind.

The last thing David wanted was to be guilty of "the great transgression," which some believe meant pride or even apostasy.

David knew his wicked heart well. He was a murderer and adulterer, and he lied to cover up both. He might even have been considered slothful, given that he didn't go out to war at the time when kings go out to battle, choosing instead to stay behind in Jerusalem (2 Samuel 11:1). That's when he spiraled out of control.

How about you? How well do you know your own heart? What sort of gross, presumptuous sins is it capable of? Do you fear being guilty of the great transgression? Use David's prayer in today's verse and make it your own. Ask God to intervene, to rule your heart, and to keep you from stumbling.

UNUSUAL KINDNESS

Once safely on shore, we found out that the island was called
Malta. The islanders showed us unusual kindness. They built a
fire and welcomed us all because it was raining and cold.

ACTS 28:1–2 NIV

Paul was a prisoner aboard a ship bound for Rome, and he was destined to stand trial before Caesar. But while they were sailing across the Mediterranean Sea, a storm arose with winds of hurricane force (Acts 27:14). The vessel was driven by the fierce winds for many days. After it ran aground and all the passengers made it safely to shore, they discovered that they had landed on an island called Malta.

Malta was inhabited by heathens. Some translations, such as the KJV, translate the word *islanders* as "barbarous people"—probably because they didn't embrace the Greek or Roman culture, though they were ruled by Rome. Either way, they were different than the shipload of people who had crashed on their island, but their first response was unusual kindness. They built a fire and welcomed everyone.

Your church may already exhibit this type of kindness to outsiders and strangers. If so, jump into the action. Find a way to help those in need. Maybe you could become an usher or start an English as a second language (ESL) program there. If your church is lacking in this type of kindness to outsiders and strangers, talk to the leadership about finding ways to change that.

WALK IN A WORTHY MANNER

Therefore I, the prisoner of the Lord, implore you to walk in a manner worthy of the calling with which you have been called, with all humility and gentleness, with patience, showing tolerance for one another in love, being diligent to preserve the unity of the Spirit in the bond of peace.

EPHESIANS 4:1–3 NASB

The apostle Paul was a prisoner in Rome as he penned this epistle to the church in Ephesus. As such, he could have asked for any number of things—a visit, support, prayer—but, under the inspiration of the Holy Spirit, he had something else on his mind.

He wanted Christians in this church to walk in a manner that was worthy of their calling, and then he spelled that out for them. For what distinguishes the Christian from the world any more than humility, gentleness, patience, tolerance, love, and unity? And what better way to show the world what a redeemed life looks like?

Gentleness, humility, and patience are often viewed as being consistent with certain personality types; nevertheless, Paul said they were basic callings for every Christian.

How are you doing in these areas? If you've fallen short in your calling, confess that to the Lord and then rely on the sanctifying work of the Holy Spirit to change you.

FINDING JOY IN THE LORD

Even though the fig trees have no blossoms, and there are no grapes on the vines; even though the olive crop fails, and the fields lie empty and barren; even though the flocks die in the fields, and the cattle barns are empty, yet I will rejoice in the LORD!

HABAKKUK 3:17–18 NLT

The prophet Habakkuk foresaw a day of trouble coming, and he took to prayer. How much better is it to be in prayer before trouble begins so your heart can be prepared and resolved to endure it joyfully, than to be surprised by it and grumble?

Habakkuk saw a time of drought in which the trees, vines, and crops would fail and most of the livestock would be dead. (This was likely the drought described in Jeremiah 14:1–6.) Yet, Habakkuk said he would rejoice in the Lord. In a preemptive strike against his own soul, he was filling himself up with faith and trust in God so bitterness couldn't creep into his heart when everything went astray.

Have you ever prayed a prayer like this? You probably aren't directly reliant on trees, vines, crops, and livestock, but you are reliant on your employer. If the economy takes a downturn and you're laid off, are you prepared to find joy in the Lord anyway? He is well able to place you in a new position. But will you praise Him during the interim time of uncertainty?

THE KINGDOM OF GOD

*For the Kingdom of God is not a matter of what we eat or drink,
but of living a life of goodness and peace and joy in the Holy Spirit.*

ROMANS 14:17 NLT

If you've been part of a church for any length of time, then you know that strong differences of opinion sometimes arise over whether Christians should listen to certain styles of music, attend movies, eat or drink certain things, and any number of other issues. Paul wrote Romans 14 to keep believers from judging one another over such matters. The specific issues were different in his day, but the same sentiment continues to modern times.

But the kingdom of God is not a matter of what you eat or drink. It's about living a life of goodness and peace and joy in the Holy Spirit. Some Christians can enjoy the blessings of wealth without sinning, while others cannot. Some can listen to mainstream music without sinning, while others cannot. The same could be said for watching movies. However, flaunting such freedom is not in the spirit of today's verse.

In Romans 14:23 (NLT), Paul said each Christian is bound by his own conscience: "But if you have doubts about whether or not you should eat something, you are sinning if you go ahead and do it. For you are not following your convictions. If you do anything you believe is not right, you are sinning."

DON'T STOP NOW

*Fight the good fight of faith; take hold of the eternal life
to which you were called, and you made the good
confession in the presence of many witnesses.*

1 Timothy 6:12 nasb

Timothy, who was called to minister, was to put off the cares of this world—namely the love of money that leads so many astray (1 Timothy 6:10). Instead, he was to fight the good fight of faith to advance the Gospel.

Timothy's vocational calling might have been different from yours, but his spiritual calling was quite similar. You're to be in the world, but not of it (John 17:15–17). You're to set your mind on things above, not on the things of this earth (Colossians 3:2). You're not to be conformed to this world, but be transformed by the renewing of your mind (Romans 12:2). As such, you're called to fight the good fight as well.

How is your fight going? If you don't sense a battle, then you probably aren't engaged in one. If, however, you feel the tension between this world and the next, and are actively engaged in overcoming your sinful habits and tendencies, then you're right where God wants you. Don't stop now. The world needs to see your witness. Wrestle, fight, and pray because eternity is at stake for all of humanity.

PERSPECTIVE ON REJECTION

*I have become all things to all people so that by all
possible means I might save some.*

1 CORINTHIANS 9:22 NIV

Witnessing for Christ has always been a challenge. In the current climate of political correctness, where truth is often replaced by opinion and personal freedom is idolized, you face unique challenges. Sharing about Jesus requires letting go of preconceived notions while still clinging to God's truth. You have freedom in Christ to share His love and grace without the shackles of shifting expectations and demands.

At the same time, those things have shaped people's opinions of God, Jesus, the church, and Christians. Earning the right to tell people about Jesus is like solving a puzzle box—you have to watch, listen, probe, learn from failure, and keep trying.

Remember a few things as you go. First, everyone matters to Jesus. They may not ever receive His gift of salvation, but that's between them and God. Your job is to treat them as Jesus did. He met people where they were—amid pain, complacency, ignorance, busyness—and told them God's truth in a way that fit their circumstances.

Also, don't fear being an imperfect messenger. Listen first, trying to learn each person's story, situation, and experience with God. If it helps, share your story of salvation. Sharing your faith carries risk, but if you're rejected, take heart. Jesus was too. Ask God for a wise and compassionate heart and for perseverance in the face of resistance.

TAKE HOLD OF GOD'S PEACE

*"You will keep him in perfect peace,
whose mind is stayed on You, because he trusts in You."*

ISAIAH 26:3 NKJV

As the spiritual leader of your family, the buck stops with you. While you're wise to discuss issues with your wife and seek the counsel of mature, experienced Christians, in the end, you're responsible for the big decisions. In those situations, how can you have peace?

When Jesus told His disciples, "Peace I leave with you, My peace I give to you" (John 14:27 NKJV), His peace was an actual thing, not an absence of something like conflict or confusion. Isaiah tied peace to trust, deliberately turning your thoughts toward God instead of your problems. Paul described peace as a shield "which transcends all understanding [and] will guard your hearts and your minds in Christ Jesus" (Philippians 4:7 NIV).

Furthermore, Paul detailed the types of thoughts you should be turning toward God—things that are true, noble, just, pure, lovely, of good report, virtuous and praiseworthy (Philippians 4:8).

When you figure all of those into your decisions—thinking about what the cost might be or what it means to follow God in your circumstances—He will *give* you His peace. And it won't be the peace the world gives, the sort that leaves you doubting, second-guessing, and feeling more alone than ever. Once you grasp God's peace, you'll make the best decision possible, entrusting your cares to Him.

DANCING WITH WORDS

"Just say a simple, 'Yes, I will,' or 'No, I won't.'
Anything beyond this is from the evil one."

MATTHEW 5:37 NLT

We've all been in situations where it's easier not to tell the truth. We do it for a variety of what seem like good reasons—protecting ourselves or someone else, or maintaining someone's high opinion of us—or sometimes, just because it's easier. And while there are subtle shades of nuance in many situations, the bottom line question may very well be: *Would my words have passed Jesus' litmus test of intention?*

For Jesus, it wasn't enough to obey the Law externally; the motives and attitude of the heart were paramount. It was against Moses' Law to cheat on your spouse, but Jesus said that if you only looked at a woman with lust, you were just as guilty in God's eyes. God doesn't want outward performance without internal obedience.

There used to be a saying that a man's word was his bond. God even said He hates liars, but that He loves trustworthy people (Proverbs 12:22). Times have changed. Telling the truth these days often carries the consequences that lying used to, but God doesn't change. He keeps His word, and He expects you to do the same. Don't dance with words; tell the hard truth, and God will have your back.

GOD'S ECONOMY

There is one who scatters, yet increases more; and there is one who withholds more than is right, but it leads to poverty.

PROVERBS 11:24 NKJV

Compared to worldly views of wealth, God's economy seems built on paradoxes: to get, you must first give, but you shouldn't give to get (Luke 6:35). Jesus' encounters with the rich—Matthew, Zacchaeus, the rich young ruler—make it clear that you can have every material advantage in the world and still lack the thing that matters most. In fact, the more you have, the more you will be held accountable for (Luke 12:48).

Consider the following financial concepts: you're not an owner but a steward; give and you will be blessed; live within your means; save so you can invest in things with no tangible value. From God's perspective, they all make sense. If they make you scratch your head, you're living in the world's economy, not God's.

Since everything belongs to God (Psalm 24:1), His business should guide your finances. Give back to Him first—don't ever give up tithing, even if you're down to a widow's mite.

Remember, God's business is seeing as many as possible receive the gift of salvation. Christ purchased a gift for you that you can never earn or purchase; the only thing you can do is share it, with your words, deeds, and resources. No other religion has Christianity's track record of helping; your involvement carries on that great tradition.

A FAITHFUL FEW

A friend loves at all times, and a brother is born for adversity.

PROVERBS 17:17 NKJV

Accountability has become one of those trendy, buzzword kinds of church ideas that people either love or hate but don't really know how to do, or why. Too often, we get caught up in some of the issues surrounding accountability—good things like confessing sins and liberty in Christ—and lose sight of the most important things—obeying God's Word, the grace of the Gospel, and faithful, committed fellowship.

You need accountability because you still need God. Sanctification is a lifelong process because you're still susceptible to temptation and sin. You have blind spots, and you need to be told about them. You still struggle with the "old man"—old habits and patterns of thinking and acting that will cause you to fall away if you let them dominate you. This is much more likely to happen in isolation. For those reasons, you need fellowship—encouragement and accountability from your brothers in Christ (Hebrews 10:25).

Accountability isn't optional. It requires commitment, as well as compassion. Pray that God would show you the men with whom you can live life, not making idols of confession or obedience but embracing God's grace together on a regular basis.

If you find yourself resisting this, ask why. Make sure you're not harboring sin. "Bear one another's burdens, and so fulfill the law of Christ" (Galatians 6:2 NKJV).

EQUAL BUT NOT IDENTICAL

God created man in His own image; in the image of God
He created him; male and female He created them.

GENESIS 1:27 NKJV

Men and women have equal standing before God. Paul observed that "there is neither male nor female; for you are all one in Christ Jesus" (Galatians 3:28 NKJV). However, God also designed male and female relationships to follow a pattern: God gave men the authority to take bottom-line responsibility for the welfare of women (1 Corinthians 11:3).

Both can show leadership and initiative, and they are "heirs together of the grace of life" (1 Peter 3:7 KJV), but there are certain responsibilities that fall to a man. And this is where too many guys have fallen short.

God meant for men and women to complement each other through physical and emotional differences. Respective roles are best defined and experienced in marriage, but they still play into everyday relationships. Even if you're not married, you can still look out for a woman's best interests and make her feel valuable, and she can still encourage you and show you respect.

If you're married, when you both submit to God and follow His design for your relationship (Ephesians 5:23–33), good things will follow. If you're single, practice emotional purity. If the woman you're friends with isn't going to be your wife, she may be another man's wife in the future. So while you can enjoy Christian fellowship, be sure to keep your relationship pure and in the proper perspective.

WAIT FOR IT

Through patience a ruler can be persuaded,
and a gentle tongue can break a bone.

<small>PROVERBS 25:15 NIV</small>

Paul said, "Love is patient" (1 Corinthians 13:4 NIV). The Greek word for *patient* means "bearing offenses" or "persevering through troubles"—the idea being that if you're being patient, you're suffering bravely.

That implies intention; you have to *want* to be patient, you have to be willing to put up with slings and arrows of outrageous fortune because you see a greater goal beyond them. Otherwise, your patience does no good. It drives you nuts, and an unappreciative recipient will just carry on as usual once the danger of your wrath is past.

In a parable, Jesus told of the king who forgave his servant a huge debt after the man begged him, "Be patient with me" (Matthew 18:26 NIV). But then the guy demanded payment from another servant who owed him far less than he had owed the king. When his pal asked for patience, he had none and had the guy thrown in jail. The king was stunned. His patience came to an end because the servant hadn't taken it to heart—didn't appreciate the gravity of his debt or the extent of his mercy.

God requires you to be patient—slow to boil, waiting for understanding. Fortunately, God offers patience as a gift of the Spirit (Galatians 5:22 NASB). You can love someone who is unlovable because God loved you first: He was patient.

GOD FORGIVES YOU

*Lord, if you kept a record of our sins, who, O Lord,
could ever survive? But you offer forgiveness.*

PSALM 130:3–4 NLT

Many men find it very difficult to forgive themselves for past mistakes and moral failures—particularly if they're living with the ongoing consequences of past actions. Daily reminded of their sins, they trudge on in condemnation and defeat, feeling that God has turned His back on them.

Though they experience His care and provision, they conclude that God is just putting up with them, barely tolerating them, but doesn't really love them. They may believe that they're saved, but often feel that they'll barely squeak into heaven.

If this describes *you*, you need to read Psalm 103:8–13 (NLT), particularly verse 12, which says, "He has removed our sins as far from us as the east is from the west." In Isaiah, He says, "I. . .will blot out your sins for my own sake and will never think of them again" (Isaiah 43:25 NLT). And in the New Testament, John tells us, "If we confess our sins to him, he is faithful and just to forgive us our sins and to cleanse us from *all* wickedness" (1 John 1:9 NLT, emphasis added).

If you've confessed your sins to God and turned from them, He has forgiven you. Now you must trust in the depth and power of His forgiveness, forgive yourself, and rest daily in His love.

LAY OFF BOASTING

Let someone else praise you, not your own mouth—
a stranger, not your own lips.

Proverbs 27:2 NLT

This verse offers very basic advice, and if you follow it, it will save you much trouble, because few people enjoy listening to a braggart.

But have you ever run into a highly successful man who, despite his accomplishments, degrees, and reputation, is very humble and down to earth? If you didn't know from speaking with him how great he was, you only found out because someone took you aside and informed you. That's what this verse is talking about.

You may feel awkward that you're forced to "boast" on your résumé. You're required to make yourself sound as good as possible, and this includes boldly proclaiming every bit of education you've received, everything you've accomplished, as well as every commendation and award you've received. But if talking about yourself and how "great" you are *bothers* you, you probably don't have much to worry about. Your heart is already in the right place.

It's when you feel smug and enjoy having others admire you, and love to hear them gush over the great things you've done, that you begin to be puffed up like a bullfrog. If you plan ways to casually drop hints of how wonderful you are, then soak it in when others praise you, you're setting yourself up for a fall. Avoid this and you'll avoid trouble.

UNCONVENTIONAL TACTICS

*So it was, when the Philistine arose and came. . .to meet David,
that David hurried and ran toward the army to meet the Philistine.*

1 SAMUEL 17:48 NKJV

One day a huge Philistine army marched up the Valley of Elah, but the Israelite army learned they were coming and blocked their advance at the town of Socoh. Then an enormous man named Goliath, covered in heavy armor, stepped forward and challenged any Israelite soldier to face him in single combat. Only David accepted his challenge.

Saul offered David his armor and sword, but after trying them on, David realized that he didn't stand a chance using conventional methods. So, grasping his shepherd's staff, he walked down to the brook, picked five stones, and slipped them into his pouch. Then he headed up toward the giant. The only weapon Goliath could see was David's staff, so he roared, "Am I a dog, that you come to me with sticks?" (1 Samuel 17:43 NKJV).

Suddenly David rushed the giant. Startled, Goliath grinned. *He really is gonna try to hit me with that stick.* At the last moment, David dropped his staff, thrust a stone into his sling, began swinging it, then let it fly with punishing force. Goliath never realized what David was about to do until it was too late.

When you face impossible circumstances, God can inspire you with crazy, unconventional solutions. Be open to them! They can work when nothing else will.

ALL THE WORLD'S A STAGE

Let everyone see that you are considerate in all you do.
PHILIPPIANS 4:5 NLT

When Paul advises you to "let everyone *see* that you are considerate in all you do," he's saying to make a conscious decision to be kind and thoughtful since others are watching you. Not that you're supposed to do it simply for show, but be aware that others are observing you and judging the Gospel by how you live it out in your daily life.

Jesus said something similar: "Let your light so shine before men, that they may see your good works and glorify your Father in heaven" (Matthew 5:16 NKJV).

Shakespeare declared, "All the world's a stage," and explained that everyone acts out the part given them to play. The world *is* a stage for Christians as well. "We have been made a spectacle to the whole universe, to angels as well as to human beings" (1 Corinthians 4:9 NIV). And how are you to act? Considerate.

In common usage, to be considerate means to show kindness and awareness for another person's feelings; it literally means to ponder, to carefully consider others and their needs. In the most intimate of relationships—marriage—the Bible advises, "Husbands, in the same way be considerate as you live with your wives" (1 Peter 3:7 NIV).

To act in a considerate manner, you need to be motivated by love.

THE MIGHTY POWER OF GOD

Finally, be strong in the Lord and in his mighty power. . .
so that you can take your stand against the devil's schemes.

EPHESIANS 6:10–11 NIV

A scheme is a methodical, calculated plan for reaching a specific goal or putting a particular idea into effect. To *scheme* often describes plans done in a devious way or with intent to bring about an evil result. The devil schemes to bring your life to ruin, and he employs time-tested methods such as hatred, fear, lust, covetousness, addictions, and so on. C.S. Lewis gave insightful descriptions of his schemes in *The Screwtape Letters*.

What's the best way to combat the evil one's schemes? To submit yourself to God and pray, "May your will be done" (Matthew 26:42 NIV).

For example, it was God's will that Jesus be crucified for the sins of the world, but Peter argued against it. So Jesus told him, "Get behind Me, Satan! . . .for you are not setting your mind on God's interests, but man's" (Matthew 16:23 NASB). Man's interests and "the will of the flesh" (John 1:13 KJV) often parallel Satan's will because both are selfish.

How do you become "strong in the Lord. . .so that you can take your stand against the devil's schemes"? Simple. "Submit yourselves. . .to God." Then you will have spiritual strength. Then you can "resist the devil, and he will flee from you" (James 4:7 KJV).

WHOLEHEARTED OBEDIENCE

He did what was right in the eyes of the LORD,
but not wholeheartedly.

2 CHRONICLES 25:2 NIV

Amaziah, king of Judah, was *sort of* a good man. . .just like his dad. His father, Joash, had lived most of his life under the shadow of the high priest, Jehoiada, and had followed God as long as Jehoiada was alive. But after Jehoiada died, Joash quickly went astray. Amaziah too had been raised all his life to worship God but in his later years strayed into idol worship.

Many people raised in the church have a similar problem. They know all about God, know what is right, and even have a relationship with Him. But as they age, they gradually depend more and more on their own reasoning, follow their own inclinations, and eventually turn away from God. And their eventual backsliding largely stems from not following the Lord wholeheartedly to begin with.

It's wonderful to attend church faithfully, give to God, and read your Bible, but if you're mainly doing these things to put on a show, to please other people, and to be accepted as a "good Christian," eventually you'll run out of steam and come to a stop.

Don't let this be you. Remember the number-one commandment: "You shall love the LORD your God with *all* your heart and with *all* your soul and with *all* your might" (Deuteronomy 6:5 NASB, emphasis added).

AN EXAMPLE TO OTHERS

*Be an example to all believers in what you say,
in the way you live, in your love, your faith, and your purity.*

1 TIMOTHY 4:12 NLT

This verse may seem like a tall order. You might be struggling with bitterness, question your faith at times, and have daily battles with lust. You don't feel like you're able to be an example to other believers. You're happy if you can hold your *own* act together enough to escape condemnation and self-doubt.

Don't give up on yourself. God hasn't thrown in the towel on you yet, and neither should you. Love and follow God today, and trust that He will continue working in your life and give you the victory in these areas as you cry out to Him to help you. Remember that when Jesus revealed God's power to Peter, the rough-hewn fisherman pleaded, "Depart from me; for I am a sinful man, O Lord" (Luke 5:8 KJV).

But Jesus *didn't* depart. He continued to work in Peter's life for the next three years. And even after all that time learning from the Master, Peter denied Him during a time of testing. But Jesus saw that coming too and said, "I have pleaded in prayer for you, Simon, that your faith should not fail. So when you have repented and turned to me again, strengthen your brothers" (Luke 22:32 NLT).

If there's hope for Peter, there's hope for you.

PRAYERS OF PROTECTION

Because he hath set his love upon me. . .He shall call upon me,
and I will answer him: I will be with him in trouble; I will deliver him.

PSALM 91:14–15 KJV

God tells the disobedient, "The LORD's arm is not too weak to save you, nor is his ear too deaf to hear you call," but "because of your sins, he has turned away and will not listen anymore" (Isaiah 59:1–2 NLT). When people are far from God, they can't claim His blessing or protection.

However, the opposite is true when you draw *near* to God. Then, you call upon Him and He *will* answer. He will be with you when you face trouble and will protect you. This doesn't mean that He will spare you from *all* trouble, but it means that He will be *with* you.

Some people, however, question why God often *doesn't* seem to be with believers who love and obey Him. Does that mean this promise isn't true? No. What it means is that God is sovereign and has His reasons for sometimes allowing suffering.

Notice in Hebrews 11:35–37 that He allowed His righteous followers to be tortured, whipped, to languish in prison, to die by stoning, to be sawed in half, and to be killed with the sword. Many others were destitute and oppressed and mistreated. Yet we remember these people not as abandoned unfortunates, but as heroes of the faith.

HELPING THOSE IN NEED

As we have opportunity, let us do good to all, especially to those who are of the household of faith.

GALATIANS 6:10 NKJV

There are generally two ways God moves you to show kindness to fellow believers. One is when you're aware of their need, are thinking about it, and realize that you're in a position to help. So you talk it over with your wife and arrange to do it. It's really a logical conclusion, done out of love for others. Often you have time to think it over and get counsel about it.

The second way is when you first become aware of their need and right on the spot the Holy Spirit speaks, telling you exactly what to do to help.

However God works to get you to loosen your purse strings—and helping someone often involves finances—be obedient. Yes, God *may* call upon you to give to someone less fortunate than yourself, even if you're a manual laborer earning minimum wage. Paul said in Ephesians 4:28 (NKJV), "Let him. . .labor, working with his hands what is good, that he may have something to give him who has need."

James asked, "Suppose you see a brother or sister who has no food or clothing, and you say, 'Good-bye and have a good day; stay warm and eat well'—but then you don't give that person any food or clothing. What good does that do?" (James 2:15–16 NLT). The answer is obvious.

INTIMIDATED BY GIANTS

"There we saw the giants. . .and we were like grasshoppers in our own sight, and so we were in their sight."

NUMBERS 13:33 NKJV

When the Israelites arrived at the border of Canaan, Moses sent twelve spies into the land. When they returned, ten of them said, "The people who dwell in the land are strong; the cities are fortified and very large. . .and all the people whom we saw in it are men of great stature" (Numbers 13:28, 32 NKJV).

They concluded, "We are not able to go up against the people, for they are stronger than we" (v. 31). Their negative report so discouraged the Israelites that they were afraid to invade Canaan, even though the Lord had promised He'd help them.

Does this ever happen to you? You're initially excited about a project and even though you're aware you'll face difficulties, you're buoyed by feelings of optimism. God has promised to be with you, and you know that He can do miracles. But when it actually comes time to launch out, you allow yourself to get discouraged by naysayers, get cold feet, and back out.

It's human nature to say, "There are giants in the land!" It's the default setting of the natural mind to see problems as huge and to feel grasshopper-sized compared to them. But have faith in God. With His help you can overcome them, no matter how big they are.

BROKEN CISTERNS

"For My people have. . .forsaken Me, the fountain of living waters, to hew for themselves cisterns, broken cisterns that can hold no water."

JEREMIAH 2:13 NASB

Israel is dry most of the year, with rain falling predominantly in the winter, so water is a precious commodity. Then as now, the best sources were springs or fountains, as their supply was fresh and clean. Also, wells tapped into underground streams, another source of running water.

God referred to Himself as "the fountain of living waters," and Jesus called the Spirit of God "a well of water springing up to eternal life" (John 4:14 NASB).

When Israelite villages lacked sufficient water, they carved out underground reservoirs called *cisterns* to store water. They sealed the walls with plaster. Then they directed the winter rain into these cisterns. A great deal of mud ended up in the bottom of it (see Jeremiah 38:6). Also, Israel had many minor earthquakes, and the plaster was constantly cracking and the water draining away.

God pointed out how senseless His people were to choose broken cisterns with muddy, stale water over fresh spring water. Unfortunately, people today are still hewing out cisterns. Ditch the stagnant water of man's philosophies and come drink of the water of life. "Let anyone who is thirsty come. Let anyone who desires drink freely from the water of life" (Revelation 22:17 NLT).

BOXING THAT BRUISES YOU

Everyone who competes in the games goes into strict training. They do it to get a crown that will not last, but we do it to get a crown that will last forever. Therefore I do not run like someone running aimlessly; I do not fight like a boxer beating the air.

1 CORINTHIANS 9:25–26 NIV

The Olympic Games were held in Paul's day too. The city of Corinth was also famous for the Isthmian Games, held every second year. Paul made many references to athletes competing in races, and here he refers to boxing, also popular in his day.

Paul had frequently seen boxers in training, shadow-boxing, striking out at nothing, and having no one strike back. He said, "I fight: not as one who beats the air. But I discipline [*bruise*] my body and bring it into subjection, lest. . .I myself should become disqualified" (1 Corinthians 26–27 NKJV, author's commentary added).

To Paul, the only kind of training that made sense was to fight an actual opponent, even though it meant taking repeated blows and getting bruised. It was far preferable to merely shadow-boxing. He didn't want to be disqualified during an actual boxing match because he wasn't tough enough to take physical blows.

Paul pointed out that athletes were willing to endure punishment to get a laurel crown that withered, so how much more willing should believers be to obtain an eternal crown?

THE DUTY OF A WATCHMAN

"As for me, far be it from me that I should sin against the LORD by ceasing to pray for you; but I will instruct you in the good and right way."

1 SAMUEL 12:23 NASB

God told Ezekiel, "I have appointed you a watchman to the house of Israel; whenever you hear a word from My mouth, warn them from Me" (Ezekiel 3:17 NASB). Watchmen stood on city walls, keeping their eyes open for danger, and sounding the alarm to rouse the people so the city wouldn't fall to the enemy. Men of God often watched over Israel. Samuel was one such man.

God declared, "I searched for a man among them who would build up the wall and stand in the gap before Me for the land, so that I would not destroy it" (Ezekiel 22:30 NASB). When the spiritual wall of a nation's defenses are weak, men of God are called to intercede for their people—to guard these gaps. You do this through intercessory prayer.

Samuel said that he'd be *sinning* if he ceased to pray for his people. Christian men today should also understand prayer as their duty. It's easy to just kick up your feet and relax after a day at work, and you *do* need rest, but it's *also* your duty to take matters to God in prayer. To do that, you must carve out some time in your schedule. Don't neglect this.

HONORED BY MEN

"I know I have sinned. But please, at least honor me before the elders of my people and before Israel by coming back with me so that I may worship the LORD your God."

1 SAMUEL 15:30 NLT

The prophet Samuel had just finished telling Saul, "Rebellion is as sinful as witchcraft, and stubbornness as bad as worshiping idols. So because you have rejected the command of the LORD, he has rejected you as king" (v. 23). Saul then admitted, "I have disobeyed. . .the LORD's command, for I was afraid of the people and did what they demanded" (v. 24).

Despite that, he *still* had the nerve to ask Samuel, "Honor me before the elders of my people."

Saul feared people, and being accepted and honored by them was all that mattered to him. He was not very concerned whether he pleased God. The religious leaders of Jesus' day were the same. "They loved human praise more than the praise of God" (John 12:43 NLT). As Jesus pointed out, "You gladly honor each other, but you don't care about the honor that comes from. . .God" (John 5:44 NLT).

The Lord understands the human need to save face and be respected. He *gets* it. Nevertheless, He insists that you seek to please Him above all. It can be difficult, but life would be so much simpler if people simply sought the praise of God first and foremost.

HOPE FOR HAPPINESS

*Make me hear joy and gladness, that the bones
You have broken may rejoice.*

PSALM 51:8 NKJV

In the ancient Middle East, a lamb that strayed from the shepherd and the flock put itself in great danger, since the surrounding wilderness was home to fierce animals. If a lamb continually strayed, a shepherd would break one of its legs. Until it healed, the lamb depended on the shepherd to carry it around and bring it grass. Once it healed, the lamb would usually stay nearer the shepherd than any other sheep.

Sometimes God allows accidents and misfortune to cause *you* to focus on Him and His doings. His desire is for your good and to draw you closer to Him, though it might not seem good at the time.

When he uttered the above verse, David was repenting for committing adultery with Bathsheba and for arranging for her husband to be slain. It almost seems inappropriate for him to pray, "Make me hear joy and gladness," and to ask that he might soon "rejoice." It seems he should have been pleading for God's mercy and forgiveness. That *is*, in fact, what he'd been doing in the rest of this psalm.

But David had tremendous faith in the Lord's loving-kindness. He knew that God was merciful, and he had the faith to look beyond his present distress to anticipate full restoration and the return of happiness. May you hope for the same.

FEEBLE FOLK IN FORTRESSES

*The conies are but a feeble folk,
yet make they their houses in the rocks.*

PROVERBS 30:26 KJV

What, you may ask, are conies? The NIV translates this verse: "Hyraxes are creatures of little power, yet they make their home in the crags." The *Hyrax syriacus*, also known as a rock badger, is found in the Sinai Desert and cliffs along the Dead Sea. It's a small, shy, furry animal that resembles a guinea pig. It lives in rock crevices, safe from predators. Hyraxes feed in groups, watched over by sentries that sound an alarm when enemies approach.

They're reminiscent of the Ewoks, short furry bipeds in the *Star Wars* movies, who lived on the forest moon of Endor. They too were a "feeble folk" who proved to be mighty.

All believers are "feeble" in *some* area of their lives—weak, incapable, and lacking power. You may be ordinary, with no special talents, yet do things that compensate for your weakness. Maybe you're thrifty and good at saving, so despite a lack of good looks, strength, or other A-list abilities, you're able to provide a secure financial future.

"Remember. . .that few of you were wise in the world's eyes or powerful or wealthy when God called you. Instead, God chose things. . .that are powerless to shame those who are powerful" (1 Corinthians 1:26–27 NLT).

FLEE SEXUAL FANTASIES

"You have heard that it was said, 'You shall not commit adultery.'
But I tell you that anyone who looks at a woman lustfully has
already committed adultery with her in his heart."

MATTHEW 5:27–28 NIV

Many men think there's a big difference between lusting and actually having sexual relations. They fail to understand how if they continually think erotic thoughts, they'll eventually attempt to follow through on them. That's because they become addicted to the rush that fantasizing gives, and their brain needs ever more stimulation. Eventually, nothing short of the actual deed satisfies.

The Ten Commandments forbade both illicit sex and fantasizing about it. Exodus 20:14 (NIV) says, "You shall not commit adultery," and verse 17 says, "You shall not covet. . .your neighbor's wife." God knew that men had to arrest lust while it was still a thought.

Resist fantasizing before it becomes a habit. The patriarch Job knew that he, like all men, was aroused by visual stimulation, so he said, "I made a covenant with my eyes not to look lustfully at a young woman" (Job 31:1 NIV).

Paul wrote, "Flee from sexual immorality" (1 Corinthians 6:18 NIV), but if you're in the habit of intoxicating yourself with lust, you'll do the *opposite* in the day an opportunity arises. So ditch licentious thoughts now, so that in the day of temptation, you'll have the willpower to put physical distance between yourself and any alluring sirens.

ACCOMPLISHING ITS MISSION

"As the rain and the snow come down from heaven, and do not return to it without watering the earth and making it bud and flourish. . .so is my word that goes out from my mouth: It will not return to me empty, but will. . .achieve the purpose for which I sent it."

ISAIAH 55:10–11 NIV

God's Word is eternal and is like buckets containing ever-fresh supplies of His Spirit. When you believe His promises and apply them to the different situations you face, it's as if you're pouring life-giving water on dry earth. This causes your situations to come to life like dormant seeds activated by water.

In the passage above, God promises that, just as water evaporates and returns as vapor to heaven, so His Word will return to Him—but not before it accomplishes the purpose He sent it to accomplish on earth.

You may sometimes wonder if the Word of God is truly effective, especially if you're claiming Bible promises for a very difficult situation. You can become discouraged if *years* go by without seeing promises fulfilled. But remember, explorers have found seeds in the deserts of Australia that have laid dormant, bone-dry, for hundreds of years, but after being watered, have miraculously and instantly sprung to life and bloomed.

If you're trusting God to do a miracle in your marriage, your finances, or your children, don't give up. God is powerful!

THE LORD'S FAVOR

*For the LORD God is a sun and shield: the LORD will give
grace and glory: no good thing will he withhold
from them that walk uprightly.*

PSALM 84:11 KJV

This beautiful passage tells you that the Lord is like the brilliant sun, giving warmth and light as you make Him your center, orbiting your life around Him. As you do so, He will bestow His radiant qualities upon you, filling your life with grace and favor, and causing you to reflect His glory. Furthermore, He's your strong defender, forming a protective shield about you.

Many people, however, fail to tune in to this overarching picture of God and His blessings and focus only on the last half of the verse: "No good thing will he withhold from them that walk uprightly." They view God as some kind of galactic candy machine and claim this truncated promise merely to get goodies.

Certainly God wants to bless you with your needs, but more than anything, He longs for you to walk close to Him, surrounded by and permeated by His presence. In turn, He wants you to shine His light upon the dark world. Only then, when you walk in the righteousness granted by His Spirit, will He be pleased to give you all good things.

A SURE SALVATION

But we are not like those who turn away from God to their own destruction. We are the faithful ones, whose souls will be saved.

HEBREWS 10:39 NLT

You can't earn salvation by your own efforts. God gives eternal life to you as an undeserved gift. Also, once you're saved, it doesn't become *your* job to *keep* yourself saved; God keeps you saved (see John 10:28–29; Ephesians 2:8–9; Romans 10:9–10).

But some Christians suffer anxiety, worrying that they'll "lose" their salvation for some sin. After all, Jesus said in Matthew 24:13 (NKJV) that "he who endures to the end shall be saved." Some Christians also worry about 1 Corinthians 9:27 (KJV) where Paul speaks of disciplining himself to ensure that he didn't become "a castaway" (see also John 15:6).

However, Jesus said, "The one who comes to Me I will by *no means* cast out" (John 6:37 NKJV, emphasis added). Your salvation isn't like so much pocket change that you casually lose. Scripture indicates that people must knowingly, completely renounce their faith to be "fallen from grace" (Galatians 5:4 NKJV; see also Hebrews 6:4–6).

However, if you love God but constantly feel unworthy and worried about your salvation, be at peace. Remember that God has promised, "Being confident of this, that he who began a good work in you will carry it on to completion until the day of Christ Jesus" (Philippians 1:6 NIV).

TRYING TO FEEL YOUR WAY

"That they would seek God, if perhaps they might grope for Him and find Him, though He is not far from each one of us."

ACTS 17:27 NASB

In Isaiah 42:19 (KJV), somewhat in exasperation, God asks, "Who is blind, but my servant?" You may be faithfully serving God, like Elisha's servant, but still struggle to sense the Lord and know His will. You're unable to perceive exactly what He's doing. The mountains might be full of horses and chariots of fire all around you, but you can't see them (see 2 Kings 6:15–17).

Like many believers, you daily seek God and grope to discover His will, much like the people in Isaiah's statement: "We grope for the wall like the blind, and we grope as if we had no eyes: we stumble at noon day as in the night" (Isaiah 59:10 KJV).

You may wonder why God made it so difficult to sense Him and know what He's doing. But the most important thing to know is that He's never far from you, and that He gently guides your hands as you struggle to feel the wall that marks the boundaries of His will.

Be encouraged! God promises, "I will bring the blind by a way that they knew not; I will lead them in paths that they have not known: I will make darkness light before them" (Isaiah 42:16 KJV).

NABAL'S FOLLY

*His name was Nabal and his wife's name was Abigail.
She was an intelligent and beautiful woman,
but her husband was surly and mean in his dealings.*

1 SAMUEL 25:3 NIV

Most men have their "Nabal days" when they're growly and ornery, like a bear that's been wakened too early from hibernation. But as your mother may have told you when you were a kid, "Don't scowl, because it could freeze on your face and you'll be stuck with it." (She never *told* you that?) Be on your guard against bad attitudes. Over time they can become habits.

Before he became king, David lived in the wilderness near Nabal's sheep farm. One day, one of Nabal's servants told Abigail, "David sent messengers...to give our master his greetings, but he hurled insults at them." The servant added, "He is such a wicked man that no one can talk to him" (1 Samuel 25:14, 17 NIV).

Do you get in moods where no one can talk to you? In Nabal's case, his attitude stemmed from the fact that he was wealthy and was used to bossing people around and getting whatever he wanted—including a beautiful wife. "The poor man uses entreaties, but the rich answers roughly" (Proverbs 18:23 NKJV).

Don't fall into that trap. You are to love your fellow man as you love yourself, and if you do, you'll treat him with consideration and be ready to listen to him.

SET FREE FROM CONDEMNATION

*Christ Jesus came into the world to
save sinners—of whom I am the worst.*

1 TIMOTHY 1:15 NIV

The Bible calls Satan "the accuser of our brothers and sisters, who accuses them before our God day and night" (Revelation 12:10 NIV). So sometimes when God is purifying your heart and you contrast yourself to His holiness, you feel great guilt. As King David grew older, he was driven to pray, "Remember not the sins of my youth" (Psalm 25:7 KJV).

The apostle Paul was also reminded of his past sins, and this caused him to declare, "Christ Jesus came into the world to save sinners—of whom *I am the worst*" (1 Timothy 1:15 NIV, emphasis added).

Paul had done some horrific things. He confessed, "I persecuted [Christians] unto the death, binding and delivering into prisons both men and women" (Acts 22:4 KJV); "And when they were put to death, I gave my voice against them" (Acts 26:10 KJV). He tortured believers and demanded that they curse Christ, admitting, "I. . . compelled them to blaspheme" (Acts 26:11 KJV).

If you find that you're constantly beating yourself up over the same past sins, it's time to throw yourself anew upon the grace of God. John Newton, who wrote the famous hymn "Amazing Grace," referred to himself as "a wretch," because he'd been on the crew of a notorious slave ship. But God forgave even him. God has already completely forgiven you too.

IN THE CAVE OF ADULLAM

David departed from there and
escaped to the cave of Adullam.

1 Samuel 22:1 nasb

The title of Psalm 142 reads: "When he was in the cave. A prayer."
David and his men had moved to Adullam when the winter rains
began, when life out in the open became miserable. For a couple
months, they hunkered down in the damp cavern near the city. In
Israel, it often rains heavily for three days nonstop, and to David
it was like a prison (Psalm 142:7).

He had been a much-loved hero of Israel. Now he was vilified,
and King Saul and his army were hunting David, seeking to kill him.
David had been forced to flee, leaving his wife, Michal, behind. It
was in this context that he poured out his complaint to God. "You
are my refuge, my portion in the land of the living" (v. 5 nasb).
God was about all David had left. So he looked to Him for help.

David was deeply discouraged, yet he prayed, "When my spirit
grows faint within me, it is you who watch over my way" (Psalm
142:3 niv). He knew that God was with him. You too can be assured
of this (Hebrews 13:5).

Are you going through a similar experience? Do you feel
hemmed in and trapped, abandoned by God? Look to Him for
help. In your darkest moments, He will be right by your side.

BEYOND THE BASICS

*Let us stop going over the basic teachings about Christ again
and again. Let us go on instead and become mature in our
understanding. Surely we don't need to start again with the
fundamental importance of repenting from evil
deeds and placing our faith in God.*

HEBREWS 6:1 NLT

You don't expect a high school senior to act like a preschooler. Good fathers work to help their children grow up, demonstrate what age-appropriate behavior looks like, and help that child understand that adult maturity is the logical end result.

In the years following Jesus' time on earth, there were Christians who were satisfied to remain babies in their faith. There was much to learn, but they essentially said, "That's interesting, but tell us our favorite story again." Where there was history, psalms, law, and prophecy the people *could* have learned, they only wanted to hear their introduction to the faith over and over.

Christians can be guilty of the same thing today. Perhaps the struggle is that the more you know, the more responsibility you have for acting on that knowledge. The apostle Paul recalled his own struggle with this issue in 1 Corinthians 3:2 (NLT), writing, "I had to feed you with milk, not with solid food, because you weren't ready for anything stronger. And you still aren't ready."

God might need to nudge the complacent so they realize that growing up into a solid faith is a vital next step for every Christ follower.

CRUSHED—BROKEN—RESTORED

*The Lord is close to the brokenhearted and
saves those who are crushed in spirit.*

PSALM 34:18 NIV

You've had bad days, lived through moments marked by heartbreak and soul-crushing circumstances. You didn't enjoy it, sought a way out, and would have welcomed relief.

God's in the business of spiritual pain relief. He's been waiting for your call. God's ability to rescue isn't influenced by things like an attractive financial portfolio, your willingness to "owe Him one," or whether you think you deserve His help.

God has always done what you can't. He paid your sin debt, made you part of His family, forgave you, fixed your broken heart, and restored your crushed spirit. You could try doing everything on your own, but if you've tried that before, you know the results are less than ideal. Let God do what He does best.

Godly wisdom recognizes who does the work—and lets Him. The God who heals loves to stand with those who need healing. He doesn't look down on those who hurt. This could be a new experience for you because while mankind values perceived perfection, God desires honesty. Transparency with God is the best way to access His help.

Bad things happen. Wounds will be inflicted. Hearts are subject to breaking. Admit the hurt and God will step in. Accept the help and let the healing begin.

EMOTIONAL DESTRUCTION

Fools vent their anger, but the wise quietly hold it back.
PROVERBS 29:11 NLT

You're an emotional creature. Certain things make you sad, angry, anxious, or ashamed. None of these emotions are reliable indicators, however, of how God views you.

Many emotions can lead to negative and sinful responses. Unhappiness can lead to discontent, anxiety to a lack of faith, anger to a lack of love, shame to believing a lie about how God sees you, despair to self-injury, and jealousy to envy.

"Be alert and of sober mind. Your enemy the devil prowls around like a roaring lion looking for someone to devour" (1 Peter 5:8 NIV). Having a "sober mind" identifies someone whose thinking is in line with God's. The call to "be alert" means to be prepared and on guard.

Emotions are a byproduct of your humanity, but to let them control you is like turning on a beacon helping your adversary find you. Negative emotions make you a *menu* option.

God's Word is filled with examples of how negative emotions led to sin. Moses couldn't enter the promised land because his anger led to disobedience (Numbers 20:12); David's lust led to adultery (2 Samuel 11); Saul's jealousy led to attempted murder (1 Samuel 19); and Peter's fear led to multiple lies (John 18:15–27). Godly wisdom recognizes negative emotions, takes those thoughts captive (see 2 Corinthians 10:5), and refuses to entertain these destructive emotions for even one minute.

LIFE GUIDANCE

I have been crucified with Christ; and it is no longer I who live, but Christ lives in me; and the life which I now live in the flesh I live by faith in the Son of God, who loved me and gave Himself up for me.

GALATIANS 2:20 NASB

If you decided to allow someone full control of your life choices, you'd want to be confident they could be trusted. You probably know people you wouldn't want applying for the job. Jesus offers full life guidance with every resource at His disposal. He owns everything after all.

To take advantage of this offer, you simply put your own selfish interests aside and let Christ take over. If it sounds like an easy trade, you can be sure it's not. While Jesus will honor His side of the offer, you will struggle to let Him. There will be times when you'll want your own way, when your way conflicts with His plan, and when His plan makes no sense to you.

You need to embrace selflessness because it's the only way Jesus can work through you. You give up your rights in order to discover the new life He designed for you.

Godly wisdom allows you to say, "My old way of thinking is gone. Jesus lives here. I will serve Him because I trust the One who loved me enough to give everything for me."

CONTENT OR COMPLACENT?

*I have learned how to be content with whatever I have. I know how
to live on almost nothing or with everything. I have learned
the secret of living in every situation, whether it is with
a full stomach or empty, with plenty or little.*

PHILIPPIANS 4:11–12 NLT

What would make you content? You're probably thinking of things like money, a particular home, or maybe a certain vehicle. If you just had whatever you're thinking about right now, all would be perfect in your world and you'd discover ultimate contentment, right?

But every time you set your eyes on the next contentment-inducing object, the target shifts. When you have what you think you want, you discover something newer that promises greater contentment. Yet with each acquisition, you schedule a new party for discontent.

The apostle Paul had almost nothing but knew contentment. He discovered contentment was the secret of living in varying circumstances. Contentment is being satisfied with where *God* places you. If He's with you, there's nothing to fear because you'll have exactly what you need.

Sometimes it's easy to exchange "contented" for "complacent." Someone who's satisfied in a circumstance he personally created is complacent. God can encourage him to move, but he doesn't want to take one step beyond the comfort zone he's made. Complacency is often found among those who've decided God can't be trusted to lead. With God in control, however, contentment can be found in multiple circumstances.

A TIME TO RETURN

*For as the heavens are high above the earth, so great is His mercy
toward those who fear Him; as far as the east is from the west,
so far has He removed our transgressions from us.*

PSALM 103:11–12 NKJV

Guilt is a peculiar thing. It can cause you to live in never-ending regret, disengage from meaningful relationships, and convince yourself to become exiled from God. However, guilt *can* serve a far better purpose.

Guilt is an internal indicator that you not only sin, but recognize you have caused hurt, demonstrated selfishness, and disobeyed God. Instead of treating guilt as a divine indictment leading to lifelong punishment, you can use the guilt to keep an appointment with God to tell Him about the sin, express sorrow, and accept forgiveness. Then? Stop feeling guilty.

Romans 8:1 (NKJV) offers this encouragement: "There is therefore now no condemnation to those who are in Christ Jesus, who do not walk according to the flesh, but according to the Spirit."

God doesn't send you a condemning voice that accuses and then is persistent in reminding you of past sin. That's something your greatest adversary does—often daily. It's important to recognize that guilt always invites you to come back to God. If you feel condemned, then you've accepted a perspective that did *not* come from God.

Guilt offers a homecoming. Stop running away.

JUSTIFICATION ACCEPTED

Since we have been justified through faith, we have peace with God through our Lord Jesus Christ.

ROMANS 5:1 NIV

The term *justification* isn't commonly used outside a courtroom, but it's a great concept. To be justified means God views you as guilt-free. Justification doesn't require any extra work on your part, you don't have to argue your case, and infractions are removed from your *sin ledger*.

Justification is difficult to understand when you're convinced you need to work to pay for every sin. Justification is foreign to social norms. People are conditioned to believe that if you want something, you work for it. But God offers a real-life benefits package as a gift. If you could pay for it, you'd have to call it something else. Gifts can't be earned. God did what you could never do, and He simply asks you to accept it.

Romans 5 says you can have peace with God because by accepting what's already been done, you can stand confident, clean, and forgiven before God. The resulting experience is a restored relationship.

Justification makes the unacceptable acceptable, the impure pure, and the stained spotless. It accepts the sacrifice of Jesus as payment for your sin. Justification restores what was lost, broken, and disbelieving. It softens hearts and changes minds. Justification is a perfect gift and the only solution for the charge of *lawbreaker*.

STANDING IN THE WAY

Not that we are sufficient of ourselves to think of anything as being from ourselves, but our sufficiency is from God.

2 CORINTHIANS 3:5 NKJV

The problem with self-sufficiency is *self*. This one little word makes the assumption that each individual can find a sense of completeness by simply following his own abilities, decision-making, and strengths. It also assumes that every individual has a complete understanding of what sufficiency means, looks like, and how to know when he's obtained it.

God made relationship a priority with and for mankind. Relationship is always improved when someone meets a need. Marriage meets many needs, but not all. Friendships meet needs, but not all. There's always something missing until you accept friendship with Jesus. You have needs that only God can meet. If you could meet all your needs, there'd be no need for God.

You'll only be sufficient when you make room for God to begin His good work in you. He will complete it, and you'll find rescue, restoration, and purpose. Wholeness can only truly be achieved when you accept friendship with the God who actually knows where you're going and how to get you there.

When you're tired of trying to do life alone only to discover failure, it's time to remove *self* from sufficiency. Wholeness is available. Don't stand in the way.

CHOICE AND REASON

The commands of the LORD are clear, giving insight for living.
PSALM 19:8 NLT

Why did God supply a list of sins to avoid? Maybe you've thought He's simply trying to keep you away from things you'd enjoy. Maybe you've thought He just wanted to make Christianity a religion of rules.

Jesus summarized God's list of laws when He said to love God and then love everyone else (Mark 12:30–31). If love is the reason to follow God's laws then the choice to sin must be fueled by a *lack* of love for God and others.

While God's grace covers your sin, and His mercy might keep punishment away, the truth is, sin grieves God. His sadness is less about your inability to follow His commands and more about the potential damage you inflict on yourself and others when you sin.

God doesn't want you to sin, because it damages your heart, mind, and soul. It also damages relationships. To be clear: avoiding sin doesn't keep you from something fun; it keeps you from grieving God, hurting others, and inflicting pain on yourself. Perhaps this thinking led the apostle Paul to say in Romans 6:1–2 (NLT), "Should we keep on sinning so that God can show us more and more of his wonderful grace? Of course not!"

God's words lead to life, promote healing, and can help restore relationships. They can serve as a warning signal and lead to rewarding life choices.

DON'T BE CONFUSED

God is not a God of confusion but of peace.
1 Corinthians 14:33 nasb

God has His own way of doing things, and He thinks differently than you do (Isaiah 55:8), so if His Word seems confusing, maybe you came to Him confused.

God offers illumination for life's next step, perspective for your purpose in life, and directions for personal choice (see Psalm 119:105; Jeremiah 29:11; Proverbs 16:9). He's never been confused, and confusion is not a part of His plan for you either.

If you hear a perspective that differs from God's Word, refuse to be confused. Always rely on the clarity of what God has actually said. John 8:32 (niv) was directed to those who follow Jesus: "You will know the truth, and the truth will set you free."

The reason God's truth may seem confusing at times is because it differs from what many accept as truth. Spending time with *common* thinking can result in a rejection of many scriptures. When that happens, there's an unintended plan to rewrite the God-given concepts.

Following God's truth will challenge your thinking, but when you understand that any confusion you experience is a result of inaccurate thinking that doesn't include God, then it becomes easier to let what He has said change your opinions, behaviors, and allegiances. Man's greatest confusion comes in trusting his own thinking—or rejecting God's.

THE ANGER LIST

My dear brothers and sisters, take note of this:
Everyone should be quick to listen, slow to speak and slow
to become angry, because human anger does not
produce the righteousness that God desires.

JAMES 1:19–20 NIV

Anger increases your heart rate, makes your blood pressure rise, and consumes mental resources that could be used for more productive responses.

Anger can lead to bitterness, unforgiveness, and invisible barriers that keep others away. Anger is rarely rational, often visible, and always results in an internal storm warning. Anger is hard to reverse when you're quick to speak, slow to give a fair hearing, and reluctant to forgive. Anger infects those you come in contact with and can cripple those you live with. It greatly affects every aspect of living. Anger causes you to struggle to love.

Anger isn't always wrong, but shouldn't be your go-to response. "In your anger do not sin" (Ephesians 4:26 NIV). And anger should always be resolved. As Paul said, "Get rid of all bitterness, rage and anger, brawling and slander, along with every form of malice. Be kind and compassionate to one another, forgiving each other, just as in Christ God forgave you" (Ephesians 4:31–32 NIV).

Maybe we're urged to keep a distance from anger because it's the perfect environment for compounding a laundry list of poor choices. Each additional rebellious choice will wound you as much, and perhaps more than, the objects of your anger.

TRUSTING THE OUTCOME

Those who trust in the LORD will find new strength.
They will soar high on wings like eagles. They will run
and not grow weary. They will walk and not faint.

ISAIAH 40:31 NLT

You're not where you want to be. You'd hoped to be further ahead, someplace different, and on track to experience contentment. You believe you're stuck, and patience is hard to find.

But patience is an exercise plan in God's gym and He wants you to work out. Unlike a physical gym, this exercise can take place wherever you find yourself and in every circumstance. You'll need to develop patience when you're not where you want to be, when people seem to find great pleasure in getting on your nerves, and when it seems God is silent to your prayers.

One of the benefits of patience goes beyond exercise to a time of rest. You may not want it, but it helps prepare you for future activity God has planned. Psalm 37:7 (NLT) says, "Be still in the presence of the LORD, and wait patiently for him to act. Don't worry about evil people who prosper or fret about their wicked schemes."

It's hard to be patient when you see other people find the success you wanted for yourself. Keep in mind that patience is a fruit of the Spirit (Galatians 5:22). God believes you can progress from an impatient state to one that trusts His future—beyond impatience.

NEVER FORSAKEN

We are afflicted in every way, but not crushed; perplexed,
but not despairing; persecuted, but not forsaken;
struck down, but not destroyed.

2 CORINTHIANS 4:8–9 NASB

Adam's sin bent every man, woman, and child toward the choice to sin (Romans 5:12). This means people will make choices that intentionally or unintentionally bring trouble to their lives. Your own choices bring trouble. Trouble is found everywhere—and you're told to expect it. Jesus said, "In this world you will have trouble. But take heart! I have overcome the world" (John 16:33 NIV).

The apostle Paul experienced trouble. He was beaten, imprisoned, and lived knowing there were plenty of people who didn't like him. When trouble came, Paul could say he wasn't distressed, didn't despair, didn't feel forsaken, and wasn't destroyed. Some who had witnessed Paul's distressing circumstances might have thought his words betrayed an advanced case of insanity.

The reason Paul could say these things is the same reason you can. Romans 8:28 (NASB) gives you the perspective: "God causes all things to work together for good to those who love God, to those who are called according to His purpose."

Paul loved God and had been called into service. He had absolute assurance that the God who accompanied him to the storm brought an umbrella. Wise men realize that the toughest of times are temporary when compared to eternity and that God never leaves and never forsakes His own (Hebrews 13:5).

BOXING GOD

You've heard the term "putting God in a box." It's usually a reference to a person who believes God only works in ways that match his preconceived ideas. Today's verse provides a different example of putting God in a box. . .and leaving Him there.

God is often placed in a proverbial box marked "Open once a weekend and only during times of absolute emergency." It's a comfort to have the box handy, but it's only intended for specific uses and is rarely opened daily. Other boxes are filled with an assortment of *life enhancements*. Usually these boxes are linked to enjoyable pursuits or personal possessions. You may find yourself drawn to these boxes because they hold a promise for immediate happiness.

You might tell others you believe God is important, but if it were a contest between which box you spend more time with, God might be hidden away in a box of your making while you keep drawing things from boxes that distract you from the neglected *God box* in the corner.

You can only serve one. Splitting time between the boxes suggests a divided loyalty. Enjoy the things God has given you, but make sure He has your love, time, and heart. Let Him out of the box.

IMPRACTICAL PRIDE

A man's pride will bring him low,
but the humble in spirit will retain honor.

PROVERBS 29:23 NKJV

Sometimes God's plan doesn't make sense, but there are practical reasons for His commands. Pride's a good example. God says He resists the proud (James 4:6). Other people recognize pride and turn away. God says pride leads to self-deception (Galatians 6:3). Other people believe those with blatant pride are delusional. God says pride leads to destruction (Proverbs 16:18). Proud but broken people make the news every day.

Pride causes an inflated view of yourself. It favorably compares personal accomplishments with others' and believes itself to be superior. Pride pays attention to personal success while minimizing personal failure. Pride has no place in God's plan because comparing personal skills and accomplishments with others is not the comparison God uses. He compares you with His Son, Jesus—and the comparison isn't in your favor.

By God's grace you're made acceptable (not superior) to God and others. He wants to use you, not to elevate you, but to advance His plan.

Proverbs 27:2 (NASB) says, "Let another praise you, and not your own mouth; a stranger, and not your own lips." Pride always has a motive for its actions. It demands to be noticed and is never really satisfied with each new accomplishment.

Honor is always a byproduct of thinking more of others and less of self (see John 3:30).

HUMILITY'S FRIEND

*True humility and fear of the Lord
lead to riches, honor, and long life.*

PROVERBS 22:4 NLT

Humility provides a correct view of who you are and the impressive power of God. Pride offends God, but humility brings unexpected benefits. There's wisdom in refusing pride, but humility doesn't seem logical when society promotes self-marketing. We often believe that if people don't know who we are, then we'll never get noticed and our talent will be wasted.

Humility promotes hard work with no demand for recognition, an advanced work ethic when no one's watching, and restful sleep because we've done our best. Humility doesn't refuse acknowledgment; it just doesn't chase it.

What Matthew 6:2, 4 (NLT) says runs parallel to humility: "When you give to someone in need, don't do as the hypocrites do— blowing trumpets in the synagogues and streets to call attention to their acts of charity! I tell you the truth, they have received all the reward they will ever get. . . . Give your gifts in private, and your Father, who sees everything, will reward you."

It's been said that humility isn't thinking less of yourself; it's not thinking of yourself at all. God knows what you do. He rewards you here or in heaven for acts of kindness and faithful service that don't seek a spotlight and don't demand applause. Humility refuses to do something positive in the name of God and then take all the credit for playing a supporting role.

FULL-TIME FAITH

God "will repay each person according to what they have done." To those who by persistence in doing good seek glory, honor and immortality, he will give eternal life. But for those who are self-seeking and who reject the truth and follow evil, there will be wrath and anger.

Romans 2:6–8 niv

God was aware that His will, Word, and way would be manipulated, contorted, and misapplied. He encouraged His people to handle His Word correctly and be workers who had His approval (2 Timothy 2:15).

Some choose to learn what God says and readjust their thinking to conform to what He wants. Some take a mental marker and blot out sections they don't want to accept as truth. There's a reward for faithfulness and a reward for disbelief. They aren't the same reward.

God didn't hide His plan, conceal His will, or confuse His people. He offered generous helpings of truth and urged you to dig in, taste for yourself, and hold tight to the promise of being made a new creature (see 2 Corinthians 5:17).

Some stop short of accepting all truth and only look to God's Word for personally comforting quotes. But Christianity is more than a spectator faith with all the benefits of the fully engaged. The pursuit of a part-time Gospel was described in 2 Timothy 4:3–4 (nasb): "The time will come when they. . .will turn away their ears from the truth and will turn aside to myths."

Keep pursuing the reward of the faithful.

ACTS OF KINDNESS

"If you lend money only to those who can repay you,
why should you get credit? Even sinners will
lend to other sinners for a full return."

LUKE 6:34 NLT

Lending to relatives is generally considered a bad idea because hard feelings can develop when the loan isn't repaid. We're conditioned to believe good deeds *must* be repaid.

Jesus didn't seem to live by the phrase, "You scratch my back and I'll scratch yours." While cooperation was important, His life, words, and deeds suggest a different phrase "I'll scratch your back because it's itchy and I can reach it." To expect a return on your time investment suggests you believe in the *wages of deeds* instead of the *gift* of time, talent, and finances.

Certainly you're entitled to lend money and expect repayment, but the bank doesn't consider that same service a good deed. It's simply a loan. If you help a friend expecting they'll help you in return, that's less a kindness than an agreement for mutually beneficial services.

In most cases, truly good deeds go unheralded and are rarely repaid. The idea of doing good without return means you'll do something for someone for a better reason. This concept is critical to understanding that Jesus paid the ultimate sacrifice to offer salvation. You can't pay for it, earn it, or return the favor. You simply have to accept the greatest intentional act of kindness mankind has ever known.

HUMILITY'S ELEVATOR

Do nothing out of selfish ambition or vain conceit.
Rather, in humility value others above yourselves.

PHILIPPIANS 2:3 NIV

We can find a kernel of cynicism in some of the good news we read. Consider this story: A little girl takes the meal she's ordered at a restaurant and gives it to a homeless man on the street outside. It's a beautiful story that gets a little cloudy when her father follows her outside with his phone camera, capturing the moment and then uploading it to social media, where it's shared repeatedly. Cynicism judges the motives of the father and the potential misuse of a child's good deed. It questions where the idea originated or whether this was a staged event.

Cynicism only sees what it wants to believe. However, cynicism can't get behind the outward gaze of the little girl who interacted with someone who had no ability to repay her. It doesn't take into account how this interaction may impact her life going forward.

If we reconstruct today's verse, it might read: "Motives associated with pride and selfish pursuits devalue others. Humility offers an opportunity for you to begin to see others with God's vision."

In God's playbook, personal ambition takes a back seat to helping others when they need help. Godly wisdom never steps on others to get to a place you want to claim, never overlooks someone because of perceived differences, and never elevates self while looking down on those with needs.

SOBER JUDGMENT

Do not think of yourself more highly than you ought, but rather think of yourself with sober judgment, in accordance with the faith God has distributed to each of you.

ROMANS 12:3 NIV

Humility is the opposite of pride, but too often Christians are only willing to convert pride to false humility, which is just a different shade of pride. It intentionally shares personal faults with others. This information then begs to be refuted.

False humility prompts others to say something nice about you. This happens when you say things like "I'm not very good at that" or "I'm not sure why I ever tried." This side of pride can be even more insidious than blatant pride because it works hard to manipulate others into verbally affirming what you already believe you're good at, and you're secretly hoping an extended audience overhears people praising you.

God asks you to consider who you are with *sober judgment*. This means you don't think too highly—or too lowly—of yourself. You're made in God's image, but pride of any shade distorts the family resemblance. You're a servant of God, but also a son of God. True humility will be inclined to express gratitude for God's good gifts while false humility wants others to compliment *your* attributes.

Sober judgment means discovering how God sees you and then refusing to let your opinion of yourself climb a stepstool that doesn't resemble sober judgment.

WORK IN PROGRESS

Clothe yourselves with tenderhearted mercy, kindness, humility, gentleness, and patience. Make allowance for each other's faults, and forgive anyone who offends you. Remember, the Lord forgave you, so you must forgive others. Above all, clothe yourselves with love, which binds us all together in perfect harmony.

COLOSSIANS 3:12–14 NLT

True humility allows you to recognize you're a sinner saved by God's grace and no better than other human beings. You're a co-recipient of God's grace, forgiveness, and love. You have fallen short of God's perfect standard (see Romans 6:23), yet God did the remarkable and offered a rescue plan so comprehensive it made you part of His family. He orchestrated His plan to encompass a restored relationship between a perfect God and imperfect people.

Humility takes the clothing of sober judgment and offers others tenderhearted mercy, kindness, humility, gentleness, patience, forgiveness, and love. You're asked to model the behavior of your Father, God. He offers all of these things to you, so He's not interested in seeing you treat others in a way that's inferior to the way He treats them.

Christians are bound together by love, and it's the choice to love that inspires harmony between God's people. God didn't love you because you deserved it. He loved you—period. The same should be said of you. Love others because you see people differently, not as wretched and unredeemable, but as loved by God and as a work in progress. Just like you.

FOR YOUR GOOD

*As obedient children, do not conform to the evil
desires you had when you lived in ignorance.*

1 PETER 1:14 NIV

Dads know it takes time, patience, and plenty of reinforcement to get children to follow directions that reinforce obedient choices.

Imagine what it's like for God, who wants to take His children from babies who don't understand much to mature believers who value godly wisdom. The early church in Corinth enjoyed their spiritual childhood a little too much. First Corinthians 3:2 (NIV) says, "I gave you milk, not solid food, for you were not yet ready for it. Indeed, you are still not ready."

God knew it would be extremely easy to fall back to the earliest days of personal belief, which is why He asked for personal maturity. Hebrews 5:14 (NIV) says, "Solid food is for the mature, who by constant use have trained themselves to distinguish good from evil."

Just like braces transform a smile, obedience transforms a life. As a dad you want your children to grow from babies to adults. You don't expect them to grow up overnight, but you do expect them to mature. God doesn't want you to stay living in ignorance either. He wants you to grow up. It's for your good.

"When I was a child, I talked like a child, I thought like a child, I reasoned like a child. When I became a man, I put the ways of childhood behind me" (1 Corinthians 13:11 NIV).

FORWARD WITH PURPOSE

You say, "I am allowed to do anything"—but not
everything is good for you. You say, "I am allowed to
do anything"—but not everything is beneficial.

1 Corinthians 10:23 NLT

When you come by faith to accept God's rescue, there's *nothing* you can do to earn His saving offer. You simply believe God can do what you can't. Ephesians 2:8–9 (NLT) says, "God saved you by his grace when you believed. And you can't take credit for this; it is a gift from God. Salvation is not a reward for the good things we have done, so none of us can boast about it."

You can't earn your place in God's family. This gift is not for sale. He offers forgiveness long after you accept His rescue. This can lead some to believe God doesn't care about behavior or life choices. Ephesians 2:10 clears that up: "For we are God's masterpiece. He has created us anew in Christ Jesus, so we can do the good things he planned for us long ago."

God has *good things* planned for your life. Those plans didn't include you sitting on the sidelines. He wants you to participate in life transformation through obedience and new thinking that aligns with His. God gave you liberty so you're free to do what He created you to do. God gave you His Spirit so you could learn to accept His best.

Come to God with nothing. Move forward with purpose.

SIMPLE, PROFOUND, AND WISE

Fear God and keep his commandments,
for this is the duty of all mankind.

ECCLESIASTES 12:13 NIV

If the God who made everything had a plan for your life, would you follow it? If the God who knew your name before you were born gave you a purpose, would it change how you live? If the God who's making a place for you in His future called you to active duty in your faith, would you do everything you could to follow the Leader? Well, He does have a plan, He's given you a purpose, and He calls you to active duty.

Today's verse is simple and profound. It contains impressive wisdom and divine directive. It contains the core of God's will for you.

While there's a *fear of God* that's connected to pending judgment (think Noah), the use of the term in this verse is positively reinforcing the view that God is awe-inspiring and worthy of the highest priority in your thinking and actions.

Keeping His commands points to your willingness to follow His leadership. By agreeing to follow, you're saying you believe He holds the key to truth and correct thinking.

By saying, *this is the duty of all mankind*, you can begin to see that even before the Bible said, "God so loved the world" (John 3:16), He had a plan for every woman, child, and man. The question isn't whether God has a plan; it's whether you'll follow.

HOLINESS

*God's will is for you to be holy,
so stay away from all sexual sin.*

1 THESSALONIANS 4:3 NLT

To be holy means to be set aside for special use, to be dedicated and blessed. It's a big deal. *Holy* is a term that easily applies to God, but it's a bit harder to embrace it for yourself. After all, you sin, go your own way, and are easily distracted (see Romans 3:23; Isaiah 53:6; 1 Corinthians 7:35).

When the term *God's will* is applied to biblical thought, it's part of His plan. In this case, God wants *you* to be holy. It's the next part of the verse that can seem troubling. How does sexual purity connect with God's will for personal holiness?

If you're set apart for God's use, then your greatest relationship will need to be with God. While God established sexual relationships within marriage, men sometimes take what He meant for their benefit and turn it into something that taints and subverts His plan. It doesn't show genuine love to the other person because it's mere physical desire. And it doesn't honor God's plan because it substitutes an enduring expression of intimacy and love for momentary satisfaction of lust.

It's not always easy to resist sexual temptation. But it's well worth the cost of refraining from sin to enjoy an unbroken spiritual relationship with God and a truly intimate, faithful relationship with your wife.

THE EXAMPLE

[Jesus] withdrew from them about a stone's throw, and He knelt down and began to pray, saying, "Father, if You are willing, remove this cup from Me; yet not My will, but Yours be done."

LUKE 22:41–42 NASB

Jesus was within hours of His death on the cross. This was God's plan from the beginning. Relationship with mankind would be restored and Jesus would defeat death, but in His human body there waged a war between the desire to live and the desire to honor His Father.

It can be a surprise to read that Jesus asked God for a second option. He prayed passionately. If Jesus' prayer ended with only a request for a way out, we might leave confused, but Jesus ended His prayer with what has become the best response of all mankind: "Not my will, but Yours be done."

No wonder we're told that Jesus understands humanity (Hebrews 4:15). If God had granted Jesus' request, salvation either wouldn't be available or God would have needed a new plan to rescue mankind. But Jesus believed in the rescue plan. He was at a critical point. Jesus chose to follow His Father's plan. . .and mankind was offered rescue.

You may not always see the wisdom of God's will. It may seem an unnecessary hardship, a burden too big to bear, or something that no longer applies. As hard as it may seem to follow God's will, it's always been perfect.

THE RIGHT KIND OF PRIDE

*I have spoken to you with great frankness; I take great pride
in you. I am greatly encouraged; in all our troubles
my joy knows no bounds.*

2 CORINTHIANS 7:4 NIV

Can you remember the last time you told a loved one or a friend or coworker, "I'm proud of you!"? The word *pride* can make many Christians nervous, because they know that God has stated repeatedly that He hates the sin of pride. But nowhere in the Bible are believers barred from speaking words of praise for a person who has done something well, and sometimes it's even fitting to use the word *proud* when you do so.

The apostle Paul gave voice to this expression of pride when he told the Christians in first-century Corinth, "I take great pride in you." The context of the apostle's kind words for the Corinthians was how they had handled an especially ugly incident of sexual immorality in their church.

There is absolutely nothing wrong with taking pride in a job well done or in the words or actions of our children or other loved ones. So when one of your children does something especially noteworthy (such as a great report card or an act of kindness toward another person) or when a coworker accomplishes something great at work, don't hesitate to let them know that you've noticed. You might even punctuate your recognition by telling them, "I'm proud of you!"

ACTING ON WHAT YOU KNOW

But don't just listen to God's word. You must do what it says.
Otherwise, you are only fooling yourselves.

JAMES 1:22 NLT

You can't be a part of our modern-day culture without knowing a little something about what it takes to be physically healthy. Almost daily you see and hear messages encouraging you to eat right and get enough exercise to keep your mind and body operating at peak efficiency.

Sadly, too many people know about these physical truths but don't act on them. The results speak for themselves. Obesity and the physical problems that accompany inactivity are at all-time highs. As a whole, North Americans aren't very physically healthy.

Today's verse gives Christian men some very simple instructions for getting and staying *spiritually* healthy. It tells you that you're not just to read what the Bible tells you that you should do, but you are also to put what you know into action. Sadly, many Christians don't consistently put what they know the Bible says into practice. The result is that they're in a spiritually unhealthy condition.

God's written Word is filled cover to cover with all kinds of truths, wisdom, and commands. And while it's a good thing to read the Bible and learn what it has to teach you, that's only the first step. The second step—and this means everything—is to act on what you learn.

THE TANGLED WEB OF DECEPTION

Do not lie to each other, since you have taken
off your old self with its practices.

COLOSSIANS 3:9 NIV

The goal of any fly fisherman is to catch fish by using hooks adorned with fur, feathers, hair, and other materials in such a way that they imitate an insect or other living creature fish like to eat. A good fisherman uses flies he knows can *deceive* a hungry fish into biting.

While no one would criticize or condemn a fly fisherman for practicing this form of deception, the Bible tells you repeatedly that as followers of Christ you are to be completely honest with others in how you speak to them and how you treat them—no "white lies," twisted truths, or spin.

You live in a world in which politicians, marketers, and many others regularly practice all sorts of deception in an effort to get people to cast their votes or spend their money in a way they want them to. But it should never be that way for believers.

As a Christian man, you damage your relationship with God—and your witness for Christ—when you speak untruthfully or when you behave in such a way as to deceive others. On the other hand, when you make honesty a big part of who you are, you please your heavenly Father and glorify Him in front of those around you.

SEEK RECONCILIATION

If it is possible, as far as it depends on you,
live at peace with everyone.

ROMANS 12:18 NIV

Think about the last time you were in some kind of conflict with another person—maybe your spouse, one of your children, a close friend, or a coworker. These kinds of situations are always uncomfortable, sometimes extremely so, simply because you and that other person are not at peace with each other.

Even after Jesus saves you, you still have your sinful nature (at least until the day you start eternity with Him), so you're still bound to make mistakes and to engage in sinful speech and actions. That often means saying and doing things that hurt or anger others. That's a two-way street, because there may be times when someone hurts or offends you.

In either scenario, there's a loss of peace and unity. At that point, someone is going to have to step up and do what it takes to remedy the situation. The ball might not always be in your court, but when it is—even partially—the Bible instructs you to choose humility, to seek reconciliation and forgiveness.

So when you find yourself in conflict with someone close to you, don't let the situation fester. Instead, search your heart, evaluate your own words and actions, and then do what you must to be at peace with that person.

COMFORT IN TIMES OF STRESS

Trouble and distress have come upon me,
but your commands give me delight.

Psalm 119:143 NIV

New Christians, or those still working to become more mature in their faith, are sometimes shocked that the Christian life isn't free of trouble and stress. Some of them can even become disillusioned when they realize that many facets of their new life are like their old one in that they face a lot of the same problems they did before they were saved.

The plain biblical truth is that God never promised you an easy or trouble-free life. In fact, many scriptures promise you exactly the opposite. Take these words straight from the mouth of Jesus: "In this world you will have trouble" (John 16:33 NIV).

If life here on earth hasn't already affirmed that truth for you, take a closer look at today's verse. Notice that the psalmist doesn't thank God for keeping his life free of trouble and stress. Instead, he freely acknowledges that he's going through a rough time and that the troubles he's enduring are affecting him internally.

But this same psalmist ends his declaration that he's going through some difficulties with these words of hope: "Your commands give me delight." He had learned an important life lesson, namely that God didn't always keep his life free of problems but was always there for him, even in the most difficult of times.

A LIFE OF INTEGRITY

*The integrity of the upright guides them,
but the unfaithful are destroyed by their duplicity.*

PROVERBS 11:3 NIV

What would you do if your server brought your check at the end of a dinner at your favorite restaurant, and you noticed that your dessert was left off the bill? Or if you were overpaid for work you had just completed? Or if someone inadvertently gave you credit for a coworker's accomplishment?

Life is filled with all sorts of tests for that character quality called "integrity." Through big tests and small (relatively, that is) tests alike, you're constantly presented with opportunities to make sure you please God by doing what you know is right.

The Christian writer C. S. Lewis noted: "Integrity is doing the right thing, even when no one is watching." That's a great definition of integrity, isn't it? And it's also a great reminder to do everything you do, even in private, with an eye toward true integrity. Here's a question to test yourself and the level of integrity by which you live: Do you do what you know is right—even in the relatively "small" areas of life—even when you know no one is looking, even when you know there are no consequences?

When you walk in integrity in all areas of your life, you please your Father in heaven and also keep a clear conscience. That's a great way to live!

SEEING SCRIPTURE ANEW

Open my eyes that I may see wonderful things in your law.
PSALM 119:18 NIV

Have you ever sat down and watched your favorite movie, one you've watched several times before, and noticed something in that particular film you'd never noticed previously—maybe a line of dialogue or an action on the part of a key character that you somehow missed during past viewings?

The same thing can happen when you read your Bible. As you read, you can find yourself focused for the first time on a particular word or phrase that hadn't made much of an impression before. On that second or third (or fourth, fifth, or sixth) reading, it's as if God has opened your eyes to some truth or some piece of wisdom you'd never before picked up on.

This is why it's important to read your Bible daily, even if you've already read it cover to cover. And this is also why it's important to devote your time of reading to the God who authored every word of it. When you sit down and read your Bible, even if you're rereading a familiar passage, first stop and ask God to reveal what He wants to reveal to you in His Word that day. You might be amazed at how He'll open your eyes to a new truth (new to *you*, that is!) you'd never seen before.

THE LOVE OF MONEY

But those who desire to be rich fall into temptation and a snare,
and into many foolish and harmful lusts which drown
men in destruction and perdition.

1 TIMOTHY 6:9 NKJV

It's not difficult to see the proof of the destructiveness of greed in the world around you. The federal prison system is filled with men whose love of money led them to commit crimes so serious that they resulted in long—sometimes lifelong—imprisonments. Just do a quick internet search of the following names for some stark examples of the consequences of greed: Bernie Madoff, Jeff Skilling, Bernie Ebbers, Dennis Kozlowski, and John Rigas.

The Bible teaches that greed, or "the love of money," is the driving force for all sorts of evil and wickedness, and sometimes the ruin of men's lives of faith: "For the love of money is a root of all kinds of evil. Some people, eager for money, have wandered from the faith and pierced themselves with many griefs" (1 Timothy 6:10 NIV).

Money, in and of itself, is not evil, and neither is the desire to better yourself financially. Money is just a tool, one you can use to care for your family, to build yourself a better life, or to bless others. But you put yourself at serious risk when you make the acquisition of material wealth your life's focus.

PROPERLY MOTIVATED PRAYER

*And we are confident that he hears us whenever
we ask for anything that pleases him.*

1 John 5:14 NLT

If you're on Facebook or some other form of social media, you've no doubt seen those posts promising amazing financial blessings from God if you'll just click on "Share" so seven of your friends can read the same post.

If you haven't already given that blessing plan a try, here's a little secret: It doesn't work, and it doesn't work because that's *not* the way God answers prayer. Your heavenly Father, as good and generous as He is with His blessings, isn't like an ATM—just shove in the right card and punch in the correct codes, and you get instant cash.

God wants to answer your prayers, and He wants to pour out His blessings on you, but, as today's verse points out, He hears you and grants your requests when you *ask for anything that pleases Him*. The apostle James put it very simply: "When you ask, you do not receive, because you ask with wrong motives, that you may spend what you get on your pleasures" (James 4:3 NIV).

In and of itself, there's nothing wrong with asking God to bless you—even bless you financially. But remember that this kind of blessing is contingent on two things: (1) Are you asking with the right motives, and (2) does blessing you financially at this time please Him?

THINK BEFORE YOU SPEAK

Out of the same mouth come praise and cursing.
My brothers and sisters, this should not be.

JAMES 3:10 NIV

Ever had someone ask you if your ears had been burning? That's a humorous way of saying that they'd been involved in a recent conversation with someone else, and *you* were the subject.

Human beings seem to love talking about other people, don't they? And sometimes those conversations aren't what the Bible would call "edifying." It's probably safe to say that every man, if he really thought about it, can recall moments in the recent past when he spoke unkind or damaging words about another person—more often than not, out of that person's earshot.

God takes the words His people speak very seriously, and He isn't pleased when you speak negatively of another person—even when what you say is factually true. That's why the apostle Paul wrote, "Do not let any unwholesome talk come out of your mouths, but only what is helpful for building others up according to their needs" (Ephesians 4:29 NIV).

So think before you speak. If the words you're thinking build up another person and enhance his or her reputation, then by all means feel free to speak them. But if they tear another down and hurt that person's good name, then keep them to yourself. . .and then see if you can't think of something good to say instead.

VICTORY OVER FEAR

The Lord is my light and my salvation—whom shall I fear?
The Lord is the stronghold of my life—of whom shall I be afraid?

Psalm 27:1 niv

If you're honest with yourself, you'd probably have to admit that the future scares you on some level. Honestly, there seem to be legitimate reasons for experiencing some fear about the prospect of economic downturns, natural disasters, terrorist attacks, crime. . .the list is seemingly endless.

This world is a scary place, and much of what happens in it gives you reason to be concerned. And while it's certainly no sin to feel some level of apprehension over the world around you and where it's headed, God tells you that you shouldn't allow fear to dominate you.

That's because you can rest in the assurance that your God isn't some distant deity but a loving heavenly Father who says, "Do not fear, for I am with you; do not be dismayed, for I am your God. I will strengthen you and help you; I will uphold you with my righteous right hand" (Isaiah 41:10 niv).

When fear attempts to make its way into your heart and your thinking—and it most certainly will try at times—you can take comfort in knowing that you have a loving heavenly Father who is bigger and mightier than any reason for fear the world can throw your way.

THE HIGH ROAD OF FORGIVENESS

*Make allowance for each other's faults, and forgive anyone
who offends you. Remember, the Lord forgave you,
so you must forgive others.*

COLOSSIANS 3:13 NLT

We live in a time when it seems that even the slightest verbal barb or insult can start a war of words—on social media or through other forms of modern technology. The exchanges can be ugly too; just think of the last time you read or heard of a "Twitter war" between two celebrities. One insult can start a seemingly endless string of messages, sometimes turning into a highly personal electronic game of "Can you top this?"

That's just fallen human nature, isn't it? In and of themselves, people aren't prone to just "take the high road" and let insults and "cuts" go without responding in kind. But God tells His people that it should never be that way with you. He challenges you in His Word to choose forgiveness, even when someone has intentionally or maliciously caused you pain.

So the next time someone cuts you off in traffic, the next time someone carelessly speaks hurtful words, or the next time you've been offended because of something someone did, take the high road and forgive that person.

That's the road God took when He extended forgiveness to you through His Son, Jesus Christ, and it's the same high road He wants you to take with those who have insulted or hurt you.

WHEN THINGS MAKE NO EARTHLY SENSE

*By faith Noah, when warned about things not yet seen,
in holy fear built an ark to save his family.*

HEBREWS 11:7 NIV

The unknown writer of Hebrews opens the eleventh chapter of his epistle by defining faith as "confidence in what we hope for and assurance about what we do not see" (Hebrews 11:1 NIV). He then goes on to show what that means through several Old Testament examples.

One of those examples is Noah, who, in obedience to God's command, built a giant ship called an ark to preserve him, his family, and representatives of every living creature from perishing during the Flood.

Noah's story is one of amazing faith on the part of one man. When you read God's instructions to him (see Genesis 6:12–22), you notice that not once did Noah question or test God. The end of this passage simply tells us that, "Noah did everything just as God commanded him" (Genesis 6:22 NIV). And because of his faith and obedience in the face of something he couldn't yet see, his family and all the animals were saved.

The apostle James tells us that even evil spirits believe in God—and tremble in fear (James 2:19). Faith, therefore, means not just believing in God, but believing God when He speaks and then acting on His promises and commands even when they don't make any earthly sense.

BE CAREFUL WHAT YOU LOOK AT

"So if your eye—even your good eye—causes you to lust, gouge it out and throw it away. It is better for you to lose one part of your body than for your whole body to be thrown into hell."

MATTHEW 5:29 NLT

In today's world, seeing visual images that can trigger your mind toward lustful thinking requires you to do just one thing—have your eyes open. Television, magazine covers, the internet, and just about any other form of communication are filled with sexually suggestive—and sometimes explicit—images that make it difficult for a man of God to keep his mind and heart sexually pure.

In today's verse, Jesus is emphasizing the importance of doing everything you can to keep your eyes from focusing on things that lure your mind toward lustful thinking. His point is the importance of ridding your life of things that can cause you to dwell on things that God deems impure and sinful. Far easier said than done in today's culture, isn't it?

Job, a man God lauded for his integrity, was onto something when he said, "I made a covenant with my eyes not to look with lust at a young woman" (Job 31:1 NLT). It's difficult, but not impossible, to keep your mind pure in the twenty-first century. It starts with simply making God, and yourself, a promise to get rid of the things that make sexually pure thinking more difficult.

CONFRONTATION TIME

But when Peter came to Antioch, I had to oppose him
to his face, for what he did was very wrong.

GALATIANS 2:11 NLT

Most men, if they're honest with themselves, have to admit that they dislike confronting another person, even when it's sorely needed. Confrontation of that kind makes most men very uncomfortable, and sometimes they choose the path of least resistance, leaving well enough alone rather than putting themselves through the trauma of speaking needed truth to another.

In today's verse, Paul recounts a moment of confrontation between himself and the apostle Peter, who because of his own fear of confrontation had behaved and spoken hypocritically concerning a thorny issue the early church faced (see vv. 12–13).

While it's highly doubtful that Paul took any pleasure in this face-to-face disagreement with Peter, what's clear is that he had the courage to say what needed to be said. In doing so, he set an example men of God can follow today.

When you find yourself in a situation that requires a face-to-face declaration of facts—with a friend, a family member, or a brother in Christ—ask God to give you the courage and wisdom to speak the words that address the problem. And when you speak, do so in a way that fosters love, reconciliation, and trust. Always seek to build up those around you, not tear them down.

TEACH YOUR CHILDREN WELL

We will not hide these truths from our children; we will tell the next generation about the glorious deeds of the Lord, about his power and his mighty wonders.

PSALM 78:4 NLT

When you think of the words "a calling from God for ministry," your mind tends to focus on some kind of vocation such as preacher, missionary, or evangelist. But far more Christian men are called to a different kind of ministry, one that is arguably as important, maybe more so, than that of a preacher or teacher—fatherhood.

When God blesses you with children, He also gives you a set of profound responsibilities that come with raising them. You must care for their physical needs (shelter, food, and clothing), their emotional needs (love and acceptance), and social needs (education and other basics). But He also tasks you with teaching your children to love and fear Him and to live and speak in ways that please Him.

This means imparting not just a belief that God exists, but a love for Him, for His written Word, and for spending time with Him in prayer.

As a father, you should never forget the importance of loving, disciplining, and correcting your children. But still more important is teaching them about the goodness and wonder of the God who loves them more than even you, as an earthly father, can comprehend.

LOVING THE UNLOVABLE

*"But I say to you who hear, love your enemies, do good to
those who hate you, bless those who curse you,
pray for those who mistreat you."*

Luke 6:27–28 NASB

Have you ever thought about where humanity would be if God had looked down on sinful, lost people and just said, "Fine! They hate Me, they curse My Name, and live lives that offend Me in every way. I'm through with them!"

The Bible teaches that you were once God's enemy (Romans 5:10), that you were alienated from Him and hostile toward Him (Colossians 1:21). But it also teaches that while you were still a sinner, Jesus, God's only Son, died for you so that you could be reconciled to Him.

God is the perfect example of Jesus' command to love your enemies and to do good to those who hate you. He tells you to love your enemies, just like He did when He sent Jesus to die for you. And He tells you to do good for those who hate you and curse you, just like He did. But more than *telling* you to do those things, He *showed* you what that kind of love and blessing really look like.

It's not easy to love and bless those who don't reciprocate. But when you do just that, you give those who dislike you and mistreat you a much-needed glimpse of what God's love is really all about.

SPIRITUAL JUNK FOOD

Anyone who lives on milk, being still an infant, is not acquainted with the teaching about righteousness. But solid food is for the mature, who by constant use have trained themselves to distinguish good from evil.

HEBREWS 5:13–14 NIV

Over the past few decades, people in America have become increasingly aware of the importance of a good diet. Now more than ever, you realize that the foods you eat have a huge impact on your longevity and on your general health.

But what about the "spiritual food" you consume daily? Living in the early twenty-first century, you're bombarded nearly every waking hour with images, music, television shows, and movies that not only don't enhance your spiritual growth but cause you to be stunted in your growth and generally unhealthy. Not only that, you can turn on your television or computer at any time of the day and find unsound teaching on any number of "Christian" broadcasts.

It's not always easy for the Christian man to consume a completely spiritually healthy diet. In fact, without a finely honed sense of spiritual discernment, it's nearly impossible. But you can give yourself a much better chance of good spiritual health when you put everything you watch and hear to two quick tests: (1) Does what I'm watching or listening to build me up in my relationship with the Lord, or does it tear me down? and (2) does this line up with the truths God has revealed in His Word?

COMPARATIVE RIGHTEOUSNESS

"The Pharisee stood by himself and prayed: 'God, I thank you that I am not like other people—robbers, evildoers, adulterers—or even like this tax collector.' "

LUKE 18:11–12 NIV

Imagine for a moment that you had to appear in traffic court after one of your locality's finest clocked you doing 55 in a 35 mph speed zone and then pulled you over and issued you a hefty ticket. Instead of acknowledging your guilt and paying the fine, you appear before the judge and offer this kind of alibi: "Hey, it's not like I was driving drunk and caused a serious accident—and I know someone who did just that. I didn't do anything as bad as what *he* did."

Your mistake in this scenario is treating your own lawbreaking in comparative terms. In other words, you thought, *Well, I'm not as bad as this other guy, so. . .*a quick word to the wise here: that won't wash in traffic court.

It doesn't wash with God either. All sins, even those you might consider "little ones," are a serious offense to God, and you won't find forgiveness and restoration by excusing your own sinful thoughts, words, and actions by comparing yourself with others whose sins you consider "worse." On the contrary, you find forgiveness and restoration only by humbly confessing your sins for what they are: falling short of the standards God has set for His people.

THE PROMISE OF A HARVEST

*So let's not get tired of doing what is good. At just the right time
we will reap a harvest of blessing if we don't give up.*

GALATIANS 6:9 NLT

If you've ever watched a tree bear fruit or tended a garden for
a summer, you're familiar with the mundane, everyday tasks of
watering, weeding, pruning, and guarding against pests. In the same
way, it's not easy to live your faith every day without any harvest
in the immediate future. There's only faithfulness and a future
hope of a reward from God—a reward that you can't quite imagine.

God's promise to you may not be as tangible and in front of
you as a garden, but it's certainly more reliable. If you continue
to faithfully love others, seek justice, and obey the Holy Spirit's
direction, there will be a harvest. Your daily faithfulness will pay
off, but you may not see it for quite some time. In fact, it's possible
that others will benefit far more from your daily faithfulness.

As you submit yourself to become a branch of God's vine,
you simplify your daily tasks, only concerning yourself with
obedience to what God has called you to do. You aren't in charge of
the results. You aren't in a competition with anyone. You only have
your small part to play as you trust God with your daily concerns.

PRAYING FOR GOD TO SET YOU STRAIGHT

The LORD knows people's thoughts; he knows they are worthless! Joyful are those you discipline, LORD, those you teach with your instructions.

PSALM 94:11–12 NLT

It's rare that you pray for discipline and correction, but living by faith in an all-knowing God means learning to trust and to even take joy in God's discipline. The last thing you want is to go off course, making destructive choices that hurt you and those you love. And so the best hope for you is to humbly know your place and to take stock of your thoughts. Compared to God's knowledge and wisdom, your own thoughts indeed are worthless.

Perhaps you can take comfort in knowing that despite being aware of the best and the worst of your thoughts, God loves you enough to seek you out for discipline. He has trusted you with the scriptures to instruct and guide you. You have His Spirit dwelling within you, assuring you that in spite of your "worthless" thoughts, you're worthwhile. You are God's beloved child whom He could never deny or abandon.

You can ask with confidence for His wisdom and instruction. He delights in directing you toward freedom and life. The only thing holding you back is your tendency to hold on to your flawed thoughts.

YOU NEED GOD'S CORRECTION

I know, LORD, that our lives are not our own. We are not able to plan our own course. So correct me, LORD, but please be gentle. Do not correct me in anger, for I would die.

JEREMIAH 10:23–24 NLT

How much of your life's direction can you control? While you're responsible for your day-to-day choices, the ultimate destination of your life isn't in your hands alone. In the midst of the destruction of his homeland, the prophet Jeremiah saw the fragility of life firsthand. So much remained out of his control; and under the crushing loss of his country, he entrusted himself to God.

You likely don't face that kind of devastation and heartbreak today, but you face the prospect of seeing your plans, hopes, and dreams unravel in an instant. One phone call can end a job you have relied on; one doctor's visit can change your future plans; and one bad decision can unravel many good ones. You're surrounded by people whose choices can dramatically impact the course of your life.

In the midst of this uncertainty, you can join with Jeremiah, who placed his trust in God to direct his life. True, he couldn't plan his own course, but he could look to God for correction and instruction in the right path for his life.

GOD BEARS YOUR LOSSES WITH YOU

*The LORD is close to the brokenhearted; he rescues those whose
spirits are crushed. The righteous person faces many troubles,
but the LORD comes to the rescue each time.*

PSALM 34:18–19 NLT

As you remember those who made tremendous sacrifices for you, those who have suffered greatly, and those who have experienced great loss, you may wonder where God is. From family tragedies to financial difficulties to serious health concerns, there are words of comfort you can offer those who are suffering, but there's no way you can mend broken hearts and crushed spirits.

When you reach your lowest moments, God remains near to you. Having suffered to the point of death on the cross, Jesus is no stranger to heartbreak. He won't leave you by yourself, and while there are some things in this life that can't be undone, the promise of God's presence in the midst of sorrow and pain can't be unraveled by any conflict or disaster.

Rescue may not look like the things you expect or want. However, in the midst of your deepest sorrows, you may find that God's comfort and presence can reach even further down than you have known. Perhaps the holidays in particular open up old wounds for you and your family. An empty seat at the table may tap into a new wave of grief. In these moments of brokenhearted grief, God is near.

ALWAYS GIVE THANKS?

And whatever you do or say, do it as a representative of the Lord Jesus, giving thanks through him to God the Father.

COLOSSIANS 3:17 NLT

It's striking to note that thankfulness is something that Paul expected representatives of Jesus to regularly practice. You could even add that you know who represents Jesus by looking for people who are thankful. Why is thankfulness so important for followers of Jesus?

For starters, thankfulness puts you in your place. You are a representative of the Lord Jesus, serving His plans and His purpose, and that requires you to live by faith. As you look to God for guidance and direction, you'll soon experience His provision as well. When you receive God's direction and provision, the only appropriate response is gratitude.

Of course, a lack of gratitude could highlight some problems to consider. Are you depending on your own wisdom and only representing your own interests? Are you looking to other people or things for your protection and guidance? The less you depend on God or remain aware of His direction for your life, the less likely you'll be thankful for His daily provision.

Then again, sometimes you need to ask God to help you see the blessings around you. Thankfulness may only be a matter of what you notice in the midst of your busy days.

THERE'S ALWAYS TIME FOR RENEWAL

Don't keep looking at my sins. Remove the stain of my guilt.
Create in me a clean heart, O God. Renew a loyal spirit within me.

PSALM 51:9–10 NLT

Renewal isn't a one-time event in your life. The mere mention of a spirit being made new again, or "renewed," means that God *expects* you to hit low points, to wander, and to struggle. Your spirit can be made new again because God sees your potential—so long as you depend on Him.

As you seek to live in the wholehearted freedom of God's kingdom, you can't create your own clean heart. Breaking you free from sin and guiding you into a life of love and service is a creative act of God.

Most importantly, for your interactions with others, the harder you work to cleanse your own heart the more likely you are to judge others—and to fail. Receiving a clean heart and right spirit from God as a pure gift is humbling and effective.

Those who recognize the depths of God's mercy live with gratitude and generosity, recognizing that all people are in need of this gift. May God's creativity reshape your life and model a right spirit for others to see.

HOW CHRISTIANS FIND UNITY TOGETHER

I appeal to you, dear brothers and sisters, by the authority of our Lord Jesus Christ, to live in harmony with each other. Let there be no divisions in the church. Rather, be of one mind, united in thought and purpose.

1 CORINTHIANS 1:10 NLT

There is no shortage of issues that Christians can become divided over, and perhaps unity seems hopeless some days. How in the world can Christians ever hope to find unity together today? Paul offers a few clues.

For starters, Paul's appeal for unity isn't just wishful thinking. He wants his readers to respond based on the authority of Christ. However, that authority of Christ isn't a top-down decree. Rather, Christ's authority comes from His Spirit dwelling within believers. He unites us together as His body.

Be that as it may, unity also doesn't necessarily mean uniformity, as there certainly will be times when Christians either misbehave or deviate from the truth. Paul admits as much elsewhere. Rather than demanding uniformity, he compels his readers to unite in their thoughts and purpose.

All Christians should aim to reach the same goals of knowing God and sharing His compassion with others. You should desire to think of God's love and salvation. In your worship and your actions you can find the unity that you may never reach in a doctrinal statement on paper.

GOD FORGETS YOUR SINS. BUT CAN YOU?

Do not hold us guilty for the sins of our ancestors!
Let your compassion quickly meet our needs,
for we are on the brink of despair.

PSALM 79:8 NLT

Everyone has the burdens of their failures and struggles, but these need not hold you back from God. Your failures don't cut you off from His compassion and mercy. In fact, when you have confessed your sins to the Lord, they're as good as forgotten. While God chooses to forget whether or not you're "worthy," it's far more difficult for you to forget how unworthy you may be. You may cling to your past, remembering how you've fallen short.

The good news is that your failures are where God's compassion goes. His mercy meets you where you're weakest and at your most imperfect. He doesn't leave you hanging, wondering if you've gone too far this time. His compassion is swift and direct.

Is God's compassion something that you have to seek, beg for, or envy others for as you see them receive it? Do you imagine yourself as particularly sinful or cut off from God's compassion? If you struggle with guilt and shame, it may be that you're holding on to your sins. The Psalms assure you that God gives you more mercy than you may think you deserve.

ONLY ONE PATH TO CONTENTMENT

Whom have I in heaven but you? I desire you more than anything on earth. My health may fail, and my spirit may grow weak, but God remains the strength of my heart; he is mine forever.

PSALM 73:25–26 NLT

Desire in and of itself can be good and healthy, but how often do you suffer grief or disappointment because you have desired the wrong thing or action? It's possible that you may think of such desires as coming from the enemy, pulling you away from God.

God doesn't delight in thwarting or stifling your desires. If you've grown up with a long list of religious rules to follow, hearing that may be a shock. However, no one has ever found God by amassing a list of things to do and stopping there. The Psalms take us one step further.

Today's psalm invites you to rethink your desires—asking where your desires are directed. Your desires can be directed toward a God who passionately loves you and who wants nothing more than to affirm your true self in union with Him.

There are a thousand ways to be discontent, lonely, and disappointed. There's only one way to find the love and acceptance that have been waiting for you since day one. The love and acceptance you seek in a thousand ways on earth have always been yours in the presence of God.

FIND JOY WHEN YOU STOP SEEKING IT

Satisfy us each morning with your unfailing love,
so we may sing for joy to the end of our lives.

PSALM 90:14 NLT

If you've ever had a difficult season or generally struggle to find joy throughout each day, you may wonder how to find joy during discouraging or difficult times. The short answer is: by *not* seeking joy!

This runs counter to advice from experts telling you to treat yourself to what you desire, to set aside time for yourself, or to create experiences that offer joy and fulfillment. While each of these actions may be fine in their place, taken at face value, they run counter to the wisdom of scripture.

Your joy is linked with the source of your satisfaction. In fact, the psalmist writes that you begin your days with the satisfaction of God's loving-kindness. When you find satisfaction in God's love and kindness, you find a stable foundation for the rest of the day.

Are you disappointed, bitter, or resentful? Perhaps consider where you have sought satisfaction. How you sought satisfaction in work, a hobby, entertainment, or a relationship that overshadowed the ever-present love of God?

God's loving-kindness gives you security and peace that no one can steal. You can only "lose" God's loving-kindness if you lose sight of it. . .but then its presence in your life doesn't rely on your seeing it.

GOD HASN'T ABANDONED YOU

"No, I will not abandon you as orphans—I will come to you.
Soon the world will no longer see me, but you will see me. Since I
live, you also will live. When I am raised to life again, you will know
that I am in my Father, and you are in me, and I am in you."

JOHN 14:18–20 NLT

If you haven't wondered if your prayers are just bouncing off the ceiling or if you're the only one struggling with doubts, you'll most likely have a crisis of faith at *some* point. In fact, Jesus' disciples frequently struggled with doubts and confusion. You're in good company if you feel like living by faith each day is a bit beyond you.

Jesus recognized this struggle in His followers and assured them that He would remain closer to them than they could even imagine. While His followers feared being left behind like orphans, Jesus assured them that He would come live within them. This mystery isn't something you'll figure out from a sermon or a prayer retreat. This is a lifelong assurance that you can cling to and experience on deeper levels throughout the highs and lows of life.

Although you probably won't see Jesus walking alongside you, He is within you much like He and the Father are one. This union with God will one day save your faith—if it hasn't already.

DO YOU HEAR PEACEFUL WORDS?

I listen carefully to what God the Lord is saying,
for he speaks peace to his faithful people.
But let them not return to their foolish ways.

PSALM 85:8 NLT

There are many different voices speaking to you today from your relationships, television, radio, and computer. Even your own internal monologues can grow quite noisy and bossy. As you hear these many voices pushing and pulling you in several directions and toward various priorities, you're challenged to stop and ask: "Am I listening to what God is saying?"

Perhaps you should work backward. Are you hearing words of peace? If you aren't hearing words of peace and hope, then it may be time to hit the pause button.

God doesn't speak fear to His faithful people. There may be people who claim to speak for God, but if they aren't speaking of God's faithfulness and peace to the faithful, then they aren't hearing from God. Even those who miss out on God's peace or who submit themselves to the many voices of this world are seeking the same thing: peace. The trouble is that so many counterfeits for peace exist in the world.

When you turn your heart toward God, you will find the peace that you crave and tend to seek in so many other places. God is already speaking peace to you. Are you listening?

WHAT SHOULD THE WEARY DO?

Then Jesus said, "Come to me, all of you who are weary and carry heavy burdens, and I will give you rest."

MATTHEW 11:28 NLT

When you carry heavy burdens, when you grow weary, when you long for rest, and when you wonder if you can take one more step, Jesus calls you to Himself. He doesn't demand any particular action or mind-set. He knows full well that you're weary, so the invitation is spare and simple.

When Jesus calls you, He only tells you to come as you are. Isn't that a relief? Rather than telling you to get your act together or to wait until you're ready for a greater commitment, He tells you to come at your worst. When you're tired, hopeless, or weighed down with many worries, Jesus tells you to stop waiting around or trying to get your act together. Come as you are, right now.

While He doesn't guarantee solutions or the removal of your burdens, He assures you that coming to His presence will result in rest. If you come to Jesus, things will get better, even if you still bear your burdens.

You don't have to keep soldiering on. Weariness and many burdens become your "qualifications" in coming to Jesus for rest and restoration. Perhaps you'll only be prepared for transformation if you first come to the end of yourself.

YOU CAN'T ESCAPE WORRIES ON YOUR OWN

When doubts filled my mind,
your comfort gave me renewed hope and cheer.

PSALM 94:19 NLT

Seasons of doubt, fear, and even panic come up frequently in the Psalms. The writers of the Psalms voiced their uneasy thoughts to God in stark, unfiltered language. They held nothing back and let God know when life became unbearable or uncertain.

What is filling your mind today? There's no escaping your worries and cares. You can't distract them to the point that they disappear altogether. You must face them as they are and then surrender them to God. The longer you run from them or deny their existence, the more persistent they will become.

The Psalms help you face your uneasy mind. They teach you to cry out for help when you're overcome. Comfort and renewed hope can be yours, but you must venture through the valley of the shadow of death first, trusting that the Good Shepherd will guide you.

Your only hope is counteracting the noise of your worries and fears with the consolation of God, seeking His direction and restoration rather than wallowing in your cares. This isn't an easy process to begin, and perhaps it may feel short on consolation at first.

The Psalms assure you that God is present, offering you the peace you seek.

GOD IS COMMITTED TO YOUR RESTORATION

"Yet I will remember the covenant I made with you when you were young, and I will establish an everlasting covenant with you."

EZEKIEL 16:60 NLT

After listing the shocking number of sins and transgressions that the people of Judah committed against the Lord, Ezekiel offered a message of consolation. After reaping what they had sown, the people had learned that God had planned something far greater and lasting than their unfaithfulness and sins. God's covenant with them was not contingent on their faithfulness.

This is precisely how God continues to treat you through the ministry of Jesus that gave you an everlasting covenant. God is committed to your restoration, even when that restoration must begin again and yet again.

When God thinks of you, He ultimately isn't focused on the ways you have let Him down. While sin must be dealt with, God's covenant stands. No matter how many times you let go, God won't abandon His people.

Perhaps you aren't shocked by God's mercy in the past, but you may have a hard time accepting it for yourself in the present. Is God *really* that merciful? There's no doubt in the pages of scripture that God's covenant stands, and you can only miss out on it if you walk away from it. The people of Israel started over again—and then started over again after that. God's mercies truly are new every morning.

DEALING WITH SIN THROUGH HOPE

*"Comfort, comfort my people," says your God. "Speak tenderly
to Jerusalem. Tell her that her sad days are gone and her
sins are pardoned. Yes, the LORD has punished
her twice over for all her sins."*

ISAIAH 40:1–2 NLT

While God loves you enough to let you make your own choices and to reap what you sow in your life, His punishment doesn't nullify His compassion and mercy. Even as you suffer the consequences of your sins and faults, God is far from smug or angry. He takes no delight in seeing you receive what you deserve. In fact, God is eager to move on and to lead you into renewal—the sooner the better.

As God spoke to the devastated people of Jerusalem, there was only a heartfelt call for mercy and compassion for people who were as guilty as anyone had ever been.

In the midst of failure or your own downfall due to sin, it's hard to imagine that God would speak words of comfort. Far from determining who is in and who is out, God's plan has always been one of rescue and restoration. True, your sins have terrible consequences and can't go unaddressed. However, God's preferred way of dealing with your sins is pardon and restoration, healing and hope.

FAITH ISN'T JUST FOR TODAY

*Then the LORD took Abram outside and said to him, "Look up
into the sky and count the stars if you can. That's how many
descendants you will have!" And Abram believed the LORD,
and the LORD counted him as righteous because of his faith.*

GENESIS 15:5–6 NLT

Some days it's hard to see beyond the challenges and trials that are
with you in the present moment. However, the story of Abram pulls
you out of the present so that you can see God at work in you for
the long term. There's much more at stake than the bills you pay
or the conflicts you face. In fact, Abram's story teaches you that
your faith today will impact generations for years into the future.

Perhaps the simple act of stepping outside to look at the stars
at night can help you remember the vastness of God's power and
the generations who will also follow you.

If you're feeling overwhelmed by your circumstances or a
particularly difficult relationship, the best thing you can do may
be to step back for a moment. In the vast movements of God
throughout your life and the years that will follow, there's a good
chance the one thing that will endure from today is your faith. How
you choose to trust God today has the greatest chance of leaving
a lasting impact for our own benefit and the benefit of others.

NEW LIFE WHERE THERE'S NO HOPE

*Out of the stump of David's family will grow a shoot—yes,
a new Branch bearing fruit from the old root. And the Spirit
of the LORD will rest on him—the Spirit of wisdom and
understanding, the Spirit of counsel and might,
the Spirit of knowledge and the fear of the LORD.*

ISAIAH 11:1–2 NLT

When the people of Israel believed that they were cut off and as good as dead, much like an old tree stump, the Lord promised new life and even fruit from this old stump that had been written off. How is new life possible when all seems lost? The answer is in the Spirit of God.

While you can't make new life spring forth from the supposedly barren parts of your life, you can trust that the Spirit of the Lord is present with you and more than capable of changing you. Jesus Himself embodied this story of resurrection, of new life springing from what appeared to be a dead stump. As He unites Himself with you, you too can take part in that story of new life, wisdom, and an awe-inspiring knowledge of God.

God's new life isn't going to match most of your expectations. Jesus certainly surprised most of His contemporaries with His message. As you look for God in this season, trust Him to bring new life and be prepared for your fruit to look different from what you'd expected.

SEEING THINGS AS THEY TRULY ARE

*Stephen, full of the Holy Spirit, gazed steadily into heaven
and saw the glory of God, and he saw Jesus standing in the
place of honor at God's right hand. And he told them,
"Look, I see the heavens opened and the Son of Man
standing in the place of honor at God's right hand!"*

Acts 7:55–56 NLT

The church remembers Stephen, a deacon in the early church who was martyred after accusing the religious authorities of killing God's Messiah. In his final moments before death, when it seemed likely that a mob would soon stone him, Stephen saw Jesus ruling in the place of honor at God's right hand.

He had faithfully shared the hard truth with great boldness. Filled with the Holy Spirit, he not only had great courage, but he also saw things as they truly were. While there may have been men standing in judgment over Stephen, God ruled in heaven with Jesus at His right hand. As he trusted his life to God, not pleading for deliverance from the mob, Stephen also had great compassion for his executioners. He pleaded with God to not hold their sin against them.

When you see yourself under God's rule, you recognize your great need for His mercy. You won't harbor illusions about what you deserve or your superiority to others. You'll see that your life depends on God not holding your sins against you.

THE GREATEST BECOME THE LEAST

Jesus called them together and said, "You know that the rulers in this world lord it over their people, and officials flaunt their authority over those under them. But among you it will be different. Whoever wants to be a leader among you must be your servant, and whoever wants to be first among you must become your slave."

MATTHEW 20:25–27 NLT

John and James wanted to take a fast track of sorts to power and authority, and their mother wasn't shy in asking for Jesus to grant them the highest positions in His kingdom. We may associate greatness in a kingdom with status, authority, respect, and attention, but Jesus flipped their notions upside down.

There are no shortcuts or fast tracks in the kingdom. Jesus challenged John and James to pursue "downward mobility" instead of trying to leap over their fellow disciples into the most prominent places in the kingdom of God. John's later epistles reveal that he received this message and took it to heart, because in them he emphasizes love for one another rather than using his authority to order his fellow believers around.

Whatever John thought he could accomplish by receiving a powerful position from Jesus, he eventually found that loving service for others carried far more power. Most importantly, service disarms critics and bridges divisions. Jesus showed John and James a new way to lead and to use authority.

YOU GROW BY BECOMING CHILDLIKE

"I tell you the truth, anyone who doesn't receive the Kingdom of God like a child will never enter it."

LUKE 18:17 NLT

Jesus holds up children to you as your teachers about the kingdom of God. What is it about children that makes them so qualified to teach you about receiving God's kingdom? Perhaps their simple dependence and trust in their parents can show you what it's like to live in the freedom of God's realm.

If you listen to enough interviews of adults who grew up in poverty, you'll notice several trends emerge. In most cases, they'll note that during their childhood they "never knew" they were poor or that their parents found ways to make things work out. Even in some of the most challenging cases of need, children found contentment and confidence in their parents. It turns out that in many cases, a loving and present parent was more than enough to compensate for the challenges of life.

Whether you're secure or in great need today, a childlike dependence on God is where you'll find long-term contentment and security. You often hear of growing in wisdom or maturity in the Christian faith, and they certainly have their place. However, Jesus also expects you to grow more "childlike" if you're going to truly live in His kingdom.

MAY GOD SAVE YOU FROM WEALTH

Jesus replied, "Friend, who made me a judge over you to decide such things as that?" Then he said, "Beware! Guard against every kind of greed. Life is not measured by how much you own."

LUKE 12:14–15 NLT

In a culture where the firstborn son enjoyed immense benefits and privileges, a younger brother pleaded with Jesus for a more equal distribution of the family's inheritance. His argument certainly appears reasonable to us today, but Jesus wasn't looking at this matter from a financial standpoint.

Jesus saw that the younger brother had become obsessed with wealth, allowing greed to determine the value of his life. By refusing to arbitrate a settlement in this family, Jesus may have saved this young man from his desires. Tempting as it is to think that Jesus deprived this young man of something reasonable, Jesus most likely gave him the hard truth that he needed the most.

It's common to treat money as the solution to almost all of your problems today. Even if there's a risk that their desire for money will soon become a never-ending pit of greed and self-indulgence, people rarely treat money as a threat to their spiritual or relational well-being. Jesus didn't mince words in this story, treating greed as a threat that you must always remain aware of. Every time you pray for more money (or "provision"), you should also pray for God's protection from greed.

REFLECTING GOD'S RADIANCE IN A DARK WORLD

*"Darkness as black as night covers all the nations of the earth,
but the glory of the LORD rises and appears over you.
All nations will come to your light; mighty kings
will come to see your radiance."*

ISAIAH 60:2–3 NLT

Where do you find your hope today? Many look to politics or some mix of religion and politics in order to bring about change in our world. However, you must place your trust in a greater power that remains at work in God's people but will one day become visible to all. In fact, God assured Israel that all rulers would one day see God's radiance over His people.

You can begin to offer hope to a world struggling in darkness by first asking God to show His radiance in you. How can you surrender to God's plans and purposes today so that His radiance overshadows the darkness of this world? If you rely on your own light, you'll only become frustrated and discouraged.

Isaiah assures you that God's radiant light in His people will be undeniable. There's no mistaking the wholeness and redemption of God in this world when lives are restored and made whole. In the face of darkness, your first step is to present yourself to the Lord so that you can more fully reflect Him to others.

MAY GOD HOLD YOU CLOSE

DAY 361 – MORNING

Yes, the Sovereign Lord is coming in power. He will rule with a powerful arm. See, he brings his reward with him as he comes. He will feed his flock like a shepherd. He will carry the lambs in his arms, holding them close to his heart. He will gently lead the mother sheep with their young.

Isaiah 40:10–11 nlt

When you think of God coming in power, do you imagine judgment or a settling of scores? While God's justice is a big part of scripture, perhaps you lose sight of how God manifests His power and justice among people. The restoration you're waiting for under God will reward you for the ways you have remained faithful to Him and will look like a shepherd finally bringing order to a flock of sheep that has long known suffering and disorder.

God's restoration will involve caring for the young and restoring families. Divisions and troubles will be resolved as the Lord brings His people together in harmony. Your fears of the future will be resolved as God Himself leads His people and cares for their daily needs.

Wrapped up in these promises from your heavenly Father is His deepest longing for intimacy with His people today, holding them close to Himself as a parent would hold a child. While you may suffer through adversity and uncertainty today, God remains present with you, willing and able to guide you through this coming year.

TO GOD BE THE GLORY

*Humble yourselves, therefore, under God's mighty hand,
that he may lift you up in due time.*

1 PETER 5:6 NIV

It's easy to take credit for your success and accomplishments when you did all the hard work. You put in long hours studying when you were in school and made many sacrifices along the way to earn that diploma. You worked tirelessly at your job and spent countless nights working overtime shifts to prove yourself worthy of that promotion. So it's no wonder you soak in all the praise when everything pays off. But, what about God? Remember Him? He created you. He blessed you with the gifts you needed to get excellent grades, to work diligently, and to achieve great things. He put you in position to be right where you are at this moment. Have you thanked Him today? Have you given Him the credit? Humble yourself, exalt Him, and tell others about the wonders He has done in your life. Stop worrying about your social standing, your position on the corporate ladder, and your status. God doesn't care about such trivial things. His recognition is more important than what anyone else thinks of you. He will bless you far greater than you can imagine. He will give you an abundance of blessings. Now, humbly obey Him, and He will honor you either in this lifetime or in the next or both.

HELP ONE ANOTHER

"The King will reply, 'Truly I tell you, whatever you did for one of the least of these brothers and sisters of mine, you did for me.'"

MATTHEW 25:40 NIV

How often do you pass the homeless person on the street corner and look away, avoiding eye contact and continuing on your way instead of offering help—food, drink, clothing, shelter, or money? Would you ignore that person if it were Jesus Himself standing right before you? Certainly, you wouldn't. So, look for opportunities to extend a hand to someone in need.

Jesus specifically says that whatever you do for someone else, you do for Him. Whether you give a drink to someone thirsty, food to someone hungry, clothes to someone who needs it, or whether you visit someone in prison or in a shelter, or look after someone who is sick, you are giving to the Lord. He's watching you.

Friend—be thankful for all your blessings and be mindful that others may not be so fortunate. Don't take what you have for granted. Share what God has given you with someone who has less than you. Perhaps you don't have much to give in the way of food or money or clothing. But it doesn't cost anything to go see an elderly person and lend a listening ear. It's free to visit someone in prison and offer a word of encouragement. Please consider doing something selfless today.

FOCUS YOUR HEART ON HIM

*What good is it for someone to gain
the whole world, yet forfeit their soul?*

MARK 8:36 NIV

Reality television has become very popular over the past decade because viewers can identify with everyday people who live out their daily routine in front of the bright lights, cameras, and microphones. But sometimes reality stars are asked to say or do things that may compromise their integrity. They have to decide whether their pursuit of fame and glory is more important than their reputation.

You don't have to be an actor or reality television personality to face similar decisions. Are power, wealth, fame, social status, and material possessions worth more to you than your soul? You may want a bigger house, a fancier car, or an exclusive membership at an elite country club, but consider the ramifications of your actions before you do whatever it takes to get to the top.

God wants you to pursue Him more aggressively than anything else. He wants you to follow the path of His son, Jesus, on your way to the top. Higher than any corporate ladder, the greatest position you can ever achieve is in heaven. Do everything in your power and focus all your energy on reaching His kingdom, and He promises that you will live abundantly now and also gain eternal life.

WALK YOUR TALK

Prove by the way you live that you have repented
of your sins and turned to God.

MATTHEW 3:8 NLT

Some Jewish leaders followed the Old Testament laws and oral traditions passed down for generations. John the Baptist criticized these leaders, calling them hypocrites for being too legalistic, and he accused them of using religion to advance their political power. John the Baptist challenged them to change their behavior and prove through their actions and by the way they lived their lives—not through words or rituals—that they had turned to God.

Friend, you've heard these sayings: "Practice what you preach" and "Actions speak louder than words." You may say that you're a Christian. You read the Bible. You go to church. You offer tithes. You follow the rigid rules in your particular denomination. But do you truly practice what you preach? Do you walk your Christian talk? Do others see Christ in you in your daily life and activities?

Only you and God know the answer to that important question. God knows your true heart. He knows your intentions. He looks beyond your words and your religious practices and ultimately will judge you based on your behavior. Your actions speak louder than your words. Today, make sure that you put your Christian faith into practice.

GIVE ME STRENGTH

I can do all things through Christ who strengthens me.

PHILIPPIANS 4:13 NKJV

The apostle Paul turned to Christianity after condemning and even murdering Christians. He eventually dedicated his life to serving Christ, and his journey led him to abundant wealth, extreme poverty, and everything in between. He was imprisoned for several years, but still wrote this joyful letter from prison. When Paul says he "can do all things through Christ," he's not talking about superhuman ability to accomplish goals that satisfy his selfish purpose. Paul learned to get by with whatever he had whether it was little or nothing. He focused on what he should do—serve the Lord—instead of what he should have. Paul set his priorities in order and was grateful for all that God gave him. Paul faced many trials and tribulations, but he found joy in spreading God's Word and was not deterred by any trouble he encountered along the way.

You also "can do all things through Christ." You can accomplish any task, overcome any adversity, and survive any trouble if you come to the Lord and ask Him to strengthen you. He will not grant you the power to accomplish anything that does not serve His interests, but He will help you every step of the way as you build your faith and develop a relationship with Him.

FORGIVE ME, FATHER

*Restore to me the joy of your salvation, and make me willing
to obey you. Then I will teach your ways to rebels,
and they will return to you.*

PSALM 51:12–13 NLT

Have you ever felt disconnected from God because of your sin? Perhaps you are so embarrassed by your actions that you feel unworthy of being in the Lord's presence at church. David felt this way when he sinned with Bathsheba. In this prayer, he cries out to God: "Restore to me the joy of your salvation." David truly repented of his sin and asked for forgiveness.

God wants you to be close to Him, but sin drives a wedge between you and Him. Unconfessed sin pushes you further away from God, and it can separate you entirely from Him if you don't confront it, beg Him for forgiveness, and learn to obey Him. You may end up suffering earthly consequences for your sin. For example, adultery may lead to divorce. Fraud may lead to imprisonment. But God's forgiveness gives you the joy of a relationship with Him.

Once you experience that joy, like David, you will want to share it with others. David wanted to teach "rebels" and help them "return" to the Lord. You can help your friends and relatives by telling them about the joy of God's forgiveness and your fellowship with Him.

A SHINING LIGHT

*Jesus replied, "My light will shine for you just a little longer.
Walk in the light while you can, so the darkness will not overtake
you. Those who walk in the darkness cannot see where they are
going. Put your trust in the light while there is still time; then you
will become children of the light." After saying these things,
Jesus went away and was hidden from them.*

JOHN 12:35–36 NLT

Jesus was speaking to a crowd of people in Jerusalem when they asked Him how the Son of God could possibly die. He explained to them He would only be with them in person for a short time and urged them to take advantage of His presence on earth. He was the light of the world, trying to show them how to walk out of darkness. If they followed Him, they would enjoy eternal salvation with His Father in heaven.

As a Christian, God wants you to bear Christ's light to the world. He wants you to let your light shine for others to see. Can those around you see Christ in you? Is your light shining brightly? Or has it dimmed? Today, get up and go out there and spread the Word of the Lord. Be a shining light for someone else to see. Be a blessing to someone. Inspire someone to come to the Lord by illuminating your light to the world around you.

DEFEATING TEMPTATION

Don't blame God when you are tempted! God cannot be tempted by evil, and he doesn't use evil to tempt others. We are tempted by our own desires that drag us off and trap us. Our desires make us sin, and when sin is finished with us, it leaves us dead.

JAMES 1:13–15 CEV

Often, you hear people say: "God is tempting me." Nothing could be further from the truth. It is not God who is tempting you. It's Satan who is tempting you. Temptation comes from the evil desires within you. It begins with a simple thought and can escalate into a wrong action if you allow it. God tests you, but He does not tempt you. He allows you to be tempted because He wants you to strengthen your faith and rely on Christ for help. You can resist temptation by praying for God's guidance and direction in those situations and obeying His Word.

People often blame others for their sins. You hear sayings like: "The devil made me do it." No, you made yourself do it. You allowed yourself to succumb to the evil one's temptation. Don't make excuses and shift the blame to someone else. A Christian will accept responsibility for their sins, confess them to God, and ask for forgiveness. You can defeat temptation by stopping it in its evil tracks before it becomes too strong and you lose self-control.

SPREAD THE WORD

For I am not ashamed of the gospel, because it is the power of God that brings salvation to everyone who believes: first to the Jew, then to the Gentile.

ROMANS 1:16 NIV

If you have a favorite pizza place, you tell your friends. You don't hesitate to tell someone about a great experience you had at a restaurant, a hotel, a vacation resort, and so much more. So why do many Christians keep quiet about Jesus Christ? You know the Savior of the universe. You know the greatest man who ever lived. Don't be shy about sharing the Good News. Don't feel embarrassed to embrace your Christian faith and share it with others.

Paul was not ashamed to preach the Gospel. He withstood strong opposition and even went to prison for his beliefs, but he boldly and consistently found ways to preach the Word of the Lord.

If the people closest to you don't know you are a Christian, you aren't doing your job. You have the best news anyone should ever want to hear. Jesus changes lives and saves souls. Tell them. Give them an opportunity to hear how the Lord has worked wonders in your life. They may be ready to hear it and accept Him if only you would speak up.

SCRIPTURE INDEX

DEVOTIONAL INSPIRATION FOR EVERY MAN!

Wise in the Word

Created just for men, here are devotional readings based on one hundred key Bible words and concepts—including Authority, Calm, Focus, Perseverance, and Victory. You'll be inspired to think deeply on God and His Word, "which is able to make you wise for salvation through faith which is in Christ Jesus" (2 Timothy 3:15 NKJV).

Hardback / 978-1-64352-219-7 / $12.99

Prayers for Difficult Times
Men's Edition

Here's a practical guide of short prayer starters that will help you pray confidently during difficult times. From illness and relationship issues to struggles with self-worth and daily life stresses, dozens of topics are covered. Each section opens with a short devotional thought and applicable scripture.

DiCarta / 978-1-68322-615-4 / $12.99